INSIDERS' GUIDE® TO
GREATER FORT LAUDERDALE

D1405396

HELP US KEEP THIS GUIDE UP TO DATE

We would love to hear from you concerning your experiences with this guide and how you feel it could be improved and kept up to date. Please send your comments and suggestions to:

editorial@GlobePequot.com

Thanks for your input, and happy travels!

INSIDERS' GUIDE® TO

GREATER FORT LAUDERDALE

Fort Lauderdale, Hollywood, Pompano, Dania & Deerfield Beaches

FIRST EDITION

CAROLINE SIEG & STEVE WINSTON

INSIDERS' GUIDE

GUILFORD, CONNECTICUT
AN IMPRINT OF GLOBE PEQUOT PRESS

All the information in this guidebook is subject to change. We recommend that you call ahead to obtain current information before traveling.

INSIDERS' GUIDE ®

Editor: Amy Lyons
Project Editor: Heather Santiago
Layout Artist: Kevin Mak
Text Design: Sheryl Kober
Maps: Sue Murray © Morris Book Publishing, LLC

Library of Congress Cataloging-in-Publication Data is available on file.

ISBN 978-0-7627-6016-9

Printed in the United States of America
10 9 8 7 6 5 4 3 2 1

CONTENTS

Directory of Maps

ABOUT THE AUTHORS

Caroline Sieg's relationship with South Florida began when she moved there at age two. She later lived in Switzerland, New York, and London, with a few stops in Florida along the way including attending University in Sarasota and Miami. These days, this half-Swiss, half-American travel writer tools around Berlin, Germany, on her much-loved Dutch bike and escapes for the warmer climes of Florida each winter. Caroline is credited with writing the Accommodations, Restaurants, Nightlife, Attractions, and Shopping chapters of this book.

Steve Winston has written or contributed to 15 books. He first saw Palm Beach County when he took a job as a cub reporter for the *Palm Beach Post*. And he's had "sand in his shoes" ever since. Steve is an adventurer and mountain climber who's traveled widely all over the world, and his articles have appeared in major media in the United States and abroad. In pursuit of "the story," he's been shot at in Northern Ireland, been a cowboy in Arizona, jumped into an alligator pit in the Everglades, flown World War II fighter planes in aerial "combat," climbed glaciers in Alaska, explored ice caves in Switzerland, and trained with a rebel militia in the jungle. He can be contacted at his website, www.stevewinston.com. Steve wrote the How to Use this Book, Area Overview, Getting Here, Getting Around, History, Performing Arts, Parks & Beaches, Spectator Sports, Annual Events & Festivals, and Day Trips & Weekend Getaways chapters, along with the Living Here Appendix.

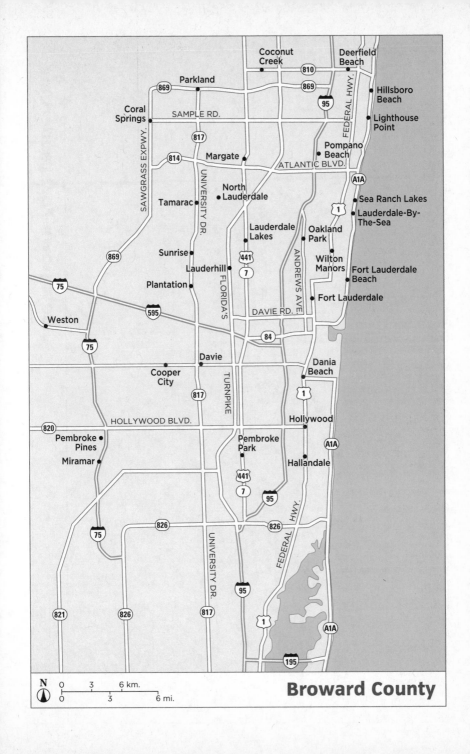

Broward County

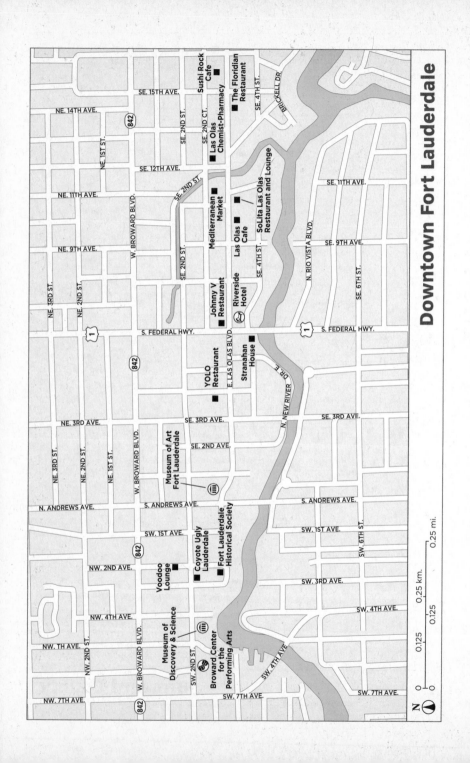

Downtown Fort Lauderdale

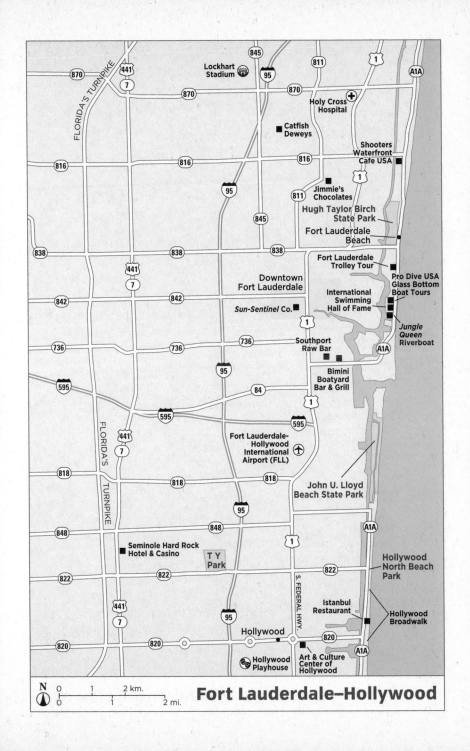

Fort Lauderdale–Hollywood

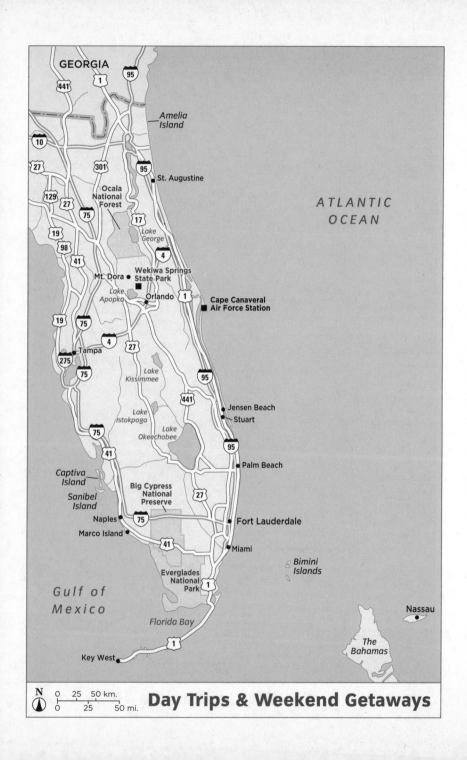

GEORGIA

441 **1** **95**

Amelia Island

10

27 **301** **95** • St. Augustine

Ocala National Forest

129

27 **17**

75

19

Lake George

98

41 **4**

Wekiwa Springs State Park

Mt. Dora •

Lake Apopka • Orlando **1**

19 **75** Cape Canaveral Air Force Station

4 **27**

75 Tampa • *Lake Kissimmee*

275

75 **95**

441

Lake Istokpoga • Jensen Beach
• Stuart

Lake Okeechobee

75 **95**

41 • Palm Beach

Captiva Island

Big Cypress National Preserve

27

Sanibel Island

75 Fort Lauderdale

Naples •

41

Marco Island • • Miami

Everglades National Park *Bimini Islands*

1

Gulf of Mexico

Nassau •

Florida Bay *The Bahamas*

1

Key West •

ATLANTIC OCEAN

N 0 25 50 km.
0 25 50 mi.

Day Trips & Weekend Getaways

HOW TO USE THIS BOOK

In the 1,205 square miles that comprise Greater Fort Lauderdale, there are some 31 municipalities, ranging from urbanized cities such as Fort Lauderdale (seat of county government) to tiny beachside villages and isolated Everglades crossroads. Although we'll cover the entire county, we'll also highlight some of the larger or more influential towns/cities, and their surrounding areas. Among them:

- **Coconut Creek**
- **Cooper City**
- **Coral Springs**
- **Deerfield Beach**
- **Davie**
- **Fort Lauderdale**

- **Hollywood**
- **Pembroke Pines**
- **Plantation**
- **Pompano Beach**
- **Sunrise**
- **Weston**

If you're visiting, or living in, a smaller town, or one of the towns not in the above list, fear not, though. We'll cover Greater Fort Lauderdale from top to bottom and from side to side. And we'll tell you everything there is to see, do, eat, listen to, watch, and everything else you need to know to maximize your experience, whether it's as a weekend visitor or a lifelong resident.

And we'll do it in alphabetical order, to make it easier for you. So, if you've heard of something that you want to find in the Attractions section, for example, all you have to do is look for it alphabetically. And if you're starting out at "base camp," as far as your knowledge of Greater Fort Lauderdale, get ready for the ride of your life. Because there's more here than you could ever hope to do or see or experience in a lifetime.

Throughout this book, you'll find a variety of Insider Tips and Close-ups about the area, often provided by those who know it best—people who have lived and worked here for many years. Some of them may be prominent people in South Florida, while others may be from the 95 percent of people who just go about their daily tasks unheralded. These may be personal vignettes; notes on local history; satirical in nature, educational, or just plain funny. But all of them will shed light on the fascinating mixture of people, cultures, and lifestyles that is Greater Fort Lauderdale.

Moving to the Greater Fort Lauderdale area or already live here? Be sure to check out the blue-tabbed pages at the back of the book, where you will find the **Living Here** appendix that offers sections on relocation, real estate, retirement, education, child care, media and more.

AREA OVERVIEW

Greater Fort Lauderdale—Broward County—has 31 cities, ranging from big ones (like Fort Lauderdale) to small ones (like Lazy Lake). From beachside (Dania, Lauderdale-by-the-Sea) to right next to the Everglades (Weston, Coral Springs). From south (in the Fort Lauderdale–Miami "orbit") to north (in the Fort Lauderdale–Boca Raton orbit). From urban/suburban development (Pompano Beach) to farmland and equestrian grounds (Parkland). This book will give you an "insider" view of everything you need to know about Greater Fort Lauderdale, whether you're moving here or just vacationing.

In this 1,205 square miles, too, you'll find some 1.75 million people (second-largest county in Florida, population-wise), representing every ethnic and national background in existence. Every religion practiced on Earth. Every conceivable political stripe. Every type of lifestyle. Every type of cuisine you've ever heard of, and some you haven't.

Our diversity—in all matters—is our strength. Because no matter your political beliefs or lifestyle inclinations, you can feel at home here.

One thing to remember: The Greater Fort Lauderdale area has witnessed tremendous—and exciting—change over the past few decades. And that change is still taking place. We're very much a work in progress, in many ways. And that's one of the reasons it's so great to visit or live here.

THE LAY OF THE LAND

Greater Fort Lauderdale sits in the middle of the region known as "the Gold Coast," a three-county area of South Florida (with a fourth, the Keys of Monroe County, added in for demographic purposes) with some six million residents. This is the most populous area of the state by far.

Most cities and towns in the region are within 20 miles of the Atlantic Ocean, so you're never very far from an ocean breeze. To the west of Greater Fort Lauderdale is the Everglades, undeveloped except for a few hardy crossroads and junctions, and the Seminole reservation at Big Cypress.

Because Broward County (and South Florida) residents tend to be clustered near the coast, "west" has a different meaning here. In fact, I'm writing this right now from the "western" town in which I live (about 20 miles from the ocean), and the Everglades dikes are just 2 miles west of my house.

Now that we've spoken about the "west," we should also mention the east: Greater Fort Lauderdale is fringed with 30 miles of Atlantic beaches.

Miami, with its magnificent skyline edging Biscayne Bay, is about 25 miles south of Fort Lauderdale. West Palm Beach, the

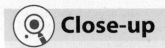 **Close-up**

Sunrises, Sunsets, and Everything in Between

This county has its share of special places and special moments:

- The **ocean at sunrise,** for instance, when the sun rises up suddenly from a darkened haze to sprinkle the horizon with burnt oranges and purples and fiery pinks and intense yellows, lightening the aquamarine waters as it moves.

- The electricity of **Las Olas Boulevard** in Fort Lauderdale on a weekend night, when thousands move happily among the bistros, sidewalk cafes, shops, and galleries.

- The **Everglades at sunset,** when the vibrations of the day are replaced by the all-consuming quiet of America's only tropical "jungle" at night.

- The **historic old neighborhoods** adjacent to downtown Fort Lauderdale, each one seeming to whisper its own personal story.

- The **Galleria** near downtown, where you can roam the elegant designer shops, or the colorful open-air shopping areas like **Town Center** in Weston.

- The **Gardens** of Pembroke Pines, or the **Promenade** in Coconut Creek.

- The **Pompano Beach Pier at sunrise,** with fishermen already loading their bait.

- **Flamingo Gardens** in southwest Broward, where you don't have to look very far to remember that this area was a wilderness not all that long ago.

- The tropical hammocks and diverse ecosystems of **Hugh Taylor Birch State Park,** whose beautiful pathways—both land and water—are sandwiched between the waters of the Atlantic on one side and the Intracoastal on the other.

- Cruising the **Intracoastal Waterway** on a crisp, clear day, under a warming sun and with no particular pressure to be anywhere else.

- The scores of **outdoor art festivals** running from autumn to spring, with their great art and their interesting artists and tons of happy people roaming through, in cool air that seems to invigorate the soul.

- And the **New River,** bordered by a red-brick **Riverwalk** and meandering through the heart of downtown, where the city meets the water, where you can explore the pioneer home of **Frank Stranahan,** considered the town's first settler, and then gaze up at the striking glass towers all around it.

urban and governmental hub of Palm Beach County, is about 40 miles north. The northern tip of the Florida Keys is about an hour and a half south, and Key West about five hours. And Fort Lauderdale is one of the cities in the southern United States closest to a foreign country; the island of Bimini, in the Bahamas, is only about 70 miles away.

Within Greater Fort Lauderdale are lifestyles and residential styles and culinary styles as diverse as anywhere. If you're interested in visiting, the place to start would be the **Greater Fort Lauderdale Convention & Visitors Bureau** (954-765-4466; 800-22-SUNNY; www.sunny.org).

If you're interested in living here—and despite the economic hardships of the past few years, many people still are—there are a number of chambers of commerce in the major cities that can help. Here are a few of the larger ones:

- **Broward County Chamber of Commerce**—(954) 565-5750; www.broward biz.com
- **Coral Springs Chamber of Commerce**—(954) 752-4242; www.cscham ber.com
- **Davie/Cooper City Chamber of Commerce**—(954) 581-0790; www.davie-coopercity.org
- **Deerfield Beach Chamber of Commerce**—(954) 427-1050; www.deerfield chamber.com
- **Fort Lauderdale Chamber of Commerce**—(954) 462-6000; www.ftlchamber .com
- **Greater Hollywood Chamber of Commerce**—(954) 923-4000; www.hollywood chamber.org
- **Miramar Pembroke Pines Regional Chamber of Commerce**—(954) 432-9808; www.miramarpembrokepines.org

- **Greater Plantation Chamber of Commerce**—(954) 587-1410; www.planta tionchamber.org
- **Greater Pompano Beach Chamber of Commerce**—(954) 941-2940; www .pompanobeachchamber.com
- **Greater Sunrise Chamber of Commerce**—(954) 835-2428; www.sunrise chamber.org
- **Weston Area Chamber of Commerce**—(954) 389-0600; www.westonchamber.com

MAJOR CITIES

Greater Fort Lauderdale spreads from the shiny beachside towers of the east to the swampy Everglades to the west. Here (in alphabetical order) are the some of the cities that most people in the county would say are "anchors."

Coconut Creek

Coconut Creek (pop. 50,500) has been changing over the past decade. For one thing, it's gotten younger; Monarch High, only a few years old, is now the second high school serving the area. For another thing, the city has gotten trendier; when the fashionable outdoor collection of shops and restaurants called the Promenade opened in 2009, it gave the city a splash of "hot" and sex appeal that it hadn't had before. Coconut Creek refers to itself as "the Butterfly Capital of the World" because it's the site of Butterfly World, where you can walk around surrounded by brilliantly hued butterflies in tropical habitats. "Creek" citizens are also proud of their environmental consciousness; their town is the first in Florida and eleventh in the country to be certified as a Community Wildlife Habitat. The town is in the northwestern part of Broward County.

Cooper City

Cooper City (pop. 29,400) is in the south-western portion of Greater Fort Lauder-dale, founded in 1959 and named after its founder, Morris Cooper. Cooper City has been voted one of the best towns for fami-lies in America by *Family Circle* magazine. And, indeed, many of its neat subdivisions are populated by young, professional fami-lies, and nearly a third of the population is under 18. One of the town's biggest gather-ing places is Brian Piccolo Park, named after a young pro football player who grew up in this area and died of leukemia in the 1960s.

Coral Springs

Coral Springs (pop. 125,800), about 20 miles northwest of Fort Lauderdale, was chartered in 1963, as one of the first planned cities in the United States. At that time a tiny dot on the map bordering the Everglades, the city has since grown to become one of Greater Fort Lauderdale's hubs, with excellent shop-ping, stylish restaurants, and nice parks. The Coral Springs Center for the Performing Arts is a first-class facility that brings in well-known singers, dancers, and theater troupes. The Coral Square Mall is a regional shopping center with an array of shops ranging from upscale department stores to one-of-a-kind boutiques. The city's main street, University Drive, is lined with good restaurants of all types. An area of University Drive called "the Walk" is the site of many of those restaurants, along with upscale jewelry, gift, and book shops.

Dania Beach

Dania Beach (pop. 28,800), just south of Fort Lauderdale, has a lot to offer. It's home to both one of the largest jai alai frontons in the United States and the International Game Fish Association (IGFA) Fishing Hall of Fame & Museum. There's a large amuse-ment park called Boomer's, with fun for the whole family. The city got its name in 1904, when most of the population—composed of Danish immigrants—changed Modello to Dania. The town also boasts "Antique Row," a string of more than a hundred antique shops housed in some of the area's original build-ings. From Victorian dressers to Persian rugs, from old baseball cards to decrepit garlic presses, if it's an antique, you'll find it here.

Davie

Davie (pop. 90,200) is a little bit western, pardner, by location and by lifestyle. It's located in western Broward County. Its main street is lined with a number of western-themed shops and restaurants. Some resi-dents still dress in western wear. And it even has the Bergeron Rodeo Grounds, scene of numerous rodeos with ridin', ropin', and calf-rasslin' events. Davie was actually carved out of the Everglades by a group of settlers who had worked on the Panama Canal in the early 1900s. In those days it was home to thousands of cattle, and today there's still a significant horse-owning population. Davie is the site of Nova Southeastern University, the well-known family attraction called Fla-mingo Gardens, and the preseason training camp (and in-season training facility) of the Miami Dolphins. Famous residents of Davie have included rapper Vanilla Ice; pro wrestler Rocky Johnson and his wrestler/movie-star son, Dwayne "the Rock" Johnson; and pro football players Jason Taylor, Chad Ocho-cinco, and Chris Chambers.

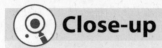

Close-up

Davie's Mysterious Pyramid

If you pass through the town of Davie, on either Davie Road or SR 575 heading east toward Fort Lauderdale, you can't miss it. It's an enormous pyramid of gold, reflecting the brilliant Florida sunlight, and shooting up more than a hundred feet into the sky. The pyramid has been here since 1974. Many—if not most—Greater Fort Lauderdale residents have no idea what it is. And many (if not most) have been passing by it for so many years that they no longer even wonder what it is, and they probably hardly even notice it after a while.

But we'll unlock the secret for you. Let's just say, to introduce it, that you don't want to find yourself there too soon. In fact, if you're on vacation here in Greater Fort Lauderdale, it would definitely put something of a kibosh on your trip if you find yourself there.

It's a mausoleum. Yes, a mausoleum. In the shape of an ancient Egyptian pyramid. And even with all the colleges and universities in Davie, it's by far the most distinctive building in town. Inside it are 4,200 crypts, half of which are already occupied, and 85 percent of which are already sold. Spokesmen for **Forest Lawn Memorial Gardens South** have noted on more than one occasion that their pyramid is a Broward County landmark—perhaps, to many, *the* Broward County landmark. (And one suspects that they're probably not at all uncomfortable with that designation.)

So, while you may not want to patronize the pyramid for a while, keep your eyes out for it as pass through Davie on SR 575. You may never see anything like it again.

Deerfield Beach

This beachside town (pop. 69,000) is located in the northeastern section of Broward County, about 10 miles north of Fort Lauderdale. It's named not for a person, but for the deer that once roamed the area. It attracts people from all over the county to its beaches, especially the strip along SR A1A near the old pier, which is lined with clubs, ramshackle—but very colorful—shops, and funky restaurants. Deerfield's the corporate home of JM Family Enterprises, one of the biggest Toyota importers and distributors in the United States. And its Quiet Waters Park is both an oasis of tranquility (with trails, canoeing on a lake, and campsites for overnight rental) and a great family center, with a lakeside beach and a water park.

Fort Lauderdale

This is the hub of Broward County, the shopping, business, entertainment, and dining mecca to which people flock—especially on weekends—from all reaches of the county. Once a low-rise town, Fort Lauderdale (pop. 183,600) now has an impressive—and imaginative—skyline. It boasts the largest cruise port in the world, a port that's always expanding. You can get just about anywhere in the world from Fort Lauderdale–Hollywood International Airport. Lauderdale is a city filled with colorful, historic neighborhoods. It has world-class arts and cultural showplaces, and world-class artists and entertainers coming in to fill them. The Broward County Convention Center attracts major corporations from all over the country.

Overview Info

A few things to know:

- The predominant area code for the county is the original one—954. Over the past few years, due to the county's growth, a 754 area code has been phased in slowly; it's still used mostly for new phone numbers, and for governmental institutions such as the Broward County school system.

- Streets run from east to west.

- Avenues run from north to south.

- Places, Terraces, Courts, etc., generally run from north to south.

Las Olas Boulevard, a smart, European-style thoroughfare filled with classy shops, galleries, and bistros, vibrates with a colorful urban pulse. Decaying—but historic—sections of the city, such as Himmarshee, have been authentically restored to their original glory. And the top of the renowned Pier Sixty-Six hotel still offers one of South Florida's most spectacular views—especially at night—from its revolving lounge. Fort Lauderdale has certainly seen some dramatic changes over the past few decades, that's for sure. But one thing hasn't changed: No matter where you are in the city, if you head east, you'll still come to one of the most famous beaches in the world.

Hollywood

Once a city on the decline, Hollywood (pop. 141,700) has rebuilt and revitalized itself over the past decade or two. Downtown, once filled with boarded-up shops and empty after dark, is now filled with interesting galleries, shops, and eateries, many in the original Art Deco style that once symbolized the city. The calendar is filled with interesting events, ranging from Latin music festivals to family celebrations. The city's famous boardwalk is filled with people on weekends, browsing through the funky little shops or watching the people parade to and from the beach. Hollywood is the favorite spot of the large French-Canadian community in South Florida, which can reach 250,000 in winter, and you'll hear plenty of French on the boardwalk and in town. The city, located just south of Fort Lauderdale, has been home to many famous people, among them model Janice Dickinson, actor Norman Reedus, pro wrestler Scott Hall, World War II pinup girl/actress Veronica Lake, and John Walsh, host of *America's Most Wanted*.

Pembroke Pines

Most Broward County residents don't think of Pembroke Pines (pop. 150,000)—in southwestern Broward—as a real "city." Yet, it's actually the second-largest city in the county, the 11th largest in the state, and the 157th largest in the country. A city of green neighborhoods and nice parks, "the Pines" really sprouted in the '80s and '90s, attracting young professional families. The Gardens of Pembroke Pines is a huge outdoor shopping area with a Main Street feel and shops ranging from funky to designer. Some say the city's named for one of the earliest residents of Greater Fort Lauderdale, a member of the British royalty called the Earl of Pembroke. That may or may not be true. Regardless, the city has a number of famous residents these days, including baseball star Manny Ramirez, model Niki Taylor, and former New York Giants superstar Lawrence Taylor.

Plantation

Plantation (pop. 83,500) is one of those suburban communities that's filled with delightful little surprises, like an incredible bagel shop, a jewelry store that sells upscale pieces for downscale prices, a great gym that the hordes haven't yet discovered, or a little pizzeria where the coal-fired pies are incredible. Plantation's also made a name for itself in the movies. Many scenes from *There's Something About Mary* were filmed at City Hall, and Mary's "childhood home" was also in Plantation. And the Plantation Golf Course was the site of the famous pool scene from *Caddyshack*. The city is located in western Broward County and is world headquarters for DHL. It's also home to the former Broward Mall, now fully refurbished and known as the Westfield Mall.

Pompano Beach

Pompano Beach (pop. 102,000) is a seaside town just north of Fort Lauderdale. Its name is derived from the pompano fish found in such profusion off the coast. It's the home of Pompano Air Park, where the Goodyear Blimp that you see overhead at so many televised sporting events is based. Pompano Park has been a popular racetrack for many years, and aficionados head here to see the trotters. In recent years, the city has made strong efforts to revitalize its downtown and beachfront areas, and these areas are emerging more vibrant and more attractive. Pompano Beach's list of famous residents includes people such as the late TV actress Esther Rolle; famous pornographer Al Goldstein; actor Kelsey Grammer;

former pro wrestler Jake "the Snake" Roberts; and numerous pro football players, among them Zack Crockett, Corey Simon, and Clint Sessions.

Sunrise

This city (pop. 90,500) is in western Broward, but it's in the center of many areas of Broward life. For one thing, it's the home of Broward's lone professional sports franchise, the Florida Panthers of the National Hockey League, who play at the 20,000-seat BankAtlantic Center. For another, it's home to Sawgrass Mills, which is not only the fourth-largest outlet shopping mall in the United States but also a vibrant entertainment and movie center with fascinating restaurants and clubs. As you wander through the corridors and courtyards, you'll hear a dozen different languages being spoken, because Sawgrass Mills is often the first place to which international visitors rush as soon as they get off the plane. Sunrise is a young city—a third of the population is under 18.

Weston

Weston (pop. 65,800) is a new city, a planned city, actually, carved out of southwestern Broward in 1996. But it's already made its mark. It's a place of wide, green boulevards, good schools, and civic involvement. In 2006, *Money* magazine ranked Weston 20th in America in the "Biggest Earners" category and also ranked it as the city with largest job growth in Florida—and 18th largest in the nation. *Business Week* called Weston one of the best affordable suburbs in the United States that same year. And in 2008, *Money* ranked it as the best place to live in Florida. One of its best places is Town Center—downtown Weston—an area of quaint

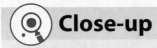

Close-up

Greater Fort Lauderdale Celebrities

PRO FOOTBALL
Isaac Bruce

Michael Irvin

Mike Mularkey

Brian Piccolo

Asante Samuel

MAJOR LEAGUE BASEBALL
Matt Murton

John Riedling

Ryan Shealy

PRO BASKETBALL
Mitch Richmond

TENNIS
Chris Evert

ACTORS AND MODELS
Catherine Hickland

Paige O'Hara

Niki Taylor

MUSICIANS
Marilyn Manson

Jaco Pastorius

OTHER NOTABLE RESIDENTS
Leo Goodwin Sr., founder of GEICO

Wayne Huizenga, business/civic leader

Dave Thomas, founder of Wendy's

D. James Kennedy, televangelist and author

streets with upscale shops and restaurants and frequent special events and festivals. And Weston's also home to Cleveland Clinic Florida, a branch of the famous Midwest medical facility. Famous residents include Hall of Famer Dan Marino, the former quarterback of the beloved Miami Dolphins.

HIGH SEASON, LOW SEASON

One of the most important things to know about South Florida is that, in contrast to much of the rest of the country, there are really only two seasons. And they're not summer and winter!

Actually, they're "High" and "Low." **High Season** starts around the first of November and continues until May. **Low Season** takes over in May and lasts through October. Each of these two main "seasons" has both advantages and disadvantages.

In High Season, for example, the weather is generally magnificent: cool, clear nights generally in the 60s, and sunny days in the 70s and 80s. This is the time of year—in contrast to the rest of America—when Greater Fort Lauderdale comes alive. There's opera, there's dance, there's song. There are art festivals and food festivals and music festivals and antique festivals and every other conceivable type of festival every weekend. Downtown Fort Lauderdale is alive with people parades often lasting into the wee hours. There's a spirit in the air as vibrant as

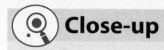 **Close-up**

Greater Fort Lauderdale Facts and Figures

- Two-thirds of the county's 1,200 square miles are protected (from development) Everglades.

- The former "cultural wasteland" is now a cultural horn of plenty—there are now nearly 600 not-for-profit arts organizations in Greater Fort Lauderdale. There are more than 10,000 working artists; 4,200 arts-related businesses; and 19,000 people who work at these businesses.

- Average year-round temperature is 75.4 degrees.

- Random facts: There are 4,100 restaurants in Greater Fort Lauderdale. There are 56 golf courses. There are 14 museums. There are 123 bridges. There are 128 parks. And 3,000 hours of annual sunshine.

- The smallest municipality in Broward County is the village of Lazy Lake—with 33 residents.

- Average annual rainfall is 65.19 inches, most of which falls between April and September.

- The county has 10 square miles of water.

- The county stretches approximately 50 miles east to west and approximately 25 miles from north to south, averaging 5 to 25 feet in elevation. The county has 23 miles of beaches and 266 linear miles of canals, with 126 miles of these canals navigable.

the air itself. Hurricane season is over. The night skies have too many stars to count. The sea breezes are almost luxurious. The colors of the buildings and the flora are more vivid. And Broward Countians—who sometimes tend to hibernate during the hot summer months—are out enjoying it all.

The only problem with all of this (according to some Broward Countians) is that everybody else—meaning visitors and "snowbirds"—is out enjoying it all, too. That means the roads are more crowded in High

Season, as are the restaurants, the movies, and the shopping centers. And if you're one of those visitors, you'll have to pay more for the privilege of wonderful weather and the joys of the season, sometimes a lot more.

During High Season, hotels can book up quickly (especially if there's a lousy winter up north); this not only impacts availability, of course, but also price. If you're visiting (and even if you live here), you'll end up doing some standing in line wherever you go. And—particularly during the holiday season—you

- There are about 806,000 housing units in Greater Fort Lauderdale.

- Broward is the 16th most populous county in the United States.

- The oldest school building in continuous use in the county is the Davie School, built by noted architect August Geiger in 1918 and still in regular use. The Deerfield School, built in 1927, is the second-oldest school still in operation in the county.

- The Hillsboro Inlet Light Station, a lighthouse in Pompano Beach, was built in 1907 and stands 132 feet high.

- The largest company in Greater Fort Lauderdale is AutoNation, a nationwide chain of auto dealerships, with $14.2 billion in revenues and 22,000 employees. The second-largest is JM Family Enterprises, Inc., the nation's largest Toyota distributor, with about $10 billion in revenues. Other notable Broward County companies include Spherion Corporation (human resources, staffing), Citrix Systems (computer network software), Elizabeth Arden (cosmetics), and Spirit Airlines, a national carrier.

- The largest employers in Greater Fort Lauderdale (besides the Broward County School Board and county government) are American Express, which employs some 4,800 people at its Plantation regional headquarters, and Nova Southeastern University, with 4,000 employees.

- Greater Fort Lauderdale is also Latin American headquarters for a number of large multinational companies, among them Siemens Building Technologies, DHL Express, Microsoft, Alcatel-Lucent, Schindler Elevator, Nortel Networks, Western Union, Stanley Works Tools, and South African Airways.

may not be able to get a rental car unless you've reserved early. And you'll pay more for the car you do get (which might easily end up being a truck or van rather than a car).

Low Season is a different story. There's no getting around it—South Florida's hot in the summer; high 70s to low 80s at night, and generally in the high 80s to low 90s in the daytime. But the humidity—often in the 80-to-90 percent range—makes it feel even hotter. The sun is very direct and very intense. There are plenty of bugs. Late-afternoon thunderstorms roll in from the Everglades (they generally clear up by evening, though). Hurricanes whose "projected paths" have to be watched very carefully in the fall. And, certainly, much less going on in the way of entertainment and diversion.

However, this is also the time when hotel rooms can be half the price (or less) they are during the winter. This is the time when restaurants run more specials (and you won't have to wait on line). This is the time when the shops offer sales (and when you

Sand in My Shoes

You may, on occasion, hear a Floridian talk about how he or she has **"sand in his/her shoes."** That's a popular expression down here, and the meaning is simple. It refers to a person who comes down to Florida, either on vacation or to live here, and who is transformed by the experience. It may be when you're walking on the beach at sunrise. It might be when you're cruising along the Intracoastal at sunset. It may be when you see the colors change as they reflect on the buildings or in the vivid color changes as the sun moves through a winter day. It may be while you're hauling in a big fish in the ocean. "Sand in your shoes" means that minute when you realize that you've really fallen in love with Florida. And that you're never "going home" again . . . because this is now home.

Winters are generally beautiful. But there's an occasional cold snap that may even leave your teeth chattering. During the winter of 2009–2010, for example, it actually got down into the 30s a couple of times (and some folks in Miami–Dade County, just south of here, actually had a few snowflakes fall). And when that happens (although even temps in the 50s are considered a "cold snap" here), it can sometimes stay that way for four or five days. Moral of the story? If you're coming in winter, sure, bring your bathing suit; the weather will probably be great. But, just in case, don't forget to also pack a sweater and a light jacket.

Then there's the H-word. And it wouldn't be fair to you if we didn't discuss it. Hurricanes—and we're not talking the University of Miami Hurricanes here, folks. Some years—such as the fall of 2009—atmospheric conditions play out in such a way that we're never really threatened, and we get a free pass. Other times—such as in '04 and '05—fuggedaboutit. We were hit hard in 2004 by Frances and then, only a few weeks later, by Jeanne. And Frances and Jeanne were no ladies. Then a year later we were dealt a glancing blow by Katrina, and then hit head on by Wilma (you probably saw the pictures on TV). After those two seasons, our previous complacency about hurricanes disappeared forever.

Hurricane season, according to the

can ramble through the malls much more easily). This is the time when you can get pretty much whatever rental car you desire, at a much more reasonable price. And this is the time when you can get a tee time pretty much whenever you want it.

EVERYBODY TALKS ABOUT THE WEATHER

. . . and in Broward County, most of the time it's beautiful. As noted previously, however, summers are hot and steamy, generally with thunderstorms during the late afternoon.

i Among the items you should always carry in your car is a water bottle—inside the car, not in the trunk. During the summer months and the early fall, it's very—*very*—humid here. And you'll sweat a lot more than you're used to. It's a good idea to keep yourself hydrated by taking a sip or two every few minutes.

books, lasts from June 1 until December 1. But there are never hurricanes brewing (out there in the ocean) in June, and almost never in July. Activity doesn't really start picking up until late August, and the peak of the season is mid-September. The "real" season then continues into mid-October. If you haven't been hit by then, you're generally home free. So there's really less than a two-month period in which we have to fret about the weather forecasts.

Bottom line? Just use common sense. If you're planning a trip here in late summer or early fall, just keep tabs on our local weather, and on what your own weather person says it's doing "down in the tropics." Do keep in mind, though, that hurricane hits—especially in a limited space like Greater Fort Lauderdale—are still relatively rare. And hurricanes that hit in other parts of the state generally don't affect our weather much, other than an increased possibility of rain.

GETTING HERE, GETTING AROUND

No matter where you are—in the country, or in the world—it's fairly easy to get to Fort Lauderdale. You can make connections to Fort Lauderdale–Hollywood International Airport from just about anywhere on the globe. And if you can't make the connections into Fort Lauderdale, you can surely make them into Miami International, only 25 miles to the south.

BY AIR

The gateway to Greater Fort Lauderdale—from just about anywhere in the world, with connections—is **Fort Lauderdale–Hollywood International Airport (FLL)** (954-359-6100; www.broward.org/airport).

In 2008, the airport processed 22,621,500 passengers, making it the 22nd busiest airport (in terms of passenger traffic) in the United States, and 14th busiest international air gateway in the United States. It's also the fastest-growing major airport in the country. And it's one of the 50 busiest airports in the world.

Fort Lauderdale–Hollywood International Airport serves as a hub for AirTran Airways, JetBlue Airways, Allegiant Air, and Spirit Airlines, which is headquartered in Broward County. The airport's close proximity to the cruise-line terminals at Port Everglades—now the busiest cruise port in the world—has also made it popular among tourists bound for the Caribbean.

"FLL" is served by 22 airlines, including all of the major domestic carriers. The airport is modern, easy to navigate, and user-friendly,

with plenty of parking and an attractive terminal and shops.

Fort Lauderdale–Hollywood International is convenient, as well. It's only 3 miles from downtown Fort Lauderdale and just off I-95, the main north–south highway in South Florida, and I-595, the main east–west highway in Broward County. And it's also convenient to the Florida Turnpike, the other main north–south road.

Car Rental

The following car rental companies are found at Fort Lauderdale–Hollywood International Airport. Most of these companies also have rentals at various locations around the county. Call ahead for information (especially during the winter High Season!).

- **Alamo Rent-a-Car**—(800) 327-9633; www.alamo.com
- **Avis Rent-a-Car**—(800) 331-1212; www.avis.com
- **Car Rentals from Budget**—(800) 527-0700; www.budget.com

- **Continental Rent a Car**—(800) 221-4085; www.continentalcar.com
- **Dollar Rent-a-Car**—(800) 800-4000; www.dollar.com
- **Enterprise**—(800) 325-8007; www.enterprise.com
- **E-Z Rent A Car**—(800) 277-5171; www.e-zrentacar.com
- **Hertz Rent-a-Car**—(800) 654-3131; www.hertz.com
- **National**—(800) 227-7368; www.nationalcar.com
- **Payless Rent A Car**—(800) 729-5377; www.paylesscar.com
- **Royal Rent a Car**—(800) 314-8616; www.royalrac.com
- **Thrifty**—(877) 283-0898; www.thrifty.com

Ground Transportation

Hotel shuttles are provided by many local hotels. Find out ahead of time if your hotel is one of them and find out where to meet the shuttle.

Taxis and Limos
TAXI/YELLOW CAB

Available on demand. Check in at the transportation podium located lower level, curbside of each terminal. Rate comparison charts are posted at each podium. Taxicabs accept up to five persons for fare stated on meters (taxi fares regulated by law in this county). Call **Yellow Cab** if you have any questions at (954) 777-7777.

SHARE RIDE/FORT LAUDERDALE SHUTTLE

Passenger sedans provide door-to-door service, usually at cheaper rates than a taxi. Check in at the transportation podium located curbside on the lower level of each

Beating the Traffic

Greater Fort Lauderdale has some very gnarly rush-hour traffic, especially during the Season. Try to avoid I-95 between the hours of 7 and 9 a.m., and also between 4:15 and 6:15 p.m.; if you get trapped behind an accident there (especially one involving a truck), you could spend a couple of hours just sitting in traffic. Also, listen for local radio reports about Florida's Turnpike. And try to avoid I-595 (which runs from the western suburbs into downtown) during rush hours; try not to head east (into town) in the morning, or west during that time. Otherwise, what is a nicely moving thoroughfare the rest of the day can become a very long parking lot.

Especially in the summer, when air-conditioning usage surges, South Florida is vulnerable to occasional electrical blackouts. It doesn't happen too often, and when it does, it's generally restricted to a compact area. But if it happens when you're in your car, you need to know the rules of the road—because traffic lights won't be working. Actually, the rules are very simple. Just treat every traffic light as if it's a four-way stop sign. Make sure you yield the right of way, rather than being a road hog. Be sure to drive defensively; we have our share of road crazies here, too. And don't panic. Police usually arrive fairly quickly to direct traffic.

terminal. Fares can be found on the rate comparison charts posted at each podium. Call **Fort Lauderdale Shuttle** if you have any questions at (954) 822-8106.

GO AIRPORT SHUTTLE

For door-to-door, shared-ride transportation, consider a luxury sedan or van from GO Airport Shuttle, which provides a "zone" fare from the airport right to your home. Private car service is also available. Check in at the transportation podium located outside the baggage area on the lower level curbside. A comparison list of fares is posted at each podium. Or for more information, contact **GO Airport Shuttle** at (954) 561-8888 or toll free (800) 244-8252.

In addition, taxis are easily found just outside the main FLL terminal. And there are numerous taxi companies throughout the county. A few other taxi and transportation companies are:
- **Ambassador Taxi Service**—(954) 779-7777
- **Fort Lauderdale Shuttle Vans**—(954) 559-9999
- **Fort Lauderdale Airport Taxi**—(954) 609-1914, (954) 744-6236

A few other limousine services are:
- **Fort Lauderdale FL Taxi & Limousine**—(954) 888-2222, (954) 733-3333; www.fortlauderdalefltaxi.com
- **Holland Limousine Service**—(954) 577-0308; www.hollandlimousine.com
- **A ABA-Cab Airport Service**—(954) 981–2354, (954) 981-0720; www.aaba-cabairportservices.com
- **A Family Limousine**—(954) 522-7455, (877) 599-LIMO; www.afamilylimo.com

Broward County Transit (BCT) bus shelters at the airport are located:
- At the west end of Terminal 1
- Between Terminals 2 and 3
- Between Terminals 3 and 4

Contact the BCT (Broward County Transit) Rider Info Line at (954) 357-8400 or 357-8320 (TTY) for more information.

Directions to FLL

- **From I-95 North or South:** Take I-95 to I-595 East. Bear right onto US 1 (South Federal Highway) and take the airport exit. Follow the directions into the airport.

- **From within Fort Lauderdale:** US 1, known as Federal Highway, runs north–south throughout Fort Lauderdale. The entrance to the airport is via South Federal Highway (see map, p. xi). **AMTRAK:** You can get to Fort Lauderdale on Amtrak from pretty much anywhere in the country. (954) 587-5387, (800) USA-RAIL (800-872-7245); www.amtrak.com.

BY BUS OR TRAIN

If you prefer the train to flying, **Amtrak** (800-872-7245; www.amtrak.com) offers long- and short-distance rail transportation throughout the United States. **Tri Rail** also offers service in Broward County, including stops in Deerfield Beach, Pompano Beach, Cypress Creek, Fort Lauderdale, Fort Lauderdale–Hollywood International Airport, Sheridan Street Station, and Hollywood Stations. A round-trip fare from Broward's northernmost station (Deerfield Beach) to its southernmost (Hollywood) is $8.45. For more information, call (800) 874-7245, or check out their website at www.tri-rail.com.

And if you prefer to "leave the driving to them," **Greyhound** (800-231-2222; www.greyhound.com) has a terminal in Fort Lauderdale. **BCT (Broward County Transit)** (954-357-8355; www.broward.org/bct), Greater Fort Lauderdale's public bus transportation, offers regular services throughout the county. Regular fare is $1.50, with reduced fares for children, seniors, and the disabled.

MAJOR ROADS

The major north–south highways in Greater Fort Lauderdale are **I-95,** which runs along the eastern corridor; **Florida's Turnpike,** which runs though the middle; and the **Sawgrass Expressway** (SR 869), which runs along the western fringe and into I-75 toward Miami.

The major east–west highway is **I-595,** which runs from southwestern Broward into Fort Lauderdale–Hollywood International Airport on the east. Another east–west corridor is the Sawgrass Expressway's (SR 869) northern leg, which runs west from Deerfield Beach before turning south in Coral Springs, in the far northwestern corner of the county.

Major north–south roads with stoplights (running through towns) include **Federal Highway** along the eastern corridor; **University Drive** in the center of the county; and **Nob Hill Road** in the western suburbs.

Major east–west roads that run through towns include **Sunrise Boulevard** (from Fort Lauderdale toward the western suburbs); **Commercial Boulevard** (ditto); **Hollywood Boulevard** (which becomes Pines Boulevard out west); and **Hillsboro Boulevard,** which runs across northern Broward.

HISTORY

If you're over a certain age, you remember that in the '60s (and '70s and '80s), Fort Lauderdale was *Where the Boys Are*. And the girls, too. There was Frankie (Avalon). James (Darren). Fabian (Forte). And guys with names like "Moondoggie" and "Gopher" and "Chug-a-lug." Annette (Funicello). Gidget. And Connie (Francis), the popular singer who sang the title song of the movie, which became sort of a badge for Fort Lauderdale.

These kids—seemingly without a care in the world—danced on the beach in the daytime and threw lavish luaus, with lobster bakes and guitars, at night. They surfed, they tossed footballs, had volleyball games, switched boyfriends/girlfriends with regularity, and generally drove the few adults in the film—often parents but sometimes local officials or hotel owners—crazy.

For an entire generation, the "beach movies" of the early 1960s—and Fort Lauderdale's center-stage role in a few of them—forever defined this provincial (at the time) small town (at the time) to the north of Miami. And that generation isn't limited to people now over 60. In fact, in large measure because of the beach movies, thousands—and then hundreds of thousands—of college students began making their way to Fort Lauderdale for what became the annual ritual called Spring Break. The phenomenon lasted nearly 30 years. In fact, to most of the country's college students during those decades, Spring Break meant only one thing—Fort Lauderdale.

For what was then a somewhat sleepy, low-rise town, those were halcyon days. Local radio hosts, eager to promote the business that Spring Break brought, began unabashedly referring to the town as "Fort Liquordale." There were all sorts of contests, from wet T-shirt to hot-dog-eating to craziest dives to limbo dancing to—of course—drinking. And no one here complained. These kids filled the hotels during the normally slower "Shoulder Season" just before or after High Season (even if they often tried to cram 10 or 12 people into a room). And they filled the restaurants, bars, nightclubs, strip joints, T-shirt shops, ice-cream shops, and surf shops as well.

Eventually, like all good things, it had to end, though. More about that later.

IN THE BEGINNING

Greater Fort Lauderdale's original inhabitants didn't do much dancing for fun; it was more for ceremonial reasons. And they had much different rituals than these latter-day revelers.

Scattered throughout Broward County are numerous Indian mounds—probably ceremonial or burial places—where archeologists have found pottery shards, arrowheads, primitive tools, shells, and, in a few cases, human remains. And the estimated dates of these mounds range from a few hundred years old to 10,000 years old.

Skeletal remains of animal hunters dating back about 10,000 years have been found here, suggesting that perhaps human beings lived here even earlier. From what we know, these first Broward Countians subsisted on fish, shellfish, deer, bear, and plants such as sea grape and prickly pear.

They apparently wandered throughout the county. The demands of their sustenance—moving where the game was—meant a life on the move, and their small villages were frequently relocated. When the Spanish came across the village of the Indians they called Tequesta in 1567, near the mouth of Miami River, it had probably not been there more than a century or two.

The relationship between the Spanish and the native inhabitants was a contentious one—pretty much standard wherever the conquistadores arrived. The Spanish established a mission on the Miami River to convert the natives. But the natives weren't buying what the newcomers were selling, and the mission was abandoned within two years.

It was about this time that the Tequesta began declining in numbers. Some historians say they began dying off because of the new diseases brought by the Spanish. Others, however, give the cause as the tribe's ongoing warfare with the stronger Calusa tribe. By the late 1700s historians believe there were actually less than a hundred Indians living in southeast Florida. And most of those left for Havana when the Spanish ceded Florida to Great Britain at the end of the French and Indian War.

At the same time as the British got Florida, another group of Indians—the Creek

nation—was moving into the state, after being driven out of Georgia by war and famine. One branch of the Creek eventually ended up in the Everglades, developed its own separate identity, and became the Seminole nation.

The British didn't reign for long, however. The loss of their American colonies resulted in the forfeiture of the region back to Spain, in the Treaty of Paris following the American Revolution. And soon after, Broward's first non-Indian settlers arrived.

The Lewis and the Robbins families arrived from the Bahamas. They weren't Bahamian though; they were British subjects who had settled in the islands. They put down roots on the south side of the New River, a channel that drains the Everglades, and began the arduous task of trying to coax crops out of this harsh land.

The Spanish didn't perceive these British people as mere farmers, however; they saw them as a potential "fifth column" that could possibly lay the groundwork for a British reoccupation of the peninsula. They sent a "supply" ship to spy on the settlers in 1793, apparently with the ultimate intention of removing them. But at the time Spain was preparing for war with France, and there were more pressing issues to be attended to. So they never removed these transplanted British Bahamians.

The Spanish apparently didn't feel all that attached to this new land, however, and they sold it to the United States in 1821. A few years later, the U.S. Army sent Colonel James Gadsden to push through the wilderness and conduct a survey of what is today Greater Fort Lauderdale. Gadsden was not impressed, to say the least. He recommended against building a road in the area, noting that "the population of the route will probably never be sufficient to contribute to [its maintenance], while the inducements to individuals to keep up the necessary ferries will scarcely ever be adequate."

WAR AND UNCERTAINTY

The Gadsden party did note the presence on the New River of two families, the Cooleys and the Williamses. We're not quite sure what the Williamses did to survive or to obtain food, but the record says that the Cooleys raised vegetables for subsistence and processed a root called coontie into arrowroot starch for cash.

In an interesting twist, the inland areas were actually showing more development than the eastern areas—but not by the British or European-Americans. The aforementioned Seminole Indians, pushed continually southward by white immigration into the lands in north Florida, began setting up camps here.

Their arrival here, of course, was part of the ongoing tragedy of Native-Anglo affairs in those days, days characterized by misunderstandings, broken promises, unwarranted fears, and demonization of the "other" side. Eventually the white settlers began requesting—and then demanding—that the Seminoles be moved from the state to someplace far out West. The Seminoles, having already been pushed out of one place, were in no mood to be pushed out of another. In what they saw as encroachment on their lands, the Seminoles' resentment began to grow as more white settlers came. One incident led to another, and before long the situation was akin to a tinderbox needing only a match.

The match was struck on December 28, 1835. The Seminoles ambushed an army column headed by Major Francis L. Dade (after whom Miami–Dade County is named), and they killed 104 of his 107 men, including Dade. This ambush actually took place far from South Florida, in the Tampa area. But it set the state aflame, and it set off the Second Seminole War.

A week after the battle, the Cooleys, still farming on the New River, became the first victims in the Broward area. A war party attacked their homestead, killing Mrs. Cooley, their three children, and the children's tutor, Joseph Flinton. But Joseph Cooley, by some quirk of fate, was not home at the time, having been on a hunting trip

Neighboring families heard the screams of the victims and hurriedly gathered a few things together. They fled south by land and eventually reached Indian Key. There they came upon Cooley and had to tell him the news.

In March 1838, a force of Tennessee Volunteers joined up with a band of army regulars and constructed a fort on the New River. The force was commanded by Major William Lauderdale, and the fort they constructed bore his name, along with a second one built later on along the beach. Major Lauderdale was the first non-Native American to explore the eastern Everglades and the canals leading from the Glades into the Atlantic. On March 22, 1838, Lauderdale's force joined other units of the United States Army in a battle with the Seminoles at Pine Island, in which the army emerged victorious.

The Second Seminole War lasted until 1842, but the mutual fear lasted much longer than that. Immigration of white families came to a stop, which was a wonderful bonanza to the Seminoles who had escaped removal to the west, as they had the area pretty much to themselves for the next 50 years. They lived quiet lives in relative obscurity for all those years, growing crops and roaming the Everglades in search of game.

The first known Anglo settlers in the postwar period were Washington Jenkins, keeper of the House of Refuge that was built for shipwrecked sailors in 1876, and John J. Brown, a pig farmer who won a scandal-plagued legislative election that same year and departed for Tallahassee (without his pigs), never setting foot in the area again.

THE TURN OF THE CENTURY

The area grew slowly; after all, it wasn't exactly paradise on Earth. The cruel summers (pre-air-conditioning) sent many a settler family back up north from whence they had come. The mosquitoes and appropriately named horsefly seemed the reincarnation of a plague. Disease—often caused by the mosquitoes—was rampant, and there were no doctors here. Realistically, if you got sick, you generally died. Towns were very tiny and very far apart from each other, and communication between them was negligible. The wild animals were everywhere, and they weren't friendly. Panthers. Bears. Alligators. Eagles and osprey. Venomous snakes such as rattlesnakes and water moccasins. Armadillos. Iguanas. And lizards—lizards that got into every article of clothing you owned, that popped up on your pillow at night, that climbed the walls of your kitchen and bedroom, that lurked in the boots you put on each morning. And the earth was loose, sandy soil, and the water table was very close to the surface; growing crops took a lot of effort and a lot of luck. Between the families who gave up and left, and the families who died, population growth was not exactly soaring.

Nonetheless, people kept trickling down in small numbers, enchanted by the opportunity to create new lives on the edge of the wilderness (and by the stories of warm winters!). In 1891 the area got its first post office. Two years later came the Bay Stage Line, operating over a shell-rock road between Lake Worth (in what is now Palm Beach County, to the north of Greater Fort Lauderdale) and Lemon City, now part of Miami. This stage line was the first real link to the outside world. And it was one of the first really tangible steps in the growth of this area.

The entire trip actually took two days. And it stopped overnight at the New River, where a transplanted (and entrepreneurial) Ohioan named Frank Stranahan was running both an overnight camp and a ferry service across the river.

In connecting the Fort Lauderdale area to the rest of the world, though, the stage brought to an end a very colorful aspect of early South Florida. With the advent of the stage line, the legendary "barefoot mailmen," who had carried the mail for seven years from Lake Worth to Miami by walking along the beach, disappeared into history.

DREAMERS AND SCHEMERS

The stages, however, didn't even last seven years. Railroad magnate and businessman Henry M. Flagler, who had built glorious hotels in North Florida, had been sent orange blossoms—in the middle of a freeze—by a Miami resident named Julia Tuttle. Upon learning that Miami was unaffected by the great freeze of February 1895, he decided to extend his Florida East Coast Railroad south from Palm Beach. A year later, the first train reached New River. And that event changed Fort Lauderdale forever.

Flagler needed workers for his various land and hotel enterprises in South Florida, and his railroad would bring them here. But he eventually found out that much of his manpower needs could be met with people already here. Swedes from the Northeast formed the nucleus of Hallandale, and Danes from the Midwest founded Dania. Southern farmers, lured by better land and milder winters, joined the Danes and Swedes and founded Pompano and Deerfield. Much of the fieldwork, however, was done by African Americans brought into town by the railroad.

Dania became the area's first incorporated community in 1904, followed by Pompano in 1908 and Fort Lauderdale in 1911. But until 1915 they were towns without a county. That year a new county was formed from portions of Dade and Palm Beach Counties and named for former Florida governor Napoleon Bonaparte Broward.

While governor from 1905 to 1909, Broward had a tremendous impact on the county that would bear his name. He had fought for drainage of the Everglades and also got the dredges working on the south and north New River canals. Draining the Everglades—especially then—was a dicey proposition at best, and the results were mixed in that area. But the drainage opened up much of today's Broward County for development, first as agricultural land and later, residential.

Growth was slow at first, but steady. But then things changed rapidly. When World War I ended in 1918, it sparked the first of Broward's two great booms.

Between 1920 and 1925, the county's population nearly tripled, climbing from 5,135 to 14,242. This boom helped spark the new development model: planned cities, not just neighborhoods. In addition, it changed the demographics of the county.

Until now, most settlers had been farmers. The newcomers, however, for the most part wanted nothing to do with the land and had little affinity for sweating over it. They were urban people, many of them retirees. In addition, with the advent of modern communications, the 1920s saw the economy morph from a crop-oriented one into an economic machine that began to be powered by tourism.

At about that time, a new breed of immigrant began coming to this area—successful developers with grandiose ideas and very deep wallets. These were men of grand accomplishment, never-give-up attitudes, and records of success up north, who saw great opportunity in South Florida. The grandest of them all was Joseph W. Young, who turned a low-lying tract between Hallandale and Dania into his dream city of Hollywood-by-the-Sea. He spent millions to build several elegant hotels, a country club, downtown office buildings to attract companies, a bridge spanning the Intracoastal Waterway, a splendid railroad station, an Olympic-sized pool, and a school. He donated his own land to create parks for his new city. His city had underground power cables—a revolutionary idea at the time (and particularly appropriate for a place that experiences occasional hurricanes)—underground water and sewers, a telephone system, sidewalks, and handsome street lighting.

All of these amenities, of course, would mean little without people to take advantage of them. So Young embarked upon a vigorous—some would say "overly aggressive"—campaign to draw residents to his new city. He took out ads all over the eastern United States. He brought prospects in by bus, train, and even ship, and treated them to lunch and tours of the city. And he certainly wasn't above the hard sell, occasionally trapping prospects in "sweat rooms" where they were bombarded by high-pressure salesmen.

In 1925, when Hollywood was incorporated as a city, Joseph Young, fittingly, was elected its first mayor. He didn't serve long, though; he resigned to develop Port Everglades.

The devastating hurricane of 1926 brought South Florida—and Hollywood—to its knees. And three years later, the Depression brought it to a crash. The era of the grand dreamers crashed with it. And Young's grand plans came to a dead end.

He died at the age of 51 in 1934, at his home in the city he loved. But he is survived by so many Hollywood landmarks that it's hard to count, among them the city's many lakes, its broad boulevard, the eastern golf course, and the famous traffic circle that now bears his name. He was the first of Broward's grand planners. And it's arguable that newer planned cities, such as Coral Springs, might never have become reality had not Young pursued—and achieved—his dream 40 years earlier.

DEVASTATION & DEPRESSION

The Depression, and the subsequent slow recovery, emphasized the fact that rough days were ahead. The growth and development of the area, in some respects, had outpaced the community's ability to manage it. Once more, access to the outside world was proving to be a considerable problem. With the spate of new settlements, there was a tremendous need for importation of both food and building material, most of which had to be brought over the single-track Florida East Coast Railroad. Henry Flagler's successors made plans to double-track the FEC. Then another railroad, the Seaboard Coast Line, was extended southward toward Miami. In turn, the newfound ability to import workers and raw materials helped Port Everglades take form.

But none of this could be done quickly enough. Goods piled up on platforms in Jacksonville because there were not enough trains to get them to South Florida in a timely manner. The backlog of goods at Jacksonville became so critical that, on October 29, 1925, the FEC had to embargo everything except food or items for which special permits had been obtained.

As a result, construction in Broward County came to nearly a complete stop. Making a bad situation worse, lending institutions took this as a sign of weakness, and credit soon dried up. In fact, these events were fodder for many Northern banks, who had long nursed the suspicion that this South Florida boom was based on fantasy, and fed by paper-thin operating margins and spiraling prices paid by speculators who were in it only for a quick buck. They had long felt the boom was too giddy to last. And when these logistical problems popped up, their suspicions were confirmed. By early 1926, the previous flow of funds was becoming more like a trickle.

The fly-by-nighters, con artists, and get-rich-quick-using-other-peoples'-money schemers were wiped out. The more-substantial investors, and visionaries such as Joseph Young, though, were prepared to wait out the downturn because they were true believers in the potential of this area. These people were prepared, even determined, to weather the economic storm.

However, they weren't prepared to weather a natural one. The great hurricane of 1926 (hurricanes didn't have names then) formed in the Caribbean' and took dead aim on South Florida. On September 17, it smashed head on into south Broward County. But it didn't hit and run. It continued into September 18, with unimaginable fury. Winds were probably what we'd call category five today. The winds treated heavy objects like little toys. Cars, trees, boats—anything that wasn't battened down, really, and many things that were—became flying projectiles, tearing into both concrete and flesh with incredible force. Beachside homes—even homes near the beach—were swept away or flooded.

Roofs ripped off buildings as if they were tin foil. The wind howled with a roar like a locomotive, except this locomotive didn't pass.

After the storm had passed, terrified residents ventured out to see the damage. Much of Joseph Young's beloved Hollywood was flattened and/or flooded. There were 34 confirmed deaths just in this one town, although most observers insisted that the real toll was much higher. Damage in neighboring Fort Lauderdale was considerable, as well, and 15 people were confirmed dead there.

Interestingly though, the communities of north Broward, which had fewer people, weren't hit as hard, suffering only minor damage and no deaths.

As native Floridians know, hurricane damage can be fixed. However, it can take a lot longer to fix a tattered reputation. Banner headlines in northern newspapers about the storm lasted long after the winds and rain had passed, scaring away both potential newcomers and potential investors. And numerous Broward residents, many of whom had lost pretty much everything,

packed up whatever belongings they still had left and headed back north.

The Depression hit the rest of America in 1929. But in reality, it had hit South Florida three years earlier. The region was—physically and psychologically—devastated.

That's not to say that everything stopped though. In 1927 Dania and Hallandale regained their independence, the latter to be its own city for the first time. Davie's charter lapsed, not to be renewed for 35 years. And the town of Floranada (for its Canadian emigrants), just outside Fort Lauderdale, was reincorporated as Oakland Park.

Eventually, after a few years, a trickle of northerners began settling in the area, perhaps because people were looking for a new start during the Depression. And as the years between the two world wars passed, the population grew from 14,242 in 1925, to 20,094 in 1930, and then to 39,794 by 1940.

BROWARD GOES TO WAR

If the Depression had come early to Broward, so did World War II. For the rest of America, it started on December 7, 1941. For Broward County, however, it had started two years earlier, on December 19, 1939. That was when the British cruiser HMS *Orion* chased the German freighter *Arauca* into Port Everglades (the rest of the world, of course, was at war two years before the United States). The *Arauca* remained tied up there until 1941, when it was seized by the United States after mutual declarations of war by Germany and the United States.

When America declared war after the attack on Pearl Harbor, it thrust this quiet, subtropical corner of the country into harsh reality. Like every other part of the country, Broward's young men streamed into recruiting offices. Civil defense units were formed, often led by men who were unfit or too old for the armed services. Ration cards were soon issued. Gasoline became scarce, as did ladies' nylons, whose material was needed for more urgent items such as parachutes.

Within a few months, German submarines (U-boats) were prowling the area for American troopships and freighters, which would most likely be carrying munitions to Britain, Russia, and other allies.

The first week of May 1942 was a costly one, as German submarines off southeast Florida torpedoed seven ships, one of which managed to limp into Port Everglades. That week served to raise the alarm level of Broward Countians. And that level went up several notches higher two months later, when four Germans were discovered after landing up the coast near Jacksonville.

Broward residents went to work. Watchtowers were set up along the ocean. The beaches were closed at night and patrolled by mounted coastguardsmen with attack dogs. The tops of headlights were blacked out, and street lights hooded as blackouts were imposed, so that it would be more difficult for ships to see lights ashore. Boaters and civil air-patrol pilots became actively involved in searching for U-boats.

Indeed Broward County went to war with a vengeance. The first Medal of Honor winner in the war was Second Lieutenant Alexander R. Nininger Jr., a graduate of Fort Lauderdale High School, who received the honor posthumously for his valiant actions in the Philippines during the Japanese invasion. Naval Air Station Fort Lauderdale trained thousands of young pilots, among them one who later became president of the United States, George H. W. Bush. And many local boys made the ultimate sacrifice.

Fifty Broward men from the Army and the Army Air Corps were killed in the war; figures are not available for the Navy and the Marines.

Broward County also became famous, however, for an event that happened a few months after the war ended. On December 5, 1945, five planes comprising Flight 19 took off from Naval Air Station Fort Lauderdale on a routine training mission—and never returned. To this day, theories abound about what really happened, most of them based on the supposition that the flight leader became disoriented and led the other planes farther out to sea, causing all of them to eventually run out of gas. The legend—and the speculation—grew even greater when another plane involved in the search for the missing squadron suddenly exploded in midair. No wreckage of any of the planes was ever found. But this episode gave birth to the stories about the "Bermuda Triangle."

During this frightening time, however, many of the seeds for Broward's future growth were planted. South Florida was one of the largest training areas for the armed forces because the weather was good all year round. Every airfield in the county, plus the future site of Broward Community College's central campus, was a World War II training facility. Port Everglades became a major naval base. And army barracks could be seen pretty much anywhere you went in the county. Literally hundreds of thousands—perhaps even millions—of servicemen passed through here during the war years. And—though their reasons for being here were, of course, serious ones—they could hardly help noticing the wonderful climate, the beaches, and the great opportunities to make a new life.

THE POSTWAR YEARS

When peace came, many of the ex-service-men couldn't get Broward County out of their minds. It was almost like a siren song that kept luring them back. Thousands of them did go back, often with their young families. And they told their friends and families, and thousands of them decided to come as well.

The greatest boom of all was officially on. When we look at the growth figures for those years, they're really hard to believe at first glance, almost otherworldly. In the 30 years from 1940 to 1970, Fort Lauderdale's population rocketed from 17,996 to 139,590. Hollywood went from 6,239 to 106,873; Pompano Beach from 4,427 to 38,587; and Hallandale from 1,827 to 23,849. Plantation, which was just getting started in 1950, had grown to 23,523 by 1970. World War II was obviously the most trying and most devastating time in history, but just as obviously, it put Greater Fort Lauderdale on the map.

Everywhere you looked, new cities were being created, and older ones were growing. In 1945, at the end of the war, the county still had only the seven active municipalities of 1929. But the growth in the number of cities and towns started soon after. Hillsboro Beach, chartered in 1939, became an active city in 1947. Hacienda Village was added in 1946, and Wilton Manors in 1947.

Then, like falling dominoes, one city after another was created. Lauderdale-by-the-Sea started it off in 1951, followed by Plantation and Lazy Lake in 1953; Margate and Miramar, 1955; Lighthouse Point, 1956; Pembroke Park, 1957; Lauderhill, Cooper City, Sea Ranch Lakes, and Pembroke Pines in 1959; Sunrise, Davie, and Lauderdale Lakes, 1961; North Lauderdale, Coral Springs, Parkland, and Tamarac, 1963; and Coconut Creek, 1967.

By 1970, the county's population was soaring toward the million mark. But, as had been shown a few decades earlier, sometimes rapid growth can bring its own set of problems. Many of the new towns had been developed by specific development companies, who had come up with master plans and who had built most of the housing in those towns. A few of these companies ran into financial problems; some of them became significantly overextended. Other developers came under intense criticism because they were seen to be too involved in the cities they created.

In addition, many newcomers to the area had a growing sense of foreboding that the rapid growth was bringing with it the same problems they had fled up north. As the 1970s dawned, many local residents became vocal in demanding that their cities put some limits on what they saw as out-of-control growth, including lower limits on the number of residences per acre. The developers, too involved in their own problems, couldn't do much to respond to these concerns. But local governments could; and they began taking some measures to cool off the growth.

Within a few years, the runaway growth had stopped all right, but it wasn't because of any governmental measures. It was because of a severe recession that swept across America. As a result, South Florida—and Broward County—was littered by half-finished condo projects. These "white elephants" eventually dotted the landscape. Even many projects that had actually been finished sat there empty—because there were no buyers. At one point, there were an estimated 50,000 unsold condominium apartments in the area. You could see them everywhere; they stuck out like sore thumbs.

And they gave ample testimony to what happens when hubris and dreams collide with a national recession.

By 1976 the building industry had begun to take baby steps toward recovery. This time, though, civic and business leaders were determined to monitor growth more carefully, to avoid a repeat of the tail-wagging-the-dog patterns of the past. A new county charter gave Broward's government broad powers to monitor and improve the quality of life and the environment. The passage of the 1977 Land Use Plan was a major step toward limiting urban sprawl and ensuring that the area's resources—natural, economic, and social—would truly be put to use for the benefit of the people who lived here.

THE MODERN ERA

By this time, the Spring Breakers had made Fort Lauderdale their yearly destination, as noted earlier in this chapter, by the hundreds of thousands. And, also as noted earlier, local merchants were delighted by the mighty influx each spring because it brought a dependable wave of business on a regular basis, which they could count on every year at the same time.

Just how "mighty" was this influx? Well, one of the best ways to explain it is this: It could easily take you 45 minutes to drive six blocks along (oceanside) SR A1A during Spring Break. Forty-five minutes to go six blocks! The sheer mass of cars with license plates from as far away as Canada and Alaska—many of them filled to the brim with students, with various body parts hanging out—was one reason. But another was that it was standard practice for cars filled with boys or with girls to stop—right in the middle of the road—and ogle, or try to make

conversation with, members of the opposite sex who were walking on the sidewalk.

Eventually, though, cracks began to show in the façade of local businesspeople who looked forward to this event every year. For one thing, as noted earlier, the kids sometimes piled 10 or more of themselves into hotel rooms—and often left without paying. For another, incidents of shoplifting and fighting always spiked during these two weeks. And for a third, the kids' behavior began growing more raunchy each year. Each year, the contests grew a little more lewd. And the alcohol flow became greater.

In addition, Fort Lauderdale began losing its appeal to families, who felt overrun and somewhat frightened by the massive influx of college kids and drinking each year. The area began getting a reputation as a place you didn't want to bring your family in the spring.

And eventually, perhaps inevitably, tragedy struck. Several drunk collegians threw themselves off their hotel balconies into the swimming pools below. And a couple of them missed.

After a few deaths, civic and government leaders made a conscious decision to withdraw the welcome mat for Spring Breakers, and to pitch wider markets that would come here all year long, not just for two weeks in March. And by this time, most of the merchants were onboard, as well.

After a particularly wild Spring Break in 1985, in which an estimated 350,000 college visitors caused disruption for several weeks, Fort Lauderdale passed a series of restrictive laws in an effort to reduce the mayhem. In an effort to staunch the damage and to get out the message, Mayor Robert Dressler actually went on *Good Morning, America* to announce that Spring Breakers were not

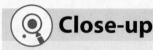

Close-up

The Strip

When I went to high school, in the late '80s, the Fort Lauderdale "Strip" was still the Strip. Those were the days when the beachside strip was swarming with kids, in all kinds of cars. We'd just drive back and forth. I can't remember meeting any girls that way, but it was probably enough that we thought we were so "cool." In fact, we almost never got out of the car. I played baseball at Pine Crest Academy, and after practice—especially on Friday nights—we'd always cruise the Strip.

Now those days are gone. The city eventually chased out all the Spring Breakers and cleaned up the Strip in order to attract a more family-oriented crowd. But I still think back fondly to those days.

—Ethan Skolnick, Sportswriter, *South Florida Sun-Sentinel*

welcome any longer in Fort Lauderdale. Overnight parking was banned near the beach, and a law prohibiting the consumption of alcohol in public places was passed. The following spring, 1986, the city denied MTV a permit to set up a concert stage on the beach. And approximately 2,500 people were arrested as the new laws were strictly enforced.

Statistics began bearing out the wisdom of the city's decision. In 1985, the 350,000 college students spent about $110 million during the four-week Spring Break season. By 2004, however, they had been replaced by some 700,000 visitors, mostly families or European tourists—who spent $800 million during the same period. By 2006, the number of college students visiting for Spring Break was estimated at only 10,000. And by that time, the college crowd had appointed other places as their Break gathering spots, such as Cancún, Mexico, and the "Redneck Riviera" of the Florida panhandle.

And the city they left behind has grown up—dramatically. Those revelers of the '80s (now, presumably, responsible

adults themselves) wouldn't recognize Fort Lauderdale.

Just as things were coming to a head with the students, the city passed a bond issue in 1986 to connect the disparate parts of town into one cohesive urban center. This plan foresaw the coalescing of different districts in and around downtown—the arts and entertainment district, the historic downtown area, and the Las Olas shopping and beach district. The twin goals were to shake, once and for all, the city's long-standing reputation as a "party" town and a cultural desert. The centerpiece of the new Fort Lauderdale was the Riverwalk, a red-brick promenade that runs along the banks of the New River and is always filled with people strolling or sitting on the benches and watching other people stroll.

Around the Riverwalk, all the nuances of a sophisticated, cosmopolitan city were put in, piece by piece. The Fort Lauderdale Museum of Art moved into a magnificent new downtown location in 1986, bringing a cultural sophistication (along with exhibits such as "King Tut" and "Bodies") to a city that admittedly had lacked it before. In 1991 the Broward Center for the Performing Arts opened (with Andrew Lloyd Webber's *The Phantom of the Opera*), bringing a world-class, state-of-the-art performance venue to the city. The next year saw the opening of the fantastic Museum of Discovery & Science, whose interactive exhibits and whimsical touches can make a child again out of the most jaded adult. By then, Las Olas Boulevard, always an attractive street, had become a true European-style urban boulevard, with horse-and-buggy rides, world-class galleries, international bistros, great jazz joints, one-of-a-kind boutiques, and a fascinating people parade.

Fort Lauderdale–Hollywood International Airport began building new terminals and bringing in new amenities. Port Everglades replaced Miami as the world's busiest cruise port. And for the first time, Fort Lauderdale began sprouting an actual skyline of striking, imaginative office or condo towers of 30 and 40 stories.

What's next? No one knows for sure. Because, unlike most areas in America, Greater Fort Lauderdale's still writing its story. And according to the locals, the best chapters are yet to come.

ACCOMMODATIONS

So you need a place to stay in Greater Fort Lauderdale. Good news: You've got choices—lots of them. This area is chock-full of traditional hotels, not to mention RV parks, hostels, and charming bed-and-breakfasts. The vast majority of accommodations here are hotels and B&Bs, and this chapter highlights some of the most centrally located accommodations, mainly hugging the beach or near-the-beach areas—after all, that's probably one of the things that drew you here, right? Additionally, we've listed a fair number of places situated near downtown Fort Lauderdale, as this is also a hub for travelers and is only a short hop or skip—or simply a water-taxi ride—from the beach. We've focused primarily on non–chain hotels, ones that offer character and a personal touch—most of those chains that are listed here have something special to offer. Additional locations can be found by consulting the phone book or visiting the website of your preferred hotel chain.

If you're traveling with family, consider staying at one of the hotels with suites or request a connecting room, which many hotels offer. Just about all hotels here are wheelchair accessible. Several accommodate guests' four-legged friends; one hotel even encourages you to bring your small pet—just note that larger dogs, as always, are difficult to tote along on your trip. Some pet-friendly hotels charge an extra fee for your furry friends to spend the night, but many don't.

There are a number of fancy, palatial hotels that cost upwards of $400 a night for a prime room or a suite, but the majority of hotels here charge between $100 and $350 a night for a room. RV parks and hostels—as well as hotels located outside of high-traffic areas like downtown and the beaches—charge significantly less. Prices are typically cheaper if you make reservations at least one month in advance—more if you are planning to come over a holiday weekend during the winter months.

OVERVIEW

If you plan to see a bit of Greater Fort Lauderdale—and reading this book suggests you do—you'd be wise to stay downtown, but then again, we're thinking part of your trip also includes beach time, in which case we recommend Fort Lauderdale Beach. That said, both of these areas are in eastern Broward County, but as the majority of sites and entertainment lie here, we've followed suit and included lodging options mostly on this side of the county. These areas are centrally located and offer easy access to restaurants, shopping, and anyplace you might want to go in eastern Broward. The Fort Lauderdale Beach hotels are just a 15-minute drive to downtown, and downtown is only a 20-minute drive to Hollywood. Anything downtown means you'll be within walking distance of trendy Las Olas Boulevard and the River-walk, and anything in Fort Lauderdale Beach means you can easily access the sand and the Intracoastal.

If you prefer something a little more off the beaten path, you've still got some excellent options. There is a range of accom-modations in the Deerfield Beach, Lauder-dale-by-the Sea, and Pompano Beach area. Lauderdale-by-the-Sea is a particularly popu-lar area to spend time in, as it has a very well-maintained community feel and offers a large selection of shops and restaurants in its tiny commercial crisscross of streets a block from the beach. Both Deerfield and Pom-pano Beaches offer beach fun too, but are sleepier. There is also a large gay and lesbian community in the Wilton Manors area, which is reflected in a number of lodging options oriented to gay travelers. Hollywood Beach is a prime choice for those wanting a small-beach town atmosphere but still lots of hop-ping nightlife and restaurants within walking distance—the Broadwalk, a long strip that runs next to the ocean, is chock full of res-taurants and bars towards its northern end.

This chapter presents a sampling of the accommodations in the Fort Lauderdale area, organized by neighborhood. This is by no means a comprehensive list of Fort Lauderdale accommodations, but it should give you many options—and save you the hassle of website–hopping to find a place to rest your head.

Price Code

Prices are based on a one-night stay in one standard room. Please note that in many cases, this chapter includes price ranges such as $$–$$$. This typically means that there are some rooms available in the lower price bracket but many options—particu-larly suites—cost more. Hotel rates often change and may be higher during the holi-days or other peak times, like during the annual Fort Lauderdale International Boat Show in late October and early November. Rates here do not include the Fort Lauder-dale hotel tax, which is 11 percent. These rates are up to date as of press time, but you should always call ahead to confirm.

$ . . . . under $100
$$ . . . . $100 to 200
$$$ . . . . $200 to $300
$$$$ . . . . over $300

ACCOMMODATIONS

The Pillars at New River Sound, Ft. Lauderdale, 38

Riverside Hotel, Ft. Lauderdale, 33

$$–$$$

Granada Inn, Ft. Lauderdale, 38

Beachcomber Resort & Villas, Pompano Beach, 40

Manta Ray Inn, Hollywood, 40

$$

By-Eddy Motel Apartments, Ft. Lauderdale, 33

Carriage House Resort Motel, Deerfield Beach, 42

Driftwood on the Ocean, Hollywood, 40

Gigi's Resort by the Beach, Ft. Lauderdale, 34

Little Inn by the Sea, A, Lauderdale-by-the-Sea, 41

Pineapple Place Apartments, Pompano Beach, 42

Schubert Resort, Ft. Lauderdale, 32

The Sea Grape House, Ft. Lauderdale, 34

$–$$

Hollywood Beach Suites, Hostel & Hotel, Hollywood, 40

$

Backpackers Beach Hostel, Ft. Lauderdale, 38

Everglades Holiday Park, Weston, 44

Floyd's International Youth Hostel & Crew House, Ft. Lauderdale, 34

Grand Palms Hotel & Golf Resort, Pembroke Pines, 43

Quiet Waters Park Camping, Deerfield Beach, 43

FORT LAUDERDALE AREA

Resorts

MARY'S RESORT $$$
1115 Tequesta St., Ft. Lauderdale
(954) 523-3500
www.marysresort.com

Small-pet owners take special note: This is one of the most inviting lodging choices you and your small pooch or cat will ever come across in the area. Named after Mary, the resort's much-loved, cheerful Boston terrier who greets guests upon arrival, the property is within walking distance to downtown Fort Lauderdale and the Riverwalk, and only a short hop to the beach. Each of the nine rooms and cottages are decorated simply with a modern, luxurious touch and feature their own private patio. Some are simple rooms with microwaves, others suitelike with kitchenettes; the biggest are two-bedroom cottages. With tropical gardens around the heated swimming pool, a bubbling Jacuzzi, and a spacious sundeck, this place makes

you feel right at home—in fact, there's even complimentary suntan lotion stocked just for guests. Free bikes are available, and the common areas stock cards and board games.

SCHUBERT RESORT $$
855 NE 20th Ave., Ft. Lauderdale
(954) 763-7434
www.schubertresort.com

This is considered one of Fort Lauderdale's premier gay resorts and draws loyal devotees back time and time again. But first things first—this is a male-only, clothing-optional resort, so, dear mister, make sure you're comfortable with that before you check in. If you choose to remain clothed, that's fine, but frankly most people strut about in the buff. The placed is housed in a former 1950s-era motel that's been transported into a playful, retro paradise. After a multimillion-dollar renovation a few years back, the resort maintained all its old-school charm but implemented modern furnishings throughout. In addition to the "loungey" pool area (which often becomes party zone any time of day or night), the property also features a 10-person Jacuzzi, complimentary breakfasts that often run until the early afternoon, and wet bars in most rooms.

Hotels & Motels

BY-EDDY MOTEL APARTMENTS $$
1021 NE 13th Ave., Ft. Lauderdale
(954) 764-7555
www.byeddymotel.com

Cute as a button, this combination motel and apartment lodging is smart and clean, with superb touches to make each guest feel at home. Rooms are cheerful and welcoming, with white tile and bedspreads flanked by colorful pillows and throws; bathrooms are spotless and shiny, often with a vase of fresh flowers or a pot of orchids. The entire complex surrounds a cheerful courtyard peppered with lounge tables and chairs (with umbrellas) and plenty of lush foliage. A superb choice in this price range, with free Wi-Fi and a communal barbecue area. The complex tends to attract European travelers—particularly French nationals—and as a result the cable-TV package includes some of the main French channels.

GALLERY ONE FORT
LAUDERDALE $$$
2670 E. Sunrise Blvd., Ft. Lauderdale
(954) 565-3800
www.galleryone.doubletree.com

Situated on the Intracoastal Waterway and directly across from the Galleria mall, this ultra-fancy Doubletree hotel reopened in 2009 after a two-year, multimillion-dollar renovation project that has transformed the property into an exceptional boutique hotel. Updates include a gallery design theme showcasing a large and unusual collection

of art and sculpture flanked by modern furniture in the lobby—most is contemporary and it changes every other month, so even repeat visits will benefit from something new to examine each time. The 231 resort residences are all one- and two-bedroom suites and feature modern kitchens, granite countertops, stainless steel appliances, and plasma TVs. Add to that a tropically landscaped terrace, water-taxi service from the hotel's dock, a substantial fitness center, and access to a private cruising yacht, and you won't get bored. An on-site restaurant and bar rounds out the experience.

i Don't leave home (or hotel) without it. And we're not talking about a credit card here. We're talking about sunscreen. Unless you live here, you have no real idea how strong the sun actually is—even in the winter. In fact, we South Florida locals are always warned by our dermatologists not to drive with our left arm resting on the window. And to always put sunscreen on, even if we're only running errands. It's advice you may come to appreciate after a few days here.

RIVERSIDE HOTEL $$$
620 E. Las Olas Blvd., Ft. Lauderdale
(954) 467-0671
www.riversidehotel.com

Fort Lauderdale's oldest hotel, which debuted in 1936, inhabits a front-row seat on Las Olas Boulevard—right in the middle of its slew of boutiques, art galleries, and restaurants. You feel transported back in time every second you're here, and the historic photos that grace the hallways give you an insight into its past. Its 205 guest rooms come in several styles—traditional is outfitted with antique oak furnishings and framed prints; classical invokes a Tommy Bahama theme; and penthouse suites in the 12-story executive tower feature balconies with sweeping views of the downtown skyline, Las Olas, and the New River. A traditional English afternoon-tea program (choose from Classic, Full, or Royal) unfolds in the lobby every day (reservations required). Frequent renovations ensure the hotel continues to be in tip-top shape, and its pub (the **Golden Lyon**) and restaurants—the stately **Grill Room** and the more casual **Indigo**—are popular in their own right—once you see patrons dining at Indigo's inviting outdoor patio tables below swirling, Old Florida ceiling fans, it's clear that this is a cut above the rest.

Bed-and-Breakfasts

THE SEA GRAPE HOUSE   **$$**
1109 NE 16th Place, Ft. Lauderdale
(954) 525-6586 or (800) 377-8802
www.seagrape.com
Oh, we love this historic bed-and-breakfast. Located at the edge of Wilton Manors (it's just 4 blocks from the bustling restaurant and nightlife scene of this predominantly gay area) and just a short hop from downtown Fort Lauderdale, this landmark house has morphed into a cozy, affordable lodging option perfect for those wanting a touch of something personal at an affordable price. The modest rooms are tenderly decorated with colorful quilts and simple furnishings, and the pool and Jacuzzi area makes you feel like you are staying in someone's home. It's also known as being a great spot to hang your hat while looking for local real estate—the staff is helpful, ready to assist, and often recommends local realtors or gives advice on where to live.

Hostels

FLOYD'S INTERNATIONAL YOUTH HOSTEL & CREW HOUSE   **$**
445 SE 16th St., Ft. Lauderdale
(954) 462-0631
www.floridahostel.com
This hostel—only a few blocks from downtown Fort Lauderdale's Riverwalk and Old Town—is a unique place to hit the hay—it serves as a travelers hostel but is also home to the countless yacht crews that pass through Fort Lauderdale, many arriving to seek work or in between jobs. The hostel also lists yacht-job links on their website, and yacht owners seeking help (sometimes just for a few days) often stop by here. If crewing is on your agenda, it's a fab spot to look for a job, trade information, and recommendations; if not, it is fun to hear the stories of those embracing a less-than-traditional way of life. The vibe is chilled and kinda groovy, and weekly rates make a longer stay quite affordable; most units are former two-bedroom apartments that share a common area and kitchen. Free Wi-Fi and local telephone calls also available.

FORT LAUDERDALE BEACH AREA
Resorts

GIGI'S RESORT BY THE BEACH   **$$**
3005 Alhambra St., Ft. Lauderdale
(954) 463-4827
www.gigisresort.com
We love Gigi's. Tucked away beyond the skyscraper beachfront hotels is sweet Gigi's, an Art Deco relic that looks like it could have been transplanted from South Beach (well, the sleepy South Beach that existed pre-1990, that is). But the Art Deco pretty much ends there—each room has its own global

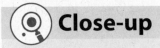

Close-up

All Hands on Deck

Fort Lauderdale is the nation's—if not the world's—biggest hub for yachting, so it's no surprise that slews of yacht crews pass though here every year in need of lodging in between contracts, or simply land here in search of a job. Fort Lauderdale offers a large number of budget-friendly hotels—hostels that largely cater to this seafaring community—and they all offer affordable options for longer stays. The hostels we've reviewed fully in this chapter are popular among both crews and regular travelers, but if they are all full, try downtown's **Bridge II/Chocolate Hostel and Hotel** (506 SE 16th St., 954-522-6350, www.yachtcrewquarters.com) or the beach's **Deauville Hostel and Crewhouse** (2916 N. Ocean Blvd., 954-568-5000, www.deauvillehostel .com). The latter is dog-friendly and offers the perk of being across from the beach. Both offer both dormitory- and private-style rooms and remain firmly in the budget category (under $100 per night).

city/regional theme, from Hong Kong to Bahamas, Paris to Nairobi. A tranquil wooden sundeck, a communal barbecue, and free continental breakfast rounds out the package. Many rooms come with kitchenettes or full kitchens. It's also possible to connect several rooms, which makes this place rather popular with the families. And with only a two-minute walk to the beach and five minutes from the main action of the Strip, you can find the hubbub easily while still resting your head in a sanctuary of calm.

HYATT REGENCY PIER
SIXTY-SIX RESORT & SPA $$$–$$$$
2301 SE 17th St., Ft. Lauderdale
(954) 525-6666
www.pier66.com
After an extensive renovation in 2009, the 384-room Hyatt Regency is sparkling yet again. The resort consists of a landmark tower (you can see the slightly retro-looking round structure from afar), which looms over the sprawling grounds with their lush

landscaping. Non-tower lanai rooms feature retro-modern appointments and a more casual feel, while the tower rooms exude business-hotel vibe—if you stay in the latter, choose from rooms overlooking the Intracoastal Waterway, downtown, or the beach (or a mix of two out of three). Other extras include a three-pool waterfall oasis to lounge around, and prime marina spots, should you arrive on your yacht (non–boat owners can simply gawk at the impressive vessels). Add a state-of-the-art spa, environmentally friendly details like reclaiming water for irrigation, no less than three hopping restaurants and bars, and a free shuttle service to the beach (less than five minutes away), and you're set for your stay.

IL LUGANO $$$$
3333 NE 32nd Ave., Ft. Lauderdale
(954) 567-4484
www.illugano.com
Directly on the Intracoastal, Il Lugano, an $80 million project, stands 14 stories high

and is located adjacent to Galt Ocean Mile. Named after a luxurious lake resort area on the border of Switzerland and Italy, the hotel's design features 105 studio and one-bedroom suites with oversized balconies and state-of-the-art gourmet kitchens, a lush pool area overlooking the Intracoastal, a full-service fitness center, deepwater boat slips (to fit all those yachts, of course), in-room washers and dryers, iPod docking stations and BOSE sound systems, and—surprising for a hotel of this caliber—complimentary high-speed Internet. Additionally, the property is home to the upscale, waterfront restaurant and lounge, **da Campo Osteria,** run by famed Boston chef and restaurateur Todd English. This place is all about service—Il Concierge offers complimentary airport and local transfers, and you truly feel like a pampered person of substance here. Rooms are palatial without feeling overdone, with both Italian and beachy nods in soothing tans and polished dark-wood touches, many with balconies overlooking the water. The pool area supplies plenty of shady and sunny spots and is also a pleasant place to relax around sunset.

LAGO MAR RESORT & CLUB $$$$
1700 Ocean Lane, Ft. Lauderdale
(954) 245-3630
www.lagomar.com
This oasis feels like a secret. Yet this secluded 10-acre tropical world wedged between Lake Mayan and the Atlantic Ocean is only a 10-minute drive from buzzing Fort Lauderdale Beach. Popular among families and older patrons, its 204 suites (many with kitchenettes) and rooms are outfitted with homey but top-quality furnishings (think toned-down Tommy Bahama), but really, you come here for the lush property. The linked buildings loop around a 9,000-square-foot lagoon pool flanked by palm trees and other tropical plants, tennis courts, beach volleyball, shuffleboard, minigolf, and a charming courtyard with a children's playground. Beyond lies a fabulous 500-foot stretch of pearly white beach—choose from the more-private sand containing a junglelike grid of palm trees, or venture closer to the ocean for some uninterrupted sun action. The resort features four restaurants (kids love the **Soda Shop**) and two bars, but most of all, this is a family-owned place, and they make sure each guest is treated like family. No other spot in the area gives you so much personal, friendly service paired with amenities like this. Lago Mar is a popular convention site, so book way ahead.

THE RITZ-CARLTON FORT LAUDERDALE $$$–$$$$
1 N. Fort Lauderdale Beach Blvd.,
Ft. Lauderdale
(954) 465-2300
www.ritzcarlton.com
Smack on Fort Lauderdale Beach, this superbly appointed luxury hotel greets you with a curving marble lobby and cool white furnishings. The entire building design is inspired by a grand luxury cruise liner, with curves that mimic ocean waves. The hotel features 192 rooms, including eight ocean-front and Intracoastal suites, with an average room size of 520 square feet. If you dare to part from your room—a bastion of creamy white and polished wood and exquisite Bulgari amenities (pure luxury—what else, this is the Ritz)—pop down to the 29,000-square-foot sundeck and loll away the day next to the infinity pool, or give your skin a treat in the 8,500-square-foot spa. Clever pluses like a personal skywalk leading to the beach,

special privileges at **Grand Oakes** Members Only Golf Course (fun factoid—this is where *Caddyshack* was filmed), a swanky pool bar, and a sophisticated on-site restaurant, lobby bar, and wine room (with a wine cellar of 5,000 bottles of wine and a rare Scotch selection) make this upscale lodging at its finest. Dog lovers take note: They also offer a **Pampered Pooch Package** (for pups 25 pounds or less—rooms prepared with a dog bed, bowls, and treats).

W FORT LAUDERDALE   **$$$$**
401 N. Fort Lauderdale Beach Blvd.,
Ft. Lauderdale
(954) 414-8200
www.whotels.com/fortlauderdale
One of the newest additions to the top-tier hotels in Fort Lauderdale is the 486-room W. This place is the definition of hip and trendy and is far more than a hotel—it's the beach's newest "in" spot. Located on a four-and-a-half-acre site straddling the swath of land between the Atlantic Ocean and Intracoastal Waterway, this W doesn't stray too far from its usual offerings, which include the W Hotel's Whatever/Whenever services (in short—get what you want, whenever you want it): a notable restaurant with a star chef, this time Stephen Starr's (of Philly restaurant-scene fame) restaurant **Steak 954**; the W signature pillow menu (yes, you choose between a body pillow, neck roll, firm foam PrimaLoft pillow, or 100 percent goose-down feather pillow); and the **Whiskey Blue** bar. Add to that a huge fitness center, the renowned **Bliss Spa,** and an oceanfront infinity edge pool. Earth tones dominate most of the modern rooms, which manage minimalism while still retaining coziness and warmth, but larger units (like the full-apartment suites) introduce bold blues in the kitchen area.

The Cruise Effect

The cruise lines, which bring people to the city from all over the country, can have a big effect on hotel prices. Most cruises depart on Friday or Saturday, sometimes driving hotel prices higher on those days. If you've got the flexibility, arriving during the week might provide better value.

To find the cheapest accommodations, try using Hotwire or Priceline when booking a hotel. Both sites offer a neighborhood search function, so you can make sure you'll be staying where you want (near the airport, near Port Everglades, near Las Olas, etc.) before booking. Before booking online, however, call the hotel and ask if any lower rates are available, particularly if you're a member of organizations such as AAA or AARP.

Hotels & Motels

THE ATLANTIC HOTEL   **$$$$**
601 N. Fort Lauderdale Beach Blvd.,
Ft. Lauderdale
(954) 567-8020
www.atlantichotelfl.com
Trend hounds take note: If you want modern digs with class and flair, the Atlantic is your mecca. Its 124 guest rooms are all significantly oversized (its 54 suites are gargantuan, and they also offer a handful

of apartment-style units that include full kitchens), and each feels breezy and beachy while maintaining a sophisticated look. For example, the decor gives a nod to Balinese-style furnishing while still feeling distinctly North American, and colors don't stray far from soft beiges, browns, and white; some rooms have large floor-to-ceiling windows opening out to the balcony and curtains billowing in the ocean breeze. Bathrooms are a shiny marble heaven with touches of Old Florida (or pre-1950s), like old-style shuttered window coverings. A full-service European spa (note to Florida residents—present your state ID and receive 25 percent off all services), the fifth floor bar and cafe (great for cocktails with a view of the ocean), and the popular **Trina Restaurant** (see p. 71 in the Restaurants chapter for a full review) round out the package.

THE PILLARS AT NEW RIVER SOUND $$$
111 N. Birch Rd., Ft. Lauderdale
(954) 467-9639
www.pillarshotel.com
Shhh . . . don't tell anyone about this place. Already dubbed a "secret hotel" by locals and visitors in the know, this gem smartly manages to hide itself on a back street of Fort Lauderdale Beach. It isn't on the beach, but once you step out into the tiny-but-charming pool area and stare out at the Intracoastal Waterway, you won't care. The property is a throwback to British colonial architecture and exudes supreme class. Most rooms face the water or the pool, and a select few contain French doors and private balconies or patios. Each space is outfitted with a wet bar, microwave, and deep cherry furnishings and floral bedspreads. Just beyond the palm-fringed pool area is a

small deck with a few tables, some with canopies, facing the water. At sunset, it can't get more romantic than this, and the area is also a calm and rejuvenating spot to have breakfast and kick back with the paper. The on-site **Secret Garden** restaurant is exclusively for hotel guests and a handpicked number of carefully selected insiders and locals. While they aren't on the standard water-taxi route, the front desk will call ahead for you, and the taxis will make a special stop on the dock.

Bed-and-Breakfasts

GRANADA INN $$–$$$
3011 Granada St., Ft. Lauderdale
(954) 463-2032 or (866) 463-4900
www.thegranadainn.com
Proprietor Cheryll Stephanoos has created a secluded paradise nestled around a lush tropical courtyard and swimming pool. Each of the 13 themed guest rooms is named after, and inspired by, an island in the Caribbean—for example you can choose between Antigua, St. Vincent, or St. Barts—but all feature plantation- or island-style furniture, crisp linens, a stereo, refrigerator, and European soap and bath amenities, and most rooms face the pool. This is yet another find tucked back in the residential area of Fort Lauderdale Beach, which means you are away from the bustle but can hop to the action with a mere 10-minute stroll. Breakfast is served poolside under the swaying coconut palms each day, and they happily lend out fluffy beach towels.

Hostels

BACKPACKERS BEACH HOSTEL $
2115 N. Ocean Blvd., Ft. Lauderdale
(954) 567-7275
www.fortlauderdalehostel.com

A short hop north of the main beach action at Fort Lauderdale Beach is this pleasant hostel. Located across the street from the ocean, you can't get better value than this—but note this is a true hostel. Depending on the night, it can be full of partygoers, and it is possible the bathroom can morph into a "barfroom," though this is the exception versus the rule. That said, there are a handful of private rooms available, and all rooms, including dorms, have their own bathroom. Also available are a few comfy common rooms, a kitchen, a tranquil garden, and a grill—free for all guests to use. There's also free Internet access and local telephone calls. Parking is also complimentary, a huge advantage in this area of town.

i Many hotels offer Internet-only deals on their websites; these frequently beat the deals you'd get by making your reservation over the phone.

HOLLYWOOD, HOLLYWOOD BEACH & HALLANDALE BEACH

Resorts

SEMINOLE HARD ROCK & CASINO   **$$$–$$$$**
1 Seminole Way, Hollywood
(954) 364-4171
www.hardrock.com

It may be miles from the beach, but most who stay here are all about the partying and the gambling anyway. The casino's Hollywood Poker Room is a wannabe Vegas floor offering over 40 poker tables and more slot machines than you can shake a quarter at. Beyond the casino lies a theater; and a 5,600-seat live-performance venue showcases top performers, touring bands, and championship boxing, 16 restaurants/bars for every budget, 14 hopping nightclubs, and over 20 retail shops. But this is just part of the story. The four-and-a-half-acre pool territory (which includes a stone mountain doubling as a backdrop to a 182-foot waterslide) is mind-blowingly impressive. Each of the 500 rooms is top-notch and includes high-tech stereo systems and Egyptian cotton–filled luxury beds. Of course the memorabilia-bedecked **Hard Rock Cafe** fills a large part of the casino, as do a number of other large restaurants. Just like in Vegas, the show and fun keep going 24 hours a day, but if you need a break that doesn't involve a pool, head to the state-of-the-art spa, in-house gym, or surrounding golf course.

THE WESTIN DIPLOMAT RESORT & SPA $$$$
3555 S. Ocean Dr., Hollywood
(954) 602-6000
www.westin.com/diplomat

Even the most well-traveled resort aficionado will be wowed by this Westin. Two looming towers, a monstrous atrium center lobby, a two-level infinity edge pool with two waterfalls cascading into a 240-foot lagoon below (the top pool also includes an eye-catching round glass bottom) make up this property. The 989 breezy, luxe rooms and suites (most with balconies facing the Atlantic) come with sumptuous, smooth tan-and-white furnishings, and many include strategically placed tubs—the bathroom's sliding wall means you can sit in the tub and look out at the ocean from beneath the bubbles. For pampering of a different kind, head to the 30,000-square-foot spa set in a lavish garden courtyard (22 treatment rooms in total). When you get hungry from all that spa, pool, and tub time, hit one of the eight on-site restaurants.

Hotels & Motels

DRIFTWOOD ON THE OCEAN $$
2101 S. Surf Rd., Hollywood
(954) 923-9528
www.driftwoodontheocean.com

We love this Hollywood lodging staple. It's been around since the 1950s, but they've maintained the property with love and care. The motel sits on a quiet south end of Surf Road and faces the beach—many rooms face the ocean, but cheaper ones don't—and most contain a full kitchen and balcony. If you get bored with the beach, the site is home to a heated pool, shuffleboard, and basketball courts. Free off-street parking and Wi-Fi make this an excellent value for its location.

MANTA RAY INN $$–$$$
1715 S. Surf Rd., Hollywood
(954) 921-9666
www.mantarayinn.com

Spread across two stories, this inn right on the ocean is a perfect escape, with its affable owners who make you feel at home and its relaxed island feel. The entire property is an old 1940s relic with all the best parts intact and the key elements newly renovated. Wicker and rattan dominate, and most units include microwaves or even full kitchens. There's no pool here, which is a turnoff for some, but with the beach on your doorstep, it's a minor issue for most.

Hostels

HOLLYWOOD BEACH SUITES, HOSTEL & HOTEL $–$$
334 Arizona St., Hollywood
(954) 391-9448
www.hollywoodbeachhostel.com

The beach's first hostel opened in 2009 to rave reviews and is already packing them in. Mixing hotel and hostel in a sublimely beach atmosphere, you're guaranteed to have fun here at any budget. Who wouldn't love the old Key West cottage; free bikes, surf boards, and Internet; simple but perky common areas—including a grilling area, large deck, and full kitchen—swathed in a fresh coat of white paint; and comfy wicker tables and chairs? Rooms are a mix of multiple-bed dorms (shared women's and shared men's are separated) and private rooms, and the entire operation is run by the respectable South Beach Group that owns several hotels in the Miami area. Many of the private hotel rooms really feel like a simple boutique hotel, and dorm rooms are a mix of beachy touches and Ikea-style metal bunk beds; you can't get better value than this on Hollywood Beach.

LAUDERDALE-BY-THE-SEA TO DEERFIELD BEACH

Resorts

BEACHCOMBER RESORT & VILLAS $$–$$$
1200 S. Ocean Blvd., Pompano Beach
(954) 941-7830
www.beachcomberresort.com

This 140-room property's beachfront location might not be in the thick of things, but it's just due south of Deerfield Beach, close to most local attractions, and about a mile from the Pompano Pier. Ocean views are in every available space on the property, from the plush, oversize guest-room balconies to the dining rooms. Villas and penthouse suites grace the top of the eight-story structure, and standard rooms reside below. Overall, the resort exudes a nice Old Florida feel and oodles of laid-back charm. The property

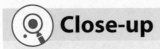

Close-up

Book It for Less

In days past, you had no bargaining power with a South Florida hotel. They were just as happy to turn you away and wait for the next person willing to pay full price—and they usually didn't have to wait more than a minute or two. But things are different now, thanks to the recession.

South Florida has been one of the hardest-hit areas of the nation. Many hotels in South Florida have had vacancy rates of 25 percent at times, and sometimes higher. And as a result, you've become a precious commodity. Some hotels are now quite willing to bargain (even if they won't admit it!). Always be sure to check the Internet price of a hotel before calling; if there's a difference in price, insist on the lower one. Always make sure you trot out whatever card in your wallet might make you eligible for a discount—AAA, AARP, your insurance company, etc. And—as a last-ditch effort—inquire about the "business rate." If you can't get a lower price, then ask about an upgrade. Or ask them to throw in the last day for free. And lastly, if you have some flexibility in your schedule, but you don't want to come during summer, try to come during "Shoulder Season"—just before or after High Season. For example, if you're thinking about coming in March, consider April instead; that's when rates start to go down. And if you're thinking about going in November, consider October instead—right before the rates go up.

includes two large outdoor pools, a tiki bar, and shuffleboard and beach volleyball courts. All guests receive complimentary passes to a fitness center located just over a mile away.

HIGH NOON BEACH RESORT $$$
4424 El Mar Dr., Lauderdale-by-the-Sea
(954) 776-1121
www.highnoonresort.com
Straddling 300 feet of prime beachfront in Lauderdale-by-the-Sea, this small resort stretches across several buildings and includes the two pool areas, a shuffleboard court, and a handful of tiki bars just to make you feel truly ensconced in a tropical paradise. The entire spread includes plenty of palms, giving it all shade and a picturesque quality. All rooms include a full kitchen and are done up in colorful spreads atop rattan

bed frames and sofa backs and modern bathrooms.

Hotels & Motels

A LITTLE INN BY THE SEA $$
4546 El Mar Dr., Lauderdale-by-the-Sea
(954) 772-2450
www.alittleinnhotel.com
Only a five-minute walk to the bustle of Lauderdale-by-the-Sea commercial area and Pelican Square, this sweet oceanfront inn-by-the-beach is favored by the over-50 set but still retains a youthful vibe. Its tranquil pool area provides a cozy respite from the 300-foot private beach beyond (including free beach chairs), and it's framed by lush tropical foliage. Breakfast consists of continental staples, but all the items are extremely fresh, and the baked goods will have you coming

back for more. Rooms—from standard hotel rooms to two-bedroom apartments—are typically Florida beachy in lots of floral patterns and coral colors; the smallest units include fridges and a microwave, the largest a full kitchen. Other perks include free bicycles and free tennis (at a nearby tennis court).

CARRIAGE HOUSE RESORT MOTEL $$
250 S. Ocean Blvd., Deerfield Beach
(954) 427-7670
www.carriagehouseresort.com

This no-frills, tidy black-shuttered colonial-style motel less than a block from the ocean is a fantastic bet for those seeking beach digs. It's spread out across a two-story building separated into two sections that are connected by a second-story sundeck. The entire structure wraps around a pool, which is rimmed by stately columns. All the cheerful units have walk-in closets, and while they do feature a handful of standard rooms, the majority are studios with kitchenettes or apartments with full kitchens. The resort-motel is popular among young families.

Condos & Apartments

PINEAPPLE PLACE APARTMENTS $$
3217 NE 7th Place, Pompano Beach
(954) 942-2424

Consistently ranked as one of the top small lodging choices in the area, this superbly renovated 1950s apartment house now rents one- and two-bedroom units at affordable rates, particularly for this part of town. Apartments are fully outfitted with modern amenities and decor of mainly white with touches of blue—you won't forget you're in a beach town here. It's situated across the street from the beach and offers a friendly

respite from everyday life, with a small but charming pool and a communal barbecue area. There is a three-night minimum, and weekly rates make the cost per night drop significantly. This is a prime place to base yourself for a slightly longer stay on a budget. Free Wi-Fi and a willingness to accept pets round out the service here.

Alternative Accommodations

If you're looking for affordable, small lodging options in and around Pompano Beach, look no further than the options provided by local entrepreneur Elaine Fitzgerald, who runs several condo/apartment properties, each with its own brand of Florida charm. We've listed a full review of our favorite, Pineapple Place Apartments, but for a full listing of properties available go to **www.4rentbythebeach.com**. Some choices include the charming **Cottages by the Sea** with its enchanting Key West–style studios and one-bedroom cottages featuring screened-in porches and lush tropical gardens; **Bahama Beach Club,** a well-maintained former apartment building painted a cheerful yellow, whose units loop around a pleasant pool; **Pelican Place** apartments, which sits adjacent to Pineapple Place (guests can use their pool); and last but not least **Sunny Place** apartments, a cheerful space housed in a triplex. All units require a three-night minimum.

Campgrounds & RV Sites

QUIET WATERS PARK CAMPING $
401 S. Powerline Rd., Deerfield Beach
(954) 360-1315
Quiet Waters Park in Deerfield Beach not only offers campsites and Rent-a-Tent sites, which include a 10-by-10-foot platform tent, grill, water, electric connections, picnic table and access to showers and restrooms, but once a week it is home to a different kind of lodging and activity experience: Saturday family campouts. The Saturday night Family Bed-and-Breakfast sleepovers run from 3 p.m. Sat to 1 p.m. Sun and include family fishing, a campfire with s'mores, and breakfast served by park staff. Some include hayrides, others have movies.

INLAND & WEST BROWARD

Resorts

GRAND PALMS HOTEL & GOLF RESORT $
110 Grand Palms Dr., Pembroke Pines
(954) 431-8800
www.grandpalmsresort.com
Compared to the other golf resort hotels in the area, this place is actually quite small: it only holds 137 rooms and suites. We think this is one of the reasons why staying here feels so comfortable and personal—each staff member is attentive but not overbearing, and it seems like they always know what you want or need before you actually ask for it. The golf course is most excellent, with 27 holes and numerous national accolades and awards, but the property doesn't end there. Six superb tennis courts, a restaurant and bar, a spacious swimming pool, tropical tiki bar, and an on-site, full-service European spa and fitness center (including yoga and spinning classes) make life after the course

extremely satisfying. Rooms are quite standard but solid, with colorful bedspreads, and many feature plush leather sofas.

MARRIOTT CORAL SPRINGS GOLF RESORT $$$–$$$$
11775 Heron Bay Blvd., Coral Springs
(954) 753-5598
www.marriott.com/fllmc
This is located on the grounds of the famous **Heron Bay Golf Club,** which features 18 championship-caliber holes along stunning waterways. It does, in many respects, seem like this hotel is really secondary when you take in the golf course, but it's a fine lodging choice with 224 guest rooms, a full-service bar and restaurant, and a decent pool and Jacuzzi area, great for resting your feet and taking a dip after a full day of golf. While the rooms are standard business-hotel accommodations, the bathrooms are particularly inviting and feature carefully selected aromatherapy toiletries.

Hotels & Motels

SHERATON SUITES PLANTATION $$$–$$$$
311 N. University Dr., Plantation
(954) 424-3300
www.starwoodhotels.com/sheraton
Conveniently located in the center of Plantation, this top-shelf business hotel is a solid choice for those seeking upscale lodging in west Broward. Its 264 rooms and suites are standard affairs with lots of beiges and touches of red—soothing but generally uninspiring, but on the flip side, service is top-notch. What really makes this lodging choice stand out, however, is its voluminous rooftop pool, which is tough to tear yourself away from. If you do manage to venture away from the sublime alfresco roof, the

ACCOMMODATIONS

Broward Mall is close by. Additional amenities include a fitness center and sauna.

Campgrounds & RV Sites

EVERGLADES HOLIDAY PARK $
21940 Griffin Rd., Weston
(954) 434-8111 or (800) 226-2244
www.evergladesholidaypark.com

You can't get much closer than this to the Everglades. For a few days near the country's most famous swampland, park your RV or pitch your tent on this pleasant and friendly camping spot. The site draws a wide variety of visitors, from retirees keen to relax and venture out to the Everglades to families interested in showing their kids what Gatorland is all about. All spaces give you access to gas, showers, laundry, and restrooms, and there's a convenience store close by with ice and groceries. *NOTE:* No matter what time of year you stay here, do not forget to bring plenty of insect repellent.

AIRPORT LODGING/DANIA & DANIA BEACH

Hotels & Motels

HILTON FORT LAUDERDALE
 AIRPORT $$$–$$$$
1870 Griffin Rd., Dania
(954) 920-3300
www.hilton.com

This may be a fairly standard business hotel, but we love its proximity to the airport (1.5 miles away)—in fact, the hotel provides complimentary airport shuttle service every 30 minutes. Add to that a cozy resort-like ambience, MP3 players in each room, and soothing Crabtree & Evelyn toiletries in the sumptuous bathrooms, and you'll feel well rested and alert for that 5 a.m. flight.

SHERATON FORT
 LAUDERDALE AIRPORT $$$–$$$$
1825 Griffin Rd., Dania
(954) 920-3571 or (866) 716-8106
www.sheraton.com

Another top-quality hotel only a mile away from the airport, the Sheraton is a step above the Hilton in terms of luxury. They also offer a complimentary airport shuttle service and a slew of standard business rooms, with plush comfy sofas and beds in soothing beige, brown, and off-white.

44

RESTAURANTS

We know. You didn't come here for the food—the beach and the sun lured you. But you're in for a treat—once you sit your newly bronzed self into a restaurant after a hard day of tanning, you'll find the dining scene scores high and offers Florida faves that don't grace many menus outside the state, plus cuisine types you know and love.

Greater Fort Lauderdale's thousands of restaurants cover every kind of cuisine you could want: American, French, Greek, Mexican, Italian, Spanish, steak, pizza, Southern and barbecue, Turkish, vegetarian, hot dogs and burgers, every kind of Asian food imaginable, hoagies and panini, breakfast and brunch fare, and, of course, the glorious seafood bounty caught straight from the Atlantic. Those looking for a fun place to socialize, cap off a great meal, or stop off for a snack will find plenty of laid-back coffee shops here.

Water plays a huge role in dining experience here—some of the best and most interesting places sit smack on the beach or the Intracoastal Waterway, are ensconced within yacht-filled docks, or provide a view of waves or boats (or both). As a result, we've listed a fair amount of restaurants where you can take in a proper waterside meal. There are many to choose from, and they fill up quickly, so be sure to reserve if you have your heart set on one.

But beyond the water there's a goldmine of excellent finds tucked into main drags and inland shopping malls. With so many eateries in the area, it's impossible to list all of the great ones in the space of a chapter. In the pages that follow, you'll find some of the best and most popular restaurants here.

If you're feeling overwhelmed by the sheer choice and you want to simply park, stroll in a restaurant-dense area, and let your nose decide, head to Las Olas Boulevard in downtown Fort Lauderdale—the street is chockablock with fine locales, most on the mid- to upscale side. For more downbeat vibe, try downtown Hollywood and tool along Hollywood Boulevard and the parallel Harrison Street. For beachside options, hit the Hollywood Broadwalk or Fort Lauderdale Beach Boulevard between East Las Olas and Castillo (but take note of our recommendations for the great finds for both; there are a tremendous amount of disappointing tourist traps along these stretches of sand and sea).

OVERVIEW

The chapter is organized to make it as easy as possible for you to find the kind of food you want in the neighborhood in which you want to dine. Restaurants (as well as coffee shops) are organized by cuisine, then organized alphabetically. The restaurants listed span the price range from highly expensive to crazy cheap, but the majority fall somewhere in between. Most offer at least a few vegetarian options; those that don't have been identified as such in these pages.

There are plenty of places to dine with children; the barbecue, diner-esque, and Floridian/seafood restaurants are particularly good candidates for family dining. Most restaurants are open seven days a week for lunch and dinner, and many serve brunch. But it can't hurt to call ahead to double-check a restaurant's hours, as these often change.

When choosing a place to eat, keep in mind that the restaurant landscape is constantly changing. By the time you read this book, some of the restaurants listed may have moved or gone out of business, so it's a good idea to call ahead before your visit.

Hours vary greatly, but if you are expecting Miami's late-night dining scene, you'll notice Fort Lauderdale eats earlier than their more Latin-influenced county to the south. Expect most venues to close their kitchens around 10 or 11 p.m. on weeknights, by 11 p.m. or midnight on weekends.

Popular restaurants—which is to say, just about every restaurant listed in this chapter—tend to fill up on Friday and Saturday nights and holidays. Keep in mind that winter sees zillions of snowbirds, sun-seeking weekenders, and beach-bound families fleeing from the cold north: As a rule, expect busier tables between November and April. Pricier restaurants take reservations so call ahead to get a table wherever possible.

Price Code

The following prices are based on a meal for two, without drinks, appetizers, desserts, or tip. Prices are also based on averages only and assume guests eat at least one pricier meat entree.

$.....................under $15
$$ .... $15 to $30
$$$ .... $30 to $50
$$$$ .... over $50

By Word of Mouth, Wilton Manors, American & Eclectic, $$$$, 48

Cafe Seville, Ft. Lauderdale, Spanish, $-$$, 71

Cafe Vico, Ft. Lauderdale, Italian, $$$, 61

Canyon Cafe, Ft. Lauderdale, Southwestern, $$-$$$, 71

Capriccio, Pembroke Pines, Italian, $$, 61

Carlos & Pepe's, Ft. Lauderdale, Mexican, $$, 65

Casablanca Cafe, Ft. Lauderdale Beach, Mediterranean, $$$, 64

Casa Peru, Hallandale Beach, Peruvian, $$, 67

Catfish Dewey's, Ft. Lauderdale, Seafood, $$, 68

Chima Brazilian Steakhouse, Ft. Lauderdale, Brazilian, $$$-$$$$, 55

Chinatown, Davie, Asian Fusion, $, 54

Coffee Scene, Pembroke Pines, Cafes & Coffee, $, 56

Country Ham & Eggs, Lauderdale-by-the-Sea, American & Eclectic, $, 49

Cove Bagels & Deli, Deerfield Beach, Delis & Sandwiches, $, 57

Cypress Nook, Pompano Beach, German, $$, 59

Dairy Belle Ice Cream, Dania Beach, American & Eclectic, $, 49

Deli Den, Hollywood, Delis & Sandwiches, $$, 58

Downtowner Saloon, Ft. Lauderdale, Seafood, $$, 68

Eduardo de San Angel, Ft. Lauderdale, Mexican, $$$, 65

El Tamarindo Cafe & Restaurant, Ft. Lauderdale, Latin American, $, 64

Emunah Cafe & Tea Room, Ft. Lauderdale, Cafes & Coffee, $, 56

Ernie's Barbecue, Ft. Lauderdale, BBQ/Southern, $, 54

Expresso, Dania Beach, Cafes & Coffee, $, 57

Ferdos Grill, Ft. Lauderdale, Lebanese, $$$, 64

15th Street Fisheries, Ft. Lauderdale, Seafood, $$-$$$, 69

Fin & Claw, Lighthouse Point, Austrian, $$-$$$, 54

Five Guys Burgers & Fries, Ft. Lauderdale, American & Eclectic, $, 49

The Floridian, Ft. Lauderdale, American & Eclectic, $, 50

Galanga, Wilton Manors, Thai, $-$$, 73

Giorgio's Grill, Hollywood Beach, Mediterranean, $$$, 64

Gourmet Greenhouse, Hollywood, Vegan & Vegetarian, $, 73

Himmarshee Bar & Grille, Ft. Lauderdale, American & Eclectic, $$-$$$, 50

Islamorada Fish Company, Dania Beach, Seafood, $$-$$$, 69

Istanbul Restaurant, Hollywood Beach, Turkish, $, 73

Jasmine Thai, Margate, Thai, $$, 73

Jaxsons Ice Cream Parlor, Dania Beach, American & Eclectic, $, 50

Jimbo's Sandbar, Dania Beach, Seafood, $-$$, 69

Jimmie's Café, Dania Beach, American & Eclectic, $$, 51

Johnny V, Ft. Lauderdale, American & Eclectic, $$-$$$, 51

Kuluck, Tamarac, Persian, $, 65

La Creperie, Lauderhill, French, $$$, 58

Las Olas Café, Ft. Lauderdale, American & Eclectic, $$, 52

LaSpada's Original Hoagies, Lauderdale-by-the-Sea, Delis & Sandwiches, $, 58

Le Café de Paris, Ft. Lauderdale, French, $-$$, 59

Le Tub, Hollywood, American & Eclectic, $$, 52

Lester's Diner, Ft. Lauderdale, American & Eclectic, $, 52

Little Havana, Deerfield Beach, Cuban, $$, 57

Lola's on Harrison, Hollywood, Seafood, $$$, 69

Lucille's American Café, Weston, American & Eclectic, $, 53

Mai-Kai, Ft. Lauderdale, Asian Fusion, $$–$$$, 54

Mama Mia Restaurant, Hollywood, Italian, $$, 62

Mediterranean Market, Ft. Lauderdale, Delis & Sandwiches, $, 58

New River Pizza, Ft. Lauderdale, Italian, $, 62

Ocean Alley, Hollywood Beach, Seafood, $$, 70

Old Heidelberg Restaurant & Deli, Ft. Lauderdale, German, $$–$$$, 60

Primanti Brothers, Ft. Lauderdale Beach, Italian, $, 62

Rosey Baby Crawfish & Cajun House, Lauderhill, BBQ/Southern, $–$$, 55

Royal India, Dania Beach, Indian & Pakistani, $$, 60

Rustic Inn Crabhouse, Ft. Lauderdale, Seafood, $$$, 70

Sage, Ft. Lauderdale, French, $$–$$$, 59

Saint Tropez, Ft. Lauderdale, French, $–$$, 59

Sea Watch on the Ocean, Ft. Lauderdale Beach, Seafood, $$$–$$$$, 70

Sol e Mar Restaurant, Pompano Beach, Portuguese, $$, 67

SoLita, Ft. Lauderdale, American & Eclectic, $$$, 53

Southport Raw Bar, Ft. Lauderdale, Seafood, $$–$$$, 71

St. Barts Coffee Company, Ft. Lauderdale Beach, $, 57

Sublime World Vegetarian Cuisine, Ft. Lauderdale, Vegan & Vegetarian, $$, 74

Sugar Reef Tropical Grille, Hollywood, American & Eclectic, $–$$, 53

Sukhothai, Ft. Lauderdale, Thai, $$, 73

Sushi Blues Cafe, Hollywood, Japanese, $–$$, 62

Sushi Rock, Ft. Lauderdale, Japanese, $–$$, 62

Taverna Opa, Hollywood Beach, Greek, $$–$$$, 60

Tom Jenkins BBQ, Ft. Lauderdale, BBQ/Southern, $, 55

Tortilleria Mexicana, Oakland Park, Mexican, $, 65

Transylvania Restaurant, Hollywood, Romanian, $$, 67

Trina Restaurant, Ft. Lauderdale Beach, Seafood, $$$$, 71

Usmania Restaurant, Plantation, Indian & Pakistani, $, 61

Wine Cellar, Ft. Lauderdale, Hungarian & Continental, $$–$$$, 60

YOLO, Ft. Lauderdale, American & Eclectic, $$$–$$$$, 53

AMERICAN & ECLECTIC

BY WORD OF MOUTH $$$$
3200 NE 12th Ave., Wilton Manors
(954) 564-3663
www.bywordofmouthfoods.com

They may eschew advertising, but the secret is out. This is a find, cherished (and rightfully so) by locals in the know and those they tell, which is everyone at this point (the media likes to talk, and it didn't take long for national food mags to catch on and sniff it out). There's no menu—display cases place dishes for inspection; your toughest job is to select only a few because they all look so heavenly. And yes, they taste as good as they look. Servers are happy to aid you in your quandary of choice, but expect sophisticated options like truffled lump crab on a bed of tender arugula, salmon braised with aged balsamic reduction over red rice, or star fruit crème brûlée. Call for hours.

BROOKS $$$
500 S. Federal Hwy., Deerfield Beach
(954) 427-9302
www.brooks-restaurant.com

If you like your dining experience refined, elegant, and accompanied by musical entertainment, Brooks is a must. Attracting a stately older crowd for over 25 years, this antiques-and-art-filled restaurant lends an air of grandeur to every decadent meal—fare is continental, with staples like lobster bisque and a New York strip steak, but regional influences sneak in with fresh shrimp from Key West and Key Largo yellowtail, but many agree their most legendary dish is their dessert soufflé (in chocolate or Grand Marnier flavors). Most evenings feature live piano entertainment, and they offer occasional opera evenings—inquire on the website for dates and details.

COUNTRY HAM & EGGS $
4405 El Mar Dr., Lauderdale-by-the-Sea
(954) 776-1666
www.countryhameggs.com

Country Ham & Eggs is the diner-style Florida neighborhood fave for down-home, gut-hugging goodness. This isn't a spot for fancy cappuccinos or trendy omelettes; here you get some eggs with greasy, crispy bacon, grits, or hash browns, and coffee served in a dull, worn brown mug. Omelettes will fill you up until dinner, and the sassy wait staff treats you like gold ("Comin' right up, honey," is the normal response to a customer request). Outdoor tables give you a breath of fresh, salty air (the beach is around the corner, but no, this is not a seat with a view). But you can watch the street traffic in the little commercial cluster at the edge of the ocean, and catch the neighbors wave to each other—Lauderdale-by-the-Sea is a friendly, tight-knit community. It's open daily for breakfast and lunch only, 7 a.m. until 2:30 p.m. Cash only.

DAIRY BELLE ICE CREAM $
118 N. Federal Hwy., Dania Beach
(954) 920-3330

Dairy Belle's full name is a misnomer, because the creamy, frozen stuff is only half the excitement at this covered, no-frills, outdoor-only space with counter service. Their claim to fame is a Montreal specialty, traditional *poutine:* fries topped with gravy and cheese curds. Really. Don't trash it before you've tried it—poutine is a highly popular, addictive street food Quebecers swear by. They fly in the gravy from Canada and the cheese from Wisconsin to ensure this sticks-to-the-ribs concoction tastes just right. You'll probably overhear some French while you stop by—Quebec snowbirds flock here for their favorite comfort food and for another treat from up north—toasted hot dogs. If burgers and sandwiches are more your thing, that's on offer too, as is soft ice cream and blizzards like that other dairy darling of American descent. Closed Mon. Call for hours.

FIVE GUYS BURGERS & FRIES $
1818 Cordova Rd., Ft. Lauderdale
(954) 358-5862
www.fiveguys.com

This may be a national chain (400-plus locations), but it's without a doubt one of the most popular places to grab a burger in town. Taking fast food to a whole new level, Five Guys prides itself on its wholesome environment (lots of red and white reminiscent of a '50s diner, with sacks of potatoes peppered around the joint), tender, juicy burgers fresh off the grill, free toppings (16, including jalapeños, grilled mushrooms, and green peppers), and hand-cut fries. Not a burger person? They also serve excellent hot dogs and grilled cheese sandwiches. A second location is in Pembroke Pines at 11097 Pines Blvd. (954-367-0167). Hours vary; call ahead.

THE FLORIDIAN $
1410 Las Olas Blvd., Ft. Lauderdale
(954) 463-4041

From the wraparound counter with round black-vinyl swivel stools to the old photos and newspapers clippings of celebrities, politicians, and news from the past and the clanking of plates carried by no-nonsense waiters, this old-school, local institution (in operation since 1937) is the diner that delivers on all fronts, 24 hours per day. Choose from a gargantuan breakfast menu with the usual suspects (various pancakes, eggs Benedict, omelettes, and buttermilk biscuits), endless sandwiches and salads, gut-filling chili, and pastel frosting–clad cakes spinning in the display case. At some point everyone lands here—retirees enjoying their eggs with the paper, businessmen grabbing lunch, or club kids winding down with comfort food at 4 a.m.

HIMMARSHEE BAR & GRILLE $$–$$$
210 SW 2nd St., Ft. Lauderdale
(954) 524-1818
www.himmarshee.com

In the sea of late-night debauchery in downtown Fort Lauderdale's kicking nightlife district, Himmarshee stands proud as the sole upmarket, quality food this side of town. The lengthy wine list (over 35 by the glass) is much fun to ponder. If you can't decide, you can order each by the half-glass—they all pair flawlessly with the New American cuisine, which can be ordered a la carte or from the three-course silver, gold, and platinum menus. Too stuffed to squeeze in dessert but seeking something post-meal? A truffletini

or nuttycino (chocolate and coffee-inspired martinis) might lure you, or ask for the expensive after-dinner drink menu that also offers cordial flights. If you're after some quiet, come for lunch or avoid the scene surrounding the tables later in the evening—though we admit it is fun to watch the antics at the open-air pub crawl that unfolds as the night wears on.

My Fort Lauderdale

My husband and I live not far from downtown Fort Lauderdale and the house where I was raised. We love to walk over our neighborhood's historic swing bridge. It was built in the 1920s and is one of just a handful left in Florida. We meander from there along the Riverwalk toward downtown, and watch all the yachts coming and going on what was the city's original thoroughfare. If it's dark outside, we try to spot the ghost in the second floor window of the Stranahan House, once a trading post for the original settlement.

We might top that off with dinner at an old Fort Lauderdale hang-out like the Southport Raw Bar, and then gorge on dessert at Jaxson's Ice Cream Parlor in Dania Beach. Perfection.

—Deborah Sharp,
Writer/Novelist *(The Mace Bauer Mysteries)*, Fort Lauderdale

---

JAXSON'S ICE CREAM PARLOR $
128 S. Federal Hwy., Dania Beach
(954) 923-4445
www.jaxsonsicecream.com

This local institution will captures the eyes of even the most distracted driver cruising by on Federal Highway—imagine an old-school fair ride gone into overdrive, and you get the picture. Flashing light bulbs framing a striped, retro sign beckon you to come in and see what all the fuss is about. Once you step in, you're in an alternate universe. First comes the old-school candy store, selling candy you didn't think existed anymore (Willy Wonka chocolate chews, anyone?) and enough toys and trinkets to make your head swim. Next come the two adjoining dining rooms—one packed with license plates, old road signs, and tatty old wooden booths, the other filled with bits of nostalgia like antique strollers, bicycles, and pots and pans hanging from the ceiling. If this place looks familiar it's because it's been featured on the *Today* show, the Food Network, and *Rachael Ray*—no surprise when you realize it's been reeling in the crowds and churning out homemade ice cream since 1956. Choose from over 30 flavors—including weekly flavors. They offer their fair share of massive sundaes, banana splits, and other classics, but smaller appetites won't be disappointed: Even a single scoop can be ordered with a dollop of whipped cream and hot fudge—it arrives at the table with a cherry, colorful sprinkles, and a tiny American flag-on-a-toothpick, guaranteed to make you smile and feel like a kid again. Aside from sweet treats, they also serve diner-style American classics like burgers, sandwiches, hot dogs, and chili. There's a massive children's menu, and kids will be endlessly entertained by the surrounds (though parents may have trouble preventing a sugar high). Open Mon through Thurs 11:30 a.m. to 11 p.m.; Fri and Sat 11:30 a.m. to 12 a.m.; and Sun noon to 11 p.m.

ℹ️ For the latest local dining news and listings online, check out www.SouthFloridaDines.com, the *Broward–Palm Beach New Times* website (www.browardpalmbeach.com), or their food blog (www.cleanplatecharlie.com). We also recommend the quirky but informative local restaurant blog at www.knife-and-fork.typepad.com, written by a few local foodies who keep their true identities under plates.

JIMMIE'S CAFÉ $$
148 N. Federal Hwy., Dania Beach
(954) 922-0441
www.jimmieschocolates.com

Jimmie's Original Chocolate Shoppe, Florida's oldest chocolate maker (see a full review in the Shopping chapter) has been open for over half a century, so it's no surprise that this cozy cafe, which opened in 2005, has caught on strong, too. Owned by two brothers who don't skimp on anything, the cafe serves delicately prepared food (if it isn't fresh, it won't be on the menu) in a converted old house. In fact, sitting at the outdoor patio almost feels like dining in someone's back yard. The cuisine is Floridian, Mediterranean, and Latin fusion; they always feature a fresh catch of the day and all their desserts come with chocolate, an ode to their original business. They're also famous for their friendly, personal service and their sangria, which comes in chunky pitchers and goes down like lemonade on a hot day. Wed night is ladies' night—all ladies enjoy two-for-one glasses of beer and wine.

JOHNNY V $$–$$$
625 E. Las Olas Blvd, Ft. Lauderdale
(954) 761-7290
www.johnnyvlasolas.com

Triple yum is an understatement at Johnny V's. Chef and co-owner Johnny Vinczencz is a South Florida celebrity chef known for his Caribbean-influenced Florida cuisine—his style has earned him the nickname "Caribbean Cowboy," but even outside the region, you may have spotted him on the *Today* show or the Food Network, or read about him in food glossies *Bon Appétit* or *Gourmet* magazine (now defunct). Known for his sharp flavors and refined Sunshine State cuisine, he reigned at the helm of Miami Beach's Astor Place in the late 1990s and opened his own 200-seat restaurant in 2003, where he continues to showcase innovative dishes like Florida stone crab shepherd's pie, blue corn–crusted calamari, and his famous "short stack" of wild mushroom pancakes. Also known for his imaginative use of game and other meats, carnivores will enjoy trying Ancho Cinnamon Grilled Pork Tenderloin or a twist on surf and turf (lobster and buffalo sharing one plate). Don't forget to ask about the cheese-tasting menu (over 30 varieties), which comes with fig-balsamic marinated grapes. It all arrives like works of art in your comfy red banquette, surrounded by deep walnut walls and an air of modish surrounds.

LAS OLAS CAFÉ $$
922 E. Las Olas Blvd., Ft. Lauderdale
(954) 524-4300
www.lasolascafe.com
Sometimes the best discoveries are hidden down alleyways right off the main action—in this case, right off busy Las Olas Boulevard. Wander down a narrow passageway and you'll encounter a tiny courtyard filled with tables and sparkling white Christmas lights. It's oh-so-atmospheric and turns into a romantic spot by night; even the inside tables feel like they are outdoors, with

interior streetlights shedding a soft glow and warm yellow tones covering the walls. Dishes run the gamut from fried green tomatoes with jumbo lump crab topping, goat cheese baked in phyllo dough, Cajun shrimp, and walnut-crusted mahimahi, to a selection of soups and salads. Closed Mon.

LE TUB $$
1100 N. Ocean Dr., Hollywood
(954) 921-9425
www.theletub.com
As one of the recipients of the Oprah effect (where a business turns into a gold mine after being featured on the *Oprah* show) this former gas station turned restaurant isn't any secret, so the crowds mean you'll wait for your table and their famous burgers. But it's worth it, and you can bide your time nursing a beer with a view of the sublime Intracoastal or inspecting the claw-foot bathtubs peppered around the interior. Open daily from noon to 4 a.m.

LESTER'S DINER $
250 SE 24th St., Ft. Lauderdale
(954) 525-5641
www.lestersonline.com
Open since the 1960s, this landmark diner is a favorite haunt of the after-bar-hopping-and-clubbing crowd, though it packs them in any time of the day. Catering to patrons of every type, age, and persuasion, this classic American diner serves staples with a Greek influence. Omelettes, gyros, Greek salads, and moussaka sit side by side with club sandwiches, burgers, and pancakes, and all the pastries are homemade. Moreover, it's the eclectic mix of customers and raspy-voiced servers that make this greasy spoon a fun stop for hungry stomachs or anyone just wanting a basic, non-fancy cup of joe

without attitude or a high price tag. Like any respectable, authentic diner, it's open 24 hours a day, seven days a week.

LUCILLE'S AMERICAN CAFÉ $
2250 Weston Rd., Weston
(954) 384-9007
www.lucillescafe.com

This replica of a 1940s luncheonette gets all the details right, including the seafoam-green wall paint, the shiny silver of the chrome swivel stools at the counter, the worn-in black booths. Even the excellent-value menu hints to a time when prices were lower and good food didn't bite the wallet so. Homemade meat loaf and three-cheese macaroni sit side by side with newer inventions like coconut-crusted shrimp and spinach-and-cheese dip. Don't forget to check out the day's blue plate special, like liver and onions (Mon dinner) or egg salad sandwich (Fri lunch). Ice cream sodas, malts and milkshakes, and root beer floats are fantastically old-school delicious, and the Sun brunch is always a big hit.

SOLITA $$$
1032 E. Las Olas Blvd., Ft. Lauderdale
(954) 357-2606
http://solitalasolas.com

Occupying a space that used to house Mark's Las Olas, a hugely popular foodie haunt, SoLita is a newcomer to the Las Olas restaurant scene. With its modern gray space, sleek white curtains in the dining room, and the cool patio, SoLita is off to a good start and the food—contemporary Italian—and drink concoctions (mixologists on a mission to seduce you with a martini glass) pave the way for a trendy spot to evolve. DJs spin smooth sounds most nights, giving it a clubby atmosphere.

i Parking on Las Olas on a busy weekend night can be a nightmare. Some restaurants offer valet parking but if yours doesn't (or you're deciding where to eat post-stroll) meander down the side streets crisscrossing the boulevard. It's safe and residential, and while you'll still have to pay you'll find a spot far quicker—and you won't be forced to parallel park with bumper-to-bumper traffic beeping behind you.

SUGAR REEF TROPICAL GRILLE $–$$
600 N. Surf Rd., Hollywood
(on the Broadwalk)
(954) 922-1119
www.sugarreefgrill.com

If you've been walking along the Broadwalk wondering which open-air spaces are worth it and which are tourist traps, Sugar Reef is the real thing. We've placed this under American & Eclectic food, but really, this place is more eclectic than anything else. With items like seafood gumbo, Vietnamese *pho* (beef or chicken noodle soup), bouillabaisse, and chicken Alfredo on the menu, you can ponder over French, Asian, Caribbean, and Southern fare. To boot, its whimsical mosaic tile decoration inside and out, dim lighting, and large fish art covering the walls lend a fun and cozy atmosphere.

YOLO $$$–$$$$
333 E. Las Olas Blvd., Ft. Lauderdale
(954) 523-1000
www.yolorestaurant.com

One of the newest additions to downtown Fort Lauderdale's swanky scene, YOLO (which stands for You Only Live Once) is as polished and fabulous as its clientele. Flickering fire pits make the patio SSAS (Swanky, Sleek, and Sexy) and after imbibing in a cocktail or munching on their new American cuisine (with Southern and seafood leanings), you can SABS (See and Be Seen) the night away. Designer clothing, stiletto heels, and cherry-red Aston Martins are de rigueur here.

ASIAN FUSION

CHINATOWN $
8934 SR 84, Davie
(954) 473-8770
www.chinatown-davie.com

You'd never guess this blah strip mall in Davie could deliver such amazing Chinese and Japanese fare at these prices—maybe it's because everything has both the touch and the eye of the owner, who never seems to take the day off. Szechuan chicken, salt and pepper shrimp, delicate rice noodle dishes, and more arrive in massive portions (it's a great place for groups and families), and while service is curt, it's consistently efficient.

MAI-KAI $$–$$$
3599 N. Federal Hwy., Ft. Lauderdale
(954) 563-3272
www.maikai.com

More a Polynesian village than just a restaurant, this sprawling complex consists of connected indoor-and-outdoor tiki huts, carved wood pillars, waterfalls, wide wood and aqua banquettes, and plenty of island music and tropical cheer to make even a cynic smile in these kitsch-but-fun surrounds. Food is Asian across the board, mainly Chinese with Southeast Asian staples, like their excellent Panang Curry Chicken and Singapore Chili Shrimp—it's all straightforward (no experimental Asian fusion here), and they offer a respectable wine list focusing on boutique wineries. It's popular among big groups and birthdays and offers a Polynesian show

(Samoan fire dancers) in the evening—be sure to reserve in advance. Special kids' performance Sun (kids under age 12 admitted free to the show every night).

AUSTRIAN

FIN & CLAW $$–$$$
2476 N. Federal Hwy., Lighthouse Point (in Shoppes at Beacon Light shopping center)
(954) 782-1060

Austrian and seafood don't generally sit together, but yes, even this landlocked country has its share of streams, rivers, and lakes, and many original recipes incorporate seafood with their more well-known fare like Wiener schnitzel (pounded and breaded veal), potato salad, kraut salad, and goulash served with hefty dumplings. This being Florida, they serve up local catches too, but whatever you order, it is delivered with a smile in this tiny mom-and-pop place tucked away in a shopping center.

BARBECUE, SOUL & SOUTHERN

ERNIE'S BARBECUE $
1843 S. Federal Hwy., Ft. Lauderdale
(954) 523-8636

It's a darn shame they don't make 'em like this anymore. Started by Ernie the bootlegger, who eschewed all rules and regulations, this blues, beer, and barbecue landmark has been churning out the good stuff since 1957—and Ernie's attitude still prevails. Regulars know to hit the tomato-heavy conch dishes, tangy slow-cooked ribs, or the succulent and enormous burgers and cheese steak sandwiches. The beer is always icy cold, and don't forget to indulge in their signature, addictive Bimini bread, served with seemingly everything. You can't miss the rounded building swathed in faded yellow paint when driving down Federal Highway, and the interior is comfy, down-home goodness.

ROSEY BABY CRAWFISH & CAJUN HOUSE $–$$
4587 N. University Dr., Lauderhill
(954) 749-5627
www.roseybaby.com
New Orleans comes to Florida in this laid-back house of crawfish (served by the bucket) and po'boys. If shellfish isn't your style, check out the burgers or the "swimmers and roamers" section of the menu (fish and meats). Evenings welcome live music and more beer-drinking patrons than diners, and the place morphs into a bar as midnight nears and dart players hover (weekday nights feature dart leagues).

TOM JENKINS BBQ $
1236 S. Federal Hwy., Ft. Lauderdale
(954) 522-5046
www.tomjenkinsbbq.com
A couple of former frat brothers from Florida A&M University run this place, and the pair is unstoppable—their barbecue sauce sells like hotcakes, and the best place to try it is here, their no-frills BBQ joint (to call it a restaurant is a stretch—you order at the counter, grub is served on Styrofoam, and picnic tables surround the space). But that's real barbecue, and you'll have fun watching the entertaining kitchen whip up your dish with flair and attitude. This local fixture is also a popular for takeout: Though we like the country memorabilia and Southern vibe inside, some may not fancy eating on picnic tables. But you can't beat their succulent ribs and pork sandwiches; their Mississippi catfish and hush puppies are a fine alternative for non-meat eaters.

BRAZILIAN

ARGENTANGO GRILL $$
1822 S. Young Circle, Hollywood
(954) 920-9233
www.argentangogrill.com
It's a carnivore's mecca: a meat-filled extravaganza, with skirt steak, filet mignon, rib eyes, and more (most cooked on a wood-fired grill), excellent mixed meat platters available for one or two people, all served with a large choice of sides, freshly baked bread and rolls with their own homemade "Chimmichurri Sauce" (a blend of herbs, garlic, oil, and vinegar, sometimes with a tomato base or red bell peppers), and soup or salad. And this isn't where it ends: Their famous sangria is whipped up tableside. Decor is reminiscent of Buenos Aires (lots of brick and wood with low lighting), and service is attentive and friendly. Best to come with a large appetite, and expect your waist to expand during your meal—but if it didn't, it wouldn't be an authentic experience anyway.

CHIMA BRAZILIAN STEAKHOUSE $$$–$$$$
2400 E. Las Olas Blvd., Ft. Lauderdale
(954) 712-0580
www.chima.cc
Flickering, modern torches lead the way into this bastion of South American class and design—walk through the impressive entrance courtyard filled with terra-cotta stones, into the main dining room with vibrant art and polished wood floors. This is a *rodizio* restaurant (one set price for a variety of selections served tableside) where a *churrasco* (grilled meat) is on offer—slabs of rotisserie meats circulate, thinly sliced upon demand at your table. Waiters are dressed as gauchos (cowboys from southern South America), and even vegetarians can fill up at

the gargantuan salad bar. Weekday evenings the courtyard hosts live music and a hopping, trendy happy hour.

CAFES & COFFEE

BON AMI CAFE $
5650 Stirling Rd., Hollywood
(954) 962-2070
Despite its French-sounding name, this is a true kosher cafe, where the menu is printed in both English and Hebrew. Clientele is always extremely mixed, and you can expect a large variety of fresh food like omelettes, salads, sandwiches, and a fair share of Middle Eastern options like Israeli salads and *kozza*, *ziva*, and *malawach*—think oodles of feta-filled concoctions. The space isn't sexy, but you come for the carefully prepared, affordable meals, not for the decor. Closed Sat for the Sabbath.

BOOMERANG COFFEEHOUSE $
1631 South Cypress Rd., Pompano Beach
(954) 783-9339
Some simply drive through and pick up a bagel or a muffin here, but that's a shame, because the comfy couches and relaxed vibes make this a prime spot to lounge with a paper and a cuppa from their extensive coffee and tea menu. Weekend afternoons are a big hit, when they showcase live jazz ensembles and local one-man bands, such as Hurricane Dave, a country-and-folk singer who's been returning to belt it out for several years.

BREW URBAN CAFE $
209 SW 2nd Ave., Ft. Lauderdale
(954) 523-7191
www.brewurbancafe.com
After 10 p.m. this area of downtown Fort Lauderdale teems with revelers and party animals, but during the day and evening it's a quiet spot of Old Town Fort Lauderdale with few options for a beverage. But Brew Cafe's popularity isn't due to being one of the sole day traders on the block—its art-filled cafe and superb coffee attract a loyal following, and their small but tasteful wine and microbrew menus encourage you to pick up your morning coffee and come back for an after-work drink, which many do. They pride themselves in their top-quality coffees, expertly trained baristas, and support of small coffee-bean farmers, as well as offering a good selection of magazines and newspapers and getting to know their regulars by name. There's a second location at 638 N. Federal Hwy, Fort Lauderdale, (954) 527-4828.

COFFEE SCENE $
15955 Pines Blvd., Pembroke Pines
(954) 441-2364
With over 50 coffee flavors to choose from, it might take a while to order. But this place won't rush you—in fact it's the slow pace that makes it distinctive and stand out from the Starbucks dotting many corners of town. Take the amazing coffee selection and add sandwiches, wraps, salads, and soups, and you've got a coffee-shop-cum-bistro that attracts families and businesspeople on a regular basis. Family owned, they always have unique touches that make them stand out, like coloring books for the little ones and live music a few days and nights per week.

EMUNAH CAFE & TEA ROOM $
3558 N. Ocean Blvd., Ft. Lauderdale
(954) 561-6411
www.myemunah.com
You don't need to be a kabbalah devotee to love this spiritual haven of calm and

tranquility—choose from a large selection of organic teas, curl up with your favorite magazine, and take in the simplicity of the sparse furnishings. If you get peckish, the kosher restaurant offers excellent vegetarian and seafood dishes, and summers feature a three-course sunset menu. Whatever you seek when you come here, you'll relax in the oasis far, far away from the maddening traffic and honking horns.

EXPRESSO $
1900 S. Andrews Ave., Dania Beach
(954) 527-1222

Blink and you might think Starbucks has joined the hippie movement, but swing by this one-of-a-kind drive-through gourmet coffee shop decorated with inlaid mosaic tiles and you can't help but grin and realize you've stumbled upon something special. Pick up coffee by the cup (nine types, plus flavored varieties that change daily) or the pound, plus a small selection of smoothies, sandwiches, salads, snacks, and light bites. It's been serving food and drink for locals on the go since 1992. Closed Sun; cash only.

ST. BARTS COFFEE COMPANY $
441 Fort Lauderdale Beach Blvd.,
Ft. Lauderdale Beach
(954) 832-9004
www.itsbetteronthebeach.com/
st-barts-coffee

Kick back and relax at this beachside space serving up simple, all-day breakfast basics like the Farmer's Favorite (two eggs, bacon, bagel, salad, and cheese) or omelettes, or get a healthy start with yogurt, granola, and fresh fruit, or oatmeal with bananas, walnuts, and brown sugar. The lunch menu adds panini, wraps, and salads to the menu. Their smoothies (we like the Tropical Tango)

hit the spot at any hour, and all can be whipped up with or without protein. This is a relaxed and friendly place—popular among the locals—to grab a bite or a coffee with the newspaper, or just let your eyes rest on the wide ocean on the horizon and inhale the sea air. The outdoor tables are where you want to land—the interior is a tad cramped and uninviting. Plus, you partially came for the ocean view, right? Open daily 6 a.m. to 6:30 p.m.

CUBAN

LITTLE HAVANA $$
721 S. Federal Hwy., Deerfield Beach
(954) 427-6000
www.littlehavanarestaurant.com

Classy Cuban cuisine (read: satisfying and gut filling) is what it's all about at Little Havana restaurant. The northern sister of this restaurant packs them into its civilized, white tablecloth setting and makes sure you don't leave until you're stuffed. Service is friendly, and the staff is helpful if you're a Cuban-food virgin. Along with daily specials, the menu focuses on standard staples like black beans, yucca, pounded plantains, shrimp in garlic sauce, baked chicken, and of course, the famous hand-pressed ham and cheese Cuban sandwich.

DELIS, BAGELS & SANDWICHES

COVE BAGELS & DELI $
1634 SE 3rd Court, Deerfield Beach
(954) 481-8600

"Gimme a toasted everything with scallion and a cuppa." That line with a New York accent and no-nonsense service makes Cove a real, authentic New York deli and bagel shop. This family-owned-and-operated affair bakes their 10-plus varieties of bagels daily (you can smell the fresh dough baking from the parking lot), and ample cream cheeses and smoked salmon means you can get your salmon bagel fix any day. Soups and salads round out the menu, but come early before your favorite choice runs out, and keep in mind they shut up shop around 3 p.m.

DELI DEN   **$$**
2889 Stirling Rd., Hollywood
(954) 961-4070
www.thedeliden.com

If you're in the mood for a classic kosher deli with all the proper trimmings—coleslaw, kosher pickles, matzo ball and split pea soups, whitefish salad, stuffed cabbage, liver and onions, beef brisket—then this is your place. Sandwiches like corned beef on rye or a grilled Reuben and potato pancakes round out the menu, and you can take everything to go or eat in the expansive dining area.

LASPADA'S ORIGINAL HOAGIES   **$**
4346 Seagrape Dr.,
Lauderdale-by-the-Sea
(954) 776-7893
www.laspadahoagies.com

If you ask locals to recommend the best restaurant in the area, don't be surprised if people respond with accolades about the most supreme hoagie ever. And it's no secret—voted Broward's number one for food and best "bang for the buck" and top rated by Zagat's—the lines stay long, but don't fret: You'll be entertained by friendly sandwich-making pros practicing their meat-flinging (it'll land smack on your sub). The end result is tall stack of ingredients crammed into a sub you'll keep devouring until your zipper begs to be undone; the flavors are far too excellent to stop eating at a sensible juncture. We highly recommend anything with

the sweet and/or spicy peppers (marinated on the premises), but some may prefer the hot, homemade meatballs. Other locations are in Coral Springs at 7893 W. Sample Rd. (954-345-8833), and in Davie at 2645 S. University Dr. (954-476-1099).

i If you're visiting LaSpada's with a friend or picking up food for two, consider splitting one of their subs. Eat an entire one (we dare you to try and stop before all is gone—they're *that* delicious) and you probably won't be hungry for the next 24 hours.

MEDITERRANEAN MARKET   **$**
1021 E. Las Olas Blvd., Ft. Lauderdale
(954) 463-1212
www.shopmedmarket.com

This gourmet food shop also dishes up excellent deli sandwiches, salads, and take-out food fit for a fancy lunch (think seared salmon with a dab of wasabi, hoisin, and jicama on tender field greens) on the beach, at the park, or its handful of outdoor tables. Open 9 a.m. to 7 p.m. Mon through Fri; 9 a.m. to 6 p.m. Sat; closed Sun.

i If you're hopping on the water taxi to downtown Fort Lauderdale for your evening meal, the closest stop to the heart of Las Olas's restaurant scene is SE 9th Avenue.

FRENCH

LA CREPERIE   **$$$**
4589 N. University Dr., Lauderhill
(954) 741-9035
www.lacreperieinternational.com

If you've never indulged in a Breton crepe (that's a crepe from Brittany), make a beeline to La Creperie. Breton crepes are made with buckwheat and filled with a concoction of your choice—cheese, mushrooms, ham— over 30 options abound—or choose a sweet version for dessert (over 10 varieties—we recommend the butter or apple), that is if you can resist their crème brûlée. The tiny bistro feels solidly European, and for those not in the mood for a thin pancake, staples like escargots and quiche grace the menu. Authentic bouillabaisse comes into play the last weekend of every month (reservations essential). Open Tues to Fri 11:30 a.m. to 2 p.m., and 5:30 to 10 p.m.; Sat 5:30 to 10:30 p.m.; Sun 5 to 9 p.m.; closed Mon.

LE CAFÉ DE PARIS $–$$
715 E. Las Olas Blvd., Ft. Lauderdale
(954) 467-2900
Craving Paris? French waiters will both welcome you (and ignore you) just enough to make you feel like you've skipped across the pond for dinner, and faux Paris touches like wrought iron rails and murals round out your stay while you munch on staples like cheese-heavy French onion soup, garlicky escargots (snails), *moules marinière* (mussels with garlic, onion, lemon, and white wine) or steak tartare. Expansive outdoor tables face busy Las Olas.

SAINT TROPEZ $–$$
1010 E. Las Olas Blvd., Ft. Lauderdale
(954) 767-1073
One of the newest additions to trendy Las Olas, this is another culinary journey through France, but this one—as opposed to the more pristine Le Café de Paris across the street—is more of a casual bistro meets cafe. Inside, you're greeted with a long, relaxed wooden bar and French newspaper–lined walls. Most of the staff is heavily accented

and seem like they left Paris yesterday, and they'll happily give you the lowdown on any menu item. Crisp sandwiches (served on crusty baguettes, *bien sûr*) and French onion soup are an excellent bet, though for larger appetites traditional coq au vin and steak frites hit the spot. What we love most about Saint Tropez is that you can pop in for a full meal or simply unwind with a newspaper, snack, and a cup of coffee, pretending you are in a traditional Parisian cafe. Sidewalk tables ensure you can people watch to your heart's content in a prime spot on Las Olas, or hit the tables out back for a more private outside space.

SAGE $$–$$$
2378 N. Federal Hwy., Ft. Lauderdale
(954) 565-2299
www.sagecafe.net/moulin.htm
French country cuisine like coq au vin and savory crepes are dished up with reasonable prices in this casual, yet sophisticated, bistro. White tablecloths lend an upscale air, but really, it's just about eating refined French fare with care and enjoyment. Sage also offers popular (and complimentary) wine tastings on the first Tues of every month from 5 to 7 p.m., free mimosas for Sun brunch, and Moulin Rouge show nights every Wed at 9 p.m. (reservations recommended).

GERMAN

CYPRESS NOOK $$
201 E. McNab Rd., Pompano Beach
(954) 781-3464
www.cypressnook.com
With a mix of both German and American classics, it's tough to know what to pick from the carefully prepared menu. But this family-owned-and-operated spot whips up some of the best breakfasts and lunches in

the area, year after year, and they've been doing it since 1979. Some favorites are their three-egg omelettes and bratwurst menus (knockwurst with sauerkraut and home-made potato salad, anyone?), tough-to-find German beer, and a renowned Key lime pie. Breakfast is served all day long, but note they're only open until 2 p.m. weekdays and 1 p.m. weekends.

OLD HEIDELBERG RESTAURANT
& DELI $$–$$$
914 W. SR 84, Ft. Lauderdale
(954) 463-3880
www.oldheidelbergdeli.com
Blink and you'll think you're rambling through a fairy tale—but no, this really is a half-timbered German house sitting at the side of a Florida state road. It only feels more authentic when you step into the interior filled with cuckoo clocks and beer steins and take a peek at the German specialties—all your typical favorites, including a long list of sausage plates and beer varieties to choose from, are there. They also sell a number of deli foods to take out, so if you haven't had your fill, swing by the deli counter on your way out.

GREEK

TAVERNA OPA $$–$$$
4010 N. Ocean Dr., Hollywood Beach
(954) 929-4010
www.tavernaoparestaurant.com
Owned by the same people as Giorgio's Grill (p. 64), Taverna Opa takes the fun of Greece and quadruples it, with late-night dancing on the tables, talented bar tricks-cum-enter-tainment (think flaming drinks and acrobatic cocktail shaking), and general raucous fun as the drinks flow. But before it gets too crazed,

tasty traditional Greek fare hits your plate like tzatziki, *kefalotiri saganaki* (flaming cheese with brandy), kebabs, and souvlaki.

HUNGARIAN & CONTINENTAL

WINE CELLAR $$–$$$
199 E. Oakland Park Blvd., Ft. Lauderdale
(in the LA Shops Plaza)
(954) 565-9021
This spot isn't just Hungarian, but it leans towards anything from the former Austro-Hungarian territory. Traditional Hungarian goulash (heavy on the paprika, of course) is one of the most popular choices, but their impressive Austrian Wiener schnit-zel (pounded breaded veal, pan fried) and chicken paprikash (chicken in a paprika-and-sour-cream sauce) are clear winners, alongside staples like cordon bleu and filet mignon. With its lacy curtains and lost in the '70s decor, you might think you have plonked yourself overseas. Interestingly, the restaurant also houses a glass-enclosed avi-ary, which gives a whole new meaning to their early-bird special. Call for hours.

INDIAN & PAKISTANI

ROYAL INDIA $$
3801 Griffin Rd., Dania Beach
(954) 964-0071
www.royalindiafl.com
One of South Florida's longest running Indian restaurants has kept its doors open for over two decades by serving reliably spicy fare at reasonable prices. Breads and chutney, tandoori chicken, and tikka masala lure in loyal addicts, but the best thing in Royal India's arsenal is its top-value $8 lunch buffet served from 11:30 a.m. to 3 p.m. daily; dinner is offered from 5 to 10:30 p.m.

USMANIA RESTAURANT $
8251 W. Sunrise Blvd., Plantation
(954) 839-7949

Indian-food lovers beware: You might not be willing to get your curry fix anywhere else after dining at Usmania. This newcomer offers traditional Pakistani fare like succulent tandoori meats, creamy butter chicken, and fragrant korma dishes. Adventurous cuisine seekers can opt away from the norm and try things like curried goat brain, though less-daring eaters can rely on seafood, meat, and veggie versions. In general, Pakistani food mimics northern Indian food, though there is more of an emphasis on flatbreads (like nan) over rice. They also serve typical street food, like *nihari*, a thick meat stew with a side of lemon, ginger, and cilantro, a staple served for breakfast by street carts in Karachi. Run by husband-and-wife team Aftab and Fouzia Katia (from Karachi, Pakistan), the place maintains a family-run air, with other members of their family helping out. It's also frequented by many burka- and sari-wearing immigrants, always a sign that the foreign fare is being done right. The flavors you'll encounter here are exceptional and more than make up for the rather bland, cafeteria-style decor. Call for hours.

ITALIAN

BEACHSIDE GRILL $$
4658 N. Ocean Dr.,
Lauderdale-by-the-Sea
(954) 489-1544

Doubling as a pseudo–sports bar and restaurant, the restaurant bit of this homey space is what dominates. The Italian menu also shares space with plenty of American classics, such as a slider-trio appetizer or chicken and fish sandwiches, but we come for classics like the tender Milanese veal chop and

the chicken scarpariello. But it's the tremendously popular Angela's Sunday Gravy (served daily) that packs in the crowds: It is a slow-cooked tomato bliss that might rival your mother's. You decide. Its aroma alone is enough to come back for more.

CAFE VICO $$$
1125 N. Federal Hwy., Ft. Lauderdale
(954) 565-9681
www.cafevicorestaurant.com

Around for ages and popular among both families and couples seeking a romantic date, Cafe Vico welcomes you like a family member. Flickering candle lamps, polished wood, terra-cotta tile, and ceilings with a faux evening sky flank yellow walls covered in photos of celebrities who've dined here. Come here for classic Italian fare like caprese salads, penne al carbonara, eggplant parmigiana, vitello saltimbocca, and homemade tiramisu.

CAPRICCIO $$
2424 University Dr., Pembroke Pines
(954) 432-7001
www.capriccios.net

It's our kind of restaurant, Frank Sinatra fans. Owner and singer Gian Piero Cangelosi circulates the dining room belting out old Frank Sinatra tunes most nights, wooing back regulars for over 30 years with his voice and menu, captivating diners old and young. And that's just entertainment; for the Northern Italian cuisine there's pastas, chicken, beef, and seafood, delicately garnished with lemon, garlic, olive oil, tangy tomato sauces, quality cheeses, and herbs from the region. If Sinatra isn't featuring, then live violin music probably will, and equally impressive is the sparkling chandelier centerpiece in the decadent lounge.

MAMA MIA RESTAURANT $$
1818 Young Circle, Hollywood
(954) 563-3272
www.miagrill.com

You won't go home hungry at this at this convivial neighborhood fave, smack on the big circle that flanks the heart of downtown Hollywood. Take your pick from uncomplicated dishes like clams casino, jumbo meatballs, salads, soups, pizzas, panini, and all the standard Italian pasta dishes, or slice into a quality steak from their butcher shop menu. They also offer an express lunch menu (in and out in under 20 minutes). Casual with lots of woodwork and crisp white tablecloths, this place is always buzzing with a healthy mix of locals, VIPs, and visitors. Open daily 11 a.m. to 1 a.m.

NEW RIVER PIZZA $
706 S. Federal Hwy., Ft. Lauderdale
(954) 618-7000
www.newriverpizzaonline.com

Do you sometimes have a hankering for anti-designer pizza—you know, the kind of pizza place you grew up with complete with canned mushrooms, thick dough, with a side of garlic knots dripping with butter? It's here at New River, where you won't find prosciutto or imported truffles anywhere in sight, and parmesan and garlic powder come in jumbo plastic containers. On our visit, our slice of pie oozed mozzarella and fat pieces of pepperoni, and we ate it at the vinyl counter, enjoying every greasy, satisfying bite. Well-seasoned meatball subs and vegetarian lasagna keep non-pizza types happy.

PRIMANTI BROTHERS $
901 N. Fort Lauderdale Blvd.,
Ft. Lauderdale Beach
(954) 565-0605
www.primantibrothers.com

A hop across the street from the north end of Fort Lauderdale Beach, this affable pizza and grill is the spot for a hefty slice of hand-tossed, made-from-scratch pizza to break up your tanning session. Entire pizzas come in 14- and 18-inch versions with the usual toppings, or choose from sandwiches made on fresh Italian bread, burgers, jumbo hot dogs (regular, cheese, or chili), and salads. There's also a trio of mains like manicotti, ravioli, or lasagna, all made in plain sight behind the diner-esque counter (watch from the vinyl swivel stools or in a comfy booth). Breakfast is offered between 8 and 10:30 a.m. Leave your diet at the door—as the menu specifies, Primanti Brothers "does not know what carbohydrates are." That's OK, you can jog it off across the street with a view of the beach. Cash only. Open 24/7; takeout service only available from 6 to 8 a.m.

JAPANESE

SUSHI BLUES CAFE $–$$
2009 Harrison St., Hollywood
(954) 929-9560
www.sushiblues.com

Family-run by Kenny Millions and his wife, Junko Maslak, expect Japanese favorites, salads, and sandwiches alongside macrobiotic choices that rarely grace the pages of a sushi menu. Take your pick from barbecued eel and papaya sushi, grilled ahi tuna salad, or honey-ginger carrot soup. Weekends bring in live music, often featuring the saxophonist owner who has clearly mastered the art of both restaurateur and musician.

SUSHI ROCK $–$$
1515 E. Las Olas Blvd., Ft. Lauderdale
(954) 462-5541

The second location of the popular South Beach restaurant, this is one of the best sushi

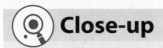

Close-up

An Insider's Guide to Florida Cuisine

Florida cuisine is tough to define, but roughly speaking, it consists of locally sourced seafood and fruit often with a Caribbean origin or influence. Its existence may be questioned, but after dining at a few local bars and grills (many on a waterside location—the beach, the Intracoastal, or a river), you'll start to notice a few usual suspects like conch fritters or blackened grouper, which might not flank most menus back home. For details about Key limes and Key lime pie, see our recipe on p. 72.

Bimini Bread: Sweet white bread originally from Bimini (a tiny Bahamian Island) but now a staple in many Caribbean Islands and popular in South Florida.

Conch Salad: Originally a Bahamian dish, the meat from large conch shells (the big, pretty white ones) is chopped and tossed with onions, tomatoes, peppers, vinegar, and spices and then marinated for a day or so—imagine a conch-meat seviche.

Conch Fritters: Conch meat mixed with a flour dough, celery, and garlic, then deep fried and served with a dipping sauce (often a creamy cocktail sauce).

Florida Spiny Lobster: Also called rock lobster, this lobster from the waters around the Florida Keys is less sweet than traditional lobster and contains skinny, spiny claws—the meat comes from the tail. It's eaten and prepared like Atlantic lobsters.

Frog's Legs: These live in and on the edge of the Everglades. The good ones are fried and taste like chicken, but be sure to ask and verify they've been caught locally (some come from a box that states "Made in China").

Gator Bites: Alligator—breaded, deep fried, and served with a dipping sauce. It's a tad chewy but tastes a bit like . . . no, not chicken. It's more like pork, or a meaty fish. Most alligator meat comes from the tail.

Grouper: This meaty white fish pops up all over menus in Florida and is often blackened or grilled, and served in a sandwich.

Key Lime Pie: Tart and yellow goodness housed in a crunchy crust. (If it's green, it isn't from a Key lime.)

Mahimahi (also often called dolphin on menus): A meaty, succulent white fish often served grilled or blackened in a sandwich with a thick slather of tartar sauce.

Rock Shrimp: A smaller version than its ubiquitous cousin, rock shrimp have a tough shell (think spiny lobster) and are best when served cracked and doused with a ton of butter, salt, and pepper.

Soft-shell Blue Crab: A blue crab after molting (it's shed its shell and has yet to grow another)—it can be eaten whole.

Stone Crab: Succulent, sweet, juicy claws of this Florida favorite are served on ice with a side of honey-mustard sauce. October to April is the season to eat it—outside these months the available claws with be frozen.

joints in town. It feels like a cross between a bar and a restaurant, and if you ignore the convertibles rolling by on trendy Las Olas and the sun-kissed shoulders and casual garb, you could almost think you're in New York City. Maybe that's why so many transplanted New Yorkers like to grab a bite here. Along with the usual suspects on the savory side, locals swear by their Banana Tempura dessert.

LATIN AMERICAN

EL TAMARINDO CAFE & RESTAURANT $
233 W. SR 84, Ft. Lauderdale
(954) 467-5114
www.eltamarindocafe.com

This family-owned-and-operated Salvadorean gem is known for its handsome portions and authentic cuisine. Crisp white tablecloths contrast the colorful array of dishes that grace the menu. Lots of succulent seafood, homemade tamales, fresh cilantro, and pungent spices and sauces (try the garlic chimichurri and the hot sauce made on site) dominate your meal, along with lots of laughs in the convivial setting. The same owners also run a coal-fired pizza joint in town (El Tamarindo Coal Fired Pizza, 712 Atlantic Shores Blvd., Hallandale Beach, 954-456-4447), which takes Latin cuisine and pizza to new heights.

LEBANESE

FERDOS GRILL $$$
4300 N. Federal Hwy., Ft. Lauderdale
(954) 492-5552
www.ferdosgrill.net

The menu clad with Middle Eastern staples like lamb chops, gyros, and mixed grill plates doesn't end there—Ferdos introduces dishes like mussels in Pernod, homemade dolmas, tiny *arayes* (seasoned minced meat stuffed in pita, grilled, and served with hummus), and the tasty kibbe (a blend of meat and cracked wheat, hand rolled, and stuffed with sautéed meat, onions, and house seasoning). Saturday nights come alive with titillating belly dancers distracting the diners, both male and female (you try focusing on a falafel when an exotic, buxom dancer jigs her way into your line of sight). It's all in good fun and makes for an entertaining evening. Open 11:30 a.m. to 10 p.m. Mon through Thurs; 11:30 a.m. to 11 p.m. Fri; 5 to 11 p.m. Sat; closed Sun.

MEDITERRANEAN

CASABLANCA CAFE $$$
3049 Alhambra St., Ft. Lauderdale Beach
(954) 764-3500
www.casablancacafeonline.com

Tuck into the most romantic restaurant in town with your honey, or just live it up sampling the exquisite cocktails and fresh Mediterranean and seafood fare with your favorite pals. Moroccan accents infuse a cozy, warm feeling, while outdoor tables sprawl across this two-story villa hidden just enough to feel exclusive, but with a view of all the beach action. Open for lunch and dinner daily at 11:30 a.m. until closing.

GIORGIO'S GRILL $$$
606 N. Ocean Dr., Hollywood Beach
(954) 929-7030
www.giorgiosgrill.com

Mediterranean food goes upscale at this enormous waterside eatery in the heart of Hollywood Beach. It's a great spot for birthdays or other celebrations—the staff really makes an effort to make groups feel special and well attended to. But it's a hit for smaller parties, too, who come for the convivial atmosphere and the consistently satisfying food. Fish dishes (including an exquisite bouillabaisse and paella) dominate and excel, but salads, pastas, and steaks satisfy all nonseafood tastes. It's one of the most popular brunch venues in town, so be sure to reserve ahead. But the Sunset Dinner menu (such a nice way to describe an early-bird special, eh?!) is the best deal they offer, and it's a steal: For $18.95 you get a glass of house wine, a three-course meal, and a view of the sun setting over the Intracoastal Waterway. Open for dinner and lunch daily; call for hours as they do vary by season.

MEXICAN

CARLOS & PEPE'S $$
1302 SE 17th St., Ft. Lauderdale
(954) 467-7192
www.carlosandpepesfl.com
This Mexican-American local fave, leaning heavy on the Mexican, dishes up your usual with oodles of options—nachos (six varieties), quesadillas (eleven varieties), fajitas (seven varieties), tacos and enchiladas with their famous tuna dip, crab enchiladas, and a mean fried ice cream. The restaurant has a sports-bar feel—lots of TVs—and a relaxed bar that concocts extra-strong, extra-mean margaritas (made with freshly squeezed juice and your choice of over 10 types of tequila). It's a popular family place that gets packed on game nights.

EDUARDO DE SAN ANGEL $$$
2822 Commercial Blvd., Ft. Lauderdale
(954) 772-4731
www.eduardodesanangel.com
Consistently voted one of the top Broward county restaurants by Zagat's, award-winning chef Eduardo Pria goes beyond the usual tacos and fajitas of your typical Mexican eatery. Expect innovative and locally inspired dishes taking Mexican cuisine to new heights, such as Florida blue crab and yellow corn cakes with chipotle-mole sauce, ancho chili crepes with a squash blossom sauce, black bean raviolis with chipotle-and-toasted-walnut cream sauce, and roast duck with spicy guava syrup and poached-pear compote. Equally impressive is its carefully selected wine list (heavy on North American wineries), which is geared to complement the dishes—the knowledgeable servers are most helpful in directing you to an appropriate choice to accompany your meal. Less experimental dishes are offered for those who like their Mexican traditional and unfussy, and you can wash it all down with expertly mixed margaritas. The relaxed but cheery dining room with lots of yellow and red is superb for any occasion. Open Mon through Sat 5:30 to 10 p.m., closed Sun.

TORTILLERIA MEXICANA $
4115 N. Dixie Hwy., Oakland Park
(954) 563-2503
Food on the run doesn't need to involve McDonald's or Burger King; if you're in the mood for a quick bite of Mexican and can't handle the fast-food feel of Taco Bell, pop into this shop-cum-deli for authentic meat-and-bean mixed plates, tacos, burritos—all the tortillas are made on-site, and service is quick and friendly, plus, we haven't tasted tamales this far east in quite some time. They've got a few tables inside if you prefer to sit, or take it to go.

PERSIAN

KULUCK $
5879 N. University Dr., Tamarac
(954) 720-6980
www.kuluck.com

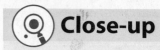

Close-up

We All Scream . . .

. . . for ice cream! It's sticky, you're perspiring, and all you can think of is an icy cone of goodness. Here are our top ice-cream parlor and gelato picks for the Fort Lauderdale area:

Grandma's French Café
3354 N. Ocean Blvd., Ft. Lauderdale
(954) 564-3671
www.grandmasfrenchcafe.com
Occupying half of a decades-old ice-cream parlor that doubles as a French cafe smack on Galt Ocean Mile/A1A, this feels like old-school sweet cream gone modern.

Razzleberry's Ice Cream
3412 E. Atlantic Blvd., Pompano Beach
(954) 943-6944
For over 30 years, beachside Razzleberry's has been whipping up fresh flavors daily—you can always try something new each time you walk in. It's named after its most popular flavor, Razzleberry (rich, oh-so-creamy black and red raspberry).

Gelato Dream
235 S. Fort Lauderdale Beach Blvd., Ft. Lauderdale
(954) 463-7677
A large and satisfying variety of gelatos hit the spot after a day at the beach (it's right across from Fort Lauderdale Beach, down an alley around the corner from legendary Elbo Room). Two dozen flavors are on offer at any given time, including mango, lemon, pistachio, tiramisu, hazelnut, and chocolate.

Marie's Italian Ice
2862 NE 17 Ave., Pompano Beach
(954) 784-8447
It's all natural, refreshing gelato—less than 10 varieties are available but oh, they're all fabulous: Faves include lemon, cherry, chocolate, strawberry, chocolate, and piña colada.

If you haven't tried Persian food yet, you haven't tasted some of the most fragrant, flavorful food on Earth. Not only that, but the divine cuisine is served way out here in Tamarac in classy surrounds: fabric-draped walls and a fun outdoor hookah lounge, which makes the place feel like a trendy evening spot later in the evening. Stews and basmati-rice dishes dominate, like chicken pomegranate stew and charbroiled chicken with saffron and barberries (a Persian specialty with a slightly tart edge). Weekends feature entertaining belly dancers and DJs. Closed Mon.

PERUVIAN

CASA PERU $$
822 W. Hallandale Beach Blvd.,
Hallandale Beach
(954) 457-3424

Between the endless list of traditional sevi-
ches and chicken-and-rice dishes, a good
selection of Peruvian beer, and a fun, laid-
back atmosphere, this is a great spot for
a quick bite or lunch. Incredible value for
lovingly prepared Peruvian staples, and the
fish is always right-off-the-docks fresh. The
setting is a bit bland, but at these prices and
the large portions, you can't complain.

PORTUGUESE

SOL E MAR RESTAURANT $$
900 E. Atlantic Blvd., Pompano Beach
(954) 941-0906

Bacalau, the staple codfish that defines Portuguese cuisine, is one of the best reasons
locals flock to this fun Portuguese find in Pompano. Seafood and saffron-heavy alternate
options, plus oodles of dishes with piri piri
peppers, enormous sardines, and delicately
spiced potatoes, keep 'em coming in. While
the food is consistently excellent, service can
be slow, but when the smiling waiter offers to
describe and explain the extensive port selection you probably won't mind. It's this type
of unrushed hospitality that makes it feel like
you've crossed the ocean to Lisbon.

ROMANIAN

TRANSYLVANIA RESTAURANT $$
113 S. 20th Ave., Hollywood
(954) 929-0777
www.restauranttransylvania.com

Check your Dracula jokes at the door. If
you've never tried Romanian cuisine, get

ready for comfort food with oomph—think
Romanian *mamaliga* (moist polenta gar-
nished with flecks of pepper and parsley),
fragrant stuffed cabbage, succulent schnit-
zel, paprika-heavy goulash, and kebabs.
Romania—literally—comes to Hollywood,
indicative of the large Romanian community
in the surrounds. Live acts, mainly Romanian
singers and dancers, perform nightly.

SEAFOOD & FLORIDIAN

ARUBA BEACH CAFE $$
1 Commercial Blvd.,
Lauderdale-by-the-Sea
(954) 776-0001
www.arubabeachcafe.com

Few beachside restaurants can do what
Aruba does—it's got the exceptional food
and valet parking, but by day you can easily
saunter up in your bikini and enjoy a Corona
on the outdoor deck. Three bars confirm this
is much more than an eating spot, but we
have to put it in this chapter because one,
the food is so damn good, and two, you'll be
missing out if all you do is drink here. You can
go fancy (Seared Sesame Ahi Sashimi melts
in your mouth, and the Crock of Escargots
are to-die-for garlic goodness) or old-school
with Macho Nachos (bedecked with bub-
bling cheddar and jack and a dollop of fresh
guacamole) or sweet and spicy Jamaican
Jerk Wings hot off the grill. Fresh salads, juicy
burgers and Florida mahimahi (on its own
or in a sandwich) round out the extensive
Caribbean-influenced menu, all of which
can be washed down with an expertly mixed
fruity martini. But we were most impressed
by the range of chilled coffee cocktails (still
dreaming about the Calypso Cappuccino).
Lunch and dinner are served Mon through
Sat from 11 a.m. to 11 p.m.; Sun from 9 a.m.

to 11 p.m. The bar is open until 1 a.m. Sun through Tues, and until 2 a.m. Wed through Sat.

BAHIA CABANA $$
3001 Harbour Dr., Ft. Lauderdale Beach
(954) 524-1555
www.bahiacabanaresort.com
Transplants from Boston swear by Bahia Cabana's homemade chowder, and judging by the number of Boston accents we overheard on our visit, plenty of northerners come here for a taste of New England, minus the nor'easters, of course. An eclectic mix of baby back ribs, fish sandwiches, and a long salad list (including a mean conch salad) rounds out the menu. Or just stop by for a daiquiri and watch the boats float by on the comfy deck beneath a palm tree—it doesn't get much more Florida than that. Open daily from 7 a.m. to midnight.

BIMINI BOATYARD $$–$$$
1555 17th St., Ft. Lauderdale
(954) 525-7400
www.biminiboatyard.com
Under new proprietorship since 2008, this waterfront landmark received a complete makeover in early 2009, and the results are fabulous. The standard fare—much-loved Florida fish thrown on the grill—is still served with a simplicity and freshness that's tough to beat for anyone on a budget. The exterior seems upscale, but really, this is a laid-back affair that demands you leave any pretensions at home.

BLUE MOON FISH CO. $$$
4405 Tradewinds Ave.,
Lauderdale-by-the-Sea
(954) 267-9888
www.bluemoonfishco.com
This spot blows everyone away—how can you not be with a wide, looming deck staring out onto the tranquil Intracoastal Waterway? There's a bit of Art Deco going on inside, but really, outside is where you want to be, enjoying the view and tucking into Florida seafood classics. At night, flickering votives and sparkling water make this a prime romantic spot, but there's always plenty of cheer and fun for family and larger groups. They're well-known for their Sun, brunch, but be sure to book in advance or risk waiting for hours. A second location is in Coral Springs at 10317 Royal Palm Blvd., (954) 755-0002.

CATFISH DEWEY'S $$
4003 N. Andrews Ave., Ft. Lauderdale
(954) 566-5333
www.catfishdeweys.com
Fried seafood is the name of the game at Catfish Dewey's, with an obvious emphasis on catfish. There's a nightly all-you-can-eat menu (variety changes), and good old hush puppies, slaw, and collard greens come on the side of everything. It's been in operation since the early 1980s and packs in the locals for its affordable cuisine and no-fuss preparation—fish done right, as the bartender said on our visit. You decide. Non-fried options include fresh Florida stone crab and fish done how you like it—baked, grilled, boiled, or blackened.

DOWNTOWNER SALOON $$
408 S. Andrews Ave., Ft. Lauderdale
(954) 463-9800
www.downtownersaloon.com
Don't be put off by the fact that the parking lot is shared with the jail next door. Hidden south of the Andrews Avenue Bridge from downtown Fort Lauderdale, this bar and grill

is worth seeking out. Savor raw oysters, fresh sandwiches, and seafood mains overlooking the New River. A water-taxi stop sits right outside the door, but you're right at the end of the Riverwalk, so you also can walk off those coated, seasoned fries you can't stop eating.

15TH STREET FISHERIES $$–$$$
1900 SE 15th St., Ft. Lauderdale
(954) 763-2777
www.15streetfisheries.com

This is hands down one of our favorite waterside seafood restaurants. Choose from the upstairs dining room, which features a larger menu and a cozy seafood-shack-gone-upscale vibe, the casual dockside cafe downstairs, or sit outside on the deck and watch the tarpon swim almost next to you (you can feed them, too, if you're inclined). Regulars swear by the sizzlin' skillet on the dockside menu—and the waiters assure us it's the most popular item on the menu: shrimp, fish (usually mahimahi or grouper), scallops, tomatoes, and artichoke hearts served on a sizzling platter with a creamy white wine sauce. Slabs of crusty, buttered French bread crown the dish, perfect for sopping up the addictive sauce. Friendly service and live music on weekends (also downstairs) make it the kind of place you want to linger long after your meal ends.

ISLAMORADA FISH COMPANY $$–$$$
220 Gulf Stream Way, Dania Beach
(954) 927-7737
www.fishcompany.com

Built on and around a massive aquarium and reef, the location alone is enough to draw the crowds, but those in the know come for the fresh seafood, namely, their renowned stone crab claws with a kickin' honey mustard sauce, or their signature sandwich (thick wedges of fried grouper, American cheese, sautéed onions, and homemade tartar on a crisp Kaiser roll). The menu also offers fried burgers, yellowtail, fried conch, clam strips, and daily grilled fish specials.

JIMBO'S SANDBAR $–$$
6200 N. Ocean Blvd., Dania Beach
(954) 927-9560
www.jimbossandbar.com

Welcome to Jimbo's Sandbar, which wins our award for best tagline: Home of the Easily Strayed and Just One More. They're so proud of this claim that they painted it out front on the entrance, just so you know how seriously they take their quote. It describes the scene here to a tee. Pop around back and you're treated to a sublime view of the Intracoastal, with the Davie Beach bridge off to your right and calm, green Florida vegetation hugging the water. A seat at the bar ensures a front-row seat to the waterway, and the crusty characters at the bar make you wonder where they've strayed in from, but no matter. You'll be as happy chewing the fat with the locals as you will chowing down on conch fritters, spicy wings, or their Jimbo's Secret Recipe BBQ (honey chipotle or original), fried fish, and dinner platters. Weekends bring live music and a more bar-like vibe, and daytime guests are less likely to encounter any drunk-as-a-skunk locals (don't worry, they're harmless). It's not everyone's scene, but it's authentically "divey" (without being dangerous) and feels a bit like you've hopped down to the Florida Keys, without the traffic.

LOLA'S ON HARRISON $$$
2032 Harrison St., Hollywood
(954) 927-9851
www.lolasonharrison.com

Glossy and upscale without attitude, Lola's is a winner on this stretch of downtown Hollywood. A menu ranging from comfort food to sophisticated cuisine keeps the masses packing it in, from caviar and down-home po'boys to Coca-Cola ribs and salmon tartare. A superb cocktail list rounds out the experience and ensures it's as popular for drinks only as it is for its food. Open Tues, Wed, Thurs, Sun 5 to 10 p.m.; Fri and Sat 5 to 11 p.m.; closed Mon.

OCEAN ALLEY $$
900 N. Broadwalk, Hollywood Beach
(954) 921-6171
www.oceanalley.net
Right on the corner, this open air space has two entire wall-free sides—inside, aqua murals depict underwater tropical fish and colorful coral. This is an excellent location on the Broadwalk, with exceptional views of the beach and the Broadwalk action. Great-value specials make this a wallet-friendly fave: For example, you get a free bottle of house wine with the purchase of two dinner entrees on Mon. Open daily for breakfast, lunch, and dinner.

RUSTIC INN CRABHOUSE $$$
4331 Ravenswood Rd., Ft. Lauderdale
(954) 584-1637
www.rusticinn.com
Relieve stress and satisfy your appetite for seafood in one swoop of the hand—at Rustic Inn, you'll crack your crab with a wooden mallet (bibs also supplied by staff, though we don't recommend you wear your Sunday best to this casual outfit with newspaper-lined tables). It's fun, but do expect to hear the banging in surround sound throughout your meal. The sound is bound to fade away as you bite into their "world-famous" garlic crabs—they're as good as they claim to be. If you're after something that'll affect your breath less, dig into lobster, off-the-boat fish, various pastas, and an array of fried bits—clams, scallops, and alligator. The space has an open airy feel, with a touch of tiki hut and round fish crates that serve as shades for the ceiling lamps. This place has been around for over 50 years, and it's more than worth the wait for the experience of dining in a Lauderdale legend.

SEA WATCH ON
THE OCEAN $$$–$$$$
6002 N. Ocean Blvd.,
Ft. Lauderdale Beach
(954) 781-2200
www.seawatchontheocean.com
Since 1974, the Sea Watch has been dishing up seafood to its faithful following on the coast. So faithful, in fact, that the restaurant carves the names of some of its most frequent guests into their own dedicated oar that hangs above the dining room. Once you step inside, it's easy to see how Sea Watch sets itself apart from the many other ocean-side venues nearby. The grounds are vast and green with wide yards of grass and oodles of palms swaying in the breeze, and it's a touch of pre-condo Old Florida. The view takes in sand dunes and protected sea grass, and you feel a bit like you've been transported away from the rapid South Florida growth, before space was so precious. Windows line the warm, marine-influenced wood interior, so you can take in all the free space and breathe free. The menu guides you from conch to chowders that cover the eastern seaboard (conch and New England versions), escargots, and San Francisco–style calamari take you to even more coasts and across the Atlantic. Main entrees see a similar mix, with

a seafood-focused array of Maine lobster, Florida red snapper, and Bouillabaisse a la Marseillaise (seafood stew inspired by the steamy Mediterranean port city).

SOUTHPORT RAW BAR $$–$$$
1536 Cordova Dr., Ft. Lauderdale
(954) 525-2526
www.southportrawbar.com

Since 1973, no-frills Southport has been dishing it up to locals who come for the mellow vibes, the freshly shucked raw oysters, and the sublime view of the Intracoastal. With its hopping happy hour (both early evening and late night versions), weekly karaoke night (Tues), and rockin' live music, this restaurant-cum-bar attracts all ages and walks of life. Seafood and Cajun themes dominate the menu, or choose from their daily menu (usually seafood heavy). Whatever you eat, the staff will make you feel at home.

TRINA RESTAURANT $$$$
601 N. Fort Lauderdale Beach Blvd.,
Ft. Lauderdale Beach
(954) 567-8070
www.trinarestaurantandlounge.com

Ensconced in the trendy Atlantic Hotel, Trina is all minimalist deep brown furnishings, cool blue lighting, and exquisite taste. The refined clientele lounges with a superb water view while enjoying imaginative seafood dishes like lobster corn dogs, oven-roasted sea bass, and fresh Florida snapper; meat lovers won't go hungry with the strip steak and filet mignon. Their islandlike outdoor terrace is bliss on a balmy summer night, where you can hear the waves and watch the pedestrian action one level down.

SOUTHWESTERN

CANYON CAFE $$–$$$
1818 E. Sunrise Blvd., Ft. Lauderdale
(954) 765-1950
www.canyonfl.com

This innovative bastion of modern Southwestern cuisine fuses its dishes with Asian, Southern, and Central American undertones. Think chipotle, wasabi, ginger, cilantro, mango, lemongrass, basil, jalapeño, and hot chiles creatively used on fresh seafood and wild game. Low lighting, earth tones, and jazzy, upbeat music keep the feel contemporary but cozy, and service is consistently exceptional. They don't take reservations, so come early or plan to wait with a cocktail in the snazzy designer bar bedecked with tequila bottles. Don't leave without trying their famously addictive Prickly Pear Margaritas, made with cactus fruit marinated in blue agave tequila. Dinner is served daily starting at 5:30 p.m.

SPANISH

CAFE SEVILLE $–$$
2768 E. Oakland Park Blvd.,
Ft. Lauderdale
(954) 565-1148
www.cafeseville.com

Transplant yourself to Spain in this authentic and dedicated Spanish fave tucked away in a bland strip mall. The food more than makes up for its location, with seafood specialties—including paella—cooked with love and care; don't expecting a quick meal, do expect lots of saffron and warm service. The accolades and awards prove this is a consistent winner, the wine list impresses oenophiles, and their extensive and one-of-a-kind tapas menu (think calamari stuffed with crab meat, scallops, shrimp, garlic, saffron, and sherry, or escargots sautéed with garlic, tomato, basil,

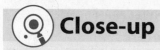

Close-up

Key Lime Pie . . . with Canned Milk?

Key lime pie was originated in Key West, Florida, by the local residents, or "Conchs." The original version was made before refrigerators were common commodities. Without any cattle on the islands, the only milk available was canned milk brought in by ship, later by train—hence the used of canned milk versus fresh. And this being Florida, heating up an oven was best avoided in the summer months, so they cleverly devised a way to make it without cooking or heating: acid from the lime juice sets and thickens the egg yolks. These days, many people still make the pie in the traditional manner, though they bake the crust (back in the day, it would have been crust-free). These days, fear of salmonella means most (including this one) are baked for 10 to 20 minutes—but it tastes exactly the same.

SUSIE'S KEY LIME PIE RECIPE

Ingredients:
Crust
18 graham crackers, crushed
3½ tablespoons sugar
1 stick (¼ lb.) butter
(Alternately, buy a 9" pie crust)

Filling
4 large egg yolks
1 14-ounce can sweetened condensed milk
½ cup fresh Key lime juice (approximately 12 to 14 Key limes)
3 teaspoons grated lime peel, green portion only

Preparation:
Crust
Mix ingredients and press into a 9" pie plate. Bake in a preheated 350 degree F oven for 10–12 minutes until lightly browned. Place on a rack to cool.

Pie Filling
Beat the egg yolks until they are thick and turn to a light yellow. Add the sweetened condensed milk and slowly beat while mixing in half of the lime juice. Once the juice is mixed in, add the other half of the juice and the zest. Continue to mix for a few seconds until it's all blended. Pour the mixture into the pie shell and bake at 350 degrees F for 12 minutes to set the yolks.

---

mushrooms, and white wine) is always on hand to keep you nibbling while you wait for your entree. Wall murals of seascapes and *toreros* (bullfighters) in a convivial, dark-wood, wine-tavern-like setting mean you'll be cozy, happy, and relaxed by the end of your meal. Lunch is served from 11 a.m. to 2 p.m., then they reopen for dinner at 5 p.m. and close when they're good and ready.

THAI

GALANGA $-$$
2389 Wilton Dr., Wilton Manors
(954) 202-0000
www.galangarestaurant.com
The wow effect starts with the massive, 700-gallon fish tank (with awesome blue lighting) that greets you in the dining room. The impressive decor continues with the giant stone head in its leafy garden patio. Once you stop pausing at the exquisite Asian art gracing the walls, the food will command your attention: spicy tuna salad with a hint of Korean kimchee, delicate steamed dumplings, scallops with basil sauce, plus gorgeous curries, teriyakis, noodle dishes, and sushi (we like the Crunch and Sexy Roll—spicy salmon wrapped in soy paper with masago).

JASMINE THAI $$
5103 Coconut Creek Pkwy., Margate
(954) 979-5530
www.jasminethai-sushi.com
It won't win any design awards, but that doesn't stop the faithful followers from returning decade after decade to this Margate Thai and sushi authority with a good selection of Chinese staples. We're particularly fond of the Thai green curry and pad thai, whipped up with care—it is clear that each dish is lovingly and delicately prepared, bringing out the best of the flavors in each dish. The sushi bar always offers a great selection of spicy tuna rolls, expertly crafted hand rolls, and surprisingly flavor-packed California rolls—we think it is due to the fresh ingredients and excellent chefs who know how to create magic with simple ingredients.

SUKHOTHAI $$
1930 E. Sunrise Blvd., Ft. Lauderdale
(954) 764-0148
www.sukhothaiflorida.com
It's rare to find a classy restaurant this hospitable and authentic, but anyone who knows great Thai cuisine will be wowed by the flavors, both fiery and delicate. Traditional Thai dishes dominate, and they cleverly separate their menu into spicy and nonspicy. Don't be surprised if you see the owners, Susie Komolsane and her son Eddie Watana, stroll through the dining room to greet regulars and newcomers. Lunch and dinner are served weekdays; dinner only on the weekend. Hours vary. Call ahead.

TURKISH

ISTANBUL RESTAURANT $
707 N. Broadwalk, Hollywood Beach
(954) 921-1263
Outstanding homemade hummus, spicy lamb kebabs, sticky baklava—it's all delicious and made with care at this tiny Turkish gem on the beach. The tiny space is light on decor, but outdoor tables add a little extra room. If there's no space you can pick up some food to go and enjoy it on the beach or a bench a few steps away.

VEGAN & VEGETARIAN

GOURMET GREENHOUSE $
5809 Hollywood Blvd., Hollywood
(954) 518-0551
www.gourmetgreenhouse.com
This raw food, vegan, and vegetarian cafe (with a tiny offering of meat items) serves sandwiches, salads, soups, and a small selection of entrees and weekly specials. Not hungry? Swing by for a fresh-squeezed juice or decadent smoothie. It's bright and friendly,

with yellow walls accented by rambling sunflower murals. On our visit, we were wowed by their weekly special (the raw pear and spinach salad with pine nuts and cranberries) and couldn't get enough of the cinnamon ice cream with candied pumpkin seed swirl. They also offer changing cooking classes (vegan, raw, vegetarian). Closed Sun and Mon.

SUBLIME WORLD VEGETARIAN CUISINE $$

1431 N. Federal Hwy., Ft. Lauderdale
(954) 615-1431
www.sublimerestaurant.com

Upscale vegan cuisine isn't that easy to find—which might be why Pamela Anderson herself came for the opening of this restaurant nearly a decade ago. Whether it was her celeb status that got it on the map initially, Sublime has held its own for nearly a decade, and it not only offers meat- and dairy-free dishes but cholesterol free, too. The interior is all modern Zen with beiges and browns, and the dishes are inventive and sure to wow the biggest carnivores—must

tries include the "caviar" appetizer (lemon, red onion, chopped tofu, chive, and a blini) and the Portobello Stack (portobello mushrooms, sautéed spinach, roasted tomato, red potatoes, cauliflower, and mashed potatoes). The intention of the owner (an active animal rights activist) is to prove that vegan is not dull, but that it is outright "Sublime." She's succeeded there. Hours are Tues through Sun, 5:30 to 10 p.m. Closed Mon.

VIETNAMESE

BASILIC VIETNAMESE GRILL $

218 Commercial Blvd.,
Lauderdale-by-the-Sea
(954) 771-5798

The recent addition is all about *pho*, the large bowls of Vietnamese soup that hit the spot in healthy, delicious goodness. You can wash it all down with a refreshing Asian beer (the selection is impressive). It's family-owned, and though the modern furnishings could be more inviting, the particularly hospitable service more than makes up for the slightly sterile vibe.

NIGHTLIFE

hat's there to see and do in the evenings and wee hours of the morning in Greater Fort Lauderdale?

Quite a bit. Scattered around the city—particularly in Hollywood and Fort Lauderdale—are bars, pubs, and lounges that range from chic to dive, from beer to wine, and from quiet to deafening. Those who like to dance can get their fix at posh dance clubs that play club and salsa.

If you prefer to kick back and listen to some live music, check out one of the city's many live music venues; clusters of beachy and casual places line Fort Lauderdale Beach and Lauderdale-by-the-Sea. The primary area to go drinking in, however, is Himmarshee, located along 2nd Street in downtown Fort Lauderdale. We've listed a few of the best places here, but frankly, most bars spill out onto the sidewalks on weekends, and the streets turn into one large party pen. Do be careful though—police patrol this area voraciously, so don't assume you can wander across the street in a drunken stupor and not be picked up for being drunk and disorderly. Many local restaurants also feature a lounge atmosphere and, in some cases, live music.

If this appeals to you, take a closer look at the Restaurants chapter, especially the areas along or around Las Olas. Most of the spots are true restaurants, but later at night the entire area feels more "loungey."

OVERVIEW

There are far too many bars, clubs, and music venues to list here, so this chapter offers up some of the city's most popular nightlife options. Before you head out, take note: Most of the bars and clubs in this chapter require guests to be 21 or older, with a valid ID. The legal drinking age in Florida is 21, and most clubs and bars don't let in anyone who is younger. Often Greater Fort Lauderdale clubs and bars charge a cover of anywhere from a couple dollars up to $10 or even $20. This does not include drinks or food; it merely gets you in the door. Bars often have higher cover charges on weekends and for special events. Many bars offer happy hour specials, although the hours, days, and discounts vary. For live music venues, it's always a good idea to purchase your tickets early. Many events—especially over holiday weekends—sell out. Tickets can be purchased at the location, on the venue's website, or by phone, unless indicated otherwise. Bars, lounges, and pubs in Greater Fort Lauderdale typically close by 3 or 4 a.m. on the weekends and earlier during the week. Hours and days do change sometimes, though, so it's a good idea to call ahead.

FORT LAUDERDALE AREA

ARUBA BEACH CAFE
1 Commercial Blvd.,
Lauderdale-by-the-Sea
(954) 776-0001
www.arubabeachcafe.com
Though this is a prime draw for those seeking a bite or a meal on this stretch of the sea, there's also live music daily, no less than three bars, excellent drink specials, and a fab location smack on the beach, so you can sip and chill with an ocean view. (See full review on p. 67 in the Restaurants chapter.)

BIERBRUNNEN PUB
427 S. Fort Lauderdale Beach Blvd.,
Ft. Lauderdale
(954) 540-2109
If you are looking for an escape from the sightseeing, tattoo shops, crowded clubs, and touristy areas dominating this stretch of the beach, this bar hides down an alley off the main drag. It's a German pub, but the best beer selection ranges from Pabst to Rogue to Oktoberfest and Holy Mackerel, and the bare bones elements for a cocktail that doesn't involve anything fancy—this is where serious drinkers come; for a fruity alcoholic slushie you'll need to head elsewhere. The place is more for drinking, but if you have a hankering for German fare, they do a good bratwurst, schnitzel, and potato salad.

COYOTE UGLY
220 SW 2nd St., Ft. Lauderdale
(954) 764-8459
www.coyoteuglysaloon.com
Yeah, it's kind of like the movie, but people flock to this Himmarshee Village staple for the beer and shots as much as they do for the hot female bartenders and random

guests strutting their stuff on the bar. It's raucous and no frills in a space that is decidedly without decor, but you've come for a stiff Jägermeister and a rowdy night out, right?

CULTURE ROOM
3045 N. Federal Hwy., Ft. Lauderdale
(954) 564-1074
www.cultureroom.net
This venue is one of the best places to go to see medium- to well-known bands (past concerts included the English Beat and Overkill), and they often offer meet-and-greet packages for fans hungry to meet their rock idol.

DICEY RILEY'S
217 SW 2nd St., Ft. Lauderdale
(954) 522-1908
www.brinyirishpub.com
This Irish-owned Irish pub does it right—cool Guinness on tap, live music most nights, a convivial, friendly atmosphere—basically, a cozy pub plonked in the middle of Fort Lauderdale party central.

ELBO ROOM
241 S. Fort Lauderdale Beach Blvd.,
Ft. Lauderdale
(954) 463-4615
www.elboroom.com
Back when Fort Lauderdale was known as "Fort Liquordale," this place was one of its staple drinking dens, and it's survived through the area's change and trend to the upscale. Perhaps it's the cheap beer, or the salty characters at the bar who merrily mix with unassuming tourists and locals in search of something real, but whatever the reason, we're glad this beachside staple has survived the odds—it's been operating since 1938. Live music (usually a one- or two-man

show spewing old favorites) dominates most nights, and the location right across the street from the beach means its always flip-flop time at the Elbo Room.

Boating it to the Bar

We all know we shouldn't drink and drive. But hopping in a taxi to or from a night out is generally a blah experience. Luckily, the water taxi (www.watertaxi.com) runs until midnight, so for a fun way to hit the bars of the River-walk, Himmarshee, and Las Olas, consider taking the water taxi to and from your nightspot of choice. Gliding along the waterways in the balmy Florida evening, coast-ing past as the lights glitter off the water is a prime way to start and end your evening out on the town.

THE GRATEFUL PALATE
817 SE 17th St., Ft. Lauderdale
(954) 467-1998
www.thegratefulpalate.net
We weren't sure whether to put this wine bar under restaurants or nightlife, but it's firmly a nightspot with food diversions. Elegant and understated, this is where true oenophiles come to sip and swirl, but you won't encoun-ter pretentious staff or snobby airs. This place is all about enjoying and learning about wine, so novices will feel most welcome, even if you don't know your Syrahs from your Sangioveses. The Grateful Palate specializes in boutique wines—that means wineries that produce a small number of barrels per year, versus, say, the large producers like Gallo or Yellow Tail. Interestingly, the place is run by a yacht provisions company, so you can be assured they have great taste—if the yachting community is happy with it, it's must be top tier. The environment is a sooth-ing mix of tan and browns, with low lighting and well-placed mirrors.

HOWL AT THE MOON/SLOPPY JOE'S
17 S. Fort Lauderdale Beach Blvd. (inside Beach Place), Ft. Lauderdale
(954) 522-5054
This popular beach spot is known for its duel-ing pianos (read, sing-along with the crowd). Vibe is Key West—in fact, the space is a takeoff on the famed Sloppy Joe's Bar in Key West. The place attracts a mainly youngish crowd and a smattering of older tourists. Even if sing-alongs aren't your thing, it's generally a fun night out, and there's always one tune you know you wanna belt your heart out to.

LULU'S BAIT SHACK
17 S. Fort Lauderdale Beach Blvd., Ft. Lauderdale
(954) 463-7425
www.lulusbaitshack.com
One of the most popular after-the-beach spots to hit (perhaps for its massive fruit cocktails—you know, the ones called "fish-bowls" that come in purple or green and arrive with 20 straws in them) . Alternatively, the requisite drink called the hurricane, plus cocktails served in souvenir glasses, are also on offer. Not your style? Normal beer is also in plentiful supply. This fun, Cajun-Creole bar and grill sits right across from the beach (stellar views) and offers a convivial atmo-sphere that's always welcoming and relaxed. They run a very popular happy hour and live music several nights a week, from rock to pop ensembles.

PARROT LOUNGE
911 Sunrise Lane, Ft. Lauderdale
(954) 563-1493
www.parrotlounge.com

First, a silly, kitschy atmosphere and decor welcome you: A buxom, bathing suit–clad siren from the '50s greets you at the door— no, not really, but a wooden mannequin version does. Next, you hit the bar, filled with locals and offering a slew of local and national favorite beer options. Then the old-school jukebox starts belting out classic rock and bam—you've found your home away from home! Cozy booths round out the space, perfect for quiet conversation in relaxed surroundings.

SHOOTERS
3033 NE 32nd Ave., Ft. Lauderdale
(954) 566-2855
www.shooterscafe.com

Whether you pull up on your boat at the dock or zip over in your car out front, this established fave is both a restaurant and bar, with a heavy emphasis on the bar bit. It's a rockin' and sometimes raucous affair, with evenings ranging from live blues nights to hot-bod contests; the flavor of the evening can be either most civilized or reminiscent of an MTV Spring Break party—to be frank, most nights the atmosphere lingers somewhere neutral in between. Be sure to check out the cozy tiki bar out back.

SUSHI ROCK
1515 E. Las Olas Blvd., Ft. Lauderdale
(954) 462-5541

Evenings sipping cocktails and Kirin at this sushi joint's sublime bar are as popular as the raw seafood they serve. See the full review on p. 62 in the Restaurants chapter.

VILLAGE PUMP
4404 El Mar Dr., Lauderdale-by-the-Sea
(954) 776-5840
www.villagegrille.com

Upscale but smack in the beach hub of Lauderdale-by-the-Sea, the low-lit Village Pump serves a casual crowd that doesn't want run-of-the-mill cheap libations and snacks. Drinks slide across a marble bar, the wine list is exceptional, and the food comes from its sister restaurant, the Village Grill, located next door. But one of the best reasons to come here is the outside tables, which pair a fab ocean breeze with fun people watching.

VOODOO LOUNGE
111 SW 2nd Ave., Ft. Lauderdale
(954) 522-0733
www.voodooloungeflorida.com

South Beach meets Lauderdale at this beautiful-people hangout. Shiny, manicured, designer-toting patrons share the venue with decadent hipsters, and our visit proved that casual people will be turned away (no jeans, unless you pair them with Prada, of course). But the excellent cocktails make this a worthy place for a well-mixed drink. There's bottle service, of course, and bouncers and a bit of a snobby attitude, but sometimes a girl or guy just wants to dance, and that's easy on this club/bar's three dance floors across 10,000 square feet in a former brewery. Music varies but expect house/trance on most nights. And if you are cool enough, there's a VIP lounge inside called Envy, and those who make it inside are indeed the envy of those who don't. If you make the cut, you'll see why.

HOLLYWOOD AREA

CLEOPATRA'S PALACE & HOOKAH LOUNGE
2032 Hollywood Blvd., Hollywood
(954) 926-5995
www.myspace.com/
cleopatraspalaceandhookah
This Hookah Lounge and bar isn't your average puffing joint—the music is loud, and the lighting is like a 1970s disco that lost its way. But somehow it all works and makes this place cozy and inviting. If flavored hookahs aren't your thing, there are a slew of cheap drinks on the menu.

HARRISON'S WINE BAR
1916 Harrison St., Hollywood
(954) 922-0074
www.harrisonswinebar.com
This is an adult bar, make no mistake. Anyone 30-plus will feel right at home. Snug and cozy sofas, velvety drapes, and low lighting make it a romantic spot as well, so late at night don't be surprised if you see a canoodling couple in the corner. But still, this is a civilized sort of place, where you don't shout or rock it out. Instead, people come for the quality wines and expert service. On balmy days check out the patio with private gazebos.

THE KINGS HEAD PUB
500 E. Dania Beach Blvd., Dania Beach
(954) 922-5722
www.daniakingsheadpub.com
Is that a building with exposed brown timber on white walls that looks straight out of the quintessentially English town of Stratford-upon-Avon? Yup. Once you head inside, it doesn't end. Am I in England, or am I in Dania Beach? The answer really is the latter, but if you are still confused, just grab a chair and order a fine beer from the former mother country and let your consternations be quelled by a large sip. This is a great place to find authentic English cider on tap, the perfect antidote to a humid Florida summer's day. Various English memorabilia lines the place, from old rail station signs to knick-knacks, and there's the requisite fireplace dart board and pub food to make your stay truly authentic.

NICK'S
1214 N. Broadwalk, Hollywood Beach
(954) 920-2800
This is one of the best bets on the Broadwalk. Leather booths, old Florida memorabilia, over 70 types of beer, and regular showings of baseball and football games on a slew of TVs across the space round out the experience here. But this isn't just any other sports bar—as it sits on the beach it's got an entire open wall, so if the game bores, you just gaze out at the beach or watch the action jog, walk, stroll, and cycle past. Sitting here nursing a beer, you often feel like you're in a glass window box, surveying beach life at its best.

PRL EURO CAFE
904A Hollywood Blvd., Hollywood
(954) 980-8945
www.prlcafe.com
Known primarily for its selection of over 100 international beers, the classy but relaxed PRL Euro Cafe also proudly serves a wide selection of wine and a good amount of ciders, so the non-beer-drinking lot won't go thirsty. If you don't know your amber ales from your Zywiecs, the helpful and knowledgeable staff will guide you to a choice to happily suit your tastes buds. Another fantastic aspect is that they regularly showcase

local artists on the walls, and DJs spin hopping tunes each weekend.

SPICE RESTO-LOUNGE
1934 Hollywood Blvd., Hollywood
(954) 923-3888
www.spiceresto-lounge.com
Latin beats and multicolored lights make this spot feel more Havana than Lauderdale, but rest assured, you haven't skipped town. Live music and performances range anywhere from merengue to salsa to bossa nova. If you prefer to wiggle your hips, the club area offers a massive dance floor where scantily clad women groove it up to the Latin beat of the night, which is often mixed with a bit of electronica and occasional Top-40 music.

SUSHI BLUES CAFE
2009 Harrison St., Hollywood
(954) 929-9560
www.sushiblues.com
This perennially popular sushi joint in downtown Hollywood feels more bar and live music venue when the live performances—mainly featuring blues and jazz —get pumping on weekend nights. See full review on p. 62 in the Restaurants chapter.

TAVERNA OPA
4010 N. Ocean Dr., Hollywood Beach
(954) 929-4010
www.tavernaoparestaurant.com
After the souvlaki and feta fade away, this Greek restaurant morphs into more of a bar than a restaurant, and the night moves on to dancing and partying—frankly, anything goes (we've seen people dancing on the tables late at night). See full review on p. 60 in the Restaurants chapter.

ATTRACTIONS

While Greater Fort Lauderdale's beaches and waterways should be at the top of your list of places to visit and experience, these are far from the only activities and sites to include on your must-see list. The area is also home to two exceptional historical houses, the Stranahan House and the Bonnet House Museum and Gardens, a magnificent museum of discovery and science, one of the Florida's top art museums. And that's just a few of the highlights.

In this chapter, you'll learn about some other places you must visit in order to get the real Greater Fort Lauderdale experience and, as it happens, places that don't fit neatly into other chapters. Several of the sights and experiences—Las Olas Boulevard, the Riverwalk, the Stranahan House, and the Museum of Art—are located downtown or just adjacent to downtown. Others like the Hollywood Broadwalk and the Bonnet House are further afield—in the northern reaches of Fort Lauderdale Beach or part of Hollywood Beach, respectively, but they are among the most definitive area attractions. Nevertheless, all of these attractions are worth a visit and offer a unique Greater Fort Lauderdale experience. You'll find nothing quite like them, even elsewhere in Florida. For that reason, among others, the attractions in this chapter are the places you shouldn't miss if you want to get a real taste of Greater Fort Lauderdale.

OVERVIEW

A few of the attractions in Greater Fort Lauderdale are free, but most cost somewhere between $5 and $15, although these prices are subject to change and do not include sales tax. Typically there are discounts for children and guests over 65. Most of the attractions listed here are open seven days a week, although hours often vary depending on the season. To be on the safe side, call ahead to make sure your attraction of choice will be open when you plan to visit.

Free parking is typically available on-site for attractions that aren't located downtown. A couple of downtown attractions have their own parking lots; others do not. For these attractions, the easiest place to park is typically in one of the municipal parking garages,

These garages are spread out around the downtown. The parking fee ranges from free for 10 minutes up to $15 for three hours or more. Parking for special events and on weekends and holidays is $7, payable upon entry.

Price Code
The following price codes are based on the cost of one adult ticket with tax.

$.......................$5 to $8
$$ ....$9 to $12
$$$ .... over $12

AH-TAH-THI-KI MUSEUM $$
Big Cypress Seminole Indian Reservation
30000 Gator Tail Trail, Clewiston
(877) 902-1113
www.ahtahthiki.com

Ah-Tah-Thi-Ki means "a place to learn, to remember" and that precisely wraps up what this museum does. Located within the Big Cypress Seminole Indian Tribe Reservation, the museum presents the culture and traditions of the Seminole Indians in Florida through carefully constructed exhibits of artifacts and reenactments of rituals and ceremonies. Additionally, the site includes a living Seminole village and nature trails. The museum is located in the Big Cypress Seminole Indian Reservation, 17 miles north of I-75 off exit 49, follow signs to park entrance. Open daily 9 a.m. to 5 p.m.

BILLIE SWAMP SAFARI $$$
Big Cypress Seminole Indian Reservation
30000 Gator Tail Trail, Clewiston
(954) 966-6300 or (800) 949-6101
www.swampsafari.com

Ah, the Everglades. It's amazing no matter how or where you experience it. But to see the Everglades through the eyes of a Native American, stop here. Billie's Swamp Safari offers daily tours of the hammocks and wetlands, and on your excursion you are likely to not only catch a glimpse of the area's ubiquitous alligators, but you'll see a wide variety of wildlife, from deer and bison to water buffalo and wild hogs. Hawks and eagles often soar above or observe you from a tree perch. Choose from the standard 30-minute airboat ride departing every half hour between 10 a.m. and 4:30 p.m., or the one-hour swamp buggy eco-tours (a swamp buggy is a special motorized vehicle that drives through the swamps on massive wheels) departing

every hour between 11 a.m. and 5 p.m. They also feature alligator and critter shows daily at 2:15 p.m., and swamp critter shows daily at 1:15 p.m.

Guided hikes, nighttime swamp-buggy safaris, and campfire storytelling are also available upon request and based on availability—call for details. Additionally, combination tickets abound, offering a variety of day, night, and overnight packages; there's an on-site lodge, the Chickee Lodge, a traditional thatched roof dwelling with no water or electricity—sort of like camping without a tent. Day packages include the swamp buggy eco-tour, an airboat tour, and either a educational show about snakes and alligators, or a swamp critter show. Night packages include a swamp buggy eco-tour and campfire storytelling—see the website for more combinations, prices, and availability. The on-site Swamp Water Cafe is a fun place to try local gator tails, frogs legs, and catfish. *NOTE:* Children four and under are not allowed on airboat or swamp buggy rides.

This attraction is located in the Big Cypress Seminole Indian Reservation, 17 miles north of I-75 off exit 49, follow signs to park entrance.

i It's a bit of a trek if you're beach bound, but a ride on an airboat is a must during any Fort Lauderdale area visit. Take your pick from two outfitters: Billie Swamp Safari or Everglades Holiday Park.

BONNET HOUSE
MUSEUM & GARDENS $$$
900 North Birch Rd.,
Ft. Lauderdale Beach
(954) 563-5393
www.bonnethouse.org

This is far more than a historic attraction. Built between the sea and a small lake by the late Frederic and Evelyn Bartlett, two artists, as a winter residence in the 1920s, the 35-acre estate holds lush grounds beautified by swans, orchids, and some rather rambunctious monkeys—it's a real ode to Old Florida. Named for the bonnet lily that grows on the grounds, the striking house is filled with exceptional art collected by the Bartletts during their wide travels. Visitors can only see the house on a 75-minute tour but can walk the nature trail on their own. In April, the property is the site of Bonnet House Jazzfest on the Green. The museum is closed Mon.

BOOMER'S   **$$**
1801 NW 1st St., west of US 1, Dania
(954) 921-1411
www.boomersparks.com
From the Sky Coaster ride (which simulates a bungee jump) to tamer rides like bumper cars, a roller coaster, go-karts, and "Naskart" racing (go-kart racing on a mile-and-a-half-long track), this small amusement-fun park has something for everyone. There's also miniature golf, batting cages, laser tag, bowling, a rock wall, and video arcades. The park is open 11 a.m. to 11 p.m. Sun through Thurs, 11 a.m. to 1 a.m. Fri and Sat. Miniature golf admission is $9; kids five and under get in for free. Go-kart rides cost $8.

BUTTERFLY WORLD   **$$$**
3600 W. Sample Rd., Coconut Creek
(954) 977-4400
www.butterflyworld.com
Founder Robert Boender's fascination with butterflies began during his childhood in Illinois, where he dutifully observed silk moths, cabbage white, and black swallowtails. After

a career as an engineer, Boender moved to Florida, switched his focus to butterflies full-time, and began raising and observing butterflies and growing butterfly food plants out of his home, which eventually grew into a butterfly farm. Later, a trip to the London Butterfly House inspired Boender to open his own butterfly house in the United States. As a result, you can now take a walk through his fantastical creation. Flowering tropical gardens house 10 acres of giant screened aviaries filled with thousands of live rainbow-hued butterflies who dwell in acres of waterfalls, orchids, roses, and tropical flora. The space is also home to fish, hummingbirds, lorikeet, insectariums, and a butterfly farm; kids love feeding the tiny parrots in the Lorikeet Encounter section. They're open Mon through Sat 9 a.m. to 5 p.m., Sun 11 a.m. to 5 p.m. (admission closes at 4 p.m.). The space also hosts a variety of educational programs and special events—check the website for details.

COCONUT CREEK SEMINOLE CASINO
5550 NW 40th St., Coconut Creek
(954) 977-6700
www.semtribe.com
Open 24 hours, seven days a week, this down-to-earth casino features over 1,500 Vegas-style and bingo-style slot machines. Betting levels start at two cents per play on up to $50 per play, and the poker room offers Seven-Card Stud, Texas Hold'em, and Omaha Hi-Lo with betting levels starting at $1. Three different restaurants and the Nectar Lounge offer live entertainment six days a week—this casino is a fantastic alternative for those who want to try their hand at gambling without the glitz and glamour of the Seminole Hard Rock Casino.

EVERGLADES DAY SAFARI, FORT LAUDERDALE $$$

No address; depart from set pickup locations only
(239) 472-1559 or (800) 472-3069
www.ecosafari.com

Everglades Day Safari is one of the only out-fitters offering guided, full-day eco-tours of the Everglades. Tours include pickup from a prearranged location in Greater Fort Lauderdale (various pickup sites available); exploration of the Everglades' four main ecosystems (saw grass prairie, mangrove estuary, cypress swamps, and pine savannah); an airboat ride and boat cruise with opportunities for viewing alligators, manatees, dolphins, and sea turtles; lunch (including gator bites as an appetizer); a wildlife drive through Big Cypress Preserve; and a tranquil nature walk with the potential for more alligator sightings and plenty of bird-watching. The staff is immensely knowledgeable and includes zoologists, herpetologists (a reptile and amphibian scientist), and various other naturalist specialists and scientists. The tour departs Fort Lauderdale each morning at 7:45 a.m. and returns about 5:30 p.m. Fee is $140 for adults and $104 for children ages 5 to 11. Children under age 5 not permitted.

EVERGLADES HOLIDAY PARK AIRBOAT TOURS $$$

21940 Griffin Rd., Ft. Lauderdale
(954) 434-8111
www.evergladesholidaypark.com

This is another prime spot to book an airboat ride or see an alligator show. Set among Everglades Holiday Park (a campground), the center also offers rides and a show. Airboat rides last about one hour and offer the chance to see alligators, exotic birds, and native fish while smoothly gliding over

the "River of Grass," a term for the Everglades made popular by the 1947 book by Marjorie Stoneman Douglas. Tours depart every 20 minutes or so between 9 a.m. and 4 p.m. daily and include alligator shows after the tour, which use an educational approach to demonstrate the power and voracity of Florida's ubiquitous reptiles.

FLAMINGO GARDENS AND EVERGLADES WILDLIFE SANCTUARY $$$

3750 S. Flamingo Rd. (3 miles south of I-595), Davie
(954) 473-2955
www.flamingogardens.org

This nonprofit nature center dedicated to protecting and preserving Florida's delicate natural environment is delightful. The best way to explore this vast place is to hop on the 25-minute tram (departing every half hour between 11 a.m. and 4 p.m.) as it takes you through the 60 acres of citrus groves, botanical gardens, a 25,000-square-foot Everglades free-flight aviary that represents five ecosystems, and habitats for flamingos, alligators, hummingbirds, and other fauna. The centerpiece is the 1933 Wray Estate, the original residence of founders Floyd L. and Jane Wray, framed by 200-year-old oaks. The gardens specialize in the cultivation of endangered heliconia plants and the protection of wood storks and roseate spoonbills. Additionally, you'll find a birds of prey center showcasing rare, endangered native Florida birds, a tropical plants center, and the xeriscape garden, which demonstrates the use of various materials appropriate for use in a low-maintenance, minimally irrigated garden. Live wildlife shows featuring Florida's native animals, such as birds of prey and reptiles and their relationship to the environment. The complex is open 9:30 a.m. to 5 p.m. Tues to Sun from June through Nov, closed Mon, but open on Labor Day. From Dec through May open Mon through Fri the same hours.

FORT LAUDERDALE ANTIQUE CAR MUSEUM $
1527 SW 1st Ave., Ft. Lauderdale
(954) 779-7300
www.antiquecarmuseum.org
This private collection of 40 prewar Packard motorcars dating from 1909 to 1940 is displayed in a re-created Packard showroom from the 1920s. During the '20s, Packard was the Rolls Royce of American automobiles, so it is only fitting they've given a nod to this relic of history. Inside the showroom you'll encounter 26 fully working Packards covering an array of models including roadsters with golf-club compartments, a doctor's coupe (check out the compartment for the medical bag!), and a pristine 1929 Dual Cowl Phaten that self-lubricates its chassis (the rectangular frame attached to the axles that holds the body and motor of an car) as it trundles down the street. Memorabilia also include dashboard clocks, hood ornaments, unique gear-shift knobs, rare carburetors, and more. The museum is open Mon through Fri 9 a.m. to 3 p.m. and occasionally on the weekends—call for details.

OLD FORT LAUDERDALE VILLAGE & MUSEUM/FORT LAUDERDALE HISTORY CENTER $$
219 SW 2nd Ave., Ft. Lauderdale
(954) 463-4431
www.oldfortlauderdale.org
Located smack on the New River, the Old Fort Lauderdale Village & Museum/Fort Lauderdale History Center tells the story of the

---

It's Spooky

If ghost and orb sightings intrigue you, **Fort Lauderdale Ghost Tours** (SE 6th Avenue and E. Las Olas Boulevard, 954-290-9328) along the historical New River is a must. The tour takes you past some of Fort Lauderdale's most haunted sights and places, and are run by Jean Mark Carr, professional ghost investigator and author of several books on ghosts including *Haunted Fort Lauderdale* (published by History Press). The walking tour runs Fri and Sat only at 8:45 p.m. (meeting point is downtown Fort Lauderdale) and lasts two hours; reservations are a must. The cost is $15 for adults, $10 for children under 10, free for children under 5 (though frankly we don't recommend it for kids). Cash only.

---

community's history from the pioneers of Fort Lauderdale to the present day through its six historic structures—only three can be visited on regular tours (a mix of self-guided and docent-led tours), but the rest can be seen from the exterior or through prescheduled appointments. The standard tour includes the a self-guided visit to the 1905 New River Inn, a hollow concrete-block structure made with sand barged from the beach (which set the standard for South Florida construction), which is Broward County's oldest remaining hotel building and the first property in the county to be listed on the National Register of Historic Places; a docent-led tour of the historic 1907 King-Cromartie House, a structure built of sturdy Dade County pine with joists made from salvaged ship's timbers; and another docent-led tour of a replica 1899 schoolhouse (constructed in the 1970s). The history center also includes the 1905 Philemon Bryan House, a foursquare vernacular-style house (now home to the administrative offices of the Fort Lauderdale History Center and the Fort Lauderdale chapter of the American Institute of Architects); the 1905 Acetylene Building; the Hoch Heritage Center (a 1949 post office annex that now serves as the home of the Fort Lauderdale Historical Society). Docent-led tours begin at 1, 2, and 3 p.m.; buildings are open for tours Tues through Sun. All six buildings are located on and around SW 2nd Avenue, and those that aren't on the tour can simply be inspected from the exterior (plaques explain what they are).

HOLLYWOOD
BEACH BROADWALK   FREE
Hollywood Beach
www.visithollywoodfl.org

When you hit the Hollywood Beach Broadwalk (not boardwalk; it's surfaced with paving stones), you're as likely to hear French accents drifting from open-air cafes as you are American voices chatting up a storm (French Canadians arrive here en masse each winter). Year-round enjoy a Riviera ambience on this award-winning, 2-mile-long promenade by relaxing under an awning at any of the cafes and restaurants that hug the strip, or just hang out and people watch as people show off their toned muscles while cycling, jogging, skating, or walking. Off to the side on the sand you'll glimpse plenty of beach volleyball action, Frisbee flinging, and various other beachy sports unfolding under the Florida sun. In addition to the sporty feel and

Trolley Me Happy

Humidity got you down? Tired of parking, paying for parking, getting lost, and generally being behind the wheel? Keen to see more than the beach? Then consider the two-hour narrated **Fort Lauderdale Trolley Tour** (419 S. Fort Lauderdale Beach Blvd., 954-522-1770, www.southflorida tourismcouncil.com). From your perch upon the rumbling trolley you'll see the cruise port, luxury yachts, marinas, homes of the rich and famous, sparkling waterways, Fort Lauderdale Beach, Las Olas Boulevard, various historic sites, Riverwalk, and more. Tour runs daily at 9:30 a.m., 11:30 a.m., 1:30 p.m., and 3:30 p.m. Complimentary trolley hat, water, and hop-on–hop-off pass valid for a day. The tour costs $25 for adults and $15 for children. The hop-on–hop-off perk means it is also a great way to get around for a day.

restaurant, cafe, and bar scene, this is also a prime place for a casual stroll, particularly late in the day or early evening when it quiets down and the palm trees sway beneath the sultry Florida sky.

The Broadwalk is located just off SR A1A/Ocean Boulevard between Monroe Street (just south of the Ramada Hollywood Beach Resort) and Sherman Street (just north of Hollywood Beach Marriott). Park around Johnson Street (off of SR A1A) to get closest to the biggest and busiest cluster of restaurants, cafes, bars, and shops. Parking is metered and strictly enforced.

IGFA (INTERNATIONAL GAME FISH ASSOCIATION) FISHING HALL OF FAME & MUSEUM $
300 Gulf Stream Way, Dania Beach
(954) 922-4212
www.igfa.org

This is utopia for anyone passionate about fishing and boating. The IGFA presents vast amounts of information and exhibits covering fish habitats and species, plus major catches by famous (and not-so-famous) anglers—the museum features a school of prize fish hanging from the ceiling with plaques set into the floor to identify the world-record fishermen who caught them. Toddlers to teens will love exploring the hands-on stuff like the virtual marlin or tarpon they can reel in, and playing the computerized "Name That Fish" game. Kids ages two to seven can also make fish prints and go fake-boating in the Discovery Room. Residents will also be interested in the Junior Angler Club and educational youth programs. Outside the structure sits a pond with Hemingway's boat and a reconstructed wetland with a short outdoor walk where you can get a peek at Florida's natural terrain. Open 10 a.m. to 6 p.m. Mon through Sat, noon to 6 p.m. Sun.

i Across the IGFA parking lot, pop over to Outdoor World, a football-field-size sports store with a huge aquarium and Florida-style shooting range.

INTERNATIONAL SWIMMING HALL OF FAME $
1 Hall of Fame Dr., Ft. Lauderdale
(954) 462-6536
www.ishof.org

This museum detailing the history of competitive swimming recognizes over 600 of the world's greatest aquatic athletes (in other words, those who embark on swimming, diving, water polo, and synchronized swimming careers) from over 100 nations through clever exhibits that contain press clippings, medals, swimsuits, and other memorabilia. This multi-faceted attraction also includes exhibits featuring the world's largest collection of objects d'art, rare photos, posters, films, trophies, and other swimming-related artifacts dating from the days of ancient Assyria to modern times. Though the bulk of the museum focuses on athletes and celebrities such as the famed Olympic athlete and *Tarzan* icon Johnny Weissmuller and the celebrated competitive swimmer and actress Esther Williams, some info also gives a nod to politicians and celebrities with some relation to swimming—for example, Ronald Reagan, who in addition to captaining his college swim team is credited with saving 77 lives as a lifeguard in his hometown, and John F. Kennedy, who was on the first Harvard swim team to beat Yale. It's run by a nonprofit that aims to promote the benefits and importance of swimming as a key to fitness, good health, quality of life, and water safety for children. The museum is open 9 a.m. to 5 p.m. daily.

JUNGLE QUEEN RIVERBOAT CRUISE $$$
801 Fort Lauderdale Beach Blvd.,
Ft. Lauderdale
(954) 462-5596
www.junglequeen.com

This traditional Mississippi riverboat is best-known and most famous for its perennially popular dinner cruise that takes guests on a fun-filled sail for an "All You Can Eat" dinner of ribs, chicken, and shrimp with all the trimmings, followed by an entertaining variety show. If you're not keen to eat while on board, try the daily three-hour fully narrated sightseeing cruises of the historic New River and "Millionaire's Row", an exclusive residential strip in Boca Raton, which includes a stop-off at the Tropical Isle on the New River to see rare birds, monkeys and an alligator exhibition.

LAS OLAS BOULEVARD   FREE
Ft. Lauderdale
(954) 937-7386
www.lasolasboulevard.com
Though we list many shops, restaurants, bars, and a hotel that line this boulevard, the section due east from South Andrews Avenue/downtown Fort Lauderdale is a sight unto itself and well worth a visit, even if you simply stroll along the concentration of businesses to get a feel for the area. Known first and foremost as a shoppers' utopia, the ambience of the boulevard is tranquil and low key, begging you to stop for a leisurely brunch at a sidewalk cafe, or browse and shop at boutiques, galleries, specialty stores, and fashion houses. In the evenings restaurants lit by flickering candlelight, atmospheric lights glittering under the soft Florida sky, and locals cramming into the street for a fine evening out on the town bring a buzz to this stretch.

LAS OLAS RIVERFRONT   FREE
300 SW 1st Ave., Ft. Lauderdale
(954) 522-6556
www.riverfrontfl.com
This prime shopping, dining, and entertainment center overlooking the New River sits in the heart of downtown Fort Lauderdale. Extending for a full 2 miles, this brick promenade with lush tropical landscaping is prime territory for a stroll, jog, or bike ride during the day or evening, and is a fantastic place to ramble or relax while soaking up

Am I in Venice?

Fort Lauderdale isn't called the Venice of America for nothing, and let's face it, you can't do Venice without a gondola ride. **Las Olas Gondola** (SE 1st Avenue, near Las Olas River House, 800-277-1390, www.lasolasgondola.com) offers gondola tours that appeal to both history enthusiasts and romantics alike. Imported Venetian gondolas are available to rent in the heart of Fort Lauderdale.

They offer many types of tours—the Casa Magnifico tour covers the area's luxury homes and gardens, and the Lovely Romantico Tour covers the same territory but includes a message in a bottle with your own personal message on parchment paper. Tours (available daily between 10 a.m. and 9 p.m.) are always private, and though they don't include food or beverages, you are welcome (and encouraged!) to bring along snacks and a drink, including alcoholic beverages (glasses and ice can be provided upon advance request). Call for reservations, rates, hours, and pickup locations.

the atmosphere and flavor of this area. It also contains entertaining educational stations, like the gizmo that lets you play with marine navigational instruments. It may be a tourist attraction in its own right, but the area is a top draw for local residents, too. The first Sun of each month also features a popular free jazz brunch between 11 a.m. and 3 p.m. (the music is free, but you can hear the music

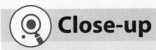

Close-up

Cruise Ship or Small Floating City?

Fort Lauderdale is the cruise ship capital, period. Home to the world's largest and busiest cruise ship ports, with 11 modern terminals serving over 48 ships that cruise to the eastern and western Caribbean, across the Atlantic, and to nowhere in particular daily. It's also home to Royal Caribbean International's Oasis ships, the largest cruise ships in the world.

You can't really enter **Port Everglades** (1850 Eller Dr., Ft. Lauderdale; 954-523-3404; www.porteverglades.net) unless you have a ticket for a cruise, but you get a fantastic glimpse of the port when you drive across the 17th Street Causeway (south of Las Olas, north of the airport), and you'll undoubtedly see a large ship entering or exiting the port from the northern tip of Dania Beach and anywhere along the southern end of Fort Lauderdale Beach.

from a table at any of the outdoor restaurant venues—all serve brunch).

**MUSEUM OF ART
  FORT LAUDERDALE   FREE–$$$**
One East Last Olas Blvd., Ft. Lauderdale
(954) 262-0200
www.moaflnsu.org
Housed within an acclaimed building designed by Edward Larrabee Barnes, this museum may never compete with the Met, but it holds its own just fine and is considered to be one of South Florida's leading cultural attractions. The museum regularly hosts world-class touring exhibits and boasts an impressive permanent collection of 20th-century European and American art, including works by Picasso, Mapplethorpe, Calder, Dalí, Warhol, and Stella, as well as an entire wing dedicated to works by celebrated Ashcan School artist William Glackens. Recent nationally acclaimed exhibitions have included the famed "King Tut" exhibit and an extensive Edward Steichen and Norman Rockwell show. Open Tue, Wed, Fri, and Sat 11 a.m. to 5 p.m.;

Thu 11 a.m. to 8 p.m., Sun noon to 5 p.m. Closed Mon.

i Check out Free Third Thursdays at the Museum of Art: free admission after 5 p.m. every third Thursday of the month.

**MUSEUM OF DISCOVERY & SCIENCE &
  AUTONATION IMAX THEATER $$$**
401 SW 2nd St., Ft. Lauderdale
(954) 467-6637 or (954) 463-IMAX
www.mods.org
The best the city has to offer to both families and science aficionados occupies two floors packed with exciting curiosity sparkers. Kids love Virtual Volleyball, the space flight simulator, and the nature section with its fascinating aquariums, spiders, snakes, and enchanted Florida forest. Games slyly teach about fitness, health, physics, and other scientific phenomena. Stop in the gift shop for learning tools of the painless variety. Ecofloat environmental boat tours showcase the beaches, barrier islands, mangrove

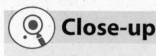 **Close-up**

Ghosts in the Attic

Ghosts in the attic? At the old **Stranahan House,** they're not only in the attic; they're also in the parlor and the bedroom and the kitchen. And, according to many people, they're often standing right behind you.

In these parts, **Frank Stranahan** is the stuff of legends. He was the first permanent settler in what is now Fort Lauderdale, and the first entrepreneur, as well. He built himself a house on the banks of the New River. Then he opened it up as a boarding house to cater to the stagecoach passengers who stopped here for the night on the way from Palm Beach to Miami. And when those passengers (and the stagecoach driver) awoke in the morning, Stranahan took them across the New River on his ferry, so they could continue their journey. In addition, this enterprising gentleman was also Fort Lauderdale's first postmaster, as well as, eventually, a banker and businessman. The trading post he established at his house was soon drawing not only new settlers but also Seminole Indians. And that trading post eventually evolved into a sort of community center/town hall for the area.

Frank eventually took a fancy to Ivy Julia Cromartie, the first schoolteacher in the area, and married her. And he took his new bride back to a house that was a marvel for its time, with electric wiring, modern plumbing, wide porches, running water, interior stairways, and bay windows.

For a while, Frank Stranahan led what seemed to be a charmed life. But his luck ran out when the Great Depression struck. His bank failed, leaving him unable to repay the many friends to whom he owed money. Like many others in that horrible time, he saw no way out. So he took his own life by drowning himself.

At the wake a few days later, Ivy stopped all the clocks in the house at what had been the hour of his death, as was the custom at that time. Later on, she lived upstairs

---

estuaries, sinkholes, and other diverse local habitat during the summer. Part of the complex, AutoNation 3-D IMAX Theater shows sky-high discovery films about nature and science. The museum is open 10 a.m. to 5 p.m. Mon through Sat, noon to 6 p.m. Sun.

**OLD DAVIE SCHOOL HISTORICAL
MUSEUM** $$
6650 Griffin Rd., Davie
(954) 797-1044
www.olddavieschool.org
The first permanent school in the Everglades opened its doors to 90 students in 1918, and the Davie School, as it was known then, was

in continuous use as a school until 1980. Placed on the National Register of Historic Places in 1988, the campus includes the oldest existing school building in Broward County, two original homes built in 1912, a replica of a 1909 early settler's shack, and an authentic chickee hut built by Seminole Tate Oceola. From the day it opened, Davie School has served as the area's source of education as well as a center for community gatherings. Today it serves as a museum of local history and culture, and continues in its role as the "Crown Jewel of Davie." It's open Tue through Sat 10 a.m. to 2 p.m.

while renting the first floor to a restaurant. She lived in the house another 42 years, passing on in 1971. Eventually, the building became a museum owned and operated by an organization called Stranahan House, Inc.

To many of the museum visitors, however, Frank and Ivy still live there. Only a few days after the house became a museum, the clock in the parlor—which Ivy had stopped some 50 years earlier—began to tick on its own. Ever since then, the burglar alarms have had a tendency to go off, but no intruders have ever been found. The mysterious smell of a woman's perfume is often detected by visitors. Many people will swear they've been tapped on the shoulder when there was no one standing behind them. Others claim to have seen shrouded visions of Frank and Ivy in the darkness. Some swear that, if you say something to Frank or Ivy, you may see them standing in the background when you look at the photos of your visit. And still others will tell you they've heard someone standing behind them, whispering their name, when there was no one there.

In addition, former doubters who have since become believers say the house is also inhabited by the ghost of a small Seminole child who mysteriously died here while Ivy was teaching her and other Seminole children; they've heard the voice of a little girl in the house. Others have heard the voice of Ivy's somewhat-surly brother, Albert, who died of tuberculosis in the house.

Want to see and hear more? Visit the **Stranahan House and Museum** when you come here, of course. But, until then, check out the videos on MySpace.com: www.myspace.com/fortlauderdaleghosttour/videos.

Then, you be the judge.

OLD DILLARD MUSEUM   FREE
1009 NW 4th St., Ft. Lauderdale
(754) 322-8828
www.broward.k12.fl.us/lddillardmuseum
The Old Dillard Museum is housed in what was the first local public school for African Americans. Today it holds three permanent displays: a hands-on, minds-on exhibit; the Jazz Gallery; and a replica of the 1920s class-room. This is a fascinating place for anyone interested in African-American culture and history. Open 10 a.m. to 4 p.m. Mon through Thurs in the summer, and 11 a.m. to 4 p.m. Mon through Fri during the school year (mid-Aug to mid June).

STRANAHAN HOUSE $$
335 SE 6th Ave. at Las Olas Boulevard, Ft. Lauderdale
(954) 524-4736
www.stranahanhouse.org
It may be increasingly dwarfed by high-rise development, but its neighboring tower can't compete with the history contained within this downtown Fort Lauderdale landmark. The area's oldest home (built in 1901) was originally built as a trading post (in other words, a bank, post office, and general store) by businessman Frank Stranahan, an ear-lier pioneer who arrived in 1892. It evolved into his home after he married his wife, Ivy

Cromartie, who also served as the city's first schoolteacher. Stranahan befriended Seminole Indians, traded with them, and taught them "new ways," which was enormously revolutionary during that time—in fact, Henry Flagler and various other prominent businessmen came to Stranahan for advice on how to build positive relations with the local community. Sadly, the story takes a morbid twist—after financial reverses in 1929, Stranahan tied himself to a concrete block and jumped into New River, leaving his widow to carry on. Ivy died in 1971, but now her home serves as one of the area's most important historic homes. It is lavishly furnished with period antiques and furnishings, as well as memorabilia from throughout the Stranahans' lives and marriage. Superb docent-led tours go into minute detail about the history of the home's owners, life as a pioneer in the early dates of settlement in Fort Lauderdale, as well as the significance of what the Stranahans accomplished and represented during their lifetime. Tours given each day at 1, 2, and 3 p.m.

PRO DIVE USA GLASS BOTTOM BOAT TOURS $$$
429 Seabreeze Blvd., Ft. Lauderdale
(954) 776-3483
www.prodiveusa.com

What's a trip to Florida without a glass-bottom boat tour? This is one of the area's finest. Float aboard their 60-foot vessel and be sure to have your camera ready—colorful fish will pop up before you know it. On the journey out to the reefs, you'll get a narrated tour of the "Venice of America." Less than a quarter mile off the coast, you'll glimpse marine life in 15 feet of water. Whatever you choose to do, there is plenty of space for sunbathing as well as shade, plus a galley with beverages and snacks. Pro Dive also offers diving

Water Taxi It

Getting around by boat is the best way to go in Fort Lauderdale. If you're like most of us and you didn't arrive by private yacht, you can jump aboard the **Water Taxi** (651 Seabreeze Blvd., 954-467-6677, www.watertaxi.com) and get a lift to shopping, restaurants, and other attractions throughout the area. Transport is swift and fun, and you'll catch plenty of glimpses of prominent homes from your perch on the water—think of it as a combo transport-tour.

You can reserve in advance or wait (for up to 30 minutes) at one of the 13 scheduled stops, which includes stops from the northern reaches of Fort Lauderdale Beach (Intracoastal side) to Beach Place (within walking distance to the heart of Fort Lauderdale Beach), the Marina Convention Center, SE 9th Avenue (with access to the prime shopping and dining area of Las Olas Boulevard), the Las Olas Riverfront, and Esplanade. Taxis run from 9 a.m. until midnight daily, later during special events and holidays. An all-day pass costs $13, $10 for seniors and ages 12 and under. Family pack ($48) covers two adults and three youths or seniors. Some boats stop everywhere; express boats make limited stops but whisk you to key areas in no time. Check the website for detailed schedules and maps.

trips; for details see p. 151 in the Recreation chapter.

SEA EXPERIENCE $$$
801 Seabreeze Blvd., Ft. Lauderdale
(954) 770-DIVE (3483)
www.seaxp.com
Sea Experience is a diving outfitter that also offers glass-bottom boat tours and snorkeling trips—see p. 152 in the Recreation chapter for details.

YOUNG AT ART CHILDREN'S
  MUSEUM $
11584 W. SR 84, Davie
(954) 424-0085
www.youngatartmuseum.org
Young At Art is one of less than a dozen children's museums in the nation that dutifully focuses on the arts and multicultural appreciation. In the past 20 years, it has served more than a million families through permanent gallery and national traveling exhibitions, art studio classes, demonstrations by professional artists, and special events. It provides interactive, hands-on exhibits and educational sessions for children of all ages, and makes a strong effort to invite kids to participate in its interactive galleries, special exhibitions, workshops, classes, and events. Always on exhibit is the EarthWorks section, which teaches about conservation and recycling. Alternatively, take a passport for the Global Village and visit an architectural dig in Israel, learn origami in a Japanese house, play in an African village (complete with about 20 drums of varying sizes), and create works of art in a Central/South American marketplace (stencils, etching, and cutting are some of the skills you'll practice). Open 10 a.m. to 5 p.m. Mon through Sat, and noon to 5 p.m. Sun.

SHOPPING

The vast amount of stores in Fort Lauderdale—including a high number of luxury ones—makes the city a fabulous place to shop. Just about anything you want or need can be purchased in the area, from quirky antiques and secondhand clothes, to surf gear and trendy flip-flops, to swanky designs perfect for a hot Florida night out. One of the most popular areas for boutique shopping is Las Olas Boulevard just west of downtown Fort Lauderdale.

If you drive around town, you're likely to notice lots of familiar stores. Greater Fort Lauderdale is home to a large amount of chain stores, ranging from cheaper retailers like Target to higher-end shops like Neiman Marcus and Chanel. Most of these are located in strip malls, shopping centers, and malls. The best and most prestigious mall in the city is the Galleria at Fort Lauderdale (2414 E. Sunrise Blvd., 954-564-1036; www.galleriamall-fl.com). The Galleria is home to elite tenants like Neiman Marcus, Saks Fifth Avenue, Swarovski, and Kate Spade, as well as less-expensive vendors such as Ann Taylor, Gap, Lucky Brand, J. Crew, Macy's, Dillard's, Williams-Sonoma, Pottery Barn, and Cole Haan.

Since the stores in this and other malls are not unique to Greater Fort Lauderdale and can easily be found by flipping through the phone book or calling information, they are not the focus of this chapter. This chapter focuses on the stores you might not discover without this book. These are primarily independent stores and smaller local and regional chains that give the city its unique flavor. Many of them are places where you can generally find more special, one-of-a-kind things.

OVERVIEW

In the pages that follow, you will find stores in just about every category. These include antiques stores and commercial art galleries, thrift and resale shops, comic-book shops, flea markets, toy stores, jewelry stores, shoe stores, gift shops and garden shops, specialty food stores, sporting goods stores, music shops, bookstores, and clothing stores for men, women, and children. You'll even find out where to buy cowboy boots and hats—used, new, and custom-made. The stores listed here are by no means the only ones in town, but they are some of the best in their respective categories. Together the stores included here range from inexpensive to luxurious, giving you options no matter what your budget is. A good number of the stores included here are located in the downtown Fort Lauderdale, Fort Lauderdale Beach, Dania Beach, and Hollywood areas. All of these areas are discussed in the Area Overview chapter and can be found using the maps in this book.

Because many of the stores listed here are small, family-owned-and-operated shops, some of them are closed one or two days a week. These closure days have been noted when appropriate in the descriptions that follow. Keep in mind, however, that stores often change their hours, especially during the holidays. It's a good idea to call ahead and make sure the store will be open when you plan to stop in. Most stores in Fort Lauderdale have parking lots or free street parking available.

ANTIQUES

ANTIQUE CENTER MALL OF DANIA
3 N. Federal Hwy., Dania Beach
(954) 922-5467
Out of all the antique spaces in Dania Beach, this one actually holds 28 antique dealers under one roof so you can hit a ton without going too far. There's a vast selection of shops—from old Victorian ware to early-1920s pieces, and everything in between. It's as fun for knickknacks as it is for that new commode you've always wanted.

DANIA BEACH'S HISTORIC ART AND ANTIQUE DISTRICT
Downtown Dania Beach
US 1/N. Federal Highway (between NE 2nd Street and Dania Beach Boulevard)
(954) 922-5467
www.visitdaniabeach.com
This tiny, sleepy area in downtown Dania may seem a tad dilapidated, but it's chock-full of some treasures—and, admittedly, some junk. But it feels like a slice of Old Florida, and a wander through the charming antique shops and art galleries is worth it.

VICTORIA'S ATTIC
1926 E. Sunrise Blvd., Ft. Lauderdale
(954) 463-6774

Brimming with Victorian to mid-century furniture—most on consignment—this is a prime spot in the area to source that new-but-old chest of drawers you need for your bedroom. Of course, you have to locate the item first, no small feat in this packed-to-capacity shop, but the genteel owner will gladly guide you through the stacks to find your treasure. In fact, if he doesn't have what you want, he'll keep a lookout for it and call you when something suitable comes up.

ARTS

VERONA ART
75 N. Federal Hwy., Dania Beach
(954) 920-0097
Like many of the antique shops and art galleries on this strip, it doesn't look like much from the outside, but this is the place to come for a lovingly restored chandelier and other crystal objects. In general, Verona Art focuses on authentic items and some reproductions from the European continent. Don't be surprised to find evocative sculptures and intriguing jewelry amidst the glitter and the glam.

BOATING & FISHING

BASS PRO SHOPS OUTDOOR WORLD
200 Gulf Stream Way, Dania Beach
(954) 929-7710
www.basspro.com
This chain is one of the top spots in the area to get your gear—from fishing tackle and poles to dive suits, snorkeling equipment, and everything in between. It is essentially a massive warehouse filled to the brim with everything a water-sports enthusiast could ever hope for, and more. Camping gear is also on offer for those who prefer to remain land bound.

Outlet Shopping to the Max—Sawgrass Mills Mall

We can't cover shopping in Broward County without mentioning the crème de la crème of South Florida outlet shopping: **Sawgrass Mills Mall** (12801 W. Sunrise Blvd., Sunrise; 954-846-2350; www.simon.com). Florida's biggest shopping and entertainment complex is a goldmine of deals, with over 350 brand-name outlets, from Nine West to Nordstrom, TAG Heuer to Tommy Bahama—plus the Saks Fifth Avenue outlet is a huge draw. It also houses movie theaters and restaurants for a great pit-stop before or after your shopping experience. Open Mon through Sat from 10 a.m. to 9:30 p.m., and Sun from 11 a.m. to 8 p.m.

BOOKSTORES

READING, ETC.
3201 SW 15th St., Deerfield Beach
(954) 363-0006
www.readingetc.com
This bookstore is more like a palace—an Egyptian-themed one, that is. Filled with exquisite stuffed leather chairs and sofas and castle-worthy thrones, Egyptian pillars and sphinx statues, delicate lighting and gorgeous polished wooden bookshelves, it is like entering the most regal zone of books you've ever encountered. The bookstore is famous not only because of its opulent decor, but it's affiliated with Heath Communications, world-renowned publisher of the

Chicken Soup for the Soul series. In addition to books, the shop sells upscale handbags, handmade paper, home accessories like candles and potpourri, handsome desk clocks, and globes and children's toys.

SECOND EDITION BOOK SHOP
6812 Stirling Rd. (in the Lincoln Park Plaza), Davie
(954) 961-5063
You won't stumble across any baggage-fee busting *War and Peace* hardcover clunker here—Second Edition has a super strict paperback-only policy. In addition to the large selection of fiction (this genre dominates), you'll find mystery and romance as well as children's tomes, literary fiction, classic, science fiction, religion, culinary, self-help, and nonfiction filling the shelves here. Tuck into anything that strikes your fancy, relax in one of their overstuffed, comfy leather chairs squeezed into most corners, and you'll be miles away from the strip mall outside. Plus, bring in any four paperback books (in decent condition) and you can grab any book off the shelf for free—it's good karma and a logical transaction. If you come without books to spare, most books sell for around half the original cover price, sometimes less. The friendly owner will gladly help you find what you need (or take your name and number and call you if the book you're seeking pops up in the shop).

CHOCOLATE

JIMMIE'S CHOCOLATES
1426 NE 26th St., Wilton Manors
(954) 563-8655
www.jimmieschocolates.com
Florida's oldest chocolatier (going strong since 1947) attracts a loyal following for good reason—its chocolates and confections

focus on the traditional (dark chocolate infused with hazelnuts, milk chocolate squares with a dollop of white on top, truffles that dissolve on your tongue like a slow, sweet drizzle), and it's all homemade. Its new digs in Wilton Manors is a classy tasting room with antique stools and a loungelike atmosphere, whereas the original Dania Beach spot (148 N. Federal Hwy., 954-922-0441) is where most of the decadent stuff is made and sold (in an old house) and also serves as home to their cafe and restaurant (see p. 51 in the Restaurants chapter).

COMICS

TATE'S COMICS
4566 N. University Dr., Lauderhill
(954) 748-0181
www.tatescomics.com

Tate's is the "superman" of comic-book stores in Florida and has been written up as one of the top shops of geekdom by national publications—it's a bit of a mecca for comic-book fans. In operation since 1993, this is a haven not just for comics of all genres, but also paraphernalia like action dolls and figures, games, and anything the comic-book addict could ever crave, and more. If you're searching for a collectible, start here and chat with the knowledgeable staff about what you're seeking, and they'll do their best to secure it for you, usually with success. Tate's is named after its owner, Tate Ottati, who opened the shop when he was still a teenager in high school. The shop has since moved and expanded, and now contains a large selection of the usual suspects plus plenty of graphic novels and Japanese anime.

Las Olas Boulevard Shops

Las Olas Boulevard Shops is a strollers' and browsers' heaven. It's a strip along the boulevard just east of downtown, home to a large number of small boutiques, trendy restaurants, offices, and a hotel. It's upscale but not snobby in the least and makes for a pleasant afternoon jaunt. It's also conveniently located near a water-taxi stop. We've included a few of our favorites from the area in this chapter, but for the full listing of shops see the website: **www.las olasboulevard.com.**

CLOTHING & ACCESSORIES

ESSENTIALS BOUTIQUE
1851 Cordova Rd., Ft. Lauderdale
(954) 463-6007
http://essentialsboutique.com

Essentials carries an eclectic but very Florida mix of accessories and women's clothing. Many of the items have a tropical, island feel, and after a few days in the area, something funny happens: Even if you don't wear these types of clothes at home, you often want to do so here. If you're more interested in jewelry, they carry a fantastic collection, and one of the owners—a gemologist—will also evaluate, appraise, and clean any jewelry you bring in. Girly handbags, shoes, and fun gifts round out the selection.

JIMMY STAR FORT LAUDERDALE— FASHION SHOWROOM

1940 E. Sunrise Blvd., Ft. Lauderdale
(954) 828-9979
www.worldofjimmystar.com

If you've ever wondered where rock stars shop, this is your place. We didn't spy any stars on our visit (though we've heard rumors), but this is as much a place to pick up perform-on-stage gear as it is decadent and over the top costumes, or just come to browse the wild outfits Bowie wore in the last century and those gracing Lady Gaga in the here and now. Anything from shiny, pink-foiled leggings to leopard-print jackets to sunglasses that make oversized shades look tiny struts its stuff on hangers across the space, and the feathered head gear (or was that a hat? We couldn't really tell) is truly fantastical.

FARMERS' MARKETS

HALLANDALE'S FARMERS MARKET

821 N. Federal Hwy., Hallandale
(888) 592-7109 or (954) 456-6695
www.bigirvs.com

Formerly called Big Irv's Farmers Market, the same establishment is now run under the name Hallandale's Farmers Market and offers fresh produce at significant discounts compared to local grocery stores. The large bins of citrus fruit are a huge draw, but you can essentially stock up on most in-season fruits and vegetables here, as well as fresh-cut flowers and a handful of baked goods. An excellent choice to stock up on fresh produce—and be sure to print out their online coupon for 10 percent off your purchase at the market.

JOSH'S ORGANIC MARKET

Corner of Harrison Street and South Broadwalk, Hollywood Beach
(954) 456-FARM (3276)

Josh's is hands-down the best organic farmers' market in Greater Fort Lauderdale. Run by a New Yorker named Josh, the market spills out along the Broadwalk every Sun from 9:30 a.m. to 5 p.m. with shoppers hungry for his extra-fresh produce, all lovingly set up on tables under white canopy tents. Many items boast the sign: FLORIDA FRESH—PICKED LAST NIGHT. Josh uses PLA plastic cups—PLA is a special kind of plastic made from corn instead of petroleum; in other words, it's compostable, so you know food doesn't get fresher or more sustainable than this. From extensive selection of herbs, nuts, and seeds to pristine tomatoes and melons (lots of tastings are on hand—in fact, Josh often mills around the crowds offering slices of fresh melon or succulent chunks of flavor-bursting tomatoes), this market is as much a beachside social occasion as it is a shopping excursion. On a sunny Sunday (read: most Sundays, this is the Sunshine State after all) it seems the entire town is here, and the atmosphere feels distinctly neighborhoody. Rounding out the space is a popular juice bar, whipping up smoothies and freshly squeezed juices. Last, any produce that isn't sold is donated to local homeless shelters.

LAS OLAS OUTDOOR GOURMET MARKET

1201 E. Las Olas Blvd., Ft. Lauderdale
(305) 775-2166

Not your ordinary farmers' market, this features exceptional products—gourmet-style, and not cheap—like straight-from-the-farm fresh fruits and vegetables; top-quality culinary herbs; a variety of nuts and dried fruits; tropical plants (including exquisite orchids), small bougainvillea, and fresh cut flowers; plus a large selection of freshly baked breads, cookie, cakes, pies, and pastries; locally made

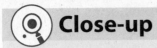

Close-up

An Old-School Chemist

We don't normally list pharmacies, but this one is special. Harking back to the days when filling a prescription involved stepping into a handsome, wooden-drawer-filled chemist, **Las Olas Chemist** (1201 E. Las Olas Blvd., Ft. Lauderdale; 954-462-4166) transports you back in time. Pharmacists are friendly and knowledgeable, and give you personal service you'll rarely find at a chain drugstore. The space evokes a feeling of a corner drugstore of yesteryear, and it's a pleasure to merely pop in to admire the space and peruse the small selection of gift items: bath and body creams, gels and salts, and lovely scented candles. Before you leave, you'll wish you had an apothecary of this standard where you live.

honey; and handmade soaps. In addition to the produce and flowers, you can also pick up delicious olive oils and balsamic vinegar blends (for those fresh tomatoes you just purchased), freshly ground coffee and interesting teas, and gift items like candles, pottery, *fleur de sel*, and various other fancy salts. This is a fun place to just browse while supping a fresh smoothie, and it's a fun window into the Sunday social scene on upscale Las Olas. Open Sun from 9 a.m. to 2 p.m.

FLEA MARKETS

FORT LAUDERDALE SWAP SHOP
3291 W. Sunrise Blvd., Ft. Lauderdale
(954) 791-SWAP (7927)
www.floridaswapshop.com

You've never seen a flea market like this. Allegedly the largest flea market in the world, the 88-acre Swap Shop is home to a flea market; a house circus with a carnival atmosphere (rides and games); a farmers' market featuring Florida goods and oodles of tropical fruits surrounded by an impressive array of food stalls with yummy snacks like seviche and homemade burritos; and a

massive drive-in movie theater (no less than 14 screens). More than 2,000 vendors sell goods—anything from art and electronics to furniture and clothing—at rock bottom prices. Open 365 days a year.

FOOD

DORIS ITALIAN MARKET
2424 Hollywood Blvd., Hollywood
(954) 921-9647
www.dorismarket.com

With no less than four locations scattered around Broward County, you don't need to venture far to find top-quality Italian ingredients such as succulent meats (prosciutto for lunch?); an impressive selection of pasta, olive oils, and vinegars straight from the mother land; fresh fish; olive bars; and mouthwatering antipasti for take out. Plus their deli is fantastic for a quick snack or sandwich. This market goes beyond the usual finds at Italian gourmet stores, so if you're searching for the elusive item you picked up on your last trip to Tuscany, this is your best bet. Additional locations are at 2077 University Dr., Coral Springs

SHOPPING

(954-346-7774); 10020 Pines Blvd., Pembroke Pines (954-499-0600); and 10057A Sunset Strip, Sunrise (954-749-1919).

GIFTS & MISCELLANEOUS

TO THE MOON MARKETPLACE
2205 Wilton Dr., Wilton Manors
(954) 564-2987
http://tothemoonmarketplace.com
While this is primarily a candy store, we'd be remiss if we classified it only as such. Past the rows and rows of candy from the United States (Jelly Belly jelly beans, Haribo Gummi Bears, pop rocks), they stock a vast array of sweets imported from across the globe (Dutch licorice, Argentine dulce de leche candies, British candy bars like Flakes and Wispas). They also sell funny, sexy novelty items (penis-shaped pasta, anyone?) and other silly, slightly erotic items that may make your grandmother blush.

MUSIC

RADIO-ACTIVE RECORDS
1930 E. Sunrise Blvd., Ft. Lauderdale
(954) 762-9488
www.myspace.com/radio_active_records
They don't make them like this anymore. It's not just that Radio-Active has a massive selection of new and used CDs and DVDs, their employees are true music hounds who happily tend to your questions, bring an encyclopedic knowledge to any music trivia, and treat all customers like fellow music-loving friends. They really stand out by specializing in that old pal, the vinyl record, ranging from modern music to electro to obscure grooves. They also expanded in the past few years and have space out back to host art openings, live bands, and a cozy seating area to take in the shows.

SPORTING GOODS

KAYAK JEFF'S
354 E. Dania Beach Blvd., Dania
(954) 926-5766
www.browardkayak.com
Specializing in kayaks and canoes, Kayak Jeff's is the best place to pick up a new vessel and learn about the ins and outs of kayaking and canoeing. From the helpful staff to their bespoke instruction courses, this is an ideal place for beginners—they'll make sure you not only understand how to safely embark on your first outing, but they'll give you tips on Florida-specific currents and other tidbits. Experienced kayakers will be in heaven, as they offer the best selection of gear in the county.

PETER GLENN SKI & SPORT
2901 W. Oakland Park Blvd.,
Ft. Lauderdale
(954) 484-3606
www.peterglenn.com
For outdoor gear, Peter Glenn is your man. From the slope to the ocean, trekking to swimming, and for the ultimate wakeboard or water skis to enjoy in Greater Fort Lauderdale's sublime Atlantic and tranquil Intracoastal waterways, this superstore has it all. While the shop stocks plenty of winter-weather clothing, they cater to their location and offer a huge selection of Florida-compatible accessories like dive suits, snorkeling equipment, and a large selection of swimwear. A second Fort Lauderdale location is at 1771 E. Sunrise Blvd. (954-467-7872).

SURF SHOPS

MAUI NIX
17 S. Fort Lauderdale Beach Blvd.,
Ft. Lauderdale Beach
(954) 522-5255
www.mauinix.com
The original store may be in Florida's surf capital Daytona Beach, but this beachside Fort Lauderdale location pulls out all the waves with its extensive flip-flop collection, endless bathing suits, and beach clothes you can happily strut your stuff in. Plus there's a good selection of shades and other beach-life paraphernalia like colorful towels, fun floppy hats, and shell jewelry. If you want to fit in with the local beach bums, this is your best bet.

THRIFT & SECONDHAND

HABITAT FOR HUMANITY RE-STORE
505 W. Broward Blvd., Ft. Lauderdale
(954) 763-7771
www.habitatbroward.org/restore
Dubbed as a home-improvement store with a conscience, this is your best bet for recycled and reused gear in an overwhelming but well-stocked warehouse filled with old sinks, used furniture, hardware galore, electrical items, and even old doors and piles of quality tile—basically, it's like a used version of Home Depot, with far lower prices. Materials sold here are largely donated from building supply and retail stores, contractors,

demolition crews, or simply from people who want to support Habitat for Humanity.

THE POVERELLO CENTER
2292 Wilton Dr., Wilton Manors
(954) 561-3663
www.poverello.org
Owned by a center that supports and helps people suffering from HIV/AIDS through local outreach programs, this thrift shop of clothes, furniture, housewares, bric-a-brac, jewelry, and dozens of items you didn't know you needed, is a great place to rummage. Anything you purchase helps support the mission of the organization. It's often got a wild and wonderful selection of gear, and you're as likely to find a pink boa as you are a black fitted skirt for the office.

VINTAGE

JEZEBEL
1980 E. Sunrise Blvd., Ft. Lauderdale
(954) 761-7881
www.myspace.com/jezebelchic
Racks and racks of vintage clothing, from 1950s swirly skirts to elegant 1920s gloves and handbags to groovy hippie boots and scarves—it's all here and more, including a very feminine negligee section and well-priced jewelry. This is the place for a smart new addition to your wardrobe that'll ensure you don't show up at a party wearing the same thing as your best friend.

PERFORMING ARTS

If you can say it, sing it, perform it, act it, express it, show it, hum it, dance it, joke about it, mime it, play it, or otherwise perform it, you'll find it—whatever "it" is—in Greater Fort Lauderdale. Particularly during the High Season, this area hums with an artistic vibe that's matched by only a few other places in America. There's a nonstop parade of world-famous actors, singers, dancers, musicians, and comedians. There's a nonstop parade, as well, of actors, singers, dancers, musicians, and comedians who will one day be world-famous. And there's a huge vein of local talent that's mined here as well.

The places where all these performances take place are as varied as the performances themselves. One night you may be sitting front-row orchestra at the Broward Center for the Performing Arts, one of America's performing-arts showpieces. The next night you may be sitting at an outdoor fountain, watching a wonderfully creative mime. And the next night . . . who knows?

People who haven't been here for awhile are always amazed at what they find in the new Greater Fort Lauderdale. This is a town, don't forget, that, until 20 years ago, was known mostly for its rowdy Spring Breaks. These days, however, you'll find so many performances you'll want to attend that you simply won't be able to attend them all. Theater here now ranges from Shakespeare to avant-garde. Musical performances range from country-and-western to opera, and everything in between. Dance performances—and local companies—run the gamut from classical ballet to modern interpretive. And singing performances range from Broadway to gospel.

OVERVIEW

The main proof of a growing arts area has always been in the number and vitality of its local organizations, and in the talents of their performers. And, if that's the case, what was once a center for spring breakers is now a center of ground-breaking entertainment.

Broward County residents appreciate the performance arts. Many of them, if not most, moved here some years back from places up north where the arts were a regular part of their lives. And many of them have gotten involved, through their hard work and their hard-earned financial contributions, in creating the vibrant performing-arts atmosphere that now characterizes Greater Fort Lauderdale. And now you can enjoy the fruits of their labors, in venues from state-of-the-art facilities hosting internationally renowned luminaries to cozy little theaters hosting homegrown talent.

THE COMPANIES

ACTORS COMMUNITY THEATER OF DAVIE

6591 Orange Dr., Davie
(954) 797-1153
www.davie-fl.gov/Gen/
DavieFL_SpclPrjcts/act

In January of 2000, a small ad in a local paper asked if there were "any thespians out there." Turned out there were. A number of people responded to the ad, and the town of Davie suddenly had its first community theater. On October 20 of that year, the fledgling company of 10 would-be actors put on *An Evening of Scenes: The Passion of Tennessee Williams, The Laughter of Neil Simon.* The audience loved it. And Greater Fort Lauderdale audiences have loved pretty much every play this company's put on since then. Shows for the 2010–2011 season included Williams's *A Streetcar Named Desire,* Herb Gardner's *A Thousand Clowns,* and Noel Coward's *Blithe Spirit.*

AMBROSIA DANCE COMPANY AND CENTER FOR CONTEMPORARY DANCE

P.O. Box 100481, Ft. Lauderdale, FL 33310
(954) 739-8795

This up-and-coming troupe offers performances in modern dance for students and audiences at both adult and children's levels, as well as professional training in dance technique and methods. In addition, the studio offers classes in yoga, intelligent exercise, and meditation. It's a multifaceted concept that reaches out to the community on several levels, including professional full-evening concert programs; lecture demonstrations; children's concerts; dance classes (modern, ballet, jazz, alignment, and creative movement); master classes; dance video programs; and performances by students who attend the classes.

ARTS BALLET THEATRE OF FLORIDA

15939 Biscayne Blvd.,
North Miami Beach
(305) 947-3998
www.artsballettheatre.org

The Arts Ballet Theatre of Florida is a company of talented young professionals founded in 1997 by ballet master Vladimir Issaev. Although it's Miami based, its venues are the Broward Center for the Performing Arts and the Parker Playhouse in Fort Lauderdale, and it also offers outreach programs to the Broward community. The company performs classics such as *Firebird, The Nutcracker,* and *Romeo and Juliet* in addition to original works by Issaev. And, although a local company, Arts Ballet Theatre of Florida has tie-ins on the international level; its summer programs have guest faculty from the Vaganova Ballet Academy of Russia.

ASHANTI CULTURAL ARTS, INC.

1350 E. Sunrise Boulevard,
Ft. Lauderdale
(954) 792-3700
www.ashanticulturalarts.com

This performing arts company provides main-stage productions and theater instruction, in addition to education, literacy, and wellness programs for the community. It's been around for two decades and has performed many premieres of innovative plays—and has won numerous awards. The company performs nationally and internationally in addition to locally. Many of Ashanti's students have gone on to notable achievements in the arts world.

BROWARD COLLEGE DANCE PROGRAM
Broward College Campus–Davie
3501 SW Davie Rd., Ft. Lauderdale
(954) 475-6840
This company takes learning out of the classroom and onto the stage, with a number of performances for the public each year.

CURTAIN CALL PLAYHOUSE
2500 SE 3rd St., Pompano Beach
(954) 784-0768
www.curtaincallplayhouse.com
This talented acting company has a unique concept: It's a true touring company, making the rounds of Greater Fort Lauderdale's theaters, libraries, and civic centers, bringing live theater "to the people," often in underserved areas of the community. In addition, they work with a variety of Broward County city governments and schools. Although they have a main-stage troupe for children's programming, they actually have no home stage of their own. And homeless or not, they must be doing something right because they've been doing it since 1998. Kris Coffelt is the founding and current artistic/executive director of the group, and she uses local actors, technical help, and stage hands. Performances in recent seasons have included *Hello, Dolly!, Broadway Nights,* and *Hay Fever.*

DRUMS OF POLYNESIA
750 NE 45th St., Ft. Lauderdale
(954) 351-5069
www.drumsofpolynesia.com
The primary mission of this group is to spread awareness of the arts and culture of the Polynesian islands, Hawaii, Samoa, Tahiti, and New Zealand through song-and-dance performances that are educational as well

as fun. Their schedule is irregular, and they do spend some time traveling around the state. So keep an eye out in the *South Florida Sun-Sentinel*'s weekend section as well as the *New Times* weekly paper.

FLORIDA GRAND OPERA
Broward Center for the Performing Arts
201 SW 5th Ave., Ft. Lauderdale
(954) 728-9700
www.fgo.org
The Florida Grand Opera is actually based in Miami, 25 miles down the road, but it performs often in Broward County. It's actually the result of the 1994 merger between the Greater Miami Opera and the Opera Guild of Fort Lauderdale, and the merger has produced nothing but success and nothing but first-class performances by a polished, professional opera company. Over the years, FGO has mounted nearly a hundred main-stage productions, among them 25 South Florida premieres. These productions have included the best that opera has to offer, including performances such as Richard Strauss's *Salome* and *Ariadne auf Naxos*; Britten's *The Turn of the Screw*; Monteverdi's *L'incoronazione di Poppea*; Handel's *Julius Caesar*; the American premiere of Rossini's *Bianca e Falliero;* and the world premieres of Robert Ward's *Minutes till Midnight* and David Carlson's *Anna Karenina*.

The FGO's Young Artist Studio provides a place where talented young opera aspirants can rehearse, learn from professionals, attend seminars and workshops with known performers, and perform before the community at various venues around South Florida. And, in addition, it provides a steady stream of local talent to continually refresh the ranks.

FLORIDA'S SINGING SONS BOYCHOIR
1229 NE 37th St., Ft. Lauderdale
(954) 563-2697
www.singingsons.org

The Boychoir is a gift to the people of South Florida from community-minded patrons who are intent on nurturing the singing talents of local youth. Every autumn, some 3,000 local third- and fourth-graders audition for the choir, but only 125 of them make it. Each of them spends the first year in the training choir before moving up to the residence choir. If they keep studying, and keep improving, the boys keep moving up. And at the end of their time in the Singing Sons Boychoir, the top ones have the skills and the experience to move up in the performing-arts world.

The Boychoir was founded in Fort Lauderdale in 1975, and since then, it has won awards all over the world. It performs a wide variety of songs, from Gregorian chants and Broadway favorites to folk music and musical theater. And members of the choir have appeared onstage with luminaries such as Liza Minnelli, Judy Collins, Lee Greenwood, Audrey Hepburn, and Bob Hope. Florida's Singing Sons Boychoir tours nationally as well as internationally.

FORT LAUDERDALE CHILDREN'S BALLET THEATER
5303 N. Dixie Hwy., Ft. Lauderdale
(954) 491-4668
www.dancedimensionsonline.com

This company features children and young adults presenting the classics. And it takes pride in reminding people that the name "Ballet Theater" emphasizes the dramatic aspect of dance, and the fact that dance tells a very real story. They perform at the Broward Center for the Performing Arts and at the Parker Playhouse.

FORT LAUDERDALE CHILDREN'S THEATRE
The Galleria Mall
2542B E. Sunrise Blvd., Ft. Lauderdale
(954) 763-6882
www.flct.org

Founded in 1952, the Fort Lauderdale Children's Theatre is the oldest documented children's theater in Florida. And it remains one of the few theaters in the world where children are not only the actors, but also the assistant directors, set designers, technicians, lighting and sound engineers, and other backstage personnel. But it's not only about the performances. This organization touches some 32,000 local children every year, and most of them never set foot on (or behind) its stages.

There's formal theater training, taught by professional actors and teachers. There is a wide variety of outreach programs to reach kids whose parents can't afford the classes, or can't get them to the classes. And the theater participates in conflict resolution, anti-bullying, and literacy programs with local public and private schools.

And then, of course, we go back to those performances. The company has won a dozen awards from local and national organizations for the quality of its personnel and its performances. Among the programs scheduled for the 2010–2011 season are *A Midsummer Night's Dream*, *Snow White and the Seven Dwarfs*, Elton John and Tim Rice's *Aida*, Disney's *My Son Pinocchio*, and *Hello, Dolly!*

GIRL CHOIR OF SOUTH FLORIDA
1350 E. Sunrise Blvd., #117,
Ft. Lauderdale
(954) 553-2809
www.girlchoir.org

The Girl Choir of South Florida, simply put, celebrates the joy of singing. Its mission is to build relationships and increase understanding by bringing this joy to the community, and by sharing with and showing young girls its belief that singing can make them better people. Founded in 2005, the girls' choir now has nearly 90 singers between the ages of 7 and 18. And it boasts a staff of award-winning professionals who are considered among the finest at their craft.

The organization consists of three different choruses, affording girls of all ages and abilities a chance to perform. Members of the choir have toured nationally, appeared on TV, and performed with the Florida Grand Opera. In 2010 they performed at the prestigious Crescent City Choral Festival in New Orleans. And their annual spring concert takes place at the Broward Center for the Performing Arts, giving these young ladies the thrill of a lifetime.

GOLD COAST JAZZ SOCIETY
1350 E. Sunrise Blvd., Ft. Lauderdale
(954) 524-0805
www.goldcoastjazz.org
If you're into jazz—moody, mellow, or boppin'—you've got to treat yourself to some performances by the Gold Coast Jazz Society. They play it hot, they play it cool, and they play it very, very well. The Society started out in 1992, performing at the historic Riverside Hotel on Fort Lauderdale's Las Olas Boulevard. They instantly began attracting live-jazz-starved South Floridians. Within four years the series had outgrown the space at the Riverside, and moved to the 110 Tower Club. As its popularity grew, so did the demand for tickets, eventually necessitating another move, this time to the 600-seat Amaturo Theater at the Broward Center

for the Performing Arts. The Amaturo is the perfect size—large enough to generate real excitement at the performances, and small enough to be intimate and friendly.

Performers have included notables such as the Frank Derrick Big Band and Quintet, the Jeff Hamilton Trio, vocalist Jackie Ryan, and the Bill Allred Classic Jazz Band.

INSIDE OUT THEATRE COMPANY
1 East Las Olas Blvd., Ft. Lauderdale
(954) 385-3060
www.insideouttheatre.org
This troupe of players has received rave reviews from the South Florida *Sun-Sentinel* and the *Miami Herald*. It's a multifaceted organization, with children's programs as well as professional players, directors, and backstage people. The theater specializes in modern plays with dramatic impact, such as *Whose Life Is It, Anyway?*, *Faith Healer*, Edna O'Brien's *Triptych*, and Paul Grellong's *Manuscript*.

MASTER CHORALE OF SOUTH FLORIDA
6278 N. Federal Hwy., #351,
Ft. Lauderdale
(954) 418-6232
www.masterchoraleofsouthflorida.com
This is a professional company of some of the finest choral voices in Greater Fort Lauderdale, so highly regarded that it has sung with such notables as world-renowned Italian tenor Andrea Bocelli and conductor James Judd. This is compelling music, with works such as Verdi's *Requiem*, Haydn's *Creation*, and Mozart's *Requiem* and *Te Deum* with the Miami Symphony Orchestra. The company has no home base; instead, it performs at local arenas (including the 21,000-seat BankAtlantic Center), schools, civic centers, performing-arts venues, and churches.

MIAMI CITY BALLET
2200 Liberty Ave., Miami Beach
(305) 929-7010
(Broward Center for the Performing Arts)
Box Office:
(954) 462-0222
www.miamicityballet.org
Miami City Ballet was blessed with stardust from its founding, in 1985, when it was announced that renowned dancer Edward Villela, formerly of the New York City Ballet, had became artistic director of the fledgling company. Since then it's become one of the most highly regarded—and innovative—dance companies in America. Miami City Ballet does the classics and the groundbreakers with equal facility. And it performs at the Broward Center several times a year.

RISING ACTION THEATRE COMPANY
840 E. Oakland Park Blvd., Ft. Lauderdale
(954) 561-2225
www.risingactiontheatre.com
The name of this young theater company characterizes its productions and its performance skills. The plays are irreverent, satirical, dramatic, and powerful, and a night here is simply a great time. The company does a mixture of plays that often reflect gay themes and multicultural and social issues, as well as more general-interest types of plays. It's performed works such as *Reefer Madness, The Musical; Flora the Red Menace* (by the writers of *Cabaret* and *Chicago*); and *Sordid Lives* ("the black comedy about white trash").

SOL THEATRE COMPANY
1140 N. Flagler Dr., Ft. Lauderdale
(954) 525-6555
This troupe prides itself on the words *cutting edge*. Its performances, in fact, are nothing

if not edgy . . . and innovative, and interesting. And there are actually two performing companies—adult and children. Adult stage has an annual schedule of one Shakespeare, one other classic, one Latin, one gay-oriented and/or female play, and one American author. The children's stage performs classic children's tales and occasional modern works.

SOUTH FLORIDA BALLET THEATER
1 Young Circle (Hollywood Boulevard and Federal Highway)
Hollywood
(954) 929-4601
www.southfloridaballettheater.com
This company dances the classics, like *A Midsummer Night's Dream, The Nutcracker,* and *Peter and the Wolf.* It's filled with talented young performers who dance with class and enthusiasm, and it's gotten good reviews from local media. SFBT's mission is to develop the skills of young local dancers, some of whom eventually move up to the company.

TRANZENDANCE DANCE PRODUCTIONS
9923 S. Hollybrook Lake Dr., #104
Pembroke Pines
(954) 260-4972
www.tranzendance.org
This group sees its mission as promoting the art of modern, multicultural, and contemporary dance through experimental and innovative performances, and to help strengthen the Broward County arts community through collaboration with other local arts organizations. The emphasis on innovation is so pronounced, in fact, that a good number of their performances are improvisational—made up right on the spot.

Many of their works have Hispanic themes and are inspired by Hispanic cultural icons such as Federico García Lorca, Salvador Dalí, and Manuel de Falla.

THE WOMEN'S THEATRE PROJECT
Sixth Star Studios
501 NW 1st Ave., Ft. Lauderdale
(954) 462-2334
www.womenstheatreproject.com
The mission of the Women's Theatre Project is simple—to explore the female voice through contemporary drama that shows life as it is, rather than how it's often depicted (and how women are often depicted) in television and the movies. Its motto, too, is simple: By Women. About Women. For Everyone. The company was founded in 2002 out of a desire to dispel the stereotypes about women that are often portrayed in the mass media. As the years have gone by, the Theatre Project has increasingly generated good reviews, both for the originality of the plays produced and for the talent displayed onstage. The company produces works from noted playwrights such as Joan Didion (*The Year of Magical Thinking*), among others. This is hard-hitting, gritty, must-see theater, performed by excellent actors.

THE VENUES

ART AND CULTURE CENTER OF HOLLYWOOD
1650 Harrison St., Hollywood
(954) 921-3274
www.artandculturecenter.org
The Art and Culture Center of Hollywood is a multifaceted facility that presents excellent art exhibitions, performing arts on stage, and special programs for children of the community. It started out as a small, beachfront art gallery in 1975. Sixteen years later,

it moved from its modest location to the beautiful Kagey Mansion downtown, a Mediterranean/Moorish masterpiece built in the mid-1920s. The move multiplied its space, and as a result, the Center was able to multiply its offerings, expanding from the visual arts alone to encompass the performing arts as well a few years later. In 1999 the Center launched its annual Ocean Dance event and has since attracted notables such as Mikhail Baryshnikov and his White Oak Dance Project. The Center's programming attracts more than 50,000 attendees annually.

Performances include dance, song, music, and also films. Recent performances have included *Fish Tales,* by the highly regarded Momentum Dance Company; *High School Musical 2;* Japanese storytelling; Delou Africa Dance Ensemble; Bits 'N Pieces Puppet Theatre; an outdoor festival called "East (the Orient) Meets Hollywood"; and a wonderful Spanish-language documentary on soccer called *Pelada.* All in addition, of course, to the great exhibitions by groundbreaking visual artists.

ARTSPARK AT YOUNG CIRCLE
Downtown Hollywood Community Redevelopment Association
330 N. Federal Hwy. (Hollywood Boulevard at US 1), Hollywood
(954) 921-3500
www.artsparkatyoungcircle.org
How ideal for Florida: the performing arts—music, dance, and song—outdoors! The city has big plans for the ArtsPark, which includes a new professional-quality amphitheater with seating for 500 people and room for 1,500 more on the lawn that slopes down to it. There will also be smaller performance pavilions for community groups. This is a thoughtfully integrated outdoor

arts complex for both community and outside performers, and a wonderful place to relax and enjoy the fresh air and the varied performers.

BAILEY CONCERT HALL
3501 SW Davie Rd., Davie
(954) 475-6880
www.broward.edu/campuslife/
culturalarts
The Bailey Concert Hall, on the Davie campus of Broward College, has long been a staple of cultural life in western Broward. It's a modern, comfortable theater that seats 1,081 and presents a variety of theater, dance, and musical entertainment, in addition to lectures by internationally known figures in government, business, and the arts. These acts have run the gamut from Broadway shows to the Dalai Lama.

BANKATLANTIC CENTER
One Panther Pkwy., Sunrise
(954) 835-7000
www.bankatlanticcenter.com
The home of the National Hockey League's Florida Panthers is also an excellent entertainment venue. And because of its size—it can hold 22,000 people—it can attract world-class events that are too big for anywhere else in Broward County. Recent acts included Michael Bublé, Eric Clapton, Roger Daltrey, Carole King and James Taylor, the renowned Dutch conductor Andre Reiu and his orchestra, Taylor Swift, John Mayer, Dane Cook, the Trans-Siberian Orchestra, Jay-Z, Jimmy Buffett, Bon Jovi, Tito Puente Jr., and Roger Waters of Pink Floyd. And since it opened in 1998, BankAtlantic Center's roster of performers is a virtual Who's Who of the greatest and most influential singers, musicians, and comics in the world.

BROWARD CENTER FOR THE PERFORMING ARTS
201 SW 5th Ave., Ft. Lauderdale
(954) 522-5334
www.browardcenter.org
When it opened on February 26, 1991, the Broward Center for the Performing Arts officially brought Greater Fort Lauderdale into the cultural major leagues. Its comfort, its beauty, its functionality, its state-of-the-art technology, and its audio clarity are second to none. And so are the quality and diversity of the acts that perform here. Great plays? How about *Wicked* or *West Side Story* or *A Christmas Carol* or *Jersey Boys*? Great Broadway performers? How about Patti Lupone or Bette Midler or Rita Moreno? Great music? How about seven-time Grammy Award–winner Gilberto Gil or the Houston Symphony Orchestra or reggae icons? And the list continues. Great singers. Great dancers and dance companies. Great lectures by renowned performing artists. Even great programs for the younger set.

An evening at the Broward Center is an evening of elegance and class, and an evening with a performance—no matter what the performance—that you'll remember for a long time.

THE BROWARD STAGE DOOR THEATRE
8036 W. Sample Rd., Coral Springs
(954) 344-7765
www.stagedoortheatre.com
In the heart of Coral Springs is a theater that utilizes the top local talent, along with well-known performers, to stage some wonderfully creative shows. The Stage Door Theatre presents a wide variety of interesting shows, ranging from comedies such as Neil Simon's *Plaza Suite,* to musicals such as *On the Town, Mame,* and *The Music Man,* to poignant stories

My Fort Lauderdale

This morning, I was doing one of the things I like most about living in Fort Lauderdale: writing on our back dock over the New River, listening to the racket of the monk parakeets, watching for the manatees that swim past every once in a while.

I was born in Fort Lauderdale in 1954. Today's urban, sophisticated community didn't exist when I was a girl. My father once shot an alligator that climbed up out of Tarpon River and went after the family dog in our front yard. Our house was on SW 12th Street, now four lanes of traffic and known as Davie Boulevard, only a couple of miles from downtown Fort Lauderdale. When I was young, I rode my horse through orange groves in western Broward County, on land now filled with subdivisions and superhighways.

Still, there are those patches of paradise to be found. I love riding my bicycle out to the beach. The beauty of the isles along Las Olas Boulevard still knocks me out. Nothing beats watching an enormous full moon rise on a summer night over the ocean. At the Bonnet House and Birch State Park, I can marvel at the beauty that remains of natural Florida. My maternal grandmother was a Griffin, and I've found all sorts of historic treasures and memories of the community her family helped settle at another favorite spot, the Old Davie School Museum.

—Deborah Sharp,
Writer/Novelist (*The Mace Bauer Mysteries*), Fort Lauderdale

like *Light in the Piazza*, to contemporary stories such as *Steel Magnolias*. The theater has an elegant, old-time ambience from the days when a theater was a *theater*. In actuality, there are two theaters inside this building, each with a different show, so you can take your pick. The shows here will make you laugh, they'll make you cry, they'll make you stop to wonder, and they'll make you snap your fingers. And Coral Springs is a city with a ton of excellent restaurants, so you'll always have your choice of post-theater options.

CORAL SPRINGS CENTER FOR THE ARTS

**2855 Coral Springs Dr., Coral Springs
(954) 344-5999
www.coralspringscenterforthearts.com**
Coral Springs, of course, became one of the earlier planned communities in America when it was incorporated in 1965. And when the doors of the Coral Springs Center for the Arts opened in 1990, it brought first-class entertainment to the city, only to be improved with a major renovation when it was only six years old. In addition to a state-of-the-art, 1,500-seat theater, the center houses a dance studio and the impressive Coral Springs Museum of Art. It's also a major venue for local and community performing-arts organizations.

The center stages performances such as *Disney's Beauty and the Beast; Bye, Bye, Birdie;* and *The Wedding Singer*, as well as singers like Frankie Avalon and TV stars from favorite shows of the '60s and '70s.

HARD ROCK LIVE

**Seminole Hard Rock Hotel & Casino
1 Seminole Way, Hollywood
(954) 797-5531
www.hardrocklivehollywoodfl.com**

This 5,000-seat arena with state-of-the-art sound and lighting has played host to many of the most popular performers in the world. It would take pages and pages to list the great musicians, singers, bands, and comedians that have played here. But a partial list would include Billy Joel; Rod Stewart; Kathy Griffin; Ringo Starr and His All-Starr Band; '60s rockers like Mickey Dolenz from the Monkees and Mark Lindsay from Paul Revere & the Raiders; Tim McGraw; Donna Summer; Earth, Wind & Fire; Van Morrison; the Gypsy Kings; John Fogerty; Aretha Franklin; Roberta Flack, and scores of others who have lit up the charts over—or for—the past few decades. This is one of Greater Fort Lauderdale's biggest places to see and be seen, and to mix with the movers and shakers of South Florida civic, business, and social societies. And after the show, of course, you can walk down the hall to the casino and try your luck.

HOLLYWOOD PLAYHOUSE
2640 Washington St., Hollywood
(954) 922-0404
www.hollywoodplayhouse.com
Opening in 1950, this may be one of the oldest continuously operating theaters in South Florida, and it's still housed in the same building it was then. It's an intimate, up-close place with only 265 seats, all of which (as you might expect) have wonderful sight lines. The facility hosts a wide variety of visiting performers and performances, among them Broadway and off-Broadway shows, comedy/improv, children's plays, concerts, and lectures. There's no resident acting company here, but there is a full slate of behind-the-scenes professionals in every theater discipline.

MIRAMAR CULTURAL CENTER/
ARTSPARK
2400 Civic Center Place, Miramar
(954) 602-4500
www.miramarculturalcenter.org
The Miramar Cultural Center is a showplace for wonderful—but less commercial—productions that wouldn't get a chance at larger venues, which means that its shows tend to take chances and, as a result, tend to be provocative and innovative. For example, some of the shows in the 2010 season included *Lil Haiti—The Untold Story,* an in-depth look at the experiences of Haitian émigrés in Miami in the 1970s and '80s; *Disney's Aladdin Jr.;* Miami Dancity Studio; and the Ballet Etudes, whose dances range from flamenco and hip-hop to Broadway and jazz.

Just because the performers here are not necessarily world renowned, however, doesn't mean that this isn't a first-class facility. On the contrary, the 800-seat theater has excellent sound and excellent sight lines. Situated adjacent to the Miramar City Hall, the facility includes (besides the theater) two art galleries, banquet facilities, rehearsal halls (open to the community), classrooms for lectures, and a botanical garden. Nearby are the Miramar Library, shops, and restaurants. It's a columned neoclassical building with a terra cotta–colored rooftop. And it's become a focal point of south Broward's cultural and social life.

MOSAIC THEATRE
12200 W. Broward Blvd., #3000
Plantation
(954) 577-8243
www.mosaictheatre.com
This is a professional company, not a community one, and it's gained a reputation for presenting cutting-edge, innovative theater.

It's won more than 50 awards over the past decade. The theater's performance schedule coincides with the arrival of the Season in Greater Fort Lauderdale, and performances run from Thurs through Sun. Productions over the past couple of years have included Tom Stoppard's *Rock 'n Roll*, Christopher Shinn's *Dying City* (a Pulitzer Prize finalist), August Wilson's *Radio Golf*, and Winter Miller's *In Darfur*. The *Miami Herald* has referred to the Mosaic as "Broward County's dramatically different theater company."

OMNI AUDITORIUM
Broward College—North Regional Campus
100 Coconut Creek Blvd., Coconut Creek
(954) 973-2233
This site hosts a variety of community and school-level performances in dance and singing.

THE PARKER PLAYHOUSE
707 NE 8th St., Ft. Lauderdale
(954) 462-0222
www.parkerplayhouse.com
The Parker Playhouse parted its curtains for the first time in February 1967, and it's been a staple in Broward County's cultural life ever since. Now managed by the Broward Center for the Performing Arts, this 1,167-seat theater still hosts important theater, dance, singing, and musical performers. It still retains an air of elegance and sophistication, from the days when it was Fort Lauderdale's only large performance facility. In recent seasons, it's featured shows such as the Fab Faux, a great Beatles cover band; Bjorn Again, a dead-on re-creation of the iconic '70s band Abba; Meg Segreto's Dance Center, which has been entertaining Greater Fort Lauderdale for more than 30 years; *Stone Soup,* an Eastern European folk tale; and the Broward Center Classical Orchestra Series.

POMPANO BEACH AMPHITHEATRE
1806 NE 6th St., Pompano Beach
(954) 946-2402
www.ticketmaster.com
This outdoor showplace in Pompano has, over the years, hosted many a famous pop and rock group, among them the Beach Boys. Concerts are scheduled sporadically though; there is no set schedule, so it pays to check the Weekend section of the *Sun-Sentinel* and to check the entertainment listings in *New Times.*

THE ROSE & ALFRED MINIACI PERFORMING ARTS CENTER OF NOVA SOUTHEASTERN UNIVERSITY
3100 Ray Ferrero Jr. Blvd., Ft. Lauderdale
(954) 462-0222
www.miniacipac.com
The Rose & Alfred Miniaci Performing Arts Center is a 498-seat auditorium that's equipped with state-of-the-art lighting and acoustics. The Performing Arts Center has become an important cog in the cultural life of western Broward, and in addition to the performances, it also stages interesting seminars and lectures for the community. This center is another facility that's managed by the Broward Center for the Performing Arts, and as a result of that connection, the Miniaci Center is able to attract a wide variety of community and professional productions. Recent productions have ranged from *Disney's The Jungle Book* to the South Florida Jazz Concert Series to the Family Fun Series' *Rapunzel.*

TAMARAC THEATRE OF PERFORMING ARTS

8761 Holly Court, Tamarac
(954) 721-9411
www.tamaractheatreofperformingarts
.org

This well-regarded theater celebrated its 30th birthday in 2010. The lineup here consists mostly of the wonderful stage classics, running from drama to musical. The plays scheduled for the 2010–2011 season are representative of the enjoyable shows in which this theater specializes: *Guys & Dolls, I Hate Hamlet, They're Playing Our Song, Laughter on the Second Floor,* and *Annie.* In addition to plays, there are also occasional musical performances, play readings, and a children's theater that puts on a performance at the end of its season.

TOWNSHIP CENTER FOR THE PERFORMING ARTS

2452 Lyons Rd., Coconut Creek
(954) 973-8094

This theater, located inside a large condo/townhouse complex in Coconut Creek, has been supplying northern Broward with good entertainment for many years, with a variety of acts ranging from Broadway to Elvis impersonators.

PARKS AND BEACHES

Greater Fort Lauderdale is blessed by nature, which is why people travel here from all over the world. The sun never stops shining with a warmth that soothes both body and soul. There's a wide diversity of natural wonders and terrain, ranging from world-famous beaches to swampy marsh. The beaches, of course, were created by nature. But it was the foresight of human beings that capitalized on this diversity by creating wonderful parks in which you can build your body, soothe your mind, enjoy a picnic, play with your kids (or your inner child), and just explore the natural beauty. Or just kick back with a cooler and a good book.

All together, there are 24 county parks, along with scores of neighborhood and city parks in Greater Fort Lauderdale. The city parks range from neighborhood pocket parks (small, "pocket-size" parks) to large, multifaceted ones with a ton of facilities and fields. There's a good chance that by the time you leave (if you leave), one of them will be "your" park.

Six of these county parks are considered "nature centers," with habitats ranging from islands to forest to sand to pine scrub to highlands to cypress to swamp. All of them are teeming with interesting plant and animal life, and all are joys to wander through.

Then of course, there are those beaches, first made famous in *Where the Boys Are* 50 years ago. They were pristine and wide and beautiful then and they're still the same today. Sink your toes into the soft sand. Let yourself float in the perennially warm waters. Smell the salt air. See the endless horizon of blue-green water flowing into soft blue sky. Feel the sea breeze. And feel, as well, the cares of everyday life slip away, if only for a few hours. Relax and enjoy. After all, you're in paradise!

STATE PARKS

HUGH TAYLOR BIRCH STATE PARK
3109 E. Sunrise Blvd., Ft. Lauderdale
(954) 564-4521
www.floridastateparks.org
This park is the former estate of millionaire Hugh Taylor Birch, who left it as a gift to the State of Florida. It's a deep-green piece of languid paradise, filled with tropical hammocks. On this one portion of the property, between the Intracoastal and the Atlantic, a number of environments and habitats can be found. And you can paddle, row, fish, hike, jog, or bike among them on trails, paved roads, paths, and seawalls. If you want to lie out on the beach, you can access it by a tunnel under SR A1A. If you're in the mood for a picnic, you can relax at a table overlooking the Intracoastal Waterway. And if you want to learn more about Hugh Taylor Birch's gift to the people of Florida—and

the wildlife that lived here long before they did—visit the Terramar Visitor Center, with its good exhibits on the area's natural and cultural history.

The following is just a sample of the activities and amenities offered by Hugh Taylor Birch State Park:

- **Biking/Skating**—There's a 2-mile paved road used by cyclists and in-line skaters alike. The road is one-way.
- **Canoeing/Kayaking**—Canoes and kayaks are available for rental.
- **Fishing**—You can fish off the seawall or in a couple of other designated areas.
- **Nature Trail**—The Coastal Hammock Trail is an easy 20-minute walk through a coastal strand–forest ecosystem of native Florida vegetation. Signs along the trail offer interesting information about the habitat. The Exotic Trail, on the other hand, gives a different perspective; it includes many nonnative plants brought here by Mr. Birch.
- **Picnics**—The park includes several picnic areas with shady trees, playground equipment, pavilions, and grills. Each of the three picnic pavilions is equipped with electricity and water and can serve about 75 people.
- **Swimming**—Swimming is permitted in designated areas.
- **Tours**—Every Friday morning during winter, a ranger leads a group walk on the Coastal Hammock Trail.
- **Visitor Center**—The Terramar Visitor Center is the former home of Hugh Taylor Birch. Built in 1940, it reflects the eclectic tastes of that time (and its owner), with strong Mediterranean elements as well as the Art Deco style popular then. You can learn more about this area and this unique coastal ecosystem here. The

visitor center is open 9 a.m. to 5 p.m., Sat, Sun, and holidays. Admission is free with paid park entrance.

- **Wildlife Viewing**—Hugh Taylor Birch State Park is a birder's heaven, with over 200 species. Here you'll see many migratory species, often from the Caribbean.

JOHN U. LLOYD BEACH STATE PARK
6503 N. Ocean Dr., Dania Beach
(954) 923-2833
www.floridastateparks.org

Miles of aquamarine water and tan sand, whether you look north or south. The sounds of the water lapping the shore, and the birds overhead. The soft caress of the sea breeze. The sensation of the salty air. And the warm softness of the sand into which your toes sink. It doesn't get much better.

The whole family can cast a line in the surf, canoe, swim, dive, go boating, have a picnic, and just luxuriate with a leisurely walk in this pristine environment. The waters of John U. Lloyd are packed with fish and colorful sea life. If you'd rather cast your line in the open water, there are two boat ramps with easy access to the ocean through the Port Everglades Inlet. The mangrove-lined waterway is filled with bird life and colorful species of plants. You can attend to those hunger pangs at the Loggerhead Cafe, or buy something to take with you on your adventure. And there's a long list of things you can rent at this park: canoes, kayaks, paddleboats, sailboats, pontoon boats, gazebos, barbecue grills, and volleyballs.

- **Boating**—After you get on the water via either of the two boat ramps, consider heading for Whiskey Creek. At this scenic spot it's easy to beach your boat and enjoy a picnic. Whiskey Creek is a manatee sanctuary that flows through the park, so you may get a chance for a close-up view—or even a close-up interaction—with the friendly "sea cow." The area's filled with wildlife on foot, on the water, and in the air. Motorboats are permitted from the Intracoastal Waterway to just south of the restaurant. There's one ramp that provides access to the Intracoastal and another, about a mile away through the Port Everglades Inlet, that provides access to the ocean. The Loggerhead Cafe is the place to rent canoes and kayaks.

- **Fishing**—Surf fishing is popular here. So somebody must be catching something.
- **Nature Trail**—At the south end of the park, you'll come upon a 45-minute, self-guided nature walk through a subtropical coastal hammock. Here things are still the way they were a thousand years ago. There's a good chance you'll see some of the residents who were here then, too—squirrels, raccoons, and all types and sizes of birds. This is a peaceful piece of Florida the way it once was.
- **Picnics**—John U. Lloyd Beach State Park has seven picnic pavilions, all of which include water, electricity, picnic tables, and a barbecue area. One of them is situated overlooking Port Everglades, where you can enjoy an imposing vista of some of the largest ships in the world coming and going. The pavilions seat between 100 and 150 people. To reserve a pavilion, call (954) 924-3859. In addition, there are over 300 individual picnic tables scattered all over the park.
- **Scuba Diving/Snorkeling**—This park offers one of the easiest and most beautiful shore dives in all of South Florida, and it's popular with snorkelers, as well. Once you swim out to the first reef, you'll see

an incredible—and an incredibly beautiful—array of sea life including tropical and sport fish, sharks, and Florida lobster.
- **Swimming**—Swimming is permitted in designated areas.
- **Wildlife**—It's all over the place!

COUNTY PARKS

Sadly, due to budget cuts, most county parks were closed on Tuesday and Wednesday during the High Season of 2010. Be sure to call ahead for current hours.

BOATERS PARK
North side of the Dania Cutoff Canal, West of Anglers Avenue/Ravenswood Road, Dania Beach
(954) 357-8811
www.broward.org
There's a reason these six-and-a-half acres are called Boaters Park—you can only get there by private boat. Up to 40 boats can dock here, and there are picnic shelters with tables, grills, and nearby restrooms. It's a quiet, pretty place where you can get away from the hubbub of city and suburbs and just spend a relaxing day.

BOULEVARD GARDENS COMMUNITY CENTER
313 NW 28th Terrace, Ft. Lauderdale
(954) 625-2988
www.broward.org
This one-acre park is a new one, opened jointly in 2006 by Broward County and the Boulevard Gardens Community Group for the benefit of a previously underserved area. There are picnic tables, grills, benches, a lighted pathway, and equipment for ball games. The park also has summer recreation programs and sports-development youth programs.

BRIAN PICCOLO PARK
9501 Sheridan St., Cooper City
(954) 437-2600
www.broward.org

This park is named after a local boy who went on to play college football at Wake Forest University, and then pro ball with the Chicago Bears. Brian Piccolo was struck down by cancer at a young age, but he has been memorialized in a famous 1971 TV movie called *Brian's Song*, and in this park that bears his name.

This 180-acre park opened in 1989, and it's been one of southern Broward's most popular places to "play" ever since. It has twelve lighted tennis courts, six lighted racquetball courts (and a pro shop), four lighted softball fields, four lighted multi-purpose fields, three lighted soccer/football fields, two lighted basketball courts, and one unlighted practice field. In fact, there are even two cricket fields—yes, cricket fields—available. And adult softball and flag football leagues are offered year-round.

But that's just the tip of the iceberg. There are biking and jogging paths. A picnic/softball complex loop (1.25 miles); a soccer complex loop (1 mile); and a gatehouse/lake/Palm Avenue loop (2 miles). There's fishing in the lake (licenses required, ages 16 and up). There are four horseshoe courts. There's a large picnic shelter (available by reservation and for a fee). There are tables and grills. There are kiddie play areas. There are 500-meter and 800-meter courses for cyclists, runners, and walkers.

There's a skate park, with 35,000 square feet of wooden ramps and courses for skateboarding, in-line skating, and BMX biking. There are two snack bars. And there's even a velodrome—the only one in Greater Fort Lauderdale—with a 333.3-meter cycling track and a 200-meter banked track for in-line skating. Bike rentals are also available.

C. B. SMITH PARK
900 N. Flamingo Rd., Pembroke Pines
(954) 437-2650
www.broward.org

This park is an old favorite. It's expansive—nearly 300 acres—and has a lot of amenities not often found elsewhere: a water park, for one, called Paradise Cove, with two large water playgrounds, a tube ride on a rushing river, and two of the longest water slides you'll ever see—450 feet each. One of the water playgrounds is designed for toddlers and the other is designed for older "kids." There's also a marina here, where you can rent a paddleboat, johnboat, kayak, or canoe. Rather get around by pedal power instead? You can rent a bike as well at C. B. Smith, but not just any bike. You can get the standard two-wheeler, of course, but you can also rent a banana bike (three wheels), a small surrey bike (seats three people), or a big surrey bike with two seats (for six people).

The AllGolf facility has a driving range, miniature golf course, a covered driving range, a putting area, and a pro shop. And there are also batting cages with variable-speed pitching machines. C.B. Smith Park also has a racquet center with tennis and racquetball courts.

As an added extra, there's even camping here; the sites have full RV hookups, picnic tables, charcoal grills, restrooms with showers, and a laundry room. The campground provides after-hours security. Spots fill up fast, so reservations are highly recommended, especially during the Season.

Oh, yes, there are the usual park facilities, picnic areas and shelters with grills and tables. This park is the site of Greater Fort

Lauderdale's Annual Chili Cook-off, which attracts country-lovin' visitors—and great chili cooks—from all over the region.

CENTRAL BROWARD REGIONAL PARK & STADIUM
3700 NW 11th Place, Lauderhill
(954) 357-5400
www.broward.org

This 110-acre facility has picnic tables scattered throughout, along with picnic shelters with grills, water, and electricity that can be reserved, and several interesting "extras." For one thing, there's a circular multipurpose field for concerts and sporting events, with 5,000 covered seats and viewing space for another 15,000 people. The field is so big—560 feet in diameter—that it can actually be used for several events going on concurrently.

Central Broward also features the Tropical Splash Water Playground, which delights children young and older, and includes a pool that offers water-safety and swimming lessons to children.

You can rent paddleboats at the park, and you can explore nature on a trail that meanders through a beautifully preserved area. Of course, there are soccer and football fields, netball courts, tennis courts, and basketball courts.

DEERFIELD ISLAND PARK
1720 Deerfield Island Park,
Deerfield Beach
(954) 357-5100
www.broward.org

Deerfield Island is a 56-acre nature park that seems a world away from the frantic life just across the water. Accessible only by boat, it's bordered by the Intracoastal Waterway and the Hillsboro and Royal Palm

Canals. There was once a freshwater wetland here, but now the area is filled with red and white mangroves, and tiny islands with thick strands of tropical trees. This park is a Designated Urban Wilderness Area, and you'll come upon its full-time residents occasionally—raccoons, squirrels, gopher turtles, and both migratory and indigenous birds.

You can get here via a free shuttle boat from the Sullivan Park dock on the hour from 10 a.m. to 3 p.m. on weekends only. The last shuttle returning to the mainland leaves the island at 4:30, so bring your watch! Or you can take your own boat; there's a marina with six slips available on a first-come, first-served basis.

There are two trails through the lush vegetation and the wildlife. The half-mile Coquina Trail has an observation platform that overlooks the Intracoastal Waterway, and the Mangrove Trail features a boardwalk through a mangrove swamp. The island has a picnic shelter with a grill, as well as picnic tables and grills scattered about. And from Oct to May on the first Sat of the month there's a free bird walk, led by a guide.

EASTERLIN PARK
1000 NW 38th St., Oakland Park
(954) 938-0610
www.broward.org

Easterlin Park is a 47-acre Designated Urban Wilderness Area and a wonderful example of a preserved mixed cypress forest in the middle of town. These trees have been here a whole lot longer than the town has—some of them are 250 years old (pre-Revolutionary War!) and more than 100 feet tall. The park seems larger than it is, as it's buffered from the outside world by thick wild coffee, ferns, dahoon holly, cabbage palm, oak, red maple, and a scenic lake. Although nature is king here, there's also a playground, a picnic shelter (reservation suggested), nature trails, horseshoes, volleyball, and an 18-hole disc golf course.

A place this beautiful should have a campground—and it does. There are 45 paved RV sites with water, sewer, and electricity (but this is "primitive" camping, there are no outlets for phone or cable). Seven of these sites are pull-through sites, and ten are for tents, six of which have water and electrical hookups. Camping is permitted on designated sites only, and one camping unit is allowed on each site. Showers and a dump station are available.

The campground is open all year. As you might imagine, however, it's busiest during the Season, especially from December through March; reservations are a good idea. A soda machine and ice are available at the park office, and a sanitary dump station is located at the campground exit for your convenience.

FERN FOREST NATURE CENTER
201 Lyons Rd. South, Coconut Creek
(954) 970-0150
www.broward.org

This area is filled with interesting wildlife, beautiful foliage, tiny ponds, and streams, and you can stroll a boardwalk right through it all.

The **Nature Center Exhibit Area** is filled with exhibits about the land's history, both natural and man-made. Inside here, you can see a number of snakes on display. At the back of the nature center—where all the trails wandering through it begin—stands the *Fern-Lore Guardian* sculpture, created by Jerome Meadows.

There are six picnic tables available on a first-come, first-served basis. (No fires or grills permitted.) The trails are wonderful. The **Cypress Creek Trail** is a half-mile wheelchair-accessible boardwalk through a tropical hardwood hammock, cypress-maple swamp, and transitional communities. The **Butterfly Bridge** overlooks a canal in which you'll see many marine animals. If you'd like a longer walk, try the **Prairie Overlook Trail,** a one-miler that goes through a prairie habitat and stands of slash pine, oak, and palm. (Don't forget to stop at the Prairie Overlook, an observation platform looking out over the prairie. If you like wet walks, bring your hiking boots and wander through the **Maple Walk Trail**—a third-of-a-mile through a red maple swamp. And keep 'em on for the **Wetland Wonder Trail,** an eighth-of-a-mile trail along a canal with a wetland community and a garden filled with beautiful butterflies.

FRANKLIN PARK
2501 Franklin Dr., Ft. Lauderdale
(954) 791-1037
www.broward.org

Franklin Park started out as a neighborhood facility in an underserved area, but the county bought it in 1999 and pumped $2 million into improvements. Now there's playground equipment, a lighted basketball court, picnic shelters, a walking trail, and a community center building with a kitchen, restrooms, and activity rooms. One of the activity rooms at Franklin Park has computers, and both children and adults are free to use them to improve their computer skills.

HOLLYWOOD NORTH BEACH PARK
3601 N. Ocean Dr., Hollywood
(954) 926-2410
www.broward.org

This is a 56-acre park to which local residents flock on weekends because those 56 acres encompass a mile of beachfront and the Intracoastal Waterway. No matter where you look or where you stand, it's a beautiful setting.

On the ocean side, the **Turtle Cafe** concession is stocked with hamburgers, hot dogs, fries, pizza, ice cream, and sodas. While you're ordering the goodies, be sure and take a look around; the concession area has a raised deck with a wonderful view of the ocean. Nearby you'll also find restrooms, picnic spots, tables, and grills. For a genuine bird's-eye view, clamber up the 60-foot observation tower that offers an incredible 360-degree panorama of the area.

The Intracoastal side of the park features two large picnic shelters, the Bridge and the Cove, each with water, electricity, a large grill, and tables. There's also a volleyball area here (and restrooms), along with other picnic areas with tables and grills. And if you're the type who'd rather grill something you've caught yourself, there's good pier fishing here.

Hollywood North also has a couple of special programs, the **Sea Turtle Program** and the **Night Hike by the Seashore.** Four different species of sea turtles use South Florida's beaches during the spring and summer months to lay their eggs and then incubate them, and hatchlings generally emerge six to eight weeks later. The Sea Turtle Program enables you to explore firsthand the mysterious life of sea turtles, and their difficult fight for survival (most of the hatchlings never make it out to sea successfully). On Wed evenings from July through Sept, you can participate in seaside releases of hatchlings; reservations required. Similarly, the Night Hike by the Seashore is a wonderful event for families.

LAFAYETTE HART PARK
2851 NW 8th Rd., Ft. Lauderdale
(954) 791-1041
www.broward.org
This is a small park—only a bit more than an acre. But it's got basketball courts, a picnic shelter, a small playground, tennis courts, and a racquetball court. The park also offers summer recreation and youth sports-development programs.

LONG KEY NATURAL AREA AND
  NATURE CENTER
3501 SW 130th Ave., Davie
(954) 357-8797
www.broward.org
This 157-acre site is a true natural wonderland, filled with interesting habitats and inhabitants. For example, among the inhabitants you'll find pileated woodpeckers, great horned owls, screech owls, ospreys, great egrets, herons, bobcats, foxes, and queen and zebra longwing butterflies. And the reason for all this wildlife is that, only a hundred years ago, this elevated oak hammock was an island, one of many surrounded by the swamps and marshes of the "River of Grass"—the Everglades. And before that, there were apparently other inhabitants of the area besides wildlife. There is archaeological and historical evidence here that this was a busy center of 19th-century Seminole life, which makes Long Key a sort of living history book on the ecology, animal life, geological forces, and human residents of this area in earlier times.

The site is filled with hardwood forests of oak, red bay, paradise tree, satin leaf, strangler fig, hackberry, cabbage palm, and the wonderfully named gumbo limbo. Long Key also has another living history "book"—a 14-acre orange grove that reminds us of the once-thriving citrus industry here—along with new marshes that have become home to various species of wetland birds. The park is dotted with ponds and canals, and there's also a bird roost/rookery. And if you're a horseback rider, this is a beautiful spot in which to take a trot; there are two equestrian trails.

There's a half-mile trail through the oak hammock that you can hike by yourself, or you can take a guided nature walk, available on request, with a park naturalist. To make a reservation for a guided nature walk, please call the nature center at (954) 357-8797, and ask to speak to a park naturalist.

You'll also find an interesting nature center that details the natural and human history of the area, with an exhibit hall, live animals, an interactive replica of an archeological "dig" pit, and a mural-like photograph of Florida's natural beauty.

MARKHAM PARK
16001 W. SR 84, Sunrise
(954) 389-2000
www.broward.org
This is a huge park, a multifaceted place that's one of the great gathering grounds for residents of Greater Fort Lauderdale. And it has some very unique activities and spaces.

For example, there's an airfield—a 50-acre parcel in which aficionados of remote-control aircraft and helicopters can have a field day. The runway has recently been expanded, and this is now considered one of the finest airfields of its kind in America. There are numerous events and competitions here, which really bring out the devotees and their planes. Both an Academy of Model Aeronautics (AMA) and a Markham Park flying card are required to fly here. You can even receive instruction in radio control;

for information contact **Fly Right** at (954) 816-4410.

But the airfield is just one of the unique aspects that make Markham Park so great. There's also a personal watercraft lake: 26 acres of open waters where you can zoom and hum in your own motorized craft to your heart's delight, on weekends and holidays from mid-Mar through the end of Oct. If you'd rather use someone else's boat, and would rather hear the breeze instead of an engine, the park has paddleboats, kayaks, and canoes for rent. There are also mountain bike trails here—11 challenging miles of them—for the novice, intermediate, and expert rider. Markham is also the home of the South Florida Amateur Astronomers Association, which opens its observatory to the public every Saturday night, without charge. There's also a playground, tennis and racquetball courts, and a campground with 88 hookups.

And there's one more surprise that Markham Park has. **Barkham** at Markham is a park specifically for—you guessed it—man's best friend. There are three-and-a-half acres for Fido and Fifi to romp with their friends and enjoy the doggie toys.

PLANTATION HERITAGE PARK
1100 S. Fig Tree Lane, Plantation
(954) 791-1025
www.broward.org
This 90-acre park was formerly a University of Florida agricultural experimentation farm. And it doesn't look all that different from those days, with flowering trees and palms all over the place. The Broward County Audubon Society's **Anne Kolb Memorial Trail** meanders through scenic plant communities, and there's a rare fruit area as well. The park has plenty of picnic areas and

playgrounds, as well as nature trails and a fitness trail, which are put to good use by local fitness buffs. There's a duck pond and a beautiful gazebo surrounded by lush vegetation. And bring your rod, because there's fishing here, too.

QUIET WATERS PARK
401 S. Powerline Rd., Deerfield Beach
(954) 357-5100
www.broward.org
Quiet Waters is one of northern Broward's great weekend hideouts. This 430-acre park is one of the most popular in Broward for the beauty of its surroundings, for the events that take place here, and for the myriad recreational options. It's particularly attractive to the extreme-sports crowd, who can stay busy all day long here. There's a lake with a cable water-skiing and wakeboarding park called **Ski Rixen.** There are 7 miles of novice and intermediate mountain-bike trails. On the large lake, you can rent paddleboats, johnboats, or canoes and spend a lazy afternoon in the sun and the quiet little coves. The lake is also open for fishing.

You can jog on any number of trails. And there's a Rent-a-Tent campground where you can rent a site with a tent or tepee already set up. Each of these sits on a platform, and each has running water and electricity, a fire ring, picnic table, and grill. There are restrooms and shower facilities, and you can buy firewood and ice at the park office. Reservations are required.

Quiet Waters Park also has two other special features. One of them is its popular **Splash Adventure water park,** an interactive watery wonderland for kids. And the other is the **Renaissance Fair,** which sets up tents (literally) here every year from mid-Feb to mid-Mar and envelops its thousands of visitors in a world of medieval magic, with period costumes and crafts, jousting on trusty steeds by knights in armor, poets and folksingers, damsels with flowing dresses, and minstrels in funny hats playing the instruments of the time.

REVEREND SAMUEL DELEVOE PARK
2520 NW 6th St., Ft. Lauderdale
(954) 791-1036
www.broward.org
This neighborhood park, on the north fork of the New River, started out as a golf course. Now it shares a 36-acre site with the **African-American Research Library and Cultural Center,** which is adorned by colorful ceramic tiles by a local artist. The park features a lake (with a fountain in the middle) with two piers for fishing and a canoe launch, basketball courts, a picnic shelter, a playground, a volleyball area, and a game room, along with computers for public use. It's named after one of Fort Lauderdale's first African-American police officers, who was shot and killed in 1977.

ROOSEVELT GARDENS PARK
2841 NW 11th St., Ft. Lauderdale
(954) 327-3888
www.broward.org
Roosevelt Gardens is a cozy neighborhood park, and some of its most frequent users live within only a few blocks. The park has three playground areas, two full-court basketball courts with lighting, and three picnic shelters (two with grills). There's also a pathway around the park for walking, skating, or strolling.

SECRET WOODS NATURE CENTER
2701 W. SR 84, Dania Beach
(954) 791-1030
www.broward.org

This is not a park; it's a nature center with all that's beautiful about South Florida on vivid, colorful display. One of the most beautiful things about the center is the peace and quiet. It's a deep forest, filled with trees such as laurel oaks, strangler fig trees, cabbage palms, and red bay, and distinctive wetland plants.

One of the newest parts of the center is **Butterfly Island,** a butterfly garden that you walk through while surrounded by different species of fluttering butterflies of a hundred colors and plants that attract them. You'll see monarch butterflies, zebra longwing, cloudless sulphur, queen, gulf fritillary, giant swallowtail, and atala hairstreak. And you'll most likely take the walk down the path several times.

Secret Woods has two nature trails, the 1,200-foot-long **Laurel Oak Trail** and the 3,200-foot-long **New River Trail,** a board-walk that winds its way out to the south fork of the New River. Each trail has benches along the way for you to stop, look, and lis-ten to nature at its most soothing. On each walk you'll see a variety of birds, squirrels, crabs, and lizards. You can learn more about what you're looking at in the **Monarch Interpretive Center,** which has exhibits about this habitat. There you'll see a live, working bee hive, and watch as the bees make honey, clean their hive, and bring back pollen. You'll also get an up-close-and-per-sonal look into a reptile habitat. History takes shape with the artifacts of Native Americans from this area, and a beautiful mural depict-ing Native Americans as they approach Frank Stranahan's Fort Lauderdale house to trade goods. And there are hands-on and interac-tive activities for children.

TRADEWINDS PARK
3600 W. Sample Rd., Coconut Creek
(954) 357-8870
Stables: (954) 357-8720
www.broward.org
This is one of northern Broward's best-loved parks; there's something for everyone here, in 627 acres of rolling meadows and forest. Here you can play on a disc golf course. You can jog. You can wander on beautiful paths. The kids can enjoy two colorful, well-equipped playgrounds. You can picnic with your friends and family under shelters and tents. You can rent sports equipment, or you can bring your own pole and try your luck at one of the various lakes and ponds on the premises. You can pedal through the park. Or, you can stand back and watch the kids yell with joy as they take a pony ride at the farm complex, which also includes the **Country House Museum** and a general store. In addition, you can mount up yourself and ride horseback on the park's numerous trails.

TREE TOPS PARK
3900 SW 100th Ave., Davie
(954) 357-5130
www.broward.org
Tree Tops Park is 243 acres of varied habitats and an incredible variety of things you can do on them. Among its many offerings are shaded equestrian trails, guided horseback rides, picnic shelters, boat rentals, three play-grounds, nature trails, a butterfly garden, a marsh observation area, primitive group camping, campfire ring, picnic tables, grills, and an observation tower from which you can watch everybody else doing all these things. The park doesn't ignore kids either; there's an area called **Safety Town,** with miniature roadways and intersections, where kids can learn bicycle safety basics.

T. Y. (TOPEEKEEGEE YUGNEE) PARK
3300 N. Park Rd., Hollywood
(954) 357-8811
www.broward.org

In the Seminole Indian language, "topee-keegee yugnee" means meeting or gathering place. And they must have known something, because residents of Greater Fort Lauderdale have been gathering in this wonderful park for years. And millions of dollars have been spent to improve the park in recent years. For example, the popular campground has been totally renovated, and now has 61 RV sites with full hookups, as well as restrooms, showers, and laundry facilities. Other improvements include a new pool, basketball courts, and replenished wooded areas, replacing the trees that were downed in 2005's Hurricane Wilma. There are 2 miles of pathways for walking, jogging, biking, or skating.

The park also now has a water park complex called **Castaway Island,** with two water-play areas. Paddleboats, kayaks, and canoes are available for rental at the lake, as are bicycles in the park. In addition, of course, T. Y. Park has all the usual amenities—basketball and volleyball courts and picnic tables.

VISTA VIEW PARK
4001 SW 142nd Ave., Davie
(954) 357-8898
www.broward.org

Vista View's loaded with things to do—picnic sites, playgrounds, basketball courts, boat rentals, equestrian corral and 2-mile trail looping around the park, an airstrip for electric radio-controlled plane and glider pilots, fishing docks, and an area for primitive group camping. Its 272 acres are somewhat hilly (for Florida) and a great place to jog or exercise for those who enjoy doing it a little bit higher than sea level. Another place enjoyed by the athletic set is the half-mile fitness trail, with stations along the way. Vista View is scenic, multifaceted, and a great place to spend a weekend afternoon.

WEST LAKE PARK
751 Sheridan St., Hollywood
(954) 926-2480
www.broward.org

West Lake Park is sacred to South Florida because there are few places that better display the region's natural diversity and water environments—and because this is pretty much what all of coastal South Florida once looked like. The park sits astride a 3-mile strip of mangrove estuary and uplands lining the Intracoastal Waterway. In fact, it's the largest remaining mangrove ecosystem between Miami and West Palm Beach. And, as it sits on the Intracoastal, you can access it from the water; there's a 175-foot dock.

On the north side of the park is the highly regarded **Anne Kolb Nature Center,** with an exhibit hall, three boardwalk trails and a gravel trail through the mangrove preserve, an observation tower with great views, dock, and a boat tour of this unique (and endangered) habitat. The Anne Kolb Center is a beautiful monument to the ecosystem of Greater Fort Lauderdale and the varied forms of life that still live here.

On the opposite side of the park, the south side, there are the more traditional trappings of a park: picnic shelters, playgrounds (one with a water feature), a fishing dock, a walking path, tennis and basketball courts, sand volleyball courts, racquetball courts, boat rentals, and a boat launch for canoes and kayaks. Bike and boat rentals are available.

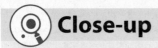

Close-up

Blue Wave Beaches

According to the Greater Fort Lauderdale Convention & Visitors Bureau, "You're in Good Sands" when you visit one of the area's great beaches. But the bureau wants to make sure you're in good *hands,* as well, by using common sense and taking some sensible precautions.

Hollywood, Dania Beach, Deerfield Beach, Pompano Beach, and Fort Lauderdale have been certified as **Blue Wave Beaches** by the Clean Beaches Council of Washington, DC.—every year for the past 10 years. That means they've been certified as clean, safe, comfortable, and user-friendly. To be certified as a "Blue Wave Beach," beaches have to abide by a code of ethics.

Seven Blue Wave Beach Ethics:
1. Leave no trace (what you carry in, carry out)
2. Move your body (walk, run, or swim)
3. Don't tread the dunes (use a walkover or walk-thru)
4. Know your limits (swim, surf, and boat safely)
5. You are what you eat (eat healthy seafood)
6. Feed your mind (read a book)
7. Respect the ocean (riptides, storms)

In the case of Greater Fort Lauderdale, we might want to add an eighth: Respect the integrity and the nesting places of sea turtles.

BEACHES

Dania Beach

This is one of Greater Fort Lauderdale's hidden gems, and it's home to some of the prettiest and least crowded stretches of ocean. **Dania Beach Ocean Park** (100 North Beach Rd., Dania; 954-924-3696) has an impressive fishing pier where you can catch your own dinner or enjoy the catch of one of the restaurants there, which offer beautiful views and fresh seafood that was in the ocean just an hour or two earlier.

JOHN U. LLOYD BEACH STATE PARK
6503 N. Ocean Dr.
(954) 923-2833
www.floridastateparks.org

This is one of South Florida's most beautiful play spots located at the north end of North Ocean Boulevard, a quarter-mile north of Dania Beach Boulevard. Here, in addition to the winding nature paths and access to both the Intracoastal Waterway and the Atlantic, you can kayak, swim, picnic, or just lie back and watch the clouds float by while listening to the ocean. Concessions, lifeguards, restrooms, picnic tables, and showers.

Deerfield Beach

The coves of Deerfield Beach are a great way to experience the sunrise over Greater Fort Lauderdale, as an orange ball peeks over the horizon and then slowly spreads its warming—and color-changing—rays over

The Secret Woods Nature Center

The **Secret Woods Nature Center,** in Dania Beach, has something of an interesting history. The land originally consisted of some 30 acres known as the Rebecca Cohen Subdivision. Local officials decided to rezone this parcel in 1971, to—pardon the pun—pave the way for a parking lot. But local folks weren't going to take the loss of their "Secret Woods" lying down. They raised a royal ruckus and they won. The officials apparently figured it wouldn't be a politically wise decision to rezone, and instead ended up selling most of the property to the Nature Conservancy. Shortly afterward, Broward County agreed to buy the land within three years.

They did so in 1975, and bought surrounding parcels over the succeeding years to bring the park up to 56 acres. Secret Woods was the first nature center in Greater Fort Lauderdale (although it's listed as a county park) when it opened in 1978. And it was all because local residents didn't want to lose their special place and fought for it.

the restaurants right across from the beach, enjoying a whiff of sea air with your food. The beach runs to the north and south of the pier, which is at the east end of 2nd Street. Concessions, lifeguards, restrooms, picnic tables, and showers are available. For more information call (954) 480-4412.

Fort Lauderdale

This, of course, is where the rest of the world first saw—and fell in love with—Broward County's beaches, in the 1960 movie *Where the Boys Are*. As we've said elsewhere in this book, Lauderdale's no longer a Spring Break mecca; it's now a family-friendly, beach-chic destination that's attracting a new type of visitor. From the "Lauderdale Luxe" hotels piercing the beachfront skyline to the funky shops and bistros, this beach is still attracting visitors from all over the globe. **Fort Lauderdale Beach,** which was widened and renovated in the '90s, has some of the best people watching in South Florida. And many of the people you'll be watching will be strolling, jogging, or skating past you, along the brick-lined beachfront promenade fringed with palm trees.

FORT LAUDERDALE CITY BEACH (CENTRAL AREA)
Sunrise Boulevard south to Las Olas Boulevard, along North Ocean Boulevard
Lifeguard Office: (954) 468-1595
Lifeguards, showers.

FORT LAUDERDALE CITY BEACH (NORTH AREA)
Oakland Park Boulevard south to Northeast 20th Street, along North Atlantic Boulevard
Lifeguard Office: (954) 468-1595
Lifeguards, showers.

the ocean and toward the shore on which you're standing. This is the northernmost beach in Broward County, and you can fish off the **Deerfield Beach International Fishing Pier.** You can also enjoy hearty American comfort food at a couple of places right on the beach. And you can dine al fresco at

FORT LAUDERDALE CITY BEACH (SOUTH AREA)
Las Olas Boulevard south to Port Everglades, along South Ocean Boulevard
Lifeguard Office: (954) 468-1595
Concessions, lifeguards, restrooms, picnic tables, and showers.

HUGH TAYLOR BIRCH STATE PARK
3109 E. Sunrise Blvd.
(954) 564-4521
www.floridastateparks.org
This has been a popular place to play—and relax in the sun—for decades. Follow Sunrise Boulevard in Fort Lauderdale east to the ocean. It's a pretty, peaceful place. Lifeguards, restrooms, picnic tables, showers, and a visitor center.

Hallandale Beach

At the southern end of Greater Fort Lauderdale, Hallandale Beach is a sportsmen's paradise, with inviting, clear waters that seem to dance in the sun. And it's the perfect place to leave everything behind and jump on a boat, either to fish or to relax (which, of course, is the same thing to a fisherman!). There are some beautiful stretches of beach here, and they're often less crowded than some of the other beaches up the coast.

Hillsboro Beach

This is the place to go when you want to unwind and when you want to feel the stresses of everyday life just slip away from your body and your consciousness. Hillsboro Beach is considered Greater Fort Lauderdale's quiet escape. The old **Hillsboro Lighthouse** still stands as a proud sentinel here at the entrance to the **Hillsboro Inlet,** where magnificent

yachts now enter, instead of the plunder-laden ships that once sought refuge here. Nearby is an impressive stone statue dedicated to the **"Barefoot Mailman."** From 1885 until 1892, mail carriers would make a seven-day journey from Palm Beach to Miami by walking 68 miles barefoot through the sand, braving all kinds of natural and wildlife hazards.

Beat the Heat . . . and the Traffic

If you're thinking of heading out to the beach on a weekend, think about doing it early or late. Early afternoon is the worst time; not only is there heavy traffic, but you could spend a while sitting at a drawbridge that's been raised for boat traffic. Certain east–west roads out to the various beaches—such as Sunrise Boulevard in Fort Lauderdale or Hillsboro Boulevard in Deerfield Beach—can get really crowded from noon until two. Add in red lights and drawbridges, and the trip may take longer than you'd like. But go in the morning, or later in the day, and you won't have nearly as much traffic. And if you're concerned about skin damage from the sun, there's an extra bonus: You won't be sitting in the sun in the middle of the day, when the rays are strongest.

Hollywood Beach

Hollywood Beach is retro—its famous **Broadwalk** runs for 2.5 miles up this sun-kissed oceanfront. And it's lined with funky, colorful, and unusual shops, selling everything from surfing gear to Canadian newspapers for the large French-Canadian population that winters here. This is a popular place for the jogging and skating crowd, and the people watching (especially during the Season) is great. The Broadwalk is lined with outdoor cafes, offering everything from "dogs" with the works to French-Canadian specialties. There's also a section of the beach for dogs and their human friends; part of the movie *Marley & Me* was filmed here.

Lauderdale-by-the-Sea

This cozy village is one of Broward County's low-key getaways, where the sounds of the ocean are the loudest ones you'll hear, rather than traffic or noise. It's only a half-mile-wide strip of beach, with a welcoming, old-fashioned "beach village" ambience. Lauderdale-by-the-Sea is one of the only locations in Florida where the three-tiered natural coral reef is close enough to swim to (and it's fantastic for snorkeling or diving). On Friday nights, the one street that runs through this sleepy town is blocked off to traffic, and most of the local folks bring their chairs to listen to live musical concerts. Follow Commercial Boulevard all the way east to the sea.

Concessions, picnic tables, and showers are on-site. Lauderdale-by-the-Sea Public Works Department, (954) 776-0576.

Pompano Beach

This town is named for the saltwater fish found exclusively in these waters, and it's home to such noted South Florida events as the annual Pompano Seafood Festival and the Fishing Rodeo. Because of a curve in the Gulf Stream, this stretch of coastline offers some of the warmest and clearest waters in South Florida, and needless to say, some of the best fishing spots in South Florida as well. The public beach is located at 10 N. Pompano Beach Blvd., at Atlantic Avenue, and offers concessions, restrooms, picnic tables, and showers. Lifeguards are on duty. For more information, call the **Pompano Beach Parks and Recreation Department,** (954) 786-4111.

NORTH OCEAN PARK
NE 16th Street and N. Ocean Boulevard
Pompano Beach Parks and Recreation
Department
(954) 786-4111
Restrooms, picnic tables, and showers.

SPECTATOR SPORTS

If you've got the time, we've got the teams in just about any sport—college or pro—and in any season. If you're the type who waits all winter long for baseball, we've got it: Major League, Minor League, and Spring Training. If you long for the color and pageantry of football, we've got it—college and pro. If basketball season brings you out of your seat (either at the game or in your living room), we've got it. If soccer is "the beautiful game" to you, as it is to much of the world, we've got it. If, to you, there's no sound quite like the crack of a hockey stick on a puck, we've got it—sorry, no college, only pro.

In fact, Broward County's got balls of all sizes, colors, and shapes flying around all year long, as well as pucks. All you have to do is pick a sport, pick a day, and get in the car. Every day of the year here, someone's playing it!

SPORTS TEAMS & EVENTS

Auto Racing

HOMESTEAD-MIAMI SPEEDWAY
One Speedway Blvd., Homestead
(866) 409-7223
www.homesteadmiamispeedway.com
From Fort Lauderdale: Go south on I-95, past Miami. Continue south on U.S.1, then look for signs to the track. Homestead, about an hour south of Fort Lauderdale in Miami–Dade County, is a place that has risen from the (almost) dead in recent years. For many years it was known as the home of the giant Homestead Air Force Base, as well as the Homestead Speedway. However, the air base closed some years back, devastating the economy of an already troubled city. Then, in 1992, Hurricane Andrew (a category five) hit head-on here, basically destroying everything in its path, and leaving the city with hardly a building still standing. But Homestead has been on the way back, thanks in no small part to the rebuilding of the racetrack (into a better racetrack) and

the emergence of the track as the site of important national competitions. And when the Season starts, the action at Homestead is almost nonstop. Major events that often take place here include the **Firestone Indy Lights Championship,** the **IZOD IndyCar Series Championship,** and the **Ford 200, 300, and 400 events**. There are now 65,000 seats around the 1.5-mile oval. And on race days they're filled with people who spend much of the time standing rather than sitting, screaming at the tops of their voices for their favorites. The color, the jet-age lines of the cars, the roar of the engines, the dramatic, fast-motion pit stops, the pre-race tailgating (and the smells of the food being barbecued and grilled), the international superstars who are racing, the international celebrities who are watching, the food, and the American pageantry all make a day at Homestead-Miami Speedway one that you won't soon forget. (There's no set schedule of events; there are events of one kind or another about 280 days of the year here.)

PALM BEACH INTERNATIONAL RACEWAY

(Formerly Moroso Motorsports Park)
17047 Beeline Hwy., Jupiter
(561) 622-1400
www.morosomotorsportspark.com

About an hour north of Fort Lauderdale on I-95, in the Palm Beach County town of Jupiter, you'll find a place to which South Floridians have been streaming for decades to enjoy all manner of stock-car races. There's a road-racing course, with an 11-turn, 2.034-mile design and some of the fastest and most challenging corners, elevation changes, and straightaways offered by any track in North America. In fact, it's an approved testing facility for Indy cars. And one of the best things about the course is that you can learn to drive a race car on it; there are several schools that give driving lessons here (Speed Karts racing league and oval league; 561-622-1400). Then there's the original drag strip, the strip that first put this place on the map. It's a well-known proving ground for hardcore hot-rodders. And the original challenge still holds true here—go fast or go home. It's a quarter-mile strip that hosts various national, regional, and local events, including the **IHRA** (International Hot Rod Association) **Palm Beach Nitro Jam.** And that's not all. At Palm Beach International Raceway, you can take to the track yourself—on the go-kart course! You'll negotiate 11 turns on this 0.8-mile course, and each one will be thrilling, whether you're an amateur or a pro. It's considered one of the best go-kart tracks in the country and, in fact, is listed as a Master Track by the World Karting Association (WKA). The track is home

to various club racing series, as well as major events like the Annual 24-hours of America and the WKA Florida Karting Championship Series. (Note: There's no set schedule; events occur randomly throughout the year.)

Minor League Baseball

JUPITER HAMMERHEADS
Roger Dean Stadium
4751 Main St., Jupiter
(561) 775-1818
http://jupiter.hammerheads.milb.com

PALM BEACH CARDINALS
Roger Dean Stadium
4751 Main St., Jupiter
(561) 775-1818
http://palmbeach.cardinals.milb.com

If you love Minor League baseball, you'll probably want to make the one-hour drive north on I-95 from Fort Lauderdale to the town of Jupiter in northern Palm Beach County. Minor League baseball is alive and well here, with affiliates of two Major League teams, the hometown **Florida Marlins** (Jupiter Hammerheads) and the **St. Louis Cardinals** (Palm Beach Cardinals). Minor league games offer really fun baseball experiences but without the cost and without the traffic. The baseball's good, the beer's cold, the hot dogs are hot, and the fans really get into it. It's a fun day or night for the whole family, without costing you an arm and a leg.

And you can get a sneak peek at the players you may be seeing in a Marlins uniform some day, and some of the players who will be performing at their new stadium in Miami when it's unveiled in 2012. Seeing good Minor League baseball is almost like going "back to the future," because you can see the future. You can see some of "the kids" who will be the next generation of

My Fort Lauderdale

When I moved to Broward County with my family in August 1974, Douglas Road was the end of the Earth. At least that's how it seemed to me, as a transplanted New Yorker. I went to Miramar High School, and to the west of that, besides the police station and bowling alley on the corner, cow pastures and fields stretched as far as the eye could see. (I wasn't much of a bowler, but I remember liking the french fries at the snack stand.)

It was in Miramar that I found the first group of friends that would smooth my way into becoming a Floridian, which is no small feat for a teenage transplant. They were a wonderful, warm group from the synagogue my family joined, and I will be forever grateful to them for making alien terrain become home.

I remember weekends dressing up and heading with friends to Fort Lauderdale beach, for no other reason than to be part of the scene on A1A, part of the moving mass of young people that made Fort Lauderdale the Spring Break capital of the world for so many years. You never knew what fleeting friendships you would make for the evening, what dance floor you would end up dancing upon for hours on end, what stories you would bring home for your friends in school the next day. It all seemed so safe, so innocent, so fun!

Fast-forward 35 years, married and moved south of the border (Miami-Dade), I visit Broward now for two big reasons—my family, who still live there; and my work as a TV news reporter. Our humble home in Miramar, what used to be the end of the Earth, is now actually the center of town—as the sprawling subdivisions of suburbia have stretched to the edge of the Everglades!

—Glenna Milberg, Reporter, ABC-TV (WPLG) Miami/Fort Lauderdale

Marlins, who will try to continue the team's somewhat-new, exciting tradition —but one with two World Series victories in its first 11 seasons.

Who will make "the Show"—the big club in St. Louis—this year? Or next? Who look like the best prospects? And who look like they'll be catching a train or plane back home pretty soon? The St. Louis Cardinals have one of the proudest histories—and possibly the best fans—in baseball. In fact, Cardinals' baseball is almost like a religion back home by the big arch on the Mississippi River. You can watch the big club train here every spring, and play their home exhibition games here. And you can take a sneak peek at who might be playing under the arch in the near future. It's a great family day, for a great family price.

But lest we forget, the big guys train here as well. Both of the parent clubs, the Marlins and Cardinals, hold Spring Training here, and both play their home Spring Training games here. So, if you're here in March, you'll get a sneak preview of what to expect from these two teams during the upcoming season.

Major League Baseball

FLORIDA MARLINS
Sun Life Stadium
2269 Dan Marino Blvd., Miami Gardens
(305) 623-6100
Florida Marlins Tickets: (877) MARLINS
www.sunlifestadium.com
www.floridamarlins.com
www.ticketmaster.com

The Florida Marlins have had one of the most successful first two decades of just about any team in Major League history; they've already won two World Series championships, in 1997 and in 2003. They habitually produce young teams that are always exciting to watch, and generally in the play-off race (if not always in the thick of pennant races).

The Marlins play at the aforementioned Sun Life Stadium, on the Miami–Dade County–Broward County line, about 15 miles southwest of Fort Lauderdale (Dan Marino Boulevard edit off the Florida Turnpike). The team's big news of late, actually, is that they're leaving Sun Life Stadium. It's a facility that was built for football, not baseball, and it's too large for the smaller crowds attracted by baseball (which, after all, has a 162-game schedule, as opposed to the 16 games of pro football). So "the Fish" are building themselves a new stadium—a *baseball* stadium—in downtown Miami. It'll be a stunningly modern showpiece with a partial roof, on the spot where the legendary Orange Bowl stood for 70 years. The new stadium will be ready for the 2012 season, and South Florida baseball fans are already watching it go up with great interest. When it opens, the Marlins will officially become the Miami Marlins, not the Florida Marlins.

In the meantime, it's still a jolly good show at Sun Life Stadium. The game is still baseball. The Marlins still field exciting young teams. The crack of bat against ball—especially to real baseball fans—still sounds the same. And the hot dogs are still just as good. Visit from April through September.

College Basketball

BROWARD COLLEGE BASKETBALL
  (MEN'S & WOMEN'S)
Central Campus
George Mayer Gym
3501 Davie Rd., Davie
(954) 201-6500
www.broward.edu/athletics/

Broward College was formerly, for many years, Broward Community College. Now it's a four-year school, playing basketball at the George Mayer Gym on its central campus in Davie (as opposed to the main campus in downtown Fort Lauderdale), about 10 miles west of Lauderdale.

FLORIDA ATLANTIC UNIVERSITY
  BASKETBALL
FAU Arena
777 Glades Rd., Boca Raton
Ticket Office: (866) FAU-OWLS
www.fausports.com
www.ticketmaster.com

The main Florida Atlantic University (FAU) campus is just across the Palm Beach County line (north of Broward) in Boca Raton. From Fort Lauderdale take I-95 north about 15 miles. Exit at Glades Road, heading east. The campus is on the left. The Owls basketball teams—both men's and women's—play in modern, comfortable FAU Arena. It's a beautiful place, although a bit unusual in one respect: The most-comfortable padded seats are actually in the upper half of the arena, rather than the lower. (The nice arena, no

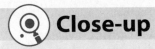

Close-up

The *Sun-Sentinel*'s Ethan Skolnick on Sports

From a sports perspective, I was very sad to see the Yankees and then the Orioles leave their spring-training home at Fort Lauderdale Stadium. It's sad to see the place now; there were so many great memories there. But there's still so much going on here. The Florida Panthers hockey games draw very passionate crowds. (And they'd draw much bigger ones if they were a bit more competitive, and made the playoffs.) And it's a very exciting atmosphere for families and kids.

And in July and August, Broward County is really the center of sports in South Florida. That's when the Miami Dolphins hold their pre-season training camp at their complex in Davie. It's the best free sports entertainment in South Florida. For all the other major-league teams we have here, the Dolphins are still the most important professional sports franchise in South Florida. And they were the first. I'm always there the first Saturday of training camp, when you can really see the way local people are looking forward to another season. I really consider the Dolphins to be sort of a Broward County team. They play on the Dade-Broward line. They run dozens of major charity events in Broward. And they train in Broward.

—Ethan Skolnick, Sportswriter, *South Florida Sun-Sentinel.*

doubt, contributes to the fact that the Miami Heat holds their preseason training camp here.) Both the men's and women's teams are generally competitive in the Sunbelt Conference, and the games are exciting. The FAU campus is very easy to get to, just off the Glades Road exit on I-95 (go east) in Boca Raton; it's a 20–30 minute drive from Fort Lauderdale, and tickets are reasonably priced. And several excellent restaurants are right across the street.

NOVA SOUTHEASTERN UNIVERSITY (MEN'S AND WOMEN'S BASKETBALL)
Don Taft University Center
3301 College Ave., Davie
(954) 262-5730
www.nsuathletics.nova.edu/index.cfm
The Nova Southeastern University Sharks play basketball in the Sunshine State Conference. The Sharks play their games in the Don Taft University Center, which has 4,500 seats; it's generally referred to as "the Shark Tank." And it's a fun—and inexpensive—way to watch college basketball. From Fort Lauderdale take I-595 west. Exit at Davie Boulevard; head south. The campus is on the left; look for signs.

Pro Basketball

MIAMI HEAT
American Airlines Arena
601 Biscayne Blvd., Miami
Ticket Information: (786) 777-1250
www.miamiheat.com
www.ticketmaster.com
The Miami Heat was born in 1988, and downtown Miami hasn't been the same since. Before, downtown was not particularly a place you wanted to be after dark. The Heat, however, has helped reinvigorate Miami, a city that now has one of the most impressive

skylines in America. American Airlines Arena is right across the street from Bayside, a harborside collection of funky shops and kiosks in a Caribbean-marketplace theme. And Gloria Estefan's Bongos restaurant is actually attached to the arena—distinguished by the two-story pineapple sticking out of the roof.

The Heat won the National Basketball Association championship in 2006. When Shaquille O'Neal played for the team for a few years—including their championship season—it was virtually impossible to get tickets. However, the team's play has been somewhat inconsistent the past few years (even though their records have been winning ones), and you can generally get seats; and, often, good seats, if you buy them in advance.

American Airlines Arena is in the heart of downtown Miami and holds 20,000 people. It's about a 40-minute drive—depending on the traffic, of course—from Fort Lauderdale. The arena's only 10 years old, and it's a comfortable place to watch a game with good sight lines no matter where you're sitting. From Fort Lauderdale take I-95 south to Miami. Exit at "Biscayne Boulevard/Downtown." Turn left (North) on Biscayne Boulevard. Go about eight blocks, the arena is on the right.

There's also a way that you can see the Heat before they actually start the season, however; they hold their preseason training camp at Florida Atlantic University (FAU) in Boca Raton (the southernmost town in Palm Beach County, and just to the north of Broward). Many of their training practices are open to the public. The pro basketball season starts in Oct, and runs into Apr (not including play-offs).

College Football

FLORIDA ATLANTIC UNIVERSITY FOOTBALL
Lockhart Stadium
1350 NW 55th St., Ft. Lauderdale
Event Information: (754) 321-1210
Ticket Office: (866) FAU-OWLS
www.fausports.com
www.ticketmaster.com

Florida Atlantic University (FAU) is a relative newcomer to major college football, having started its football program in 2001. In 2007, it became the first team in history to go to a bowl game in only its seventh season, and it won that bowl game. Then it received another invitation to a bowl game in 2008 and won that one, too. Although FAU's main campus is in Boca Raton, in Palm Beach County, the Owls play in old Lockhart Stadium in Fort Lauderdale, with a seating capacity just under 20,000. However, FAU may not be there that much longer. The university is on an aggressive fund-raising campaign for an on-campus stadium, and plans have been developed for a 30,000-seat stadium and a surrounding area of shops and restaurants. One of the driving forces behind the new complex is the legendary coach of the Owls, Howard Schnellenberger, who won a national championship as coach of the down-the-road Miami Hurricanes in 1983. As of this writing, ground-breaking has not taken place. But hopefully, by the time you're reading this, it may have.

In the meantime, it's not hard to get to Lockhart Stadium, which is just off I-95 in northern Fort Lauderdale. Exit at Commercial Boulevard west. Look for stadium signs on the right.

And there's not a bad seat in the house. The Owls play in the Sunbelt Conference, with opponents such as Troy University, Arkansas State, North Texas State, and Louisiana Tech. And the tickets are very reasonably priced.

FLORIDA ATLANTIC UNIVERSITY
FOOTBALL—SPRING PRACTICE
FAU Campus
777 Glades Rd., Boca Raton
(561) 297-3000
No admission charge

FAU's football team takes the field for three weeks of practice in the spring. The team holds three scrimmages, all of which are free to the public, and you can get some idea of how the Owls will look in the coming season, and who are the players to watch. The practice fields are behind the Tom Oxley Athletic Center on the main FAU campus in Boca Raton, just across the Broward–Palm Beach County line. The entrance to the campus is on Glades Road, just east of I-95. After you come in the entrance, take the first left after the traffic light, and follow the signs to the Oxley Center. There's limited seating in the bleachers, so it's a good idea to bring a folding chair. There's a concession stand that sells food and drinks. From Fort Lauderdale take I-95 north about 15 miles. Exit at Glades Road, heading east. The campus is on the left.

UNIVERSITY OF MIAMI FOOTBALL
Sun Life Stadium
2269 Dan Marino Blvd., Miami Gardens
(800) GO-CANES or (305) 623-6100
www.hurricanesports.com
www.ticketmaster.com
www.sunlifestadium.com

The fabled University of Miami Hurricanes left their beloved Orange Bowl for newer pastures in 2007, and the grand old stadium, scene of so many legendary games and championship contests in both college and pro football, was torn down shortly afterward. In these parts, you can still find a lot of people who mourn the loss of the Orange Bowl. However, you won't find too many who wouldn't admit that Sun Life Stadium (in the town of Miami Gardens, on the border of Miami–Dade County and Broward County) is a much nicer place to watch a game than the Orange Bowl, which had been built in 1937. This stadium is modern and comfortable, with easy access, clean restrooms, better food, and better seats, and it's much more easily accessible from Broward County than the Orange Bowl (in downtown Miami) was. The Hurricanes transformed the game of college football forever in the '80s and '90s, winning five national championships in the years between 1983 and 2001—a feat that may never be repeated. They're not quite that dominant any more, although they still produce winning—and very exciting—teams. The college game is fun to watch, and the pageantry, with marching bands and cheerleaders and chanting fans and the alma mater songs, is a colorful slice of Americana.

The 'Canes play in the Atlantic Coast Conference, against opponents such as Georgia Tech, Virginia Tech, Boston College, and their in-state rivals, the Florida State Seminoles. Games against Florida State sell out, as do games against other national powers such as the University of Oklahoma. However, there are generally seats to be had against most of the other teams on the schedule. On a sunny autumn Saturday, there aren't many better places to be than here. As Hurricanes fans will tell you—and anyone else who's in the stadium—"it's a 'Canes thing." From Fort Lauderdale head west on I-595. Exit at Florida Turnpike, heading south (toward Miami). Get off the turnpike at the Dan Marino Boulevard exit.

Pro Football

MIAMI DOLPHINS
Sun Life Stadium
2269 Dan Marino Blvd., Miami Gardens
(305) 623-6100
www.sunlifestadium.com
www.miamidolphins.com
www.ticketmaster.com

The Miami Dolphins were the pioneers of the South Florida sports scene and the first professional franchise in the region. The approach of their season still generates more anticipation than any other franchise here since. And they still attract more passion—positive or negative—than any of the other South Florida teams. Their first season was 1966, and they were the laughingstock of the National Football League, winning only one game that year. They didn't stay a laughingstock for very long though. They won the Super Bowl in 1972 (when they were undefeated; as of 2010, they're still the only team in history to go through a season undefeated). Then they won the Super Bowl again in 1973. And, in so doing, they captured the hearts of South Florida sports fans forever. It's been a long time since that last Super Bowl victory, of course. But almost as soon as one season ends, the fans start talking about prospects for the following season.

Sun Life Stadium holds 77,000, and about 55,000 of those seats go to season-ticket holders. However, there are generally a few tickets available as late as the week before the game. The stadium is clean and modern (and also newly renovated). It's a nice place to watch a football game—and it's the focus of most of South Florida's attention on game days.

The stadium is located in the town of Miami Gardens, right on the border of Miami–Dade County and Broward County. It's easy to get to, as it's just off the Florida Turnpike. Traffic, as you might expect, is very dense on game days, so head out early if you've got tickets. Don't worry; there's no such thing as *too early* here; tailgate parties start hours before kickoff, by which time the parking lot is a sea of grills, coolers, and tables. If the Dolphins are not having a particularly good season (they've been up and down the past decade), you may even be able to walk up to the ticket window and get a ticket the day of the game—but don't count on it. If you do get in, you'll find yourself enveloped in a sea of aqua and orange. From Fort Lauderdale, head west on I-595. Exit at Florida Turnpike, heading south. Exit from the turnpike at Dan Marino Boulevard.

MIAMI DOLPHINS TRAINING FACILITY
Miami Dolphins Ltd.
7500 SW 30th St., Davie
(954) 452-7000
www.miamidolphins.com
No admission fee

If you're in town in late-July and August, you can watch the Dolphins practice at their facility in the town of Davie, about 10 miles west of Fort Lauderdale. The facility is on the campus of Nova Southeastern University. It's a state-of-the-art complex.

The bleachers can accommodate 2,000 people. But you'd better get there early. Dolphin fans—known hereabouts as Dolfans—are a passionate bunch. And, as the opening of training camp is one of the most anticipated events of the year here, they pack the place. In addition to the grass field, the Dolphins inaugurated a huge indoor "bubble" in 2006, sort of a tent the size of Cleveland, in which they can practice even if the usual rains come in July and August. It's a 2.2-acre, air-supported structure.

Keep in mind, though, that once the regular season starts, it's all business at the training facility. And—just as is the case with other NFL teams—the general public won't be allowed in then.

Pro Hockey

FLORIDA PANTHERS
BankAtlantic Center
One Panther Pkwy., Sunrise
Tickets: (954) 835-PUCK
www.ticketmaster.com
www.floridapanthers.com
In how many other parts of the country can you drive to a major league hockey game with the top down or the sunroof open? Where else can you take your jacket off when you leave the arena at the end of a game, rather than put it on? Although the Florida Panthers came into being in 1993, it still seems like a novelty for many fans—especially those who grew up in the northerly climes—to be able to do these things, and to walk out of the arena into a winter night that's 60 degrees and clear, with swirls of stars overhead, instead of into snow and ice. The Panthers play in BankAtlantic Center, off the Sawgrass Expressway in the western Broward County town of Sunrise. It's about a half hour from downtown Lauderdale and easily accessible off this wide, smooth-flowing highway. From Fort Lauderdale take I-595 west. Go approximately 15 miles to the major interchange. Exit onto Highway 869

on the right. Head north on Highway 869 about 5 minutes. Exit at Panther Parkway.

The arena is a modern, airy place with 20,000 seats. As of 2010, the Panthers haven't been in the playoffs for nine years (even when they've had winning teams). As a result, even though they have a dedicated core of fans, there are generally some tickets available even on the day of the game. And the arena has a very exciting atmosphere, with cowbell-clanging fans who are very vocal in their support of "the Cats." The arena is also very family-friendly, with special kids' fun zones and a lot of contests and activities to keep the younger set very involved. There are always a lot of fun things going on here, in fact, for adults as well, including on-ice musical chairs, trivia contests, free prizes, and more. And the game of hockey itself is fast and intense and colorful. The puck flies toward the goalie at upwards of 90 miles an hour, the hits are bone-jarring, and the skills of the players as they backpedal on skates or weave through opposing defenders while still controlling a puck are breathtaking.

Pro Soccer

MIAMI FC
Lockhart Stadium
1350 NW 55th St., Ft. Lauderdale
Tickets: (305) 377-2700
www.miamifc.com
After splitting its games between Miami and Fort Lauderdale's storied soccer venue, Lockhart Stadium, Miami FC (Football Club) has made a permanent switch to Fort Lauderdale. And even after the switch, the club will still be called "Miami" (don't ask!). But Broward soccer aficionados are very excited. Over the years, Lockhart has seen numerous memorable international matches, along with former franchises such as the Fort

Lauderdale Strikers and the Fusion. Broward County has always had a dedicated core of soccer fans; the old Strikers, in fact, used to routinely draw 20,000 people to their games here in the late '70s and early '80s. The soccer season here runs from mid-April to early October. And tickets are very reasonably priced. From Fort Lauderdale take I-95 north. Exit at Commercial Boulevard west. The stadium is on the right.

Golf Tournaments

No major golf tournaments are played in Broward County. But there are a couple of majors played nearby.

CA CHAMPIONSHIP
Doral Golf Resort & Spa
4400 NW 87th Ave., Miami
(305) 592-2000
www.doralresort.com
The legendary course at Doral known as "the Blue Monster" is the site of the annual CA Championship in March. And after watching this tournament, you'll know exactly why the course got its name. (P.S.: The purse is close to $9 million.) Doral's about an hour south of Fort Lauderdale, to the west of Miami. Head west on I-595. Go approximately 15 miles to the major interchange. At the interchange, get on to I-75 south (toward Miami). Go about 20 miles; look for signs.

THE HONDA CLASSIC
PGA National Resort & Spa
400 Ave. of the Champions,
Palm Beach Gardens
Resort: (800) 863-2819
Honda Classic: (561) 799-2747
www.thehondaclassic.com
The famous Honda Classic is played every March at the PGA National Resort & Spa,

about an hour north of Fort Lauderdale, on the Champion course. The purse here isn't exactly chump change, either—close to $6 million. This is also the headquarters of the PGA. From Fort Lauderdale: Head north on I-95, for approximately an hour. Exit at Palm Beach Gardens Boulevard heading west. Look for signs.

Tennis Tournaments

BMW TENNIS CHAMPIONSHIP
Sunrise Tennis Club
9605 W. Oakland Park Blvd., Sunrise
(954) 572-2286
www.sunrisefl.gov/grandslam.html
Each March, Sunrise Tennis Club hosts the BMW Tennis Championship, a prestigious tournament that gives South Floridians a rare opportunity to see some of the top men's professional tennis players in the world. It's one of only three major tennis tournaments in the state of Florida. And it's the only event in Broward County that's sanctioned by the Association of Tennis Professionals (ATP)—the organizer of the principal worldwide men's tennis tour. From Fort Lauderdale: Head west on Sunrise Boulevard.

DELRAY BEACH INTERNATIONAL
TENNIS CHAMPIONSHIPS
Delray Beach Tennis Center
201 W. Atlantic Ave., Delray Beach
(561) 243-7360
The Delray Beach International Tennis Championships (ITC) is a nine-day extravaganza spread out over two weekends. It takes place at the Delray Beach Stadium & Tennis Center every year, generally in February, right in the heart of downtown Delray. The twin bookends of the tournament are an ATP World Tour event and an ATP Champions Tour

event. The week attracts current top tennis pros such as Mardy Fish and Aaron Krickstein, and old favorites such as John McEnroe. Delray Beach is about a half-hour north of Fort Lauderdale. Go north on I-95, approximately 22 miles. Exit at Atlantic Avenue, heading west. Proceed toward downtown area. The stadium will be on your left.

SONY ERICSSON OPEN TENNIS CHAMPIONSHIPS
Crandon Park Tennis Center
6800 Crandon Blvd., Key Biscayne
(305) 365-2300
www.sonyericssonopen.com

Every late March/early April, you'll see most of the world's greatest tennis players gather in picturesque Key Biscayne, over a causeway from downtown Miami. You'll also see some of the world's biggest celebrities here. It's become a glamorous international event, and the competition is thrilling. Key Biscayne is about 45 minutes south of Fort Lauderdale. From Fort Lauderdale: Head south on I-95 for about 30 miles; you'll pass downtown Miami. Get off at the exit for Rickenbacker Causeway/Key Biscayne.

Horse Racing

CALDER RACE COURSE & CASINO
21001 NW 27th Ave., Miami Gardens
(954) 523-4324
www.calderracecourse.com

Here's where the thoroughbreds roam, adjacent to Sun Life Stadium (where the Dolphins and the Marlins play). The season generally runs from late April until mid-October. From Fort Lauderdale: Head west on I-595. Exit onto Florida Turnpike, heading south. Look for signs.

GULFSTREAM PARK RACING & CASINO
901 S. Federal Hwy., Hallandale Beach
(954) 454-7000
www.gulfstreampark.com

Gulfstream Park is the home of the Florida Derby, and you may see a horse or two from that race entered in the Kentucky Derby. The racing season takes place during the winter months. And the complex has been revitalized, with a shopping village and new restaurants. From Fort Lauderdale: Head south on Federal Highway.

POMPANO PARK (ISLE CASINO RACING POMPANO PARK)
777 Isle of Capri Circle, Pompano Beach
(954) 972-2000
pompano-park.isleofcapricasinos.com

The excitement really builds as the trotters near the finish line here, several nights a week during the winter months and into early May.

Dog Racing

HOLLYWOOD GREYHOUND TRACK & MARDI GRAS CASINO
831 N. Federal Hwy., Hallandale Beach
(954) 924-3200
www.playmardigras.com

This greyhound track opened in 1934—before TV and computers, when radio was still in its infancy and the only people who flew in airplanes were wealthy celebrities. And it's been providing exciting racing for South Floridians (and visitors) ever since. From Fort Lauderdale: Head south on Federal Highway.

Jai Alai

DANIA JAI-ALAI
301 E. Dania Beach Blvd., Dania
(954) 920-1511
www.betdania.com

If you've never seen this ferociously fast game imported from the Basque country of Spain, you're really missing something. The ball (pelota) ricochets off the walls with astounding speed, and the fleet-of-foot players have to catch it in 2-foot-long baskets on their hands, and then hurl it back against the wall. It's colorful and it's fun. The competition runs all year long, from Tues night through Sat night (there are also matinees on Tues and Sat afternoons). From Fort Lauderdale: Head south on Federal Highway. Turn left on Dania Beach Boulevard.

High School Sports

Broward County fields boy's teams in all the major high school sports—football, soccer, basketball, baseball, and volleyball—and girl's teams in all but football (although girls' flag football has now started to catch on in the high school ranks). Broward schools—both public and private—regularly supply major college teams across the country with All-American athletes. And many of these athletes eventually end up playing professional sports. Football games are generally played on Friday nights across the county (and occasionally on Thursday night). The crowds are large and excited, and the games are colorful and competitive. High school basketball—both boys' and girls'—also draws nice crowds. Contact the high school in your area for more information.

RECREATION

OK, let's start with the obvious. The only skiing you're going to be able to do around here is on water, not on snow. We're not that big on dogsledding either, or snowboarding or ice-skating. But if you don't need snow or ice to do it, you can do just about any other form of outdoor recreation here in Greater Fort Lauderdale. And you can do it just about any day of the year. Because—while we don't have snow—we do have sunshine (tons of it!). We do have water . . . in lakes, rivers, the Intracoastal Waterway, and the Atlantic Ocean. And we do have the Everglades—which no one else in the world has.

In addition, we have tons of leagues, for folks just like you. So, whatever your favorite participant sport or form of outdoor recreation, you can do it here in Greater Fort Lauderdale.

In fact, you'll run out of time long before you run out of things to do!

ADULT RECREATION LEAGUES

The starting point for information about the listings below is the **Broward County Parks and Recreation Division**, located in Oakland Park at 950 NW 38th St. (954-357-8100, www.broward.org/parks).

Basketball

DEERFIELD BEACH ADULT BASKETBALL LEAGUE
City of Deerfield Beach
150 NE 2nd Ave., Deerfield Beach
(954) 480-4200
www.deerfield-beach.com

HOLLYWOOD ADULT BASKETBALL LEAGUE
Washington Park
(954) 967-4606
www.hollywoodfl.org/Parks_rec/
Athlet.htm

LAUDERDALE LAKES
City of Lauderdale Lakes
4300 NW 36th St., Lauderdale Lakes
(954) 535-2700
www.lauderdalelakes.org

TAMARAC
City of Tamarac
7525 NW 88th Ave., Tamarac
(954) 553-5538 or (954) 720-7103
www.tamarac.org

Beach Volleyball

POMPANO BEACH ADULT COED SAND VOLLEYBALL LEAGUE
1650 NE 50th Court, Pompano Beach
(954) 363-3315
www.leaguelineup.com

RECREATION

Cricket

NORTH LAUDERDALE
City of North Lauderdale
701 SW 71st Ave., North Lauderdale
(954) 724-7061
www.nlauderdale.org/Parks

Flag Football

COCONUT CREEK
Coconut Creek Community Center
1100 Lyons Rd., Coconut Creek
(954) 545-5670
www.coconutcreek.net

FORT LAUDERDALE
Mills Pond Park
2201 NW 9th Ave., Ft. Lauderdale
(954) 828-8942
http://info.ci.ftlaud.fl.us/leagues/
monday/default.htm

PLANTATION
Plantation Adult Athletic Leagues
9151 NW 2nd St., Plantation
(954) 452-2509
www.plantationadultathletics.com

Soccer

CITY OF PEMBROKE PINES
Contact Assistant Athletic Coordinator
Renee Nunez
(954) 538-3696
www.ppines.com/parks/locator/west
pinessoccerpark.html

**CORAL SPRINGS MEN'S SOCCER
 LEAGUE**
10697 Wiles Rd., Coral Springs
(954) 907-3234
www.csmsl.com

MIRAMAR
Miramar Regional Park
16801 Miramar Pkwy., Miramar
(786) 797-6466
www.ci.miramar.fl.us/

**NORTH LAUDERDALE (MEN'S AND
 WOMEN'S)**
City of North Lauderdale
701 SW 71st Ave., North Lauderdale
(954) 722-0900
www.nlauderdale.org/Parks

**PLANTATION ADULT ATHLETIC
 LEAGUES**
9151 NW 2nd St., Plantation
(954) 452-2509
www.plantationadultathletics.com

TAMARAC
City of Tamarac
7525 NW 88th Ave., Tamarac
(786) 367-0972
www.tamarac.org

Softball

For a comprehensive listing of adult softball leagues, go to **www.floridaadultsoftball .com**.

**TOWN OF DAVIE ADULT SOFTBALL
 PROGRAM**
Davie Town Hall
6591 Orange Dr., Davie
(954) 327-3928
www.davie-fl.gov

FORT LAUDERDALE
Mills Pond Park
2201 NW 9th Ave., Ft. Lauderdale
(954) 828-8943
http://ci.ftlaud.fl.us/cityparks/mills_
pond/index.htm

LAUDERHILL
Lauderhill Sports Park
(954) 572-1478
West Wind Park
(954) 572-1471
http://lauderhill-fl.gov/html/dept_pals_
athletics.html

**PLANTATION ADULT ATHLETIC
LEAGUES**
9151 NW 2nd St., Plantation
(954) 452-2509
www.plantationadultathletics.com

TAMARAC
City of Tamarac
7525 NW 88th Avenue
Tamarac, FL 3321
(954) 726-2013
www.tamarac.org

Tennis

WESTON
Midtown Tennis Club (members only)
2300 Royal Palm Blvd., Weston
(954) 384-2582
www.midtown.com/Weston/Pages/
MemberTennisPrograms.aspx

WATER ACTIVITIES &
WATER SPORTS

With the Atlantic Ocean, the Intracoastal Waterway, and the Everglades so close by, there are plenty of opportunities for water sports, such as fishing, boating, waterskiing, surfing, Jet Skiing, and kayaking around the Greater Fort Lauderdale area.

Be sure to wear a life vest and practice water safety when you participate in water activities in and around the Greater Fort Lauderdale area. Water can rise quickly, jellyfish and Portuguese man-of-wars can suddenly take over the water without much notice, and dangerous currents can whisk you away quicker than you can blink. Also check the weather before you head out. It's not unusual for Florida days to start out sunny before abruptly turning stormy, though do remember that in the rainy season (roughly May through October) and the hurricane season (officially June through November, though most storms come between August and October) there is a thunderstorm nearly every afternoon. Also make sure someone on land knows you are on the water, just in case conditions get rough. Gear for water activities can be rented at smaller outfitters listed here, as well as at the sporting goods stores mentioned in the Shopping chapter. Additional shops can be found in the yellow pages or by contacting the local visitor bureau. If you're in the area in late October, also be sure to visit the **Fort Lauderdale International Boat Show** (www.showmanagement.com). More details on this widely attended boating extravaganza are included in the Events chapter. Below are some of the most popular options for water activities in and around Greater Fort Lauderdale.

Airboat Rides

BILLIE SWAMP SAFARI AIRBOAT RIDES
Big Cypress Seminole Reservation
30000 Gator Tail Trail, Clewiston
(800) 949-6101
Take in a bit of history and culture in addition to your airboat ride, which will be piloted by

RECREATION

a member of the Seminole Tribe who knows every inch of this Everglades wilderness. In addition to the ride, you can marvel at the glorious history of the Seminole Nation (the only tribe that has never signed a peace treaty with the United States) at the Ah-Tah-Thi-Ki Museum. You can wander through an authentic Seminole village. You can enjoy Indian food, such as fry bread, Indian stew, or frog's legs. You can watch tribal craftspeople creating wonderful blankets, dresses, jewelry, or flutes. And you can even rent an authentic "chickee" (a thatched-roof hut) for the night, or for as many nights as you wish. To reach Big Cypress Seminole Reservation from Broward County, go west on I-75 and get off at exit 49; continue north for about 16 miles.

LOXAHATCHEE EVERGLADES TOURS
15490 Loxahatchee Rd., Parkland
(800) 683-5873 or (561) 482-6107
www.evergladesairboattours.com
Whir through the "River of Grass" on pretty much the only type of boat that can successfully navigate it—an airboat, with a booming engine and a huge propeller on back. You'll get an up-close-and-personal view of America's only subtropical jungle and hundreds of species of wildlife found nowhere else on Earth. You may see otters. Red-shouldered hawks. Brilliantly colored birds called purple gallinules. And, yes, those shredded old tires on the banks are not really old tires—they're alligators.

SWAMP BUGGY ECO-TOUR
Big Cypress Seminole Reservation
30000 Gator Tail Trail, Clewiston
(800) 949-6101
The swamp buggy is a unique vehicle that's as much at home on land as it is in the

swamps and hammocks of the Everglades. This 90-minute private tour will take you through the tropical hammocks and mangroves of the River of Grass and past all sorts of wildlife. You may see deer, antelope, bison, snakes, or wild hogs, and more unusual wildlife such as red-shouldered hawks or purple gallinules. And you'll almost definitely see alligators. To reach Big Cypress Seminole Reservation from Broward County, go west on I-75 and get off at exit 49; continue north for about 16 miles.

Boating

Greater Fort Lauderdale offers more than 300 miles of navigable waterways; after all, the Greater Fort Lauderdale area is known as "the Venice of America." And the **Broward County Division of Parks and Recreation** offers a lot of these navigable miles, and boat rentals, at a number of its parks. Whether you want to launch your boat into the edge of the Everglades at Markham Park, pull into a slip for a leisurely picnic at Boaters Park, or pedal your way around a lake in a boat shaped like an oversized swan at T. Y. Park, there's a park to fit your needs. In fact, two county parks—Boaters Park and Deerfield Island Park—are accessible only by boat. For more information on any of these parks and their facilities, visit the Broward County Division of Parks and Recreation website (www.broward.org/parks).

Boat Ramps
- Markham Park
- Quiet Water Park
- Tradewinds Park
- West Lake Park

Boat Docks
- Boaters Park
- Deerfield Island Park
- West Lake Park (no fossil-fueled boats allowed)

Boat Rentals
- C. B. Smith Park
- Central Broward Regional Park
- Markham Park
- Plantation Heritage Park
- Quiet Waters Park
- Tradewinds Park
- Tree Tops
- T. Y. Park
- West Lake Park

Canoeing, Kayaking & Rowing

Launch Sites
DEERFIELD ISLAND PARK
1720 Deerfield Island Park,
Deerfield Beach
(954) 360-1320
www.broward.org/parks
Deerfield Island is a Designated Urban Wilderness Area island park, and as you might have guessed, you can only get there by boat. It's a heavily wooded 56-acre site with some swamp, in the protected waters of the Intracoastal Waterway and the Hillsboro and Royal Palm Canals. If you're lucky, you might see some gopher tortoises, raccoons, and armadillos, along with a wide variety of sea birds. Exit I-95 at Hillsboro Boulevard east, and turn left at NE 5th Avenue, which takes you into Pioneer Park, where you get on the boat.

EVERGLADES HOLIDAY PARK
21940 Griffin Rd., Ft. Lauderdale
(954) 874-1124
www.evergladesholidaypark.com
Located in western Broward, Everglades Holiday Park offers access to the Water Conservation area, where the fishing is good, the canals are straight, and the wildlife is everywhere. The airboat areas are a bit more scenic than the other waters, but of course then you'll have to deal with the noise and the wakes. The area's filled with a brilliantly colored bird called a purple gallinule. And, of course, plenty of snakes, ibises, egrets, herons, red-shouldered hawks, and gators. From Fort Lauderdale take I-95 south to Griffin Road. Take the Griffin Road exit and head west. Cross US 27 (pretty much the westernmost road in Broward County). And when you can't go any further, you're there.

FORT LAUDERDALE BEACH
Just north of the "the Strip" (and Sunrise Boulevard) on SR A1A in Fort Lauderdale, there's a stretch with on-street parking (marked in pink), where you can park, unload, and leave your car only about 20 yards from the water. It's the easiest place to get a canoe or kayak into the ocean. There are some showers at the south end of this section. Be advised, though, that motorboats come closer to shore here than in a lot of other places.

GEORGE ENGLISH PARK
1101 Bayview Dr., Ft. Lauderdale
(954) 396-3620
http://ci.ftlaud.fl.us/cityparks/george_english/index.htm
Paddling here will bring you past the multimillion-dollar homes of the Las Olas area where you can see both dream homes and rather unusual homes, to put it mildly. From here, you can head north to the Middle River, west to the New River, or south toward Port Everglades. Take I-95 to Sunrise Boulevard east. When you see the Galleria mall on your

right, look to your left and you'll see George English Park. Turn left into Bayview Drive.

HOLLYWOOD BEACH

Take I-95 to Sheridan Street east. Go over the drawbridge over the Intracoastal and turn left onto SR A1A. Go north past North Beach Park, then turn right after a few blocks, being careful since the streets are all one way, alternating east- and westbound. Turn left at the end of the street (also one way); watch for cyclists and skaters. The put-in is at Meade Street, a block north of Custer Street. You can drive onto the beach to unload and load, then park in metered parking.

MIDDLE RIVER—WILTON MANORS

The town of Wilton Manors is just north of Fort Lauderdale. Because it's pretty much surrounded by a loop of the Middle River, it's called (by some) the Island City. The river isn't very wide, or very deep, but it does wind past a lot of parkland, so you'll see plenty of green rather than just seawalls. Rolling tarpon inhabit these waters, along with manatees (who will sometimes come right up to your boat). The full loop is 7 miles long, with another 3 if you continue on to George English Park. Take I-95 to Oakland Park Boulevard, going east. Island City Park has a parking lot off 28th Street.

NEW RIVER—DOWNTOWN FORT LAUDERDALE

Here, you'll go on a genuine urban paddle, past the glorious old Riverside Hotel and the Broward Center for the Performing Arts, and past the magnificent homes dotting the Las Olas Isles area off Las Olas Boulevard. (This area is considered the main reason why Fort Lauderdale is called "the Venice of America.") The launch site is called Cooley's Landing at Sailboat Bend. Take I-95

to Broward Boulevard East, turn right at NW/SW 7th Avenue (Avenue of the Arts) and go straight onto Cooley Avenue.

NEW RIVER—SOUTH FORK

Although hardly untracked wilderness, this section of the New River is less "urban" and a bit more "wild." The section between I-595 and the Dania Cutoff Canal has no buildings, and mangroves have been planted along the west bank. Tarpon and snook are found here, and the lovable manatees (sea cows) are common in winter. There's a little bit of fantasy on this trip, too; you'll be able to get a good look at how the other half lives, as you glide past the gleaming white mega-yachts moored in the boatyards by I-595. For Riverland Wood Park (3950 Riverland Rd., Fort Lauderdale) turn east on Riverland Road off SR 441 just north of I-595, then make the first right turn past some convenience stores. The park is at the end of the road.

POMPANO BEACH

This is a beach launch, just south of the Pompano Fishing Pier. Exit I-95 heading east on Atlantic Boulevard and keep going until you see the Atlantic. Go across SR A1A, and you'll see a small parking lot on your left. If you're going, go early because this is also a public beach, and parking spaces are at a premium.

WEST LAKE PARK
751 Sheridan St., Hollywood
(954) 926-2480
www.broward.org/parks
There's a 175-foot dock on the Intracoastal Waterway, which is available on a first-come, first-served basis. This area is affected by the tides, so it's important to consider the depth of the water when docking. Overnight docking is not permitted.

WHISKEY CREEK/JOHN LLOYD STATE PARK
6503 N. Ocean Dr., Dania Beach
(954) 923-2833
www.floridastateparks.org/lloydbeach/
Located in John U. Lloyd State Park, Whiskey Creek is a shallow 2.25-mile paddle between the beach and the mangroves. In addition to paddling in the creek, other options are dragging the kayak over to the beach, or shoving into the Intracoastal and looking at cruise ships steaming in and out of Port Everglades (don't get too close, though—Homeland Security is watching!). The creek got its name from the smugglers who used it as a hiding place for themselves (and a storage "facility" for their liquor) during Prohibition.

Fishing

There's some good fishing at Broward County parks, particularly at the places listed below. If you don't own a boat, you can still enjoy some great fishing here. T. Y Park, C. B. Smith Park, and Quiet Waters Park all rent boats—pedal boats or rowboats—that you can use for fishing on weekends and holidays. Or, you can bring your own electric trolling motor and battery to use with a rowboat. It's best to call ahead for boat rental hours and availability.

BRIAN PICCOLO PARK
9501 Sheridan St., Cooper City
(954) 437-2600
www.broward.org/parks
There are no boats allowed here. But people fish along the back lake, both from the dock and west of the dock.

C. B. SMITH PARK
900 N. Flamingo Rd., Pembroke Pines
(954) 437-2650
www.broward.org/parks
This park has some fair bass fishing, along with the exotic spotted tilapia and a growing population of peacock bass. You can rent a boat at the marina. But it's no problem if you'd prefer to keep your feet on terra firma; there are some good spots on the shoreline as well.

DEERFIELD ISLAND PARK
1720 Deerfield Island Park,
Deerfield Beach
(954) 360-1315 (contact Quiet Waters Park for information)
www.broward.org/parks
For the best fishing, stake out a position at the marina or west of the picnic area on the Hillsboro Canal.

HOLLYWOOD NORTH BEACH PARK
3601 N. Ocean Dr., Hollywood
(954) 926-2410
www.broward.org/parks
Fishing is allowed off all the fishing piers on the east side of the Intracoastal Waterway, as well as from the park shorelines.

MARKHAM PARK
16001 W. SR 84, Sunrise
(954) 389-2000
www.broward.org/parks
Markham Park has several lakes, as well as access to the levy leading out to the Everglades, so the fishing here is excellent. People also find fish in the canals that run along the south and west sides of the park.

PLANTATION HERITAGE FISH
  MANAGEMENT AREA
Plantation Heritage Park
1100 S. Fig Tree Lane, Plantation
(954) 791-1025
www.broward.org/parks

The Plantation Heritage Fish Management Area has pretty good fishing for bream (bluegill and redear sunfish), bass, and catfish. There are three fish feeders on site, and those feeders also happen to be the best locations to find bream and catfish. Channel catfish are stocked annually (4,000 fish/year), and catfish up to 12.5 pounds have been caught at Heritage. Fishing is allowed from the shore only, not from any of the rental boats. Because this is a Fish Management Area, you'll have to be cognizant of other restrictions as well, such as only one pole per person—even with a cane pole. And you need a freshwater fishing license if you're between the ages of 16 and 65.

QUIET WATERS PARK
401 S. Powerline Rd., Deerfield Beach
(954) 357-5100
www.broward.org/parks

The bass are really runnin' at Quiet Waters, and you can catch 'em from a rental boat or from the shoreline. This is one of Greater Fort Lauderdale's prettier parks, with a large lake and plenty of woods. There are boats for rent and food stands at the Lakeview Marina, and you're welcome to bring your own electric trolling motor. There is fishing is all along the shoreline except at the Splash Adventure swimming beach and the Ski Rixen Lake.

REVEREND SAMUEL DELEVOE PARK
2520 NW 6th St., Ft. Lauderdale
(954) 791-1036
www.broward.org/parks

There are no boat rentals here; fishing is permitted only from the shore of the lake.

TRADEWINDS PARK
3600 W. Sample Rd., Coconut Creek
(954) 357-8870
www.broward.org/parks

There's good shoreline fishing on both north and south sides of Tradewinds. In fact, this is considered the best Broward County park for catching peacock bass (which seem to be more abundant on the south side).

TREE TOPS PARK
3900 SW 100th Ave., Davie
(954) 370-3750
www.broward.org/parks

Fishing is allowed along lake banks.

T. Y. (TOPEEKEEGEE YUGNEE) PARK
3300 N. Park Rd., Hollywood
(954) 357-8811
www.broward.org/parks

T. Y. Park is a good spot for bass fishing. The best fishing is from boats, which you can rent here.

WEST LAKE PARK
751 Sheridan St., Hollywood
(954) 926-2480
www.broward.org/parks

The fishing here is fine, and there are a bunch of different places from which you can do it. For one thing, boats are allowed. In addition, fishing is allowed from the Sheridan Street bridge that crosses the lake, as well as off the Fishing Trail boardwalk/fishing pier. You can also toss a line into the Intracoastal Waterway from the path running under the west side of the Intracoastal bridge. One proviso where boats are concerned: You can't use boats requiring fossil fuels; they have to be

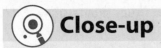

Close-up

Regulations and Licenses

The **Florida Fish and Wildlife Conservation Commission** (888-347-4365; www .myfwc.com) regulates fishing and boating in the area. Here's what that means for you: The department requires everyone 18 or older who wants to fish in public water to get a fishing license. Fishing license pricing varies depending on whether you want to fish in freshwater or saltwater (though both licenses cost the same amount for nonresidents) and whether you are a Florida resident (residency is defined as any person who has resided in Florida for six continuous months prior to the issuance of a license and who claims Florida as his/her primary residence; or any member of the United States Armed Forces who is stationed in Florida). Nonresidents pay $47 for the annual license, $17 for the seven-day version and $17 for a three-day license for either a freshwater or a saltwater license. Residents pay $32 for an annual license to fish in freshwater and saltwater. Combination licenses that permit fishing in freshwater and saltwater, as well as fishing-and-hunting license combo packages, are also available, as well as special licenses for only catching tarpon or spiny lobster. Also check the website for certain license exemptions.

Licenses can be purchased at dozens of locations around Broward County, including sporting goods stores, gun shops, bait and tackle shops, and even grocery stores. They can also be purchased online at the Florida Fish and Wildlife Conservation Commission's website (www.myfwc.com). The department also limits the number and size of fish you may take out of Florida waters; these numbers vary based on location and fish type. Visit the Florida Fish and Wildlife Conservation Commission website to review these regulations before your trip if you're thinking about taking home more than a few fish.

Before operating any kind of personal watercraft, any vessel over 10 horsepower, or a sailboat over 14 feet, aspiring boaters must also be in possession of a **Boater Education Identification** card, which essentially means you've been taught how to operate a boat safely and correctly, for the benefit of yourself and other boaters on the water. Boater education courses are available from a large number of outfitters and range between $14 and $30; for details about where to take this course visit www.myfwc.com/safety.

either electric or propelled by the force of your arms.

Boat Charters
ACTION SPORTFISHING
(954) 423-8700
actionsportfishing.com

CHARTERBOAT QUETZAL
Hillsboro Inlet Marina
2705 N. Riverside Dr., Pompano Beach
Boat: (954) 782-2982
Cell: (508) 237-6714
www.charternet.com/charters/quetzal

Lake Fishing

Broward County has plenty of other lakes outside of the county parks as well, and the fishing's great in most of them:

- **Fort Lauderdale North Area**— Lake Margate, North Lake, Rock Pit Lake, South Lake
- **Fort Lauderdale South Area (and south of Fort Lauderdale)**—Cliff Lake, Crystal Lake, Lake Eden, Lake George, Playland Lake, Silver Lake, Stirling Lake
- **Pompano Beach Area (and North Broward)**—Cypress Lake, East Coral Lake, Lake Cayuga, Lake Melva, Lake Seneca, Lettuce Lake
- **Port Everglades Area**—Lake Mabel, Lake Sylvia, Mayan Lake, North Lake, South Lake, Sunset Lake, West Lake

FLAMINGO FISHING
801 Seabreeze Blvd., Ft. Lauderdale
(954) 462-9194
flamingofishing.com

GOODFELLAS CHARTERS
2510 NE 33rd St., Lighthouse Point
(954) 254-7700
www.goodfellascharters.com

INTOXICATION SPORTFISHING
2629 N. Riverside Dr., Pompano Beach
(954) 785-8604
www.southfloridasportfishingtrips.net

NEW LATTITUDE SPORTFISHING CHARTERS
301 Seabreeze Blvd., Ft. Lauderdale
(954) 707-2147
www.newlattitude.com

POSEIDON TOO SPORTFISHING
Cove Marina
Intracoastal and Hillsboro Blvd.,
Deerfield Beach
(954) 224-FISH
www.poseidontoo.com

TACO'S HOOKED UP SPORTFISHING
801 Seabreeze Blvd., Ft. Lauderdale
(954) 764-4344
www.tacohookedup.com

TOP SHOT SPORTFISHING
(954) 439-8106
www.topshotfishing.com

ULTIMATE SPORTFISHING CHARTERS
4560 NE 3rd Terr., Ft. Lauderdale
(954) 673-3616
www.ultimatesportfishing.com

Sailing

Schools
BLUE WATER SAILING SCHOOL
922 NE 20th Ave., Ft. Lauderdale
(954) 768-0846
http://bwss.com

SOUTHEAST YACHTING SCHOOL
2601 Acacia Court, Ft. Lauderdale
(954) 812-8540

TIGERTAIL LAKE CENTER
580 Gulfstream Way, Dania Beach
(954) 201-4500
www.broward.edu/maps/tigertail.jsp

Charters

CAPTAIN CRAIG'S CHARTERS
5533 Ravenswood Ave., Ft. Lauderdale
(954) 989-3296

ENCHANTMENT YACHT CHARTERS
5721 NW 54th Way, Ft. Lauderdale
(954) 270-1932
www.enchantmentyachts.com

SEATREK CHARTERS
801 Seabreeze Blvd., Ft. Lauderdale
(954) 463 4304
www.seatrekcharters.com

Scuba Diving & Snorkeling

PRO DIVE USA
429 Seabreeze Blvd., Ft. Lauderdale
(954) 776-3483
www.prodiveusa.com

In operation since 1973, Pro Dive offers daily scuba diving and snorkeling trips on their 60-foot dive boat, the *Pro Diver II*. The outfitter also has a retail dive shop featuring Aqua Lung, Aquatic Atomics diving gear; they also offer scuba training and certification. Courses and excursions are available for divers of any level and experience. Pro Dive is also the world's first and only SEA&SEA School of Underwater Photography with "demo days" aboard the *Pro Diver II*, where divers can explore the world of underwater digital photography. One-day dive trips (including two tanks and weights) cost $75 ($55 if diver supplies own tanks and weights); with full scuba equipment, $115. They also offer daily 2.5-hour glass-bottom boat tours where you have the option of coral-reef snorkeling: $28 (tour only) or $35 (tour and snorkel, including masks, snorkels, fins, and snorkeling vests). They will instruct you on how to snorkel if you have never

Public Swimming Pools

Central Park Pool
9151 NW 2nd St., Plantation
(954) 452-2525
www.plantation.org

Coral Springs Aquatics Complex
12441 Royal Palm Blvd.,
Coral Springs
(954) 345-2121
www.aquaticcomplex.com

Croissant Park Pool
245 W. Park Dr., Ft. Lauderdale
(954) 423-1068

Cypress Park Tennis Center
1300 Coral Springs Dr.,
Coral Springs
(954) 345-2109

Roarke Pool
1720 NW 60th Ave., Sunrise
(954) 572-2460

Royal Palm Pool
6200 Royal Palm Blvd., Margate
(954) 972-3478

Village Beach Club Pool
6767 NW 24th St., Sunrise
(954) 572-2480

Welleby Pool
9605 W. Oakland Park Blvd.,
Sunrise
(954) 572-2285

Wolk Park Swimming Pool
1080 NW 42nd Way, Lauderhill
(954) 321-2466

done it before. For details about the glass-bottom boat tour, see p. 92 in the Attractions chapter.

SEA EXPERIENCE
801 Seabreeze Blvd., Ft. Lauderdale
(954) 770-DIVE (3483)
www.seaxp.com

Located on the Bahia Mar Resort, this is the only dive-boat and dive shop in South Florida located in a resort marina on the beach, most convenient if you are staying nearby or at the resort. They offer dive excursions (including night dives), snorkeling trips, and glass-bottom boat tours on one of their three boats; all snorkeling trips are part of their glass-bottom boat tours. Daily dive trips cost $75 ($55 if diver supplies own tanks and weights); with full scuba equipment, $105. Snorkeling/glass-bottom boat tours cost $35 ($28 for ride only) and depart twice per day, at 10:15 a.m. and 2:15 p.m.

SOUTH FLORIDA DIVING
2621 N. Riverside Dr., Pompano Beach
(954) 783-2299 or (800) 771-DIVE (3483)
www.southfloridadiving.com

This friendly dive center offers both diving and snorkeling trips to local reefs (destination varies according to season and weather), plus diving instruction for those keen to get certified. They also offer a free shuttle from many area hotels—call to inquire if your hotel is on the list. Two-tank dive trips cost $55, snorkel trips $30 (around two hours).

Wave Running & Jet Skiing

The Broward County Division of Parks & Recreation offers one area for personal watercraft. The 26-acre lake at **Markham Park** (www.broward.org/parks), is open to motorized personal watercraft such as Jet Skis and WaveRunners. The park is open seasonally on weekends and holidays from mid-Mar through the end of Oct. A launching fee is required. Session times run from 8:30 to 11:30 a.m., noon to 3 p.m., and 3:30 to 6:30 p.m. Call the park at (954) 389-2000 for more information.

Windsurfing

For information about the windsurfing scene in Florida, get in touch with **South Florida Windsurfing Association, Inc.** (9655 SW 159th Court, Miami; www.sfwa.info), or to learn more about windsurfing and equipment, contact **Watersports Unlimited, Inc.** (301 Seabreeze Blvd., Fort Lauderdale, 954-763-4020).

Locations
FORT LAUDERDALE BEACH/SOUTH BEACH PARK

This beach is a popular place for kitesurfing, and there are also people sailing catamarans and enjoying other water sports. The winds are good, with an easterly component from north to south. Sailing is open ocean with little or no protection from shore break. Waves are fair. And bars, restaurants, picnic sites, and bathrooms are just a short walk away.

The launch is at a boat ramp with a water-sports concession and a kitesurfing school. Accordingly, the area can get very crowded—especially on weekends—with sailboats, catamarans, Jet Skis, kitesurfers, and beachgoers

During the week, you can usually park on the boat ramp directly off SR A1A. On weekends, you should park at the adjacent (fee-based) parking lot. Because of moderate wave and shore break, and the often-crowded conditions, Fort Lauderdale beach requires at least an intermediate sailing-ability level. You should be confident in deepwater starting, and in launching and returning through whitewater and breaking waves.

Diving & Snorkeling Shops

American Dive Center
8092 W. Sample Rd., Coral Springs
(954) 346.0174
www.americandivecenter.com

Anchor Scuba, Inc.
37 N. Ocean Blvd. (SR A1A and Atlantic Boulevard),
Pompano Beach
(954) 788-DIVE
www.anchorscuba.com

Deep Blue Divers
4348 Ocean Dr., Lauderdale-by-the-Sea
(954) 772-7966

Divers Cove
2333 S. University Dr., Ft. Lauderdale
(954) 473-1220
www.diverscovefl.com

Divers Discount
2701 S. Federal Hwy., Ft. Lauderdale
(954) 761-1426
www.diversdiscountflorida.com

Force E Scuba
2700 E. Atlantic Blvd., Pompano Beach
(954) 943-3483
www.force-e.com

Lauderdale Diver
1334 SE 17th St., Ft. Lauderdale
(954) 467-2822
www.lauderdalediver.com

Scuba School and Dive Center
3331 E. Oakland Park Blvd., Ft. Lauderdale
(954) 566-6344
www.scuba-school.com

Undersea Sports
1450 N. Federal Hwy., Ft. Lauderdale
(954) 564-8661
www.underseasports.com

From I-95, take Broward Boulevard east. Go south a few blocks on Brickell Avenue, then make a left (east) on Las Olas Boulevard. Take Las Olas to the beach and then turn right (south) on SR A1A, for several blocks. Get in the left lane and make a U-turn at the parking lot. Look for the catamarans and the boat ramp on your immediate right.

Hollywood Beach

This is a good spot for open-ocean and wave sailing, with easterly winds from north to south. There's a small sandbar offshore (which doesn't offer much protection from shore break). Waves can be fair to very good; they're generally best on strong east–wind days. The launch area is small and can get very crowded, especially on weekends. During the week, you can usually park right at the boat ramp, directly off SR A1A. On weekends, you should park at the adjacent (fee-based) parking lot.

Hollywood Beach requires at least an intermediate sailing-ability level, because of moderate wave and shore break, and the often-crowded beach and water conditions. This means that you should feel very comfortable with deepwater starting, and launching and returning through whitewater and breaking waves.

From I-95, take the Sheridan Street exit east to the beach. Make a left (north) at SR A1A and go 5 blocks to Pershing Street. Drive an additional block along the beach (Surf Road) to get to Meade Street.

Pompano Beach

A popular wave-sailing spot—good for winds with an easterly component from north to south. However, you've got to be wary of the reef and rocks to the north when sailing southeast winds. The reef provides some measure of protection from shore break, and it creates a zone of whitewater (the "washboard") 50 to 100 yards from the beach. This is a large beach, and there's a small park with picnic and bathroom facilities. This is also a popular kitesurfing spot, so be careful to avoid getting caught up in those lines.

Due to the moderate wave and shore break, and the fact that water depth increases rapidly as you head out from the shore, Pompano Beach mandates at least an intermediate sailing-ability level. You should be experienced in deepwater starting, and in launching and returning through whitewater and breaking waves.

From I-95, take Atlantic Boulevard east to the beach. Turn left and take SR A1A north about 1.5 miles. Make a right into NE 16th Street, where there's metered parking.

BIKING

The **Broward Metropolitan Planning Organization** (Broward MPO) has developed an Internet site that allows you to really plan your biking routes through Greater Fort Lauderdale. Cyclists can enter their start and end locations, and receive turn-by-turn directions on how to reach their destination. Bike Broward includes five types of route selections users can choose from, including short, fast, least interaction with traffic, simple, and scenic. When planning your trip you can also include multiple travel points along your designated route. Check it out at **http://bike.browardmpo.org.**

Broward County Parks

Twelve Broward County Parks offer biking trails. For more information about any of

Bike Rentals in Greater Fort Lauderdale

Atlantic Bicycle
6350 W. Atlantic Blvd., Margate
(954) 971-9590
www.atlanticbicycle.com

Bicycle Evolution
977 W. SR 84, Ft. Lauderdale
(954) 318-2453
bicycleevolution.com

Bicycle Generation
1346 E. Hillsboro Blvd., Deerfield
Beach
(954) 427-1484
bicyclegeneration.com

Big Wheel Bicycle USA, Inc.
7029 Taft St., Hollywood
(954) 966-5545
www.big-wheel-bicycles.com

Bike America
10194 W. Sample Rd., Coral Springs
(954) 752-2544
www.bikeam.com

Blue Planet Bikes Inc
2155 NW 37th Ave., Coconut Creek
(954) 972-7100

Dan's West Broward Bicycle Center
13612 W. SR 84, Davie
(954) 424-9394
www.westbrowardbicyclecenter.com

Downtown Bicycles
400 N. Federal Hwy., Ft. Lauderdale
(954) 761-9920
downtownbicycles.com

Mega Cycle
1334 SW 160th Ave., Sunrise
(954) 384-0400
megacycle.cc

Z's Bike & Fitness
2600 Glades Circle, Weston
(954) 888-9030
www.zbikes.net/Zs_Bike_Shop/
Home/Home.html

them, visit the county's website at www
.broward.org/parks.

- **Brian Piccolo Park;** also has a bicycle-racing facility called the Velodrome
- **Central Broward Regional Park**
- **Hollywood North Beach Park**
- **Markham Park**
- **Plantation Heritage Park**
- **Quiet Waters Park**
- **Reverend Samuel Delevoe Memorial Park**
- **Tradewinds Park**
- **Tree Tops Park**
- **T.Y. Park**
- **Vista View Park**
- **West Lake Park**

Bicycle rentals are available at two Broward County Parks—**T. Y. Park** and **C. B. Smith Park.**

The nearest mountain to South Florida is some 600 miles north, just beyond Atlanta. But that doesn't mean you can't go mountain biking here. You can! Both Markham and Quiet Waters Parks have miles of trails, maintained by volunteer groups that are members of the International Mountain Bicycling Association. These groups organized a major cleanup and rebuilding effort after Hurricane Wilma in 2005, and continue to maintain the trails on a regular basis.

The **Broward County Parks and Recreation Division's Special Populations**

Section offers a **Tandem Bicycle Program** designed for adults who are blind or visually impaired. This six-week program offers basic biking skills, leisure rides, fun, and socialization. Call Special Populations at (954) 357-8160/8170 to find out when the next program is scheduled.

BOWLING

AMF DAVIE BOWLING
8200 W. SR 84, Davie
(954) 473-8822
www.amf.com

AMF PEMBROKE PINES LANES
1940 N. University Dr., Pembroke Pines
(954) 432-5500
www.amf.com

BRUNSWICK MARGATE LANES
2020 N. SR 7, Margate
(954) 972-4400
www.brunswickbowling.com

DON CARTER LANES, LTD.
8501 N. University Dr., Tamarac
(954) 722-2700

FORUM LANES BOWLING CENTER
8500 NW 44th St., Ft. Lauderdale
(954) 749-1400

HOLIDAY LANES
106 E. Pembroke Rd., Hallandale
(954) 458-3111

HOLIDAY SPRINGS LANES
8034 W. Sample Rd., Coral Springs
(954) 752-5270
www.holidaybowlingcenter.com

MANOR LANES, INC.
1517 NE 26th St., Ft. Lauderdale
(954) 566-7457
www.manorlanesfl.com

POMPANO BOWL
2200 N. Federal Hwy., Pompano Beach
(954) 941-0968

RINALDI DOLPHIN LANES
3900 NW 37th St., Ft. Lauderdale
(954) 731-3222

UNIVERSITY BOWL
5325 S. University Dr., Davie
(954) 434-9663

WEST HOLLYWOOD BOWL, INC.
2965 SR 7, Hollywood
(954) 983-8153

CAMPING

Five Broward County parks offer campgrounds: C. B. Smith, Easterlin, Markham, Quiet Waters, and T. Y. All but Quiet Waters offer sites with full RV hookups, and all have picnic tables, charcoal grills, and restroom complexes with hot showers. C. B. Smith and T. Y. also have laundry rooms, while T. Y.'s restrooms are air-conditioned.

At Quiet Waters, you can take advantage of the Rent-a-Tent package. Each site includes a platform with 10-foot-by-10-foot canvas tent (already set up for you) with capacity for six, a fire ring, a grill, a picnic table, electricity, and running water. Or, you can try one of the two tepee sites, each with a grill, a fire ring, and a picnic table.

All county campgrounds provide after-hours security. Two pets per campsite are allowed, with proof of current vaccinations and appropriate licenses. Pets must be registered at check-in, and must be kept on a leash no longer than six feet at all times when not inside the RV or tent.

Camping fees vary, with residents of the tri-county area of Broward, Palm Beach, and Miami-Dade receiving discounts.

Reservations are highly recommended, especially during High Season, from Nov through Apr.

You can make reservations by calling the individual park offices. Visit the website (www.broward.org/parks) for more information.

- **C. B. Smith Park**—(954) 437-2650
- **Easterlin Park**—(954) 938-0610
- **Markham Park**—(954) 389-2000
- **Quiet Waters Park**—(954) 360-1315
- **T. Y. (Topeekeegee Yugnee) Park**—(954) 357-8811

RV Parks

BREEZY HILL
800 NE 48th St., Pompano Beach
(954) 942-8688
www.hikercentral.com/
campgrounds/103217.html

CAMP VISTA
10193 NW 31st St., Coral Springs
(954) 752-7571
www.hikercentral.com/
campgrounds/122842.html

CAREFREE COVE RV RESORT
3273 NW 37th St., Ft. Lauderdale
(954) 731-2387
www.hikercentral.com/
campgrounds/103257.html

C. B. SMITH PARK
900 N. Flamingo Rd., Hollywood
(954) 437-2650
www.hikercentral.com/
campgrounds/103229.html

EAGLES LANDING CAMPS
7600 Lyons Rd., Coconut Creek
(954) 571-8709
www.hikercentral.com/
campgrounds/125321.html

EMBASSY RV PARK
3188 Lake Shore Dr., Hallandale
(954) 961-8892
www.hikercentral.com/
campgrounds/103326.html

GOLF VIEW ESTATES TRAVEL TRAILER PARK
901 NW 31st Ave., Pompano Beach
(954) 972-4140
www.hikercentral.com/
campgrounds/103385.html

HIGHLAND WOODS TRAVEL PARK
900 NE 48th St., Pompano Beach
(954) 942-6254
www.hikercentral.com/
campgrounds/103425.html

HOLIDAY PARK
3140 W. Hallandale Beach Blvd.,
Hallandale
(954) 981-4414
www.hikercentral.com/
campgrounds/103435.html

KIDS IN MOTION
11246 Wiles Rd., Coral Springs
(954) 344-1661
www.hikercentral.com/
campgrounds/122086.html

KOZY KAMPERS RV PARK
3631 W. Commercial Blvd., Ft.
Lauderdale
(954) 731-8570
www.hikercentral.com/
campgrounds/103495.html

NORTHCOAST PARK & MARINA
4500 Ravenswood Rd., Ft. Lauderdale
(954) 983-2083
www.hikercentral.com/
campgrounds/129981.html

RECREATION

PARADISE ISLAND RV RESORT
2121 NW 29th Court, Oakland Park
(954) 485-1150
www.hikercentral.com/
campgrounds/130248.html

RV HIDEAWAY
3001 N. SR 7, Hollywood
(954) 966-3421
www.hikercentral.com/
campgrounds/103736.html

SEMINOLE PARK
3301 N. SR 7, Hollywood
(954) 987-6961
www.hikercentral.com/
campgrounds/103805.html

TRINITY TOWERS RV PARK
3300 Pembroke Rd., Hollywood
(954) 962-7400
www.hikercentral.com/
campgrounds/103944.html

TWIN LAKES TRAVEL PARK
3055 Burris Rd., Davie
(954) 587-0101
www.hikercentral.com/
campgrounds/130001.html

T. Y. PARK
3300 N. Park Rd., Hollywood
(954) 985-1980
www.hikercentral.com/
campgrounds/103897.html

GOLF

If you're a dedicated duffer, you're in luck, because you could play golf in Broward County for 68 days in a row, without ever playing on the same course twice! Here's a brief rundown of each.

ADIOS GOLF CLUB
7740 NW 39th Ave., Coconut Creek
(954) 574-1440
www.adiosgolfclub.org
This club is exclusively for male players; ladies are not permitted to play here. A chain-link fence runs down the east and west sides of the course, which is an out-of-bounds marker for six holes. Several holes have water hazards, among them #6, a 559-yard, par 5, requiring a tee shot over a water hazard.

AMERICAN GOLFERS CLUB
3850 N. Federal Hwy., Ft. Lauderdale
(954) 564-8760
This is a nice executive course on flat terrain (after all, this is Florida!) with small greens and no water hazards. There's also "pitch and putt" course for novices, with holes ranging from 40 to 63 yards.

ARROWHEAD GOLF COURSE
8201 SW 24th St., Davie
(954) 475-8200
You'd better be a straight hitter, because this is a narrow course, with thick rough lining the fairways. The course has several dog-leg fairways. The greens are medium-size, and there are plenty of mounds and sand bunkers. Eleven of the holes feature canals. There's also a driving range.

BONAVENTURE COUNTRY CLUB—GREEN MONSTER COURSE AND RESORT COURSE
200 Bonaventure Blvd., Ft. Lauderdale
(954) 389-2100
www.golfbonaventure.com
The Bonaventure Country Club has a reputation for great golf, and there are two outstanding courses from which you can

158

choose (or you can play both!). The East Course (Green Monster) is the championship one, and you'll encounter water on 14 holes. The signature hole is #3, a 173-yard, par 3, with a waterfall looming ominously across the front of the green. The West (Resort) Course has less length, less water, and two extra par 3s. The club hosts the Dixie Amateur and a Pro Family Tournament each year.

BROKEN WOODS COUNTRY CLUB
9001 W. Sample Rd., Coral Springs
(954) 752-2140
This course has greens of average difficulty and tight fairways—and if you like water challenges, you'll run into them on 15 holes. The 5,290-yard men's also has a ladies' course rating of 68.9 and slope of 119.

CAROLINA GOLF CLUB
3011 N. Rock Island Rd., Margate
(954) 753-4000
www.carolinagolfclub.com
The Carolina Golf Club is a favorite of golfers in the northern part of the county. The fairways are narrow and challenging, with houses and trees on both sides. The greens are somewhat fast. And there are water hazards on 17—that's right, 17—holes. Bring your best game, if you're not an experienced golfer. But even if you don't do well on the course, you can relax afterward in the club, which resembles a plantation home of the pre–Civil War South.

CLUB AT EMERALD HILLS
4100 N. Hills Dr., Hollywood
(954) 961-4000
www.theclubatemeraldhills.com
The sixth hole is the most challenging on this course, because it features a green that has three levels. It's a pretty course, with rolling fairways. And there are water hazards on 10 holes.

COLONY WEST COUNTRY CLUB—CHAMPIONSHIP COURSE AND GLADES COURSE
6800 N. Pine Island Rd., Tamarac
(954) 726-7710
www.golfcolonywest.com
These are considered very good courses, and they're almost on the edge of the Everglades. The fairways are wide open, and there seem to be water hazards everywhere you look. On the Championship Course, water comes into play on 12 holes. The most challenging hole here is the twelfth, a 452-yard, par 4, on which you'll have to make a tee shot through a cypress forest onto a green surrounded by water. The Glades Course is easier, with water on only five holes. Walking is permitted on this course, but you'll need a cart on the Championship Course.

COOPER COLONY COUNTRY CLUB
5050 SW 90th Ave., Cooper City
(954) 434-2181
This course has well-bunkered fairways, along with rolling greens that are pretty fast. And—of course, in Florida—there's water on several holes.

CORAL RIDGE COUNTRY CLUB
3801 Bayview Dr., Ft. Lauderdale
(954) 566-4746
www.coralridgecc.com
This course is owned by Robert Trent Jones, so you know it's a good one. The signature hole is #16, a 181-yard, par 3, requiring a tee shot from an elevated tee to a green surrounded by water on three sides. Sand bunkers are situated both in front of and behind the green, so your shot better be precise.

And the fairways are bordered by palm trees on both sides.

COUNTRY CLUB OF CORAL SPRINGS
10800 W. Sample Rd., Coral Springs
(954) 753-2930
www.countryclubofcoralsprings.com
Don't lose focus on this course because you'll end up paying for it. It's a tough course, with trees snuggled up close along the edges of the fairways. And there are roughs all over the place, so you'll need to be accurate.

i If you hit a ball into the water, do not go in after it! Repeat, do *not* go in after it. Alligators spend most of their time in water, or seeking out water. And they're not all that particular about the location of the water they choose. Forget about the ball. Forget about any stroke penalty. It's not worth losing an arm—or worse!

CRYSTAL LAKE COUNTRY CLUB & TAM O'SHANTER GOLF COURSE—NORTH COURSE AND SOUTH COURSE
3800 Crystal Lake Dr., Pompano Beach
(954) 942-1900
www.crystallakecc.com
You can't do much better than two wonderful courses designed by the legendary Rees Jones—and that's what you have here. On the North Course, designed for the more experienced duffer, the toughest hole is #8, a 410-yard, par 4. You've got to avoid the water on your tee shot, and then you've got to approach the elongated green by hitting up a severe dogleg. The Crystal Lake South Course is great for the average golfer. The fairways are narrow and tree lined, and the greens are small and fast.

DEER CREEK GOLF CLUB
2801 Country Club Blvd.,
Deerfield Beach
(954) 421-5550
www.deercreekgolfclub.net
This is not your usual Florida course. In fact, Deer Creek's rolling hills and steep bunkers are more characteristic of good courses up north. The signature hole, fittingly, is the one you have to wait a few hours to approach. Number 18 is a 423-yard, par-4, overlooking the water and the beautiful old Key West–style clubhouse (elements of nautical, Key West "gingerbread"/Victorian style designs). All of the greens, tees, and fairways have been purposely over-seeded, giving the grass a vibrant green effect. This course has long been a favorite of visiting movie stars and golf celebrities.

DEERFIELD COUNTRY CLUB
50 Fairway Dr., Deerfield Beach
(954) 427-6326
www.dccfl.com
This course's greens are moderate and fairly flat, and the fairways are open. There are some sand bunkers, but no water hazards. The ladies' par is actually 70.

DIPLOMAT RESORT COUNTRY CLUB
501 Diplomat Pkwy., Hallandale
(954) 457-2000
www.diplomatcentral.com
This course is wide open and flat, with a medium-cut rough. There are scattered lakes on the course, which come into play on nine different holes.

EAGLE LAKES GOLF COURSE
7590 W. Atlantic Blvd., Margate
(954) 979-9446

If you've got an "A" game, you probably wouldn't want to take it here. But if you're not an experienced golfer—or simply just not a very skilled golfer—you'll like this course. All holes but one (which is a par 4) are par 3s.

EAGLE WOODS GOLF & COUNTRY CLUB
3700 S. Douglas Rd., Miramar
(954) 431-3800
This is a semiprivate club with a nice course and plenty of water that you'll have to go over or around. There's a stream, in fact, that runs right alongside holes #4, 5, and 6. And, if the stream isn't enough of a challenge, you'll probably really enjoy the lake on the fairways on #8 and 9.

ECO GOLF CLUB
1451 Taft St., Hollywood
(954) 922-8755
www.ecogolfclub.com
This is a well-maintained executive course with nine holes, for all experience levels. It's in a rather unusual setting—surrounded by a water-treatment plant, with channels running on both sides of the course. Not surprisingly, three of the nine holes require tee shots over water to the green. Perhaps surprisingly, though, the course is a fairly scenic one. Sand bunkers are spread throughout the course, and there are plenty of palm trees around the holes. Accuracy—rather than power—is the key at Eco, because of all the hazards.

FLAMINGO LAKES COUNTRY CLUB
701 SW Flamingo West Dr.,
Pembroke Pines
(954) 435-6110
You've got to be an accurate golfer here because the fairways are narrow, and you'll

run into water hazards on 16 of the 18 holes. This course was designed for all skill levels—novice to pro. The signature (and most fun!) hole is #14, a 140-yard, par 3, requiring a tee shot to the green—which is on an island.

FORT LAUDERDALE COUNTRY CLUB— NORTH COURSE AND SOUTH COURSE
415 E. Country Club Circle,
Ft. Lauderdale
(954) 587-8040
www.fortlauderdalecc.com
You can take your pick here—a longer course with less hazards, or a shorter course with more. The tees and greens on the North Course (the longer one) are rolling and somewhat elevated, waste bunkers line many of the fairways, and there are water hazards on six holes. The South Course is shorter and has less water, but it's filled with challenging doglegs and greens.

GRAND PALMS GOLF & COUNTRY CLUB—CHAMPIONSHIP COURSE AND GRAND/ROYAL COURSE
900 S. Hollybrook Dr., Pembroke Pines
(954) 431-4545
Grand Palms is a private club with two great courses. The Championship Course has plenty of trees along the fairways, elevated greens (although the rest of the terrain is mostly flat) that are medium speed, and several lakes around which you'll have to navigate. The most difficult hole is #6, a 394-yard, par 4, which is guarded by sentry-like trees on one side and two lakes on the other. In addition, there's a hill that slopes down to the water, so you'll want to hit your tee shot with a slight fade. Next, you'll need to hit an approach shot to a green that's elevated . . . and well-protected by more sentries (bunkers!). The Championship Course

is so well-regarded that it hosts an annual Pro-Am. The other course is a par 3: much shorter, more open, and perfect for beginners and perhaps some seniors. The fairways are not particularly scenic, unless you like the sight of condominiums. However, there are some canals that you'll have to get past.

GRAND PALMS HOTEL & GOLF RESORT
110 Grand Palms Dr., Pembroke Pines
(954) 437-3334

This club has three nine-hole courses that are played in 18-hole combinations. And the courses are interesting; each of them has water obstacles on almost every hole. This is true "placement" golf, so accuracy is at a premium. Of the three courses, the Royal Course is the toughest.

GRANDE OAKS GOLF CLUB
3201 W. Rolling Hills Circle,
Ft. Lauderdale
(954) 916-2900
www.grandeoaks.com

This resort has an 18-hole regulation course, and a 35-acre practice facility with four actual holes. The Grande Oaks Course is on rolling terrain, with fairways lined with scenic Spanish oaks and Australian pines, and an occasional water hazard. In addition, when you play here, you're not only playing a good course—you're actually playing on a piece of cinematic history. Grande Oaks was the location for the hilarious 1980 movie *Caddyshack*.

HILLCREST GOLF CLUB
4600 Hillcrest Dr., Hollywood
(954) 983-3142
www.hillcrestgcc.com

Hillcrest has two courses, an 18-holer and a 9-holer. The most challenging hole on the

Championship Course is #9; it's a 421-yard, par 4, and you'd better be accurate because the green is on an island. Both the fairways and greens are expansive, and the greens have a bit of a "wave" to them. The Executive Course is small—but it, too, is somewhat challenging, with wide fairways, small greens, and plenty of bunkers.

HILLSBORO PINES GOLF COURSE
2410 Century Blvd., Deerfield Beach
(954) 421-1188

This executive course has a lot of interesting features; the fairways are very diverse, and so is the undulation in the greens, several of which are multilevel. And there are enough roughs to make things challenging. The terrain is mostly flat, but here and there you'll run into a mound which will require your concentration. Six of the holes have water hazards.

HOLLYWOOD BEACH GOLF & COUNTRY CLUB
1650 Johnson St., Hollywood
(954) 927-1751
www.hollywoodbeachgolf.com

This course is affiliated with the Hollywood Beach Hotel, and is sort of a landmark for local golfers. The terrain is mostly flat, with open, tree-lined fairways. You'll run into water hazards on eight of the holes, and you'll hit from elevated tees on a few others. The greens are large and fast, and to reach them, you'll need to get by a number of sand bunkers.

INVERRARY GOLF CLUB—EAST COURSE, WEST COURSE, EXECUTIVE COURSE
3840 Inverrary Blvd., Lauderhill
(954) 733-7550
www.inverrarygolf.com

Inverrary's one of the true centers of golf in Greater Fort Lauderdale, and you'll find three courses here: two 18-hole regulation courses and one executive course. In fact, if you're a real golf fan, the name may ring a bell—the Jackie Gleason Tournament, along with an LPGA event, were played here in 1991 and '92. The East Course is wider and longer than the West Course. But the West Course is trickier; the greens are all elevated, and you'll run into sand bunkers almost everywhere you look, requiring you to be a bit of a magician on some shots.

JACARANDA GOLF CLUB—EAST COURSE AND WEST COURSE
9200 W. Broward Blvd., Plantation
(954) 472-5836

Jacaranda's been a hangout for the good-golf-and-good-times set for a long time, with two nice courses and an active clubhouse. If you play the East Course, you'd better like water—'cause you'll run into it on 16 of the 18 holes. And you won't have to wait long for the toughest hole. It's arguably #1, a 549-yard, par 5, on which you'll have to engineer a tee shot up a dogleg left fairway. The greens on the East Course are very fast. The West Course is shorter, not as fast, but has more sand bunkers and nicer natural scenery. This club offers all the amenities of a private country club. U.S. Open Qualifying and PGA Tour Qualifying Tournaments were here in 1993.

LAGO MAR COUNTRY CLUB
500 NW 127th Ave., Plantation
(954) 472-7047
www.lagomarcc.com

This is a tight course that has enough tricky touches to make it really interesting. It's laced with canals (ubiquitous in Florida, of course), and you'll encounter one on pretty much every hole. The fairways have a lot of trees, and a lot of roughs. Many of the greens are sloped, and all of them are fast. And the trickiest hole of all—even though it's only 178 yards and par 3—is #17, on which you'll have to angle a shot over the water.

LAUDERHILLS GOLF COURSE
4141 NW 16th St., Lauderhill
(954) 730-2990

This is a short nine-hole course. The fairways are narrow, and the greens are fast and flat. Canals ramble throughout the course.

LEISUREVILLE FAIRWAY
2921 W. Golf Blvd., Pompano Beach
(954) 946-0350

This is a short nine-hole course in a retirement community, reserved only for the residents and their guests. And it's a fun course, both to walk and to play. There are no sand bunkers to be found, but there is, however, a lake. The signature hole is #8; it's only a 100-yard, par 3, but to get to the hole you've got to take a shot over water.

MAINLANDS GOLF COURSE
4500 Monterey Dr., Tamarac
(954) 731-6710

This is an executive course, easy to walk and popular with seniors. The fairways are wide, and there are a couple of ponds around which you'll need to maneuver.

OAK TREE COUNTRY CLUB
2400 W. Prospect Rd., Ft. Lauderdale
(954) 733-8616

This course is part of the Lauderdale-by-the-Sea Resort & Beach Club. The greens are up-and-down, and they're very fast. You'll have to deal with narrow fairways, along with water on a couple of holes. It all makes for an interesting challenge . . . even for experienced golfers.

ORANGEBROOK COUNTRY CLUB—
EAST COURSE AND WEST COURSE
400 Entrada Dr., Hollywood
(954) 967-4653
www.orangebrook.com
Both of these courses are basically flat. The greens run the gamut in size, and there are enough sand bunkers scattered around to make for some challenging holes. The East Course features more water hazards, while the West Course is more open and easier to hit (and to plan your shots). The big hole on the West Course is the thirteenth (and the longest), a 580-yard, par 5.

ORIOLE GOLF & TENNIS CLUB OF
MARGATE
8000 W. Margate Blvd., Margate
(954) 972-8140
www.oriolegolfclub.com
A lot of local folks really enjoy playing this course. The fairways are tight, and you'll deal with water on nine of the holes.

PALM-AIRE COUNTRY CLUB—CYPRESS
COURSE, OAKS COURSE, AND PALM
COURSE
2600 Palm Aire Dr. North,
Pompano Beach
(954) 974-7699
www.palmairegolf.com
If you can't find a course you like here, you better give up because there are five of them, all very good. The Palms Course has rolling greens with a lot of bunkers and a lot of water hazards. The Pines Course is favored by long-ball hitters; but after they hit their long drives, they've got to deal with large

bunkers. The Sabal Course is an executive course with a lot of bunkers, and, with 14 par 3s and four par 4s, it's a great place to work on your short game. On the Oaks Course, you'll run into water on 10 holes, and in addition, you'll have to navigate the many doglegs. The Cypress Course, too, has doglegs, along with water hazards on 11 holes and sand bunkers seemingly wherever you look. On this course, the toughest hole may be #18. It's 430 yards, par 4, and you'll have to come up with a creative approach shot to the green, which is elevated.

PEMBROKE LAKES GOLF AND
RACQUET CLUB
10500 Taft St., Pembroke Pines
(954) 431-4144
www.pembrokelakesgolf.com
The narrow fairways require a high degree of accuracy, and the water—on 13 holes— requires a great deal of strategy, and a steady hand. The last four holes are without any water hazards, but don't breathe a sigh of relief yet; there are plenty of sand traps. It doesn't get any easier as you head toward the final holes, either. Number 14 is a monster—a 519-yard, par 5 that requires a tee shot to reach a fairway with water on both sides. And the approach is a green with water on three sides and sand bunkers both in front and back.

PINE ISLAND RIDGE COUNTRY CLUB
9400 Pine Ridge Dr., Ft. Lauderdale
(954) 472-1080
www.pircc.com
This is an executive course—but a difficult one, to be sure. There are trees all over the place. And there are obstacles aplenty; if a hole doesn't have out-of-bounds markers, it's sure to have water hazards. The fairways are narrow, and the greens are small.

PINES PAR 3 GOLF COURSE
315 SW 62nd Ave., Hollywood
(954) 989-9288

This is a "pitch and putt" course without sand bunkers or water hazards. You'll hit all your tee shots from mats, onto a wide course. This is a great place for novice golfers, and for experienced golfers whose short game needs some improvement. And the course is lighted, so you can work on your game at night, as well.

RAINTREE GOLF RESORT
1600 S. Hiatus Rd., Pembroke Pines
(954) 432-4400
www.raintreegolfresort.lbu.com

Raintree Golf Resort has a par 72 championship course measuring 6,456 yards. There are six par 3s, six par 4s, and six par 5s, and the course is appropriate for a wide range of players. Accuracy is key to this course—because it's got water hazards at every hole but one! Many of the greens are somewhat elevated. You'll have to earn your cold drink in the clubhouse, because the toughest hole is the last; it's a 385-yard, par 4, and you'll have to leapfrog a large lake to get to a small green. There are practice facilities here, as well, with putting greens, a sand trap, and a lighted "aqua range."

SABAL PALM GOLF COURSE
5101 W. Commercial Blvd., Tamarac
(954) 731-2600

This is a good course for beginners and seniors, but that doesn't mean there aren't challenges. Every hole but two, in fact, has bunkers. And, as there are five ponds and six canals, you'll come up against water hazards on almost every hole. The ninth hole is the star here: a 575-yard, par 5. It'll take several well-hit balls to reach the green.

SPRINGTREE COUNTRY CLUB
8350 Spring Tree Dr., Sunrise
(954) 572-2270

This executive course is fairly flat, with medium-size greens that are slow to medium. But it's a thinker's course nonetheless, because there are water hazards or out-of-bounds markers on every hole but one.

SUNRISE COUNTRY CLUB
7400 NW 24th Place, Sunrise
(954) 742-4333

The greens on the course have recently been redesigned by noted architect Charles Ankrom. There is a lake here and a canal, and they come into play on some holes. This course looks much like one you'd see up north, because it has a lot of trees.

SUNRISE LAKES PHASE-3 GOLF COURSE
9361 Sunrise Lakes Blvd., Sunrise
(954) 741-8352

This executive course is for residents and their guests only. Canals run all through the course, and you'll run into them on a number of holes. The fairways are open, but guarded by a lot of bunkers.

TPC AT EAGLE TRACE
1111 Eagle Trace Blvd., Coral Springs
(954) 753-7600
www.tpceagletrace.com

If you're of a certain age, you've seen this course on TV before; it was the home of the PGA Tour's Honda Classic in the '80s. And it achieved plenty of fame afterwards, as well—*Golf Digest* chose this course the "Best in State" for 1995–1996. Situated in the swanky development of Eagle Trace, the course itself is a showpiece. It's filled with lush tropical vegetation, and its rolling fairways and narrow greens are often angled away from the player. Both lakes and streams run through the course.

TPC AT HERON BAY
11801 Heron Bay Blvd., Coral Springs
(954) 340-9160
www.heronbaygolfclub.net
This magnificent course, set amidst the upscale Heron Bay area of north Coral Springs, became an instant sensation the moment it opened in 1996. For one thing, it was designed by well-known pro Mark McCumber. For another, it's the site of the Honda Classic. Exactly how challenging is this course? Well, McCumber, for one, says it "has 18 signature holes." The fairways are generous, but your driving will have to be on-point, because there are a lot of big bunkers. There isn't much water here, somewhat unusual for a good Florida course. But there are 109 bunkers that'll keep you busy, both mentally and physically.

WESTON HILLS COUNTRY CLUB—
PLAYERS COURSE AND TOUR COURSE
2600 Country Club Way, Ft. Lauderdale
(954) 384-4653
www.westonhillsgolfclub.com
Weston Hills is the former host of the PGA Honda Classic, so you know the two courses here are excellent. The Tour Course has water hazards on six holes. The biggie is the eighteenth, which will ensure that you enter the clubhouse bushed both mentally and physically. It's a 585-yard, par 5 that'll have you really sweating, with a large water hazard running down the entire left side of the fairway and a green that slopes from front to back—which can make your approach shot a very interesting proposition. The Players Course is flowing with lakes and ponds, and

many of them will stand between you and a decent score.

WOODLANDS COUNTRY CLUB—
CYPRESS COURSE AND PINES COURSE
7801 NW 80th Ave., Tamarac
(954) 722-4300
www.woodlandscountryclub.net
There are two courses here, each with plenty of water and plenty of bunkers. The Pine Course has small fairways, while the fairways on the Cypress Course are larger.

WOODLANDS COUNTRY CLUB—EAST
COURSE AND WEST COURSE
4600 Woodlands Blvd., Tamarac
(954) 731-2500
www.woodlandscountryclub.net
This club has two regulation courses, very similar in design, with greens that tend to be long and narrow. Both courses were designed with all skill levels in mind.

GYMS

You don't have to abandon your workout routine when you come to Fort Lauderdale. Here you'll find dozens of gyms and fitness centers—some owned by the city, others private facilities that allow short-term visitors to purchase a day pass, or sometimes even a week- or monthlong pass. Some even offer free day or week trial memberships, although you should be prepared for endless phone calls encouraging you to up your membership if you opt for a free trial.

Chains such as **Gold's Gym** (www .goldsgym.com), **Bally's** (www.ballyfitness .com), and **24 Hour Fitness** (www.24hour fitness.com) all have several locations in and around the area. Fort Lauderdale also has a number independent health clubs and gyms, many of which cost a little more than the larger chains. These gyms offer a broad range of workout equipment and classes and offer personal training opportunities for an additional cost. A small sampling of some of the most popular gyms in town can be found here. See the phone book for more gyms near you.

BETTER BODIES GYM CORP.
1164 E. Oakland Park Blvd., #100
Oakland Park
(954) 561-7977

BEYOND FITNESS
9900 Griffin Rd., Cooper City
(954) 680-8755

BODY SOLUTIONS
10199 Cleary Blvd., Plantation
(954) 475-4966
www.bodysolutionsinc.com

CLASSICAL PILATES
1425 S. Andrews Ave., Ft. Lauderdale
(954) 524-2939
www.classicalpilates.net

CLUB FORT LAUDERDALE
110 NW 5th Ave., Ft. Lauderdale
(954) 525-3344
www.the-clubs.com

DOWNTOWN GYM & FITNESS CLUB
713 E. Broward Blvd., Ft. Lauderdale
(954) 462-7669
www.downtowngym.net

DYNAMIC BODY WELLNESS CENTER
13242 W. Broward Blvd., Plantation
(954) 916-8888

1164
1164 E. Oakland Park Blvd., Oakland Park
(954) 561-2920

SAMSON'S IRON HOUSE GYM
2700 NW 44th St., Oakland Park
(954) 484-0068

SIMPLY FITT
6842 Stirling Rd., Hollywood
(954) 987-2322

TAMARAC FITNESS CENTER
7935 W. McNab Rd., Tamarac
(954) 726-1070

UNIVERSITY FITNESS & TANNING
7166 N. University Dr., Tamarac
(954) 718-8200

WELLNESS CENTER
Broward General Hospital
1600 S. Andrews Ave., Ft. Lauderdale
(954) 355-4386
www.browardhealth.org/bgwellness

X-PRESS FITNESS & METABOLIC
8415 W. McNab Rd., Tamarac
(954) 718-7100

YOGAROSA INC.
110 N. Federal Hwy., Ft. Lauderdale
(954) 456-6077

YMCA Broward County

For more information on various YMCA locations throughout the Greater Fort Lauderdale area, check out **www.ymcabroward .org.**

EAST BROWARD YMCA FAMILY CENTER
1830 W. Broward Blvd., Ft. Lauderdale
(954) 334-9622

GREATER HOLLYWOOD YMCA FAMILY CENTER
3161 Taft St., Hollywood
(954) 989-9622

L.A. LEE YMCA FAMILY CENTER
408 NW 14th Terrace, Ft. Lauderdale
(954) 467-2444

LAUDERHILL COMMUNITY YMCA CENTER
1901 NW 49th Ave. (inside the Lauderhill Middle School), Lauderhill
(754) 322-3608

PARKLAND YMCA FAMILY CENTER
10559 Trails End, Parkland
(954) 384-9622

PEMBROKE PINES YMCA FAMILY CENTER
501 SW 172nd Ave., Pembroke Pines
(954) 727-9622

SHEINBERG FAMILY YMCA OF WESTON
20201 Saddle Club Rd., Weston
(954) 424-9622

HORSEBACK RIDING & LESSONS

BAR B RANCH
3500 Peaceful Ridge Rd./SW 121 Avenue, Davie
(954) 424-1060
www.bar-b-ranch.com
In the heart of western-themed Davie, Bar B offers riding lessons as well as trail rides. The ranch reaches both English or Western riding styles, and experienced riders or those confident enough to go it alone can simply rent a horse for the day (from $35 per hour). Riding lessons cost $50 per hour (appointments required); 1.5 hour ($45) trail rides through nearby Robbins Open Space Preserve offer a glimpse of Old Florida and resident Longhorn cattle while riding through one of Broward County's few remaining oak hammocks. Kids are keen on the ponies available for hire ($12 for half hour; $20 per hour) and the ranch's summer camps (ages 7 to 16) are

a favorite with both local and out-of-state kids and teenagers.

THE BRITISH BARN
17640 SW 52nd Court, Southwest Ranches
(954) 252-5574
www.thebritishbarn.com
This is a full-service equestrian facility, offering private lessons, Saturday day camp, and summer camp. You can board your horse here as well. And you can buy one.

GALLOWAYS FARM
5400 Pinetree Rd., Parkland
(954) 255-5856
www.gallowaysfarm.com
Trainer Ellie Schofield is considered one of the best at what she does, and she has the medals to prove it. She specializes in teaching adults, amateurs, and advanced junior riders.

HORSE TALES RANCH
2995 SW 121st Ave., Davie
(954) 240-6080
www.horsetalesranch.com
The "tale" of this ranch started in 2004, with the rescue of a horse named Baby Girl. And now, the total number of rescued horses stands at over a dozen. You can board horses here, buy them, or learn how to ride them. There's also summer camp and spring-break camp for kids.

MALACHI ACRES
4701 Godfrey Rd., Parkland
(954) 464-1239
www.malachiacres.com
Malachi Acres is in the community of Parkland, which is about as "horsey" as you can get. They offer lessons for all ages and all skills, as well as boarding.

PONY PALOOZA CLUB
Wattland II Barn
8000 NW 84th Ave., Parkland
(954) 383-0044
www.ponypaloozaclub.com

As you might have guessed from the name, this is a good place for your children to learn horseback riding and to learn it with other children. At this working barn in the heart of horse country, children learn about horses before they ever mount one. And they'll get hands-on experiences in the feeding and care of the horses. In fact, they'll actually be given notebooks in which to record their notes.

TRADEWINDS PARK
3600 W. Sample Rd., Coconut Creek
(954) 357-8870
Stables: (954) 357-8720
www.broward.org/parks

Tradewinds is one of two Broward County parks that offer horseback riding and pony rides. Guided Trail Rides are available on Sat, Sun, and designated holidays, weather permitting. Trail rides are an hour long, and are on a first-come, first-served basis. Trail ride sales close 30 minutes prior to the scheduled ride time. Children must be 9 years old or at least 52 inches tall, and must be accompanied by an adult. Weekday trail rides are available from Oct through May by appointment only. The littlest ones can have fun here, too. Pony Rides are offered on Sat, Sun, and designated holidays from 11 a.m. to 3:30 p.m., weather permitting. Children must be less than 52 inches tall to ride the ponies.

TREE TOPS PARK
3900 SW 100th Ave., Davie
(954) 370-3750
www.broward.org/parks

Tree Tops is the other Broward County park offering horseback and pony rides. Call AAD Horse Adventures at (954) 830-7800. Hours of operation are Sat, Sun, and most holidays from 9:30 a.m. to 4 p.m. (last one-hour trail ride leaves at 2 p.m., last half-hour ride leaves at 3:30 p.m. and last pony ride is at 4 p.m.) Horse trail rides are $35 per hour or $25 per half hour. Pony rides are $1.50 for once around the circle or $5 for four times around the circle. Weekday rides are available by appointment. All horse and pony riders (as well as pony walkers) must wear closed-toe shoes, and long pants are strongly suggested for all riders. An equestrian trail map of the park is on the park's map page.

ICE SKATING & ICE HOCKEY

You might think—ice-skating and Fort Lauderdale? What's up with that? But yes, Floridians love ice-skating, and on a sweltering August afternoon, stepping into a cool, slippery world and a spin on a smooth slab of ice spells utopia. All of the following rinks offer skating parties and group events.

GLACIER ICE & SNOW ARENA
4601 N. Federal Hwy., Lighthouse Point
(954) 943-1437
www.glaciericeandsnow.com

This 40,000-square-foot ice-skating rink offers ice-skating classes, hockey leagues, and free skating for those who just want to drop by and have fun. They also feature sleigh rides, snowball competitions, and other wintery fun from up north. Access to the rink for public skating costs $8, renting skates costs $3. Check out their website for an up-to-date public ice-skating schedule and hours of operation.

Little Leagues

Coconut Creek Little League
(954) 968-3643
www.creekbaseball.com

Coral Springs American Little League
(954) 825-8172
www.csall.com

Coral Springs National Little League
www.csnll.org

Deerfield Beach Little League
www.eteamz.com/DeerfieldBeach/sponsors/index.cfm

District 21 Little League Baseball, Inc. (Plantation)
(954) 792-7924

Fort Lauderdale Federal Little League
(954) 525-4910
www.eteamz.com

Fort Lauderdale Little League
www.fortlauderdalelittleleague.com

North Pompano Beach Little League
(954) 783-7083
www.leaguelineup.com

North Coral Springs Little League
www.eteamz.com/northsprings/locations/index.cfm

Northeast Little League (Oakland Park)
(954) 771-4980

Northeast Little League (Fort Lauderdale)
(954) 771-7151

Parkland Little League
www.active.com/baseball-league/parkland-fl

Pembroke Pines Little League
(954) 983-0004

Southside Little League (Fort Lauderdale)
(954) 327-1882
www.eteamz.com/southsidelittleleague/sponsors

Sunrise Little League
(954) 741-2580
www.sunrisefl.gov/2park_sunrise.html

Tamarac Little League
(954) 720-0301
www.eteamz.com/tamaraclittleleague/index.cfm

Weston Area Little League
www.wallbaseball.org/safety.asp

Wilton Manors Little League
(954) 390-2104
www.leaguelineup.com

INCREDIBLE ICE
3299 Sportsplex Dr., Coral Springs
(954) 341-9956
www.incredibleice.com
With 125,000 square feet, this place is massive. But what else could it be as the home of the Florida Panthers? Check the website for the schedule and drop by to catch a training session (free). Alternatively, come here to skate the heat away, take figure-skating classes, do some curling, or play some ice hockey. Public-skating sessions vary each month (and are subject to hockey-practice schedules), so check the website for details. Every weekend they jam out with live DJs and a light show projected onto the wall

(trust us—it's groovy). Public skating costs $6.50 to $9 (depends on when you go); skate rental will set you back $3.

PINES ICE ARENA
12425 Taft St., Pembroke Pines
(954) 704-8700
This great neighborhood ice-skating rink might not be the area's biggest or snazziest, but it's got all the basics: public skating, figure-skating lessons, and ice hockey. Public skating is available Mon to Fri 10 a.m. to 3 p.m., Sat and Sun 10 a.m. to 5 p.m., and 8:30 to 11:30 p.m. and costs $7 to $9 (depends when you go); skate rental is $4.

MARTIAL ARTS

A USA KARATE
6473 Taft St., Hollywood
(954) 966-8005
www.usakaratedo.com/

ACADEMY OF KOEI-KAN KARATE DO
2526 N. SR 7, Hollywood
(954) 894-8244

AIKIDO OF FLORIDA AIKIKAI
3326 Farragut St., Hollywood
(954) 981-4824
www.aikidoonline.com

AMERICAN INTERNATIONAL KARATE
7107 W. Broward Blvd., Plantation
(954) 587-5008
www.mudokai.com/main.html

AMERICAN PRIDE TAE KWONDO
2670 N. University Dr., #206, Sunrise
(954) 578-1000
www.americanpridetkd.com/

AMERICAN SHORIN RYU KARATE
12349 SW 53rd St., #203, Cooper City
(954) 252-1950

AMERICAN TKA MARTIAL ARTS
8604 W. SR 84, Davie
(954) 472-2554
americantka.com

AMERICAN TOP TEAM
7340 W. Atlantic Blvd., Margate
(954) 935-9497
www.americantopteam.com/index.php

ATEMI-RYU SCHOOL OF SELF-DEFENSE
3253 Ridge Trace, Davie
(954) 452-9419

ATEMI RYU JU-JITSU
6936 Stirling Rd., Hollywood
(954) 967-8272
www.atemi-ryu.com

ATEMI RYU BUSHIKAN SCHOOL OF SELF-DEFENSE
1323 SE 17th St., Ft. Lauderdale
(954) 763-8611
www.atemi-ryu.com

BART VALE'S ISFA
10162 NW 50th St., Sunrise
(954) 746-0202
www.livestrong.com/
business-bart-vales-isfa_954-746-0202

BILL CLARK'S ATA BLACK BELT
1153 N. Federal Hwy., Ft. Lauderdale
(954) 567-5686

BLACK BELTS KENPO ACADEMY INC.
5107 Coconut Creek Pkwy., Margate
(954) 971-3877

BLACK BELT STUDIOS INC.
10115 Sunset Strip, Sunrise
(954) 370-0001

BRAZILIAN JIU-JITSU CENTER
1750 E. Commercial Blvd., #4,
Oakland Park
(954) 771-0084
www.bjjcenter.com

CHUNG'S WORLD MARTIAL ARTS
8337 W. Atlantic Blvd., Coral Springs
(954) 344-7000

DRAGONS DEN
4932 NW 88th Ave., Sunrise
(954) 741-3069

DYNAMIC TAE KWON-DO ACADEMY
5892 Stirling Rd., Hollywood
(954) 961-0910

EAST WEST KARATE
1311 N. University Dr., Coral Springs
(954) 346-9300
www.eastwestcoralsprings.net

KIMLING'S ACADEMY OF MARTIAL ARTS
3550 N. Andrews Ave., Oakland Park
(954) 564-3833
www.kimlingsacademy.com/kickboxing
.html

ROGER KRAHL'S ULTIMATE KARATE
4553 N. Pine Island Rd., Sunrise
(954) 742-5753
www.attwolfpack.com

SANG'S MARTIAL ARTS
3367 N. University Dr., Hollywood
(954) 431-6000

SOUTH FLORIDA WING CHUN KUNG
4426 N. University Dr., Lauderhill
(954) 741-3373
www.wingchunacademy.us

SOUTH FLORIDA WING CHUN KUNG FU ACADEMY
11300 NW 45th Place, Sunrise
(954) 749-2905

STEVE'S HOUSE OF KARATE
10016 Griffin Rd., Cooper City
(954) 680-4204
www.steveskarate.com/bo-staff-steves-
house-of-karate.htm

TEAM KUNG FU & KICK BOXING
4943 Sheridan St., Hollywood
(954) 964-7400

TOTAL FITNESS KICKBOXING
830 E. Oakland Park Blvd., Oakland Park
(954) 568-2707

UNIVERSITY OF MARTIAL ARTS
5107 Coconut Creek Pkwy., Margate
(954) 977-7820

USA KENPO KARATE INC.
740 Riverside Dr., Coral Springs
(954) 575-1030

WARRIOR & SCHOLAR KENPO KARATE
7230 Taft St., Hollywood
(954) 981-1646
www.warriorandscholar.com/contact-us
.html

ROCK CLIMBING

CORAL CLIFFS ROCK CLIMBING CENTER
3400 SW 26th Terr., #A4, Ft. Lauderdale
(954) 321-9898
www.coralcliffs.com
If you're into extreme sports or preparing for a challenging hike, consider visiting Fort Lauderdale's indoor rock-climbing gym with the clever name, Coral Cliffs (get it? Florida has lots of coral, and this facility offers you the cliff you won't find in the state). They offer

over 55 top-routed routes, 25 lead routes, and oodles of overhangs. At press time they were planning to expand to include a bouldering cave in late 2010. Employees at the rock-climbing gyms can spot you and hold the other end of your rope during your climb, but it's more fun to bring along a buddy to help you out. The facility also offers lessons to give you the skills necessary to be a better climber both at the gym and on real mountains. First-time climbers, rest assured: this gym emphasizes safety, and employees will—literally—show you the ropes beforehand and help you out on the ground throughout the climb.

There's no minimum age to rock climb at either location, but parents are required to sign a liability waiver for children under 18.

Keep in mind that the required harness can't be worn with skirts or dresses. Rock climbing can be a little pricey but a day pass is good for an entire day, even if you leave for lunch and come back. A day pass at Coral Cliffs costs $15. That doesn't include the requisite gear, which can be rented for an additional $10 (shoes, harness, belay device, and chalk bag). If you can't come with a friend and need someone to belay you, you can pay a staff member to belay you for $25 per hour.

RUNNING & WALKING

This being sunny Florida, running and walking are two of the most popular activities for all age groups. Running and walking paths flank the beaches and parks, and for the most part roads are equipped with well-maintained sidewalks. See the Parks & Beaches chapter for additional information on these training sites as well as running trails around Greater Fort Lauderdale.

There are scores of running and walking races in Greater Fort Lauderdale during the course of the year, particularly in the fall and winter months. Here are just a few; keep your eye on the sports section of the *South Florida Sun-Sentinel* for news of upcoming events, as well as the website of the **Greater Fort Lauderdale Road Runners Club** (www.gflrrc .net).

GREATER FORT LAUDERDALE ROAD RUNNER'S CLUB
(954) 461-5515
gflrrc.net

This friendly, local running club is a great place to find a running partner, meet new people (newcomers and transplants who recently relocated are most welcome), or train for that marathon you've always dreamed of completing. The club meets regularly—every Thurs night is a fun run/walk night which is a walk or run for three to seven miles; it meets at 6:30 p.m. at George English Park (1101 Bayview Dr., Fort Lauderdale). Every weekend features training runs. Sat morning you can join at 6:30 a.m. at the Galleria mall (2414 E. Sunrise Blvd., Fort Lauderdale), and Sun runs start at the Deerfield Beach Pavilion (on A1A just north of Hillsboro Boulevard). Additionally, training courses are scheduled throughout the week (check the website for details), and they hold a pizza social the fourth Thurs of every month (it takes place after the Thurs run—pizzas are delivered to the park). Membership is required and starts at $35 per year (discounts for multiple-year, family, and student memberships), but everyone is welcome to try it out for one run before they commit.

Races & Marathons

DANIELLA'S JOURNEY 5K RUN, WALK, AND KIDS FUN RUN
1059 SE 6th Ave., Dania Beach
www.daniellasjourney.org/Race/index
.shtml

Daniella Folleco was a Broward County resident who died in 2007 from a vicious form of bone cancer that took her life when she was only 12. But in her short life, and in the three years of her illness, Daniella displayed a rare courage, insight, and appreciation for every minute of life. Now her memory—and her life—are memorialized in an annual road race that helps raise funs for the Joe DiMaggio Children's Hospital in Hollywood and the Pine Crest School in Fort Lauderdale. Daniella wrote, "My journey has changed my life forever," and by participating in this race—and using your participation to help raise funds for these two worthy recipients—you can help change another child's journey. The race attracts more than a thousand participants from all over South Florida. And you couldn't ask for a more unique course. It takes place on the Hollywood Beach Boardwalk, from the south end to the northern, and then back again. And you'll be able to enjoy the salt air as you run, past the many colorful shops and hundreds of cheering spectators routing you on. Registration fee; held in April.

GREATER FORT LAUDERDALE ROAD RUNNERS FALL FLING 5K
Tradewinds Park
3600 W. Sample Rd., Coconut Creek
(954) 357-8870

This run takes place in September. And, let's face it, where else can you find an Over the Hill 5K and a Young and the Restless 5K on the same day, and at the same place (Tradewinds Park in Coconut Creek). In addition, there's a Fitness Walk, a Kids Fun Run, and a Youth Fun Run. Registration fee.

POMPANO BEACH RUN LIKE A BUNNY 5K RUN
City of Pompano Beach
100 W. Atlantic Blvd., Pompano Beach
(954) 786-4600
www.mypompanobeach.org/events

The City of Pompano Beach and the South Florida Racewalkers hold this event every April, combining a 5K HealthWalk and 5K Judged RaceWalk to benefit the Dynamos of Pompano Beach and the Juvenile Diabetes Foundation. It's a scenic course, running along Ocean Boulevard, and the fun doesn't stop when the runners cross the finish line. There's a post-race party on the beach, with refreshments, music, prizes, a Kids' Beach Dash, and an Easter Egg Hunt (and, usually, an appearance by a floppy-eared visitor who loves carrots and makes his rounds during this holiday). Registration fee.

RUN FOR TOMORROW HALF MARATHON
Cypress Bay High School
18600 Vista Park Blvd., Weston
(954) 384-7521
www.runfortomorrow.com/

This event is staged by the Rotary Club of Weston to raise money for worthy local charities, especially those involved with children and families in Broward County. There's a half marathon; a 5K Run/Walk competition; and a 1.5-mile Fun Walk. And afterwards there's a family festival and a pancake breakfast. There's a Get Fit Wellness Festival right after the run, along with a Kids Get Fit competition. The event takes place every December. And there's a new starting/finish line—Weston Town Center. So you can bulk up at some of the wonderful restaurants here before you start—or celebrate afterwards. Registration fee.

WALK FOR THE ANIMALS
Huizenga Plaza
Corner of Las Olas Boulevard and
Andrews Avenue, Downtown
Ft. Lauderdale
(954) 266-6817
www.walk4theanimals.com/
This event to benefit the Broward County Humane Society has been going on every March for more than two decades. And, if you love animals, here's your chance to show it! (And—surprise!—it's a dog-friendly event.) Registration fee.

ROLLER SKATING

GALAXY GATEWAY ROLLER SKATING
RINK
7500 Southgate Blvd., Margate
(954) 721-0580
Skate yourself happy at this roller rink that's been open since the 1986 (you can pretty much tell; even the Pacman video games look like they're straight out of a 1980s arcade). While the place is most popular among teenagers looking for some off-the-mall fun and birthday parties for kids of all ages, adults also enjoy tooling around the rink. Open daily 10 a.m. to midnight.

GOLD COAST ROLLER RINK
2604 S. Federal Hwy., Ft. Lauderdale
(954) 523-6783
This popular skating rink is a popular spot for people of all ages to strut their stuff on roller skates—their Thursday night Drink and Skate parties features DJs and a fun atmosphere, though do watch out for those who

can't hold their liquor. Whether drinking and rolling-skating are a good combination is questionable, but for the most part people come to have fun and grab a drink. They also host regular Roller Derby nights. Open Sun through Wed, 11 a.m. to 11 p.m., Thurs 11 a.m. to 2 a.m., Fri and Sat 11 a.m. to midnight.

My Fort Lauderdale

I've lived in all three South Florida cities, and while Fort Lauderdale lacks the Latin-tinged international sophistication and energy of Miami, on the one hand, or the Old Florida charm of West Palm Beach, it has a subtle quality all its own. You just have to cock an ear and pay close attention. You can see it lazing down the New River, which runs through the heart of the city. Or in the faded space-age architecture of the Mid-Century modern buildings and homes that survive here and there. And you can sense it on A1A, where the famous Fort Lauderdale beach retains its distinctive flavor under a new coat of paint.

—Chauncey Mabe,
Fort Lauderdale; Writer, Former
Reporter for the *South Florida
Sun-Sentinel*

TENNIS

Greater Fort Lauderdale is home to dozens of tennis courts. Many are located inside member-only country clubs, schools, or neighborhood parks that restrict court access to residents. The **Broward County Parks and Recreation Division** contains tennis courts at seven area parks (Brian Piccolo, C. B. Smith, Central Broward Regional, Lafayette Hart, Markham, T. Y., and West Lake) which you can learn more about on www.broward.org/parks or in the Parks and Beaches chapter.

There are far too many private tennis clubs, public courts and tennis associations in the area to include here, but below we are including some of the most popular clubs in town:

BRIAN PICCOLO RACQUET CENTER
9501 Sheridan St., Cooper City
(954) 437-2661
12 courts

BROWARD TENNIS FOUNDATION
11370 Lakeshore Dr., Cooper City
(954) 452-2530

CARDINAL GIBBONS HIGH SCHOOL
4601 Bayview Dr., Ft. Lauderdale
(954) 427-5827
6 courts

CORAL RIDGE COUNTRY CLUB
3801 Bayview Dr., Ft. Lauderdale
(954) 564-7386
11 courts

DAVID PARK TENNIS CENTER
510 N. 33rd Court, Hollywood
(954) 967-4237
12 courts

DEER CREEK RACQUET CLUB
2950 Deer Creek Country Club Blvd.,
Deerfield Beach
(954) 421-7890
17 courts

DEERFIELD BEACH TENNIS CENTER
222 N. Dixie Hwy., Deerfield Beach
(954) 480-4422
8 courts

GOLDEN ISLES TENNIS PARK
100 Egret Dr., Hallandale
(954) 457-1459
10 courts

GRAND PALM RACQUET CLUB
110 Grand Palms Dr. (150th Avenue),
Pembroke Pines
(954) 435-4242
6 courts

HILLSBORO CLUB, INC.
901 Hillsboro Mile (SR A1A), Hillsboro
(954) 941-2220
10 courts

LAGO MAR COUNTRY CLUB
500 NW 127th Ave., Plantation
(954) 472-3017
8 courts

LAKESHORE PARK/MIRAMAR TENNIS
8501 S. Sherman Circle, Miramar
(954) 436-1953
10 courts

LAUDERDALE TENNIS CLUB
600 Tennis Club Dr., Ft. Lauderdale
(954) 763-8657
23 courts

**LAUDERHILL PARK & RECREATION
(WOLK AND WESTWIND PARKS)**
2000 City Hall Dr., Lauderhill
(954) 245-2320
5 courts

**LIGHTHOUSE POINT COMMUNITY
TENNIS ASSOCIATION**
3500 NE 27th Ave., Lighthouse Point
(954) 946-7306
9 courts

MAXWELL PARK/PEMBROKE PINES
1200 SW 72nd Ave., Pembroke Pines
(954) 435-6759
8 courts

NORTH LAUDERDALE (CITY OF)
1300 Interlachen, North Lauderdale
(954) 974-2742
5 courts

PARKLAND (CITY OF)
6500 Parkside Dr., Parkland
(954) 757-1910
5 courts

POMPANO BEACH TENNIS CENTER
920 NE 18th Ave., Pompano Beach
(954) 786-4115
16 courts

ROSE PRICE PARK/PEMBROKE PINES
901 NW 208th Ave., Pembroke Pines
(954) 437-1287
4 courts

SILVER LAKES/PEMBROKE PINES
17601 SW 2nd Ave., Pembroke Pines
(954) 431-4147
6 courts

**SOUTH FLORIDA YOUTH
DEVELOPMENT TENNIS PROGRAM**
9441 SW 20th St., Hollywood
(954) 435-8476
6 courts

SUNRISE (CITY OF)—WELLEBY
9601 W. Oakland Park Blvd., Sunrise
(954) 572-2286
18 courts

TENNIS CENTER OF CORAL SPRINGS
2575 Sportsplex Dr., Coral Springs
(954) 344-1840
16 courts

TOWNGATE PARK/PEMBROKE PINES
901 NW 155th Ave., Pembroke Pines
(954) 450-6895
4 courts

**TOWNSHIP COMMUNITY MASTER
ASSOCIATION**
2424 Lyons Rd., Coconut Creek
(954) 968-3450
10 courts

**WILTON MANORS PARKS &
RECREATION DEPARTMENT**
524 NE 21st Court, Wilton Manors
(954) 390-2132
6 courts

YOGA

Yogis can breathe easily: There are plenty of opportunities to practice yoga in the Fort Lauderdale area. In addition to yoga classes offered at many local gyms, there are many studios around the city.

Most studios offer classes early in the morning and in the evening on weekdays, as well as at various times on weekends. Individual classes or week-, month-, or yearlong passes are available for purchase.

AMERICAN YOGA
1645 SE 3rd Court (inside the Cove Shopping Center), Deerfield Beach
(561) 789-8080
www.americanyoga.net
American Yoga offers classes in vinyasa and power yoga styles. Vinyasa basically merges several styles of yoga with breath-synchronized movement. In other words, you will move from one pose to the next on an inhale or an exhale. The center is run by Monica Schmidt, who has been teaching yoga and fitness classes for 13 years. Expect plenty of aromatherapy in each class, too. The center also offers massage therapy and yoga teacher training courses.

BIKRAM YOGA FORT LAUDERDALE
1777 South Andrews Ave., Ft. Lauderdale
(954) 523-0047
www.bikramyogafortlauderdale.com
This is the only certified Bikram yoga center in Fort Lauderdale, which means that all instructors have been trained according to the method devised and trademarked by Bikram Choudhury, the founder of this type of yoga. Bikram yoga consists of a series of 26 asanas (postures) and two breathing exercises performed in a room that is heated up to approximately 105 degrees Fahrenheit (the heat warms your muscles and facilitates increased flexibility while preventing injury). The heavy sweating also helps to detoxify the body. A single class costs $15, a set of 10 classes is $120, monthly unlimited is $145. Beginners can take advantage of the special one-week unlimited package for $20.

RED PEARL YOGA
918 NE 20th Ave, Ft. Lauderdale
(954) 828-1651
http://redpearlyoga.com

Few yoga studios manage to give you a serious workout and adhere to key yoga standards and philosophies yet still be friendly and accommodating. Set in a loftlike space with large windows facing the Middle River, Red Pearl is a judgment-free zone where you don't need to feel bad if you can't remember the last time you did a down dog. But you'll feel equally at home if you've diligently practiced yoga for a decade. Ever the crowd-pleaser, they offer a variety of yoga styles and free tea in their lounge. No wonder they won *New Times*'s Best Yoga Studio in 2009.

THE YOGA CONNECTION
6555 Nova Dr. (inside Nova Commons shopping center), Davie
(954) 577-5777
www.theyogaconnection.com
The Yoga Connection offers a wide variety of yoga classes (vinyasa, hot, hatha) as well as ample mat Pilates classes in their fantastical space replete with runny waterfalls. They also offer massage therapy, courses on teaching yoga, and excellent package deals for those who'd like to try a little bit of everything.

THE YOGA INSTITUTE OF BROWARD
10400 Griffin Rd., #205, Cooper City
(954) 452-4424
http://yogabroward.com
This Iyengar yoga institute is run by Ruth Ann Bradley, who has been teaching Iyengar for over a decade. Iyengar yoga, named for B. K. S. Iyengar, emphasizes alignment, and the asanas are done in a precise, safe, and healthy manner, paying special attention to the body's joints. Classes are offered every day except Sun, and they generally run at least one prenatal yoga class per week.

YOGA ROSA
110 N. Federal Hwy., Hallandale Beach
(954) 456-6077
www.yogarosa.com

Specializing in Iyengar yoga, this intimate studio is particularly relaxing (even by yoga studio standards). They also offer special needs classes geared to those with limited mobility, such as people with Parkinson's, multiple sclerosis, and lymphedema.

YOGA WAREHOUSE
508 SW Flagler Dr., Ft. Lauderdale
(954) 525-7726
http://yogawarehouse.org

This place focuses on classic hatha yoga, which means there is a strong emphasis on *pranayama* (breathing), and they do it well (this is not the best place for those wanting a hard-core workout like ashtanga). Classes are generally on the moderate side and take place in a warehouse space next to the train tracks (it can be a tad noisy so stay focused, people) and instructors are friendly but firm, emphasizing correct posture and form at all times.

YOGI HARI
12750 SW 33rd St. (Miramar Parkway), Miramar
(954) 843-0319
www.yogihari.com

This ashram offers traditional hatha, ratha, and nada classes, plus a variety of other interesting options like cooking classes with an emphasis on yoga principles, teacher certification, and many retreats, should you require an intensive yoga session. Yogi Hari is a respected Yogi (recognized beyond Florida), so you can rest assured you are in excellent hands.

ANNUAL EVENTS & FESTIVALS

South Florida—and Broward County—used to be very quiet places during the late spring and the summer. They used to be the sort of laid-back, subtropical places where things really slow down (or come to a complete stop!) during the hotter weather, where you don't have to worry about marking upcoming special events on your calendar. And, while things certainly still do slow down some when the temperature rises, Greater Fort Lauderdale has become a place where you shouldn't put that calendar marker away, even in the summer. Though the area can hardly be said to be humming with activity at that time of year, there are certainly some interesting events taking place. The calendar is now busy year-round.

But when the temperature breaks—usually in early October—that's when the area really starts to come alive! When the rest of the country is gathering its firewood and getting ready to stay indoors for several months of hibernation, Greater Fort Lauderdale blooms like a brilliant rose with colors, festivals, one-of-a-kind events, sound, and fun. There are numerous art and music festivals, food festivals, and special events, virtually every weekend from early October through April. Often, in fact, you'll have a hard time choosing, because there are so many great events—and not enough days on the calendar—that some of them have to take place at the same time.

One caveat: We've all seen the effects of a recession by now. And, of course, even in the best of times, some "annual" events get canceled or postponed for a variety of reasons. So it's possible that a few of the events listed here may not be taking place this year, or any more. So you might want to make sure you call ahead—or read about it in the paper or online—before getting in the car and going.

But don't be too concerned. Because one thing's for sure—you'd better buy an additional marker for your calendar. You're going to need it!

ART & ANTIQUE SHOWS

January

DANIA BEACH FOLK ART & ANTIQUE FESTIVAL
Downtown Dania
West of US 1 at Dania Beach Boulevard
(954) 816-3324
www.gracecafeandgalleries.com

There's live music and dance, great food, and a motorcycle show along with some wonderfully creative artists and some fascinating art forms. You never know what you'll find here—and it could be anything from antique Samurai swords to Cabbage Patch dolls (yes, for those of you who grew up in the '80s, Cabbage Patch dolls—including the ones you threw away—are now considered collectibles!). Much of this art is edgy and funky, and the folks who create it will be happy to talk with you about it. *NOTE:* The Folk Art & Antique Festival has also been held in February in the past, so it's best to check before making any plans to attend.

My Fort Lauderdale

My favorite spot in Greater Fort Lauderdale is right outside my screen door—it's my balcony, which overlooks the ocean. It relaxes me, and gives me the serenity I need to create my abstract paintings. I sit out there for the sunrise, or at sunset. Or right in the middle of the day, when I need a quiet getaway. How many people in this world are lucky enough to say that their favorite spot in the whole world is right on their own balcony?

I love where I live, also, because I'm right in the middle of everything . . . and there's so much to do here. The Fort Lauderdale Museum of Art, the Broward Center for the Performing Arts, the restaurants and galleries on Las Olas, which is such a pretty street . . . I'm close to everything. On Friday nights, there's live music at the square at A1A and Commercial Boulevard; and I can just walk down there. To me, there's no better place than where I live.

—Arleen Mark, Artist, Fort Lauderdale

DEERFIELD BEACH FESTIVAL OF THE ARTS
34 S. Ocean Way, Deerfield Beach
(954) 480-4433
www.deerfieldbeachfestivals.com

It's hard to imagine a more beautiful setting for a festival celebrating the arts. The Deerfield Beach festival takes place right on the ocean. Simply drive east on Hillsboro Boulevard until you come to the ocean, and you'll see hundreds of artists and thousands of people talking, eating, listening, watching, and buying. Media on display here encompass all that you can possibly conceive of and some you can't. There's painting, of course (in oils, acrylics, watercolors, batik, and various stains). There's magnificent photography, running the gamut from extraordinarily beautiful panoramas to incredibly "human" portraits. There's bonsai. Bottles (yes, bottles can be art). Candles. Ceramics. Painted glass. Wood carvings. Natural wood furniture. Ceremonial masks. Jewelry. Sculptures made from plywood. Puppets. Stained glass. Drawings. Etchings. Blown glass. Metal artwork. Fountains and garden art. And so much more. And if it can be barbecued, grilled, fried, stir-fried, pan-fried, sautéed, popped, spun, roasted, battered, buttered, steamed, twirled, or frozen, you'll find it to eat here! *NOTE:* The Festival of the Arts has also been held in February in the past, so it's best to check before making any plans to attend.

LAS OLAS RIVERFRONT ARTS & CRAFTS SHOW
Las Olas Boulevard between SE 3rd Avenue and SE 1st Avenue, Ft. Lauderdale
(772) 336-6060
www.myfairsandfestivals.com

This show highlights arts and crafts, fine arts, and fine crafts. It takes place, of course, on fashionable Las Olas Boulevard—which means there's a whole lot to do in addition to eyeing the imaginative pieces of art. In addition to the art outdoors on the street, you'll have plenty of opportunities to duck into the excellent galleries all along the street. A second Las Olas Riverfront show takes place in April.

MUSEUM OF ART FORT LAUDERDALE NATIONAL ART FESTIVAL
Huizenga Plaza (across from the Museum of Art Fort Lauderdale)
Southeast corner of Andrews Avenue and Las Olas Boulevard
Ft. Lauderdale
(954) 525-5500
http://moaflnsu.org

In 2008, after a hiatus lasting several years, the Museum reintroduced the original Las Olas Art Festival to the area. For over thirty years, this festival was a landmark Fort Lauderdale event, known to many people by its acronym (LOAF). And now it's back. The art and artists are first-rate, and they come here from all over the country. And the event is a definite calendar marker for the area's real art lovers. You'll see award-winning artists in media such as painting, drawing, photography, ceramics, fiber arts, and jewelry, along with live music and a wide variety of treats for the palate. And if your appetite for great art isn't quite sated by the festival, you can just walk across the street and visit the Museum. *NOTE:* This festival has also been held in February in the past, so it's best to confirm the date before you plan on attending.

WESTON TOWN CENTER ART FESTIVAL
Weston Town Center
1675 Market St., Weston
(954) 349-8123

There are close to 200 artists' booths here, with a variety of interesting works ranging from steel sculptures to oil paintings, from metal statues to fine jewelry, and from blown glass to exotic furniture pieces and clay and ceramic creations. The artists are only too happy to talk with you about their work. And Town Center itself is a wonderful place for a festival—an all-American village with a clock tower, atmospheric shops, and interesting restaurants and cafes. Weston is one of Broward County's most upscale, sophisticated towns with a very cosmopolitan population; as a result, it attracts a large number of wonderful artists and craftspeople to this festival.

February

ANNUAL WESTON ART WALK
Weston Town Center
1675 Market St., Weston
(954) 389-4321
www.artscouncilweston.com

In just a few short years, this has grown to be a "must" stop on the calendar for Broward County art lovers and artists. There are some very talented photographers, painters, sculptors, carvers, ceramists, glassblowers, and mixed-media artists here, along with a wide variety of craftspeople whose work is not only beautiful, but, in many cases, extremely practical for your home. There's music, as well, with talented local bands. Young dancers from the Weston area perform, in addition. There are mimes and every other conceivable type of street performer you can imagine. And it all takes place amidst a turn-of-the-century (20th, not 21st!)

atmosphere of brick sidewalks and buildings, street lamps, and unique shops. You'll probably want to try one of the interesting restaurants, as well, before heading home with the art you've purchased!

COLLECTIBLE GLASS SHOW AND SALE
War Memorial Auditorium
800 NE 8th St., Ft. Lauderdale
(954) 828-5380
Event Information: (305) 884-0335
The South Florida Depression Glass Club has been staging this show for more than three decades, and it attracts dealers from across America and guests from all across South Florida. The focus here is on Americana—vintage glass, pottery, and china that celebrates and illuminates American tradition. Here, you just might find that glass set from Revolutionary War times, or Depression-era pottery, or that fine china set from the Gilded Age of the 1890s. If you're a collector, there's a good chance you'll finally find that piece for which you've been searching. And if you're just curious about the American heritage of creating beautiful glass and ceramic objects, there's a good chance you'll fall in love with a piece you never even knew you wanted.

March

ART FESTIVAL IN THE PINES
River of Grass Arts Park
Sheridan Street and 172nd Avenue, Pembroke Pines
(954) 986-5027
www.ppines.com
Fine arts and crafts in the early spring—it's a hard atmosphere to beat. The festival also features plenty of food booths—too many if you're on a diet!—and live music, a hands-on art children's area, and demonstrations

of their processes and approaches by local artists. This is a juried competition, with over 100 artists. And there's always something fun going on here.

CORAL SPRINGS FESTIVAL OF THE ARTS
The Walk
2900 University Dr., Coral Springs
(954) 340-5992
www.csfoa.com
Picture two bright, beautiful early spring days, where the sun is warming but not hot, and the skies are a perfect blue. Then picture a 3-block-long strip of distinctive shops and restaurants (ranging from Japanese to Greek, and pretty much everything in between). Add to that a fairly new art festival (started only in 2004) that's already become one of the finest (and largest) in South Florida, one that already attracts well-known artists and craftspeople from all over the country. Then, to top it all off, throw in some talented dance and musical groups, some marching bands, some ethnic organizations presenting their own exciting cultures with stirring performances, some theatrical presentations, and literary workshops with well-known writers from the Greater Fort Lauderdale area. Combine all these elements, and you have the Coral Springs Festival of the Arts. It all takes place on the Walk, the finest concentration of upscale shops and restaurants in "the Springs." You should probably plan to go on the first day, which is Saturday, because you'll definitely want to come back again on Sunday.

HOLLYWOOD FESTIVAL OF THE ARTS
Artspark at Young Circle
Downtown Hollywood
(954) 921-3404
www.hollywoodartsfest.org

This is a juried show with a wide variety of artistic forms and styles, along with music and food. *NOTE:* After many years, this festival was cancelled in 2009. However, a number of organizations were hoping to hold it again. Please call or go to the website for up-to-the-minute information.

QUILT SHOW BY THE SEA
War Memorial Auditorium
800 NE 8th St., Ft. Lauderdale
(954) 987-8827

This is a juried competition, and you'll see quilts that are truly works of art. You'll find a nice selection of sewing machines on sale, along with a merchant mall, a silent quilt auction, special exhibits, and a quilt raffle. But there's much more: This is truly a place to listen and learn for anyone interested in the quilting arts. There are lectures and workshops, live demonstrations by quilting masters, and the opportunity to speak with teachers of the craft.

April

ART IN THE PARK PLUS FESTIVAL
Oakland Park Library
1298 NE 37th St., Oakland Park
(954) 561-6289

This juried art show gets better each year and provides an excellent showcase for local and statewide artists. There are cash awards for the best-in-class artists, along with plenty of music, food, and children's programs. In addition—as you might expect from a festival that takes place at the Oakland Park Library—there's a book sale.

COOPER CITY FOUNDERS DAY ARTS & CRAFTS SHOW
Brian Piccolo Park
9501 Sheridan St., Cooper City
(954) 434-4300

This art fair and historic remembrance day features plenty of free activities, kiddie rides and games, a car show with all types of crazy (or cool!) makes and models, and free main-stage entertainment. And it's all capped by a spectacular fireworks display at night. And, because it's Founder's Day, there's also a host of other activities, including a 1-mile walk/run, a parade, baseball games, bingo, and more by the Broward County Sheriff's Office. And there's a golf tournament the following day.

CORAL SPRINGS INDOOR JURIED SPRING EVE CRAFT SHOW
La Quinta Inn
3701 N. University Dr., Coral Springs
(954) 345-6404
www.coralspringscraftguild.com

This annual event is sponsored by the Coral Springs Craft Guild, which has worked for the past 30 years to promote the handicraft arts in South Florida. Among the media represented are basketry, candles, fiber art, glass crafts, jewelry, metal work, mixed media, paper, textile, woodworking, and much more. This is a juried show, and the quality of the crafts—and the imagination that went into them—is very high.

SEASIDE CRAFT FAIR
The Broadwalk at Hollywood Beach, Hollywood
(813) 962-0388
www.artfestival.com

This fair is unique in that it takes place right on the Broadwalk that runs along Hollywood's replenished beach and along scores of colorful, eclectic shops selling things you may not see anywhere else. As Hollywood is headquarters for the considerable French-Canadian population in South Florida, this event definitely has an international feel. As you walk along the Broadwalk, with an ocean breeze flowing over your face, you'll see stunning handmade crafts, including jewelry, ceramics, wall art, personalized gifts, wall hangings, paintings, photography, and much more. You'll also come upon a large Green Market with interesting foods and sauces, plants, orchids, and homemade soaps and cosmetics.

May

ANTIQUE & COLLECTOR FAIR
War Memorial Auditorium
800 NE 8th St., Ft. Lauderdale
(954) 828-5280
The lobby at the War Memorial Auditorium is filled with historical items commemorating veterans of Vietnam, Korea, and World War II. The facility was constructed in 1949, but was renovated a few years ago. For two days, you'll be able to browse around hundreds of displays of antique jewelry, furniture, clocks and watches, paintings, ceremonial items, art-glass, sculpture, ceramics, decorative art, glassware, handicrafts, all manner of avant-garde objets d'art, and handwoven rugs and carpets.

September

ANNUAL HORTT MEMORIAL EXHIBITION
Fort Lauderdale Museum of Art
One E. Las Olas Blvd., Ft. Lauderdale
(954) 525-5500
moaflnsu.org

This competition is proof positive of South Florida's emergence as a vibrant center of creativity and artistic forms. It's an annual competition featuring some of South Florida's finest artists, and no medium is too outrageous. And it's been going on since 1959 (before South Florida was a center of the arts!).

October

ANNUAL COCONUT CREEK CRAFT FESTIVAL AT THE PROMENADE
The Promenade Shops
4401 Lyons Rd., Coconut Creek
(954) 472-3755
www.artfestival.com
The Promenade is the newest place to meet in Coconut Creek, a Main-Street–type setting that's filled with distinctive boutiques, shops, and eateries, many of which have alfresco dining outside; all the shops are open to the street. Arrayed along the street will be fine artists and artworks in a wide variety of media, including painting, sculpting, woodworks, glass works, ceramics, bronze, sand, and more.

LAS OLAS ART FAIR
600 E. Las Olas Blvd., Ft. Lauderdale
www.artfestival.com
This show—ranked by art lovers as one of the top 100 in the nation—has become a fall tradition in Greater Fort Lauderdale. The fair attracts nearly 200 artists and craftspeople (picked from a much wider pool of applicants), who display their art amidst the stunning shops boutiques, galleries, and sidewalk cafes of this wonderful European-style street.

All exhibiting artists are required to be at the festival—they can't send someone in their place. As a result, you'll have the opportunity to talk with the artist about their work, about a piece you might like to commission, and about their techniques or their backgrounds. (And, of course, about their prices, which they are obviously at greater liberty to negotiate than a representative or salesperson is.) And, though the art is truly world-class, that doesn't necessarily mean all the prices are; there are plenty of beautiful items in the $15–$20 range. The Las Olas Art Fair takes place on the Boulevard between SE 6th Avenue and SE 11th Avenue.

November

ART IN THE PARK
Liberty Tree Park, Plantation
(954) 797-9762
www.plantationjuniorwomansclub.org/
ART-IN-THE-PARK.html
This festival is put on annually by the Plantation Junior Woman's Club, and they do a heck of a job. This is a juried fine arts show with $10,000 in prize money. There's a separate section for craftspeople to show off their works. The show attracts over 130 artists from all over Florida and the United States. All kinds of good jazz, folk, and swing groups perform here, along with groups representing other musical genres as well. And there's a Kid's Korner with plenty of entertainment for the younger set, including singing, dancing, baton twirling, cheerleading, and animal shows.

LAUDERDALE-BY-THE-SEA
 CRAFT FEST
Commercial Boulevard and SR A1A,
Lauderdale-by-the-Sea
(954) 472-3755
www.artfestival.com
The main street of this picturesque town (by the sea!) comes alive every year with an art festival that has an atmosphere and a vibe all its own. The winter sun seems to glance off the buildings with a vivid impact, and the nearby bars and cafes are blasting the Dolphins game from dozens of TVs. This event has a nice scale; it's big enough to see everything, but small enough to not be jostled by swarms of fellow art lovers. And the art is eclectic and interesting.

December

WOODSTOCK ARTS & CRAFTS
 FESTIVAL
Welleby Park
11100 NW 44th St., Sunrise
(954) 748-8370
www.woodstockartsfest.com/home.html
What started out as a small homeowner's association arts-and-crafts/flea market in 1980 has morphed into an annual event worthy of the name Woodstock (that other "artsy" town up north!). And it's not small anymore. There are now close to 250 artists and craftspeople displaying their works, along with community-service booths and vendors whose food tastes as good as it smells (and looks!). And if you're like most of the folks who come by here, you should clean out your car before you come 'cause you'll be hauling home some treasures in it when you leave.

MUSIC FESTIVALS
April

FLORIDA'S NEWPORT GUITAR
 FESTIVAL
Seminole Hard Rock Hotel & Casino
1 Seminole Way, Ft. Lauderdale
(954) 327-7149
www.newportguitarfestival.com

If you love guitars—playing them, listening to other people playing them, or even just touching them or talking about them—you've got to make it to this event. There are great concerts, of course—more than 200 of them (finger-style, jazz, and rock)—by the world's greatest guitarists on three different stages. But there's so much more, in addition. There are literally thousands of guitars for sale, from vintage to state-of-the-art, from traditional to exquisite masterpieces. (You can even bring your own guitar to sell, or, at least, to get an idea what it's worth.) There are the artists who built them, with whom you're welcome to talk and swap stories. And there are seminars, where you can learn the inside secrets of becoming a master guitar maker from master guitar makers.

MUSIC ON THE PLAZA
The Village at Gulfstream Park
501 S. Federal Hwy., Hallandale Beach
(954) 378-0900
www.thevillageatgulfstreampark.com
Every Friday night from early April to late May, the new Plaza outside Gulfstream Park Racetrack—which is filled with atmospheric shops and restaurants—comes alive with great musical performances. You'll hear jazz, salsa, blues, rhythm and blues, flamenco, country, and classic rock 'n' roll. And afterwards you can stop for dinner at one of the wonderful eateries, or head inside the racetrack to root on the thoroughbreds for a night of real excitement.

SEMINOLE MUSIC AND ARTS FESTIVAL
Junior Cypress Rodeo Grounds
Big Cypress Seminole Indian Reservation
(in the Everglades)
30000 Gator Tail Trail, Clewiston
(954) 985-2300, ext. 10670

It doesn't get much better than this in South Florida. And it's definitely worth the ride into the Everglades, as much for a look at the 'Glades as for the music, art, and insight into the culture of Broward County's first residents. There are plenty of country-and-western artists here, as well as Seminole singers and bands, affording a glimpse into a Native culture that you might not find anywhere else. (And you'll also hear some hybrid fusion versions—a combination of country and Native American.) There are carnival rides, from kiddy to fast and furious. There's a classic car show (maybe you'll see that '64 Mustang you've been dreaming abut since '64!). There's all kinds of interesting art, ranging from traditional Seminole to abstract to "Floridian" to avant-garde. There's constant entertainment. There's all sorts of clothing for sale, much of it created by hand by very creative artisans, and much of it authentic Seminole garb created by tribal artisans, brilliantly hued and festooned with beads and jewels.

Then, of course, there are all the options offered by the reservation itself. One of them is the Museum ("Ah-Tah-Thi-Ki" means "a place to learn"), offering a wonderful look inside the tradition and history of this people who are the only tribe never to sign a peace treaty with the United States. Another option is Billie's Swamp Safari, which gives you an up-close-and-personal look at the Everglades by way of an amphibious vehicle that can cruise on this "River of Grass" while also driving on land. And, if you really want to experience life the way the early Seminoles did, you can stay overnight in a *chickee* on stilts (to keep the critters away!).

To reach Big Cypress Seminole Indian Reservation, take exit 49 off I-75 and continue 19 miles north on Snake Road.

May

RED, WHITE & BLUEGRASS
Hollywood Beach
SR A1A
(954) 924-2980
www.visithollywoodfl.org/bluegrass
.aspx

Get ready for some gen-yoo-ine strummin' and pickin' and cloggin' and front-porch singin', friends, 'cause this is the real thing. Bluegrass music—an authentic form of purely American music—has been rediscovered lately. And some of the country's best are here in Hollywood for this weekendlong event, doing all that pickin' and strummin'. Toss in some folk, blues, and country artists as well, performing at several stages along the beach, and you've got a real hoedown. This festival has played host to a number of Grammy-nominated artists, and a number of Male/Female Artists of the Year, along with plenty of musicians and singers who perform regularly at the Grand Ole Opry in Nashville. And there are workshops that'll teach you to harmonize or pick that banjo with the best of 'em.

June

BANK OF AMERICA STARLIGHT MUSICALS
Holiday Park
1000 E. Sunrise Blvd., Ft. Lauderdale
(954) 828-5363
www.fortlauderdale.gov/events/
starlight/starlight.htm

Grab a few folding chairs, a cooler with some goodies in it, and a thermos and head out to Holiday Park on Friday nights in summer from mid-June through early August. Here, you can relax on the lawn as a variety of musical groups perform a variety of musical styles, ranging from pop and country to rock and rhythm and blues. It's all very friendly, very casual, and very comfortable. And it's free, as well.

July

SUMMERTIME BLUES JAM
Fort Lauderdale Stadium Festival Grounds
5301 NW 12th Ave., Ft. Lauderdale
(954) 489-3255
www.fortlauderdale.gov/festivals

This event helps to raise funds for the nationally acclaimed Blues in the Schools program. The finest blues musicians in South Florida are rounded up to prove that "the thrill" is definitely not gone (to paraphrase B. B. King's famous blues classic).

October

AMERICAN MUSIC FESTIVAL
Fort Lauderdale Stadium
5301 NW 12th Ave., Ft. Lauderdale
(954) 489-3255
www.ci.ftlaud.fl.us/festivals

American music is a treasure-trove of styles, sounds, influences, and instruments. And, according to many, it's perhaps our greatest gift to the world. The American Music Festival is meant to publicize and promote all these sounds and styles and influences. Among these styles are bluegrass, traditional country, gospel, folk, and Dixieland—along with American dancing and other aspects of the American musical quilt. For details on the admission fee, check out the festival website.

November

RIVERWALK BLUES & MUSIC FESTIVAL
Downtowner Saloon
10 S. New River Dr. East, Ft. Lauderdale
(954) 463-9800
www.riverwalkbluesfestival.com
The first South Florida Blues Festival was held in the legendary, gone-but-not-forgotten Musicians Exchange Café in Fort Lauderdale, in 1987. Even though it was a brand-new festival, it was able to attract world-renowned headliners—Buddy Guy, John Lee Hooker, and John Mayall. The Musicians Exchange Café was condemned by the city in 1996, and the event is now held along the beautiful Riverwalk running through the heart of downtown. But one thing hasn't changed: It's still attracting some of the finest musicians in the world—more winners of a Grammy, Blues Music Award, Blues Blast Award, and International Blues Challenge Award than you could possibly list here. You'll hear these artists in an outdoor setting on the New River as, one by one, the lights of the city sparkle on. And you never know when a Delbert McClinton, Johnny Winter, Taj Mahal, Buckwheat Zydeco, James Cotton, Rick Derringer, Bobby Blu Bland, Buddy Miles, Elvin Bishop, Mose Allison, Edgar Winter, or the Fabulous T-Birds might pop up to perform, because at one time or another, all of them have.

**FLAMENCO IN THE SUN SUMMER
 FESTIVAL**
Bailes Ferrer Flamenco Music and Dance
700 Pine Ridge Terr., Davie
(954) 288-0882
www.bailesferrer.com
Bailes Ferrer was founded in 1995 by Damaris I. Ferrer as a way to bring the art and

beauty of flamenco music and dance to South Florida. The company premiered its first concert in April 1996 and has since earned quite a reputation for excellence . . . and for exciting, colorful performances. The company has since, also, expanded its repertoire to incorporate other types of dance, in addition, merging flamenco with classical, tango, Middle Eastern, and jazz movements and dances. Every summer the company stages a festival for Broward County dance aficionados.

FOOD & WINE FESTIVALS
Year-Round

RIVERWALK TRUST'S GET DOWNTOWN
In the Courtyard Plaza at Las Olas Place
333 E. Las Olas Blvd., Ft. Lauderdale
(954) 468-1541
www.goriverwalk.com
This event was originally started with the goal of attracting more people downtown to enjoy the city. And apparently it worked; more than 1,000 people now come to this several-times-a-year event, at which they can sample foods from some of Greater Fort Lauderdale's distinctive restaurants, ranging from the elegant to the funky. You can sip superb vodkas, liqueurs, wines, and beers (among them Landshark Beer, of which Jimmy Buffett is one of the owners). You'll sample all of this while enjoying lively local bands. The event is produced by and benefits the Riverwalk Trust, which was the force behind the successful Signature Brick Program (over 24,000 bricks sold) and serves as the catalyst in nurturing Riverwalk as a community connected by the New River.

January

KISS COUNTRY CHILI COOK-OFF
C. B. Smith Park
900 N. Flamingo Rd., Pembroke Pines
(954) 523-3309
www.wkis.com

If you're country—and you'd be surprised how many folks in Greater Fort Lauderdale are—you can't afford to miss this! The music is foot-stompin', the cowboy hats and boots are everywhere, and the food is just what you'd expect—fried, barbecued, and served with a bunch of chilis that are competing for best-in-contest. (The hotter the better!) This is no small-time event, folks. Recent musical guests have included country music royalty—Alan Jackson and Montgomery Gentry—along with Jessica Simpson (admittedly not known for her country songs) and a bunch of other talented performers. And the prizes aren't chicken feed (pardon the expression) either; the team that cooks the best chili can advance to the World Championship Chili Cookoff. And if they win there, they'll walk away with $25,000. Tickets are on sale at many area Wal-Marts and Pet Supermarkets, as well as Ticketmaster (www .ticketmaster.com). *NOTE:* This event has also been held in February in the past, so it's best to confirm what month it'll be this year before planning on attending.

April

ANNUAL WINE & CULINARY CELEBRATION
Museum of Discovery & Science
401 SW 2nd St., Ft. Lauderdale
(954) 713-0954
www.mods.org

A city that was once considered a cultural wasteland—and that includes the areas of food and wine—is now anything but. And the Annual Wine & Culinary Celebration is proof positive that Broward Countians' taste buds are now every bit as sophisticated as their musical and artistic tastes. The event (and it truly is a celebration) takes place at the Museum of Discovery & Science in downtown Fort Lauderdale.

This celebration was named one of the "10 Best Annual Fort Lauderdale Events" in 2007 by *Gold Coast* magazine, a local chronicler of the good life on the Gold Coast. It features a progressive sequence of wine and food pairings, with the intention of both delighting and educating the guests. More than 30 top restaurants in the region will be represented, generally by their chefs and owners. In addition, of course, guests will be treated to the fruit of the vines of vineyards all over the world. There's also a silent auction. And every guest walks away with a complimentary wine glass.

The evening starts off with an exclusive VIP Martini Reception, and these guests will also be able to attend wine-tasting seminars and the Grand Tasting. For these guests, the evening concludes with exclusive access to the VIP Lounge. VIP tickets are $150 per person, and general admission tickets are $85 per person. Attendance now exceeds 1,000 people. And they'll long remember this special night.

EXPO ALFRESCO
Hollywood's ArtsPark at Young Circle
Downtown Hollywood
(954) 923-4000
www.expoalfresco.com

A food festival outdoors in April, as the sun goes down. It just doesn't get much better than that. You'll sample all sorts of gourmet foods. Try all types of interesting wines.

Listen to great live music. Watch the Battle of the Chefs, in which chefs from two top local restaurants compete against each other for bragging rights. Your little ones will enjoy the Kidz Corner (and if they're under 10, they get in free). This festival now attracts upwards of 3,000 attendees, and a great time is had by all.

NEW TIMES INTERNATIONAL BEERFEST
Esplanade Park
400 SW 2nd St., Ft. Lauderdale
(954) 233-1534

This is a buffet of brews: top-quality domestic and imported microbrews, specialty ales, and lagers. *New Times* is South Florida's alternative weekly newspaper, hip and award-winning. And they really know how to throw a party. There are dark beers, light beers, wheat beers—pretty much every type, color, and taste of beer you can conceive of. There will be more than 50 breweries showing off their products. There are always good live musical performances. A number of local restaurants provide the food, which is included with the price of admission. There's a VIP area located in the Museum of Discovery & Science, from where you can watch the entire festival as if you were a king. Beer-fest veterans will tell you that there are a few unwritten rules that must be followed: Come early. Stay late. And don't make any plans for the next day.

POMPANO BEACH SEAFOOD FESTIVAL
On the Beach
Just north of Atlantic Boulevard,
Pompano Beach
(954) 570-7785
www.pompanobeachseafoodfestival
.com

This, to many people in Greater Fort Lauderdale, is the Big One. It's not called "Florida's Biggest Beach Party" for nothing! Three days of the freshest seafood you'll ever find (much of it caught in local waters just a few hours earlier) and plenty of "American" food, as well. Big-name musical acts. Arts and crafts of all types. Top local bands ranging from country to funk. Hundreds of local vendors in their tents, selling everything from offbeat jewelry creations to decorative items of shell and stone to tempting taste treats. And it's all strung out on the beach, with the Atlantic Ocean as the backdrop.

Stay Street Smart

Greater Fort Lauderdale is much like any other urban-suburban area in America—there's some crime. Don't feel that because you're on vacation in sunny South Florida you don't have to take the same common-sense precautions that you would anywhere else. Lock your door, in your hotel room and in your car. Don't flash a lot of money. Don't flash a lot of bling (jewelry!). If you have doubts about a certain neighborhood—particularly after dark—don't go there. And always look around at your surroundings, which—again, like other areas of our country—can change quickly. Just use common sense. Your hotel desk will be happy to advise you about any unsafe areas in the town in which you're staying.

May

ANNUAL LAS OLAS WINE AND FOOD FESTIVAL
2010 Las Olas Blvd., Ft. Lauderdale
(954) 524-4657
www.lasolaswineandfood.com

When the first Las Olas Wine and Food Festival was held in the late '90s, it was in November, to commemorate Beaujolais Nouveau (the new Beaujolais vintage). After a few years it was moved to March, and then, a couple of years ago, to May. The third date, apparently, was a charm; May worked out so well that it's now become the regular date.

The first festival had somewhat modest origins; it took place on an open street (with traffic), and wine tastings were held in shops and on the sidewalk. As the event grew, however, and more vendors began participating and more guests began coming, the activity began spilling over into the street. And eventually the street was closed for those days.

In the early years, this was a three-day event. On Thursday and Friday evenings there were tastings along the boulevard (both inside and out), and afterward many restaurants held special wine dinners hosted by guest vineyards. On Saturday afternoon a grand tasting was held, usually under a tent. Saturday evening was the finale, a grand wine dinner in the dining room of the legendary Riverside Hotel, which still adorns Las Olas Boulevard with the style, grace, and ambience of the 1890s.

Over the years, many changes took place as the festival evolved. The wine dinners were discontinued and then brought back. The tastings moved back onto the street. Eventually gourmet foods were offered along with the wines. And rather than being spread out over three days, the event now takes place on one elegant Saturday evening, starting with a VIP reception, and ending with the street festival. Great food, fine wine, musical entertainment, and the beauty of this storied boulevard all combine to create a memorable evening under the stars. And it's all for a great cause: The proceeds go to the American Lung Association of Florida.

June

THE HUKILAU
Mai-Kai Restaurant
3599 N. Federal Hwy., Ft. Lauderdale
(954) 563-3272
www.thehukilau.com

They call this "the Most Intimate Tiki Event in the World." Well, they should call it, as well, "the Coolest Tiki Event in the World." Because it's a real hoot—a four-day South Seas bacchanal of Polynesian food, drink, dance, song, and ceremony—along with a lot of things that are about as far from Polynesian as you can get. It takes place at Mai-Kai, one of Fort Lauderdale's legendary restaurants (established 1956). The first Hukilau was in 2002, and since then it's grown every year, attracting a wild and woolly assemblage that's intent on having fun. There's all kinds of alternative and unusual music (not necessarily Polynesian), from bands with names like the Bikini Beachcombers and the Stolen Idols; live alternative theater, storytelling, avant-garde cinema; fashion shows (Sarong-arama); and drum banging, imaginative artistic creations, and chanting. Pretty much everyone and everything is a tribute to tiki culture, including films such as *Tikimentary*. So check your hang-ups at the door, don some South Seas apparel, claim a good spot, order a tall drink, and enjoy the merriment. It may well be the most unusual party you'll ever attend!

October

DINE OUT LAUDERDALE
**Area restaurants in Greater
Fort Lauderdale**
www.sunny.org/dineout/

This is your chance to experience the best cuisine Fort Lauderdale has to offer—and to do it at a discounted price. Every year at this time, some 30 to 40 local restaurants offer a three-course dinner at $35 per person. It's your chance to eat at some wonderful restaurants that might normally cost a lot more—without breaking the bank. And you could eat at a different place every night and never be in the same restaurant twice. The diversity is outstanding—American, Asian, Brazilian, Chinese, French, fusion, Greek, Italian, Spanish, Polynesian, seafood, steak house, and Thai, among others. There are no corners cut here; you'll feast on signature dishes by many of South Florida's finest chefs. So sit back, relax, and enjoy!

SPECIAL EVENTS

January

CANADAFEST
**The Broadwalk at Hollywood Beach
Hollywood
(954) 924-9705**
www.canadafest.com

During the winter, Hollywood becomes the third-largest city in French Canada. In fact, there are about 250,000 Quebecers in South Florida during the Season. And Hollywood is their epicenter, the place where their fascinating culture and cuisine and music and merchandise are on proud display all over. This is particularly so on the Broadwalk, and it's only right that this festive tribute to our neighbors to the north should take place here. Each year, more than 150,000 people fill the Broadwalk for the festival, and they come from all over the region. Singers, dancers, and other Quebecois performers light up the stages. Vendors selling French-Canadian culinary specialties (the food is delicious!), crafts, clothing, and specialty items fill up more than a hundred kiosks on the beach. CanadaFest is the largest French festival in the United States. The entire weekend is a pure joy.

FORT LAUDERDALE ORCHID SOCIETY SHOW
**War Memorial Auditorium
800 NE 8th St., Ft. Lauderdale
(954) 563-3548**
www.flos.org/show_info.htm

The Fort Lauderdale Orchid Society was founded back in 1951 for the purpose of stimulating interest, providing education, and enhancing opportunities for the exchange of information among those interested in the culture of orchids. And they certainly accomplish those objectives—and more—with this show, in which some two-dozen orchid growers participate and present orchids of startlingly beautiful colors and arrangements.

February

DANIA BEACH BLAST
**Dania Beach Ocean Park
SR A1A and Dania Beach Boulevard
(954) 926-2323**
www.greaterdania.org

"Blast" is a perfect word for this event—because you're sure to have one. This is a good old-fashioned street fair, but on the beach. And there's something for everyone. A talented group of artists and craftspeople will display their works, ranging from vintage to avant-garde. There will be unusual merchandise, for your home and for your hobbies, as well. The International Game Fishing Association is generally involved, which means that you can learn a lot if you like throwing a line. Students and professors from Florida Atlantic University will usually be on hand to show you equipment used in oceanographic exploration and photography. There'll be plenty of activities for the kids, including a colorful shoebox regatta. There's a classic car show, at which you might see everything from a '64 Mustang to a 1955 Jaguar. A nice parade of local bands will be taking the bandstand, and they'll keep you movin' your feet all day long. And if you feel like moving the rest of yourself as well, see if you can procure a spot in the Lions Club's One-Ton-Tug. Afterwards, you can refresh yourself at one of the many food stands.

FLORIDA RENAISSANCE FESTIVAL
Quiet Waters Park
401 S. Powerline Rd., Deerfield Beach
(800) 373-6337
www.ren-fest.com
Hear ye! Hear ye! The King doth proclaimeth thusly: That every year, from mid-February to mid-March, Quiet Waters Park will turneth into Sherwood Forest and Nottingham, verily, that the King's loyal subjects shall partake of the merriment of court jesters, blacksmiths, sword-wielding knights of the Round Table, fair maidens playing harps and flutes, horses decked out in the coats of arms of their royal owners, carvers, weavers, jugglers, damsels in distress, assorted ne'er-do-wells, ladies of the court, poets, games of skill, jousting rides for the wee ones, puppet shows, and wonderful storytelling. Whereby, in addition, said merriment shall also encompass medieval knights of the Realm jousting in the lists, to see who stands tall on his steed and with his long pole. Ye may read notices of the day nailed into trees, starting with "Hear ye! Hear ye!" Whosoever shall attend this Kingly festival shall feast on the biggest—and best—turkey legs he or she (or Henry the Eighth) have ever seen. Furthermore, the Court of the King announce that all manner of crafts shall be available for purchase by the loyal subjects (and the not-so-loyal ones, as well!). Ye can wander through dusty medieval villages eerily reminiscent of those you've seen in history books. Thereby, the King doth proclaim that this event shall be a world of wonder and of color, or surprises and delights for the whole family. So it shall be written. And so it shall be done.

FOUNDERS' DAYS
Main Stage is at SE 2nd Street and
Ocean Way
Deerfield Beach
www.foundersdays.com/home.html
This four-day festival celebrates this town at the northern end of Greater Fort Lauderdale—its history, its red-letter dates, and the people who have helped create and nurture it. The festivities start on Thursday with a colorful nighttime carnival with rides and food. The carnival continues on Friday night, when the music starts and the motorcycles—sometimes hundreds of them of all shapes, sizes, and designs—roll in. On Saturday there's a bed race and a parade that's a lot of fun. Then the kids' events start, generally along with a motorcycle show. The music starts, too, with genres ranging from rock to reggae, and from calypso to country. Saturday night ends with a spectacular fireworks display. The fun rolls over into Sunday, with the crafts, the food, the music, and the parade of people from all over Broward County. No doubt, Deerfield Beach's founders and pioneers would be amazed if they

could see this festival, and see what their efforts hath wrought.

MARDI GRAS FIESTA TROPICALE/FAT TUESDAY ON HOLLYWOOD BEACH
Broadwalk at Hollywood Beach
(954) 924-2980
(954) 214-2456
www.mardigrasfiesta.com

If you like hot sauce, spicy gumbo and jambalaya, Cajun and Creole cuisine, zydeco music, instruments like the fiddle and the harmonica, and the soulful sounds of N'awlins R & B, this four-day festival should be on your must-do list. And if you like Tabasco sauce, so much the better. The food is hot and spicy here, and you'll find yourself sweating even though it may not be warm out. The spirit is sky-high, as the area's filled with revelers. There are a bunch of stages here at the Broadwalk, and they'll all be filled with the songs and the ceremonies from back home on the Bayou. So get on your most outrageous outfit—maybe even a mask?—and throw on some colorful strings of beads, and come ready to party!

POWWOW AND SEMINOLE TRIBAL FAIR
Seminole Hard Rock Hotel & Casino
One Seminole Way, Ft. Lauderdale
(954) 502-7529
www.semtribe.com

From all over America they come, descendants of the first Americans, to help Florida's Seminole tribe celebrate their illustrious history and culture. From the deserts of the Southwest come the Navajo. From the forests of upstate New York come the Iroquois. From the Oklahoma prairies come the Cherokee. And from all over Florida come the Seminoles, members of the only tribe never to

sign a peace treaty with the United States. And when they are all here, on land owned by the Seminoles and visited (because of the Hard Rock Hotel & Casino) by people from all over the world, dozens of tribes from all across America are represented. Native American cowboys and cowgirls participate in the rodeo at the Bill Osceola Rodeo Grounds, and, in addition, there are actually rodeo events for kids (with parents running alongside!). The rodeo grounds are also where you can watch colorful traditional dances, drum circles with chanting, and timeless ceremonies. There's a replica of an authentic Seminole village, complete with *chickees* (huts) and work stations where the Indians carve their canoes by hand, and tribal members are there to answer your questions. There are dance competitions, in which brilliantly costumed (and plumed) participants festooned in beads and feathers retrace the ancient ceremonial steps of their ancestors.

At the Rodeo Hall, you can buy that pair of cowboy boots you've always dreamed about, as well as hand-carved saddles, hand-woven blankets, spurs, and other accessories. And there are stunning Native crafts for sale, from intricately woven and beaded skirts and blouses to beautiful jewelry, from Seminole dolls to necklaces, from beaded decorative items to shirts and jackets with Seminole symbols.

SEMINOLE TRIBE OF FLORIDA ORANGE BLOSSOM FESTIVAL, PARADE & RODEO
Town Hall
6591 Orange Dr.; from Davie Road west to SW 66th Terrace, Davie
(954) 797-1000
www.davie-fl.gov/Pages/DavieFL_Spcl-Prjcts/orangeblossom2011

This is a good, old-fashioned country hoe-down, bringing alive the "western" roots of this area, and its multiethnic background. More than 250 vendors, artists, and craftspeople will exhibit their products and art. And everything is free, including an arts-and-crafts show, fine-arts show, an authentic recreation of a western town, diverse musical groups, a Native American exhibit, an animal farm/petting zoo, a display of real western wagons and carriages, a "commerce corner," a motorcycle show with everything from "Hogs" to Vespas, and a display of military vehicles. There's a Kids' Corner with bounce house, giant slide, climbing wall, magic show, and arts-and-crafts activities. Do you like to think that you're a master in the kitchen? Then enter the Orange Cook-Off Contest, where the prize-winner is the one who comes up with the best orange-based recipe. Have a way with strawberries? Then craft a strawberry-based creation to offer at the Strawberry Shortcake Festival (where you can also sample some delicious cakes and berries and cream offered by other bakers!). There's a farmers' market, street concerts and dancing, and—true to Davie's western roots and western identity— a rodeo. The Davie Pro Rodeo has actually been voted the Best Rodeo East of the Mississippi. There'll be bull ridin', bronc bustin', cattle rasslin', barrel races, and team roping competitions, along with the most incredible barbecue and fixin's you've ever tasted. The whole festive weekend kicks off with a giant parade on Sat morning.

SISTRUNK HISTORICAL FESTIVAL
540 NW 4th Ave., Ft. Lauderdale
(954) 687-3472
www.sistrunkfestival.org

Sistrunk Historical Festival, Inc., is a cultural organization that celebrates the accomplishments of people of African descent, in the wider world as well as in the communities of Greater Fort Lauderdale. The organization was founded in 1980 and is named in honor of Dr. James Sistrunk, one of the first African-American doctors in Broward County, and a pioneer community organizer. In addition to the Annual Sistrunk Historical Festival, the organization is involved with a number of educational, historical, and recreational events in the area. And this event attracts thousands of people from all over the tri-county region of South Florida, as well as from elsewhere in the state. The festivities kick off with a large parade, followed by a variety of international foods, top entertainment provided by both local and national personalities, and activities with an emphasis on the family. If you'd like to learn more about Greater Fort Lauderdale's rich African-American history—and have a great time while doing it—this is the place.

March

ANNUAL MAROONE HISPANICFEST
Pines Recreation Center
7400 Pines Blvd., Pembroke Pines
Next to Broward College South Campus
(954) 987-2665
www.hispanicunity.org/hispanicfest
The name "Maroone" doesn't sound very Hispanic. And, truth be told, Mike Maroone, an executive with Auto Nation (a Fort Lauderdale company) and a successful auto dealer in these parts for many years, is not Hispanic. But he sure knows how to throw a great party! Having started back in 1989, this is the oldest Hispanic festival in South Florida. And it brings in Hispanics—and everyone else, as well—from all over the region. Famous

Hispanic singers and musicians come here to perform from all over Latin America, and in a wide variety of styles. There's a Kids Zone for the younger set. The food, representing most of the cuisines of Central and South America, is wonderful. And the rhythms are mesmerizing and exciting at the same time. The sights, sounds, smells, and experience are all unique. And be prepared to boogie, Latin-style! *NOTE:* This event has also been held in April in the past, so it's best to confirm when it'll be this year before you plan on attending.

ANNUAL SPRING GARDEN EVENT AT FLAMINGO GARDENS
Flamingo Gardens & Wildlife Sanctuary
3750 S. Flamingo Rd., Davie
(954) 473-2955
www.floridaattractions.org/en/rel/470
Flamingo Gardens is one of those places that feels like it's been here forever. In the midst of ever-growing South Florida, it's a place of quiet natural beauty, unusual experiences, and learning about the land and the environment and the wildlife of Greater Fort Lauderdale. Every year the Gardens greets the coming of spring with this special weekend-long event. You'll see a variety of plants and trees, some of which you haven't seen before. You'll also see displays of garden supplies, along with accessories and decorative items for the yard and patio. And there will be knowledgeable people there to answer your questions about the items. You'll see all types of flowering plants and orchids, butterfly and hummingbird plants, and herbs you can use in your cooking. On Sunday there's an auction, the proceeds of which go to special projects in Flamingo Gardens. You'll walk through the botanical gardens; the free-flight aviary with 43 species of birds; and the Birds of Prey

exhibit with eagles, owls and hawks. But that's not the only wildlife you'll see here; there are also brilliantly plumed flamingos (naturally!), Florida panthers (of which there are only a couple of hundred still left), bobcats, otters, alligators, tortoises, and turtles. You can watch Wildlife Encounter Shows. Take your family on a tour through the Wray Home, a typical Old Florida house from the 1930s. The kids will love the 20-minute narrated tram tour. And, if you're hungry, there's plenty of food from which to choose.

BMW TENNIS TOURNAMENT
Sunrise Tennis Club
9605 W. Oakland Park Blvd., Sunrise
(954) 572-2286
www.sunrisetennis.com
If you're looking for some serious tennis competition in the heart of Greater Fort Lauderdale, you should check out the BMW Tournament, which often attracts 10 to 15 of the world's men's top tennis players. The BMW Tennis Championship is one of only three major tennis tournaments that take place in Florida. It's also the only event in Broward County that's sanctioned by the Association of Tennis Professionals (ATP), the organizer of the principal worldwide men's tennis tour. The tourney offers invitations to 50 top players around the world, and special wild-card invitations to the world's premier players. And the Sunrise Tennis Club itself is a world-class facility. It's an award-winning tennis spot—a winner, in fact, of the United States Tennis Association's (USTA) 2001 Outstanding Facility award, and *Tennis Industry* magazine's 2001 Court of the Year award. In 1999, while being built, the Tennis Club was recognized by both the USTA and the United States Tennis Court and Track Builders Association as an example of excellence in the

design and construction of a tennis facility. And that may be one of the reasons so many elite players come here in March.

COLLECTOR CARS OF FORT LAUDERDALE
Greater Fort Lauderdale/Broward County Convention Center
1950 Eisenhower Blvd., Ft. Lauderdale
(954) 765-5900, (519) 352-4575
www.rmauctions.com

Have a hankerin' for that 1930 DeSoto four-door sedan? Check out this show. Nursing a thirst for that 1930 Ford Model A Woody (with wooden paneling on the sides)? Check out this show. Got a craving for that classic '67 Camaro Coupe? You might find it here. Do you still turn up the volume on the TV when *Bullitt* (1968) comes on, so you can hear that throaty roar of Steve McQueen's green Mustang hatchback? Ditto. Remember the first Corvette you ever saw? Maybe it was a 1972 yellow convertible. Are you old enough to remember the *real* Volkswagen Beetle or, better yet, the Volkswagen Van (into which, if you are a certain age, you may have stuffed 12 to 15 of your most intimate friends)? Every year in March, the Fort Lauderdale Convention Center becomes a feast for the eyes, filled with the chrome and wood and velvet and shark fins and dual exhausts and wooden dashboards and fancy wheels and racing steering wheels and the British racing green of yesteryear—when a car was a car! And it's not just cars we're talking about here. It's also antique Texaco oil cans, model-car collections, vintage road signs, antique tools and repair kits, hubcaps with logos, old coin banks, even a carhop's serving tray from the 1950s. You can buy, sell, learn, marvel, ogle, swap stories, and just generally schmooze to your heart's delight.

DANIA BEACH MARINE FLEA MARKET
Dania Beach Jai Alai Fronton
301 E. Dania Beach Blvd., Dania Beach
(954) 920-7877
www.daniamarinefleamarket.com

The promoters call this the largest event of its type anywhere, and they may be right. This is a flea market, but it isn't like any flea market you've seen before. Here you don't buy old furniture or homemade candy. You buy boats, all types of marine equipment, antiques that conjure up images of the raging sea in olden times (some actually brought up from those raging seas), fishing tackle, diving gear, nautically related artwork, and just about any other knickknack or accessory that has anything to do with the sea (on it or under it!). You can actually find a lot of very usable things—and interesting antiques—and you'll get them at a much lower price than you would at retail. There's new and used, treasured and throwaways. If you love the sea, you'll find plenty of things to love here. And if it's even peripherally related to the sea—such as sunglasses to reduce the glare—you'll find it here. There's also food and drink. It's like a big block party for the marine set.

FLORIDA DERBY
Gulfstream Park Racing & Casino
901 S. Federal Hwy., Hallandale Beach
(954) 454-7000
www.gulfstreampark.com

This is the big horse race in Florida, with a $750,000 purse and a national reputation. It's a mile and an eighth, for three-year-olds—one or two of whom you may be watching in the Kentucky Derby two months later. There's an electricity running through the park as they get into the starter's gate. And when the gate lifts up, the crowd rises to its feet with a roar. If you enjoy watching talented thoroughbreds and world-class riders make a run for the money on a beautiful day in March, head for Gulfstream Park.

FORT LAUDERDALE INTERNATIONAL AUTO SHOW

Greater Fort Lauderdale/Broward County Convention Center
1950 Eisenhower Blvd., Ft. Lauderdale
(954) 765-5900
www.ftlauderdaleautoshow.com/
index.php

This four-day show, managed by the South Florida Automobile Dealers Association, is now in its third decade. It's grown dramatically in that time, and it's become a "must" stop for automobile manufacturers and the industries associated with them. If you want to see the latest in technology and design—and the next big things in the automotive industry—don't miss this show. And if you want to see the cars that people will be talking about over the coming year, make a beeline for the convention center. More than 500 cars, trucks, SUVs, motorcycles, and every other conceivable type of motor-driven vehicles (on land) will be on display for you to see, hear, touch, and feel. The event benefits the Boys and Girls Clubs of Broward County, and since the first show in 1991, more than $3 million has been raised. It will certainly make you feel good to contribute to this organization. And it will make you feel good, as well, to sit in a prototype Porsche or Jaguar or hybrid or electric car of the future that the rest of the world won't be seeing for a while.

FORT LAUDERDALE IRISH FESTIVAL AND ST. PATRICK'S DAY PARADE

Huizenga Plaza, at the southeast corner of Las Olas Boulevard and Andrews Avenue, Ft. Lauderdale
(954) 828-5804
www.ftlaudirishfest.com

Erin go Bragh! There's a bit o' the green in all of us, and everyone's Irish on this festive occasion. And Fort Lauderdale celebrates it with a flair. The culture of this ancient land is on vivid display here, with Irish step dancing and jigs (and no matter what your own ethnic or national heritage, you'll soon find yourself dancing along!); the wearin' o' the kilts (and don't bother asking if they're wearing anything underneath) wonderful songs; Irish crafts; exhibits on the contributions of Irish people to America (and to Greater Fort Lauderdale); good food, from steak and kidney pie to bangers and mash; and the distinctive Celtic sounds of bagpipes, telling the story of an ancient culture with every note. Oh, and you'll also hear Gaelic, which is still used in many parts of western Ireland. You'll see demonstrations of Irish cooking, clogging (a form of dance), and Gaelic football (which is something of a mix between soccer and rugby). And then, of course, is the parade, a wonderful procession that runs along Las Olas Boulevard chock-full of great floats, pipe bands, green hats and vests and bowties and suspenders, and people just plain having fun. *Slainte!*—Gaelic for "To your health!"

HOLLYWOOD ST. PATRICK'S DAY PARADE & FESTIVAL

**Hollywood Boulevard west of
Young Circle, Downtown Hollywood
(954) 921-3404
www.downtownhollywood.com/St
PatricksDay/tabid/770/Default.aspx**

Few cities anywhere do St. Patrick's Day quite like Hollywood. Here there's a bit o' the green in all of us, and the culture and history and folklore and music of Ireland are on brilliant display. You'll hear Irish bands, from folk to rock. You'll see—and shortly after, participate in—authentic step dancing. Of course you'll try some Irish coffee, food, and Irish beer, such as Guinness Stout, Smithwick's, or Harp. You'll see pipe and drum bands, and hear the lilting sounds of the bagpipes summoning that Celtic spirit. And of course, no one does a parade like the Irish. There will be kid's activities, plenty of interesting arts-and-crafts exhibits (both Irish and non-Irish). The storytelling will bring back the atmosphere and the aura of the Auld Sod (and will probably include, we suppose, more than a bit o' the blarney thrown in for good measure!). And, for one day at least, we'll all be Irish.

April

ANNUAL PEOPLE & PLANET FAIR

**Snyder Park
3299 SW 4th Ave., Ft. Lauderdale
(954) 524-0366
www.peopleandplanetfair.org/index
.htm**

If you're old enough to remember it, it probably doesn't seem like more than 40 years since the first Earth Day. This fair serves a dual purpose: To remind us that our Earth is still very much in peril, from a variety of forces, and to show us what we can do about it. This is an all-day affair, starting at seven in the morning and running until five in the evening. And, in addition to the message, it's just plain fun. There's a 5K run. There'll be a lot of talented artists displaying their works, and a lot of vendors with items you suddenly realize you might need. There's an art contest for the kids. There's a tree planting ("Plant It For the Planet")—and what better possible symbolism for Earth Day? There's live music from good local bands. And, of course, plenty of good things to eat.

CITY OF SUNRISE EARTH DAY

**Sawgrass Sanctuary
237 N. New River Circle, Sunrise
(954) 747-4600
www.sunrisefl.gov/earthday.html**

This is a day to love Mother Earth—and a great place to bring the family. There's live music, including some notable children's performers. And the kids will also enjoy the many rides and activities geared to them. You will love browsing through the farmers' market, where you might find anything from antique canning jars to spicy pickles, soy candles, eclectic quilts, and handcrafted kitchenware. You can sample "green" foods (along with some wonderful ethnic specialties, and—let's face it—some foods that are not so green, but they are really good). You can wander amongst rows of unique handicrafts created by Broward County artisans. There's an eco-chic fashion show; you'll be surprised what can be done with natural materials. And there are books, pamphlets, and experts who can help you learn more about green living, and leading a sustainable lifestyle.

FLEET WEEK
Port Everglades
Fort Lauderdale

This week, as the old song goes, "the fleet's in." The U.S. Navy fleet, to be exact. Port Everglades fills up with guided-missile cruisers, frigates, destroyers, amphibious assault ships, submarines, Coast Guard cutters, and various attack and supply ships of the Navy. Sometimes you can even see a giant aircraft carrier, its crew all dressed in their whites and standing at attention, waiting for the "Dismissed" command that will let them rush to the gangplanks to go ashore. And the streets of Fort Lauderdale fill up with the thousands of sailors who've been waiting impatiently for their boats to dock. Occasionally, ships from foreign navies also come into port; recent years have seen ships from Great Britain and Germany participating among others. In earlier (or more innocent) days, more of the ships were open for tours. But in our post-9/11 world, more caution is exercised, and things can change quickly. In addition—also post-9/11—there's not as much notice as there used to be about when Fleet Week will take place (usually late April or early May), which ships will be visiting, and where they will be berthed. However, there are a number of ceremonies—including marching bands and color guards—on shore. And it's truly a stirring sight to see these grey behemoths that protect our country resting in the harbor. If you're interested, many local folks serve as hosts to sailors for the week, treating them to home-cooked meals, a welcoming family atmosphere, and some warm conversation. And there's an official All Hands on Deck Party to welcome the visitors, at the Hard Rock Hotel & Casino in Hollywood (www.seminoleparadise.com). Check the *South Florida Sun-Sentinel* for information as springtime nears.

OCEAN FEST DIVE AND ADVENTURE SPORTS EXPO
Fort Lauderdale Beach
(954) 839-8516
www.oceanfest.com

Fort Lauderdale's the perfect place for a festival celebrating the richness and diversity of the world's oceans because it's home to an extensive system of artificial reefs, as well as one of America's only natural coral reefs that's accessible from the shore. This event takes place in giant tents at the ocean's edge and features more than 150 exhibitors from the diving and adventure-sports worlds. There will be food, music, treasure hunts, raffles and prizes, and seminars about the ocean waters that make up three-quarters of the Earth's surface. In addition, there will be introductory scuba-diving courses, and an underwater treasure hunt for dive boats and one for shore diving. It is located on A1A just south of Las Olas Boulevard, north of the Yankee Clipper Hotel, the Bahia Mar Resort and Yacht Club, and Bahia Cabana Hotel.

May

AMERICA'S RED CLAY TENNIS CHAMPIONSHIP
Jimmy Evert Tennis Center
Holiday Park
1300 E. Sunrise Blvd., Ft. Lauderdale
(954) 828-5378
http://venueguide.com/fort_lauderdale

Jimmy Evert, of course, is the father of renowned tennis star Chris Evert; and he also trained Jennifer Capriati, who achieved some measure of stardom. He's considered one of the finest tennis teachers in America, and his Tennis Center is considered one of the best facilities. America's Red Clay Tennis Championship brings together top players from throughout the United States.

POMPANO BEACH FISHING RODEO
Alsdorf Park
2901 NE 14th St., Pompano Beach
(954) 942-4513
www.pompanofishingrodeo.com

This rodeo don't take place on land, pardner . . . but it's as wild and woolly as they come! The Pompano Beach Fishing Rodeo began in 1965, and it's since become one of the signs of spring in these parts. The original intent was to keep winter tourists in South Florida a bit longer by showing them that this is a springtime destination, as well, in addition to bringing attention to the local charter-boat business. It's a two-day fishing tournament held annually on the third weekend of May. The idea of calling it a rodeo came because it's sort of a "roundup" of the most popular species of fish. Through the years, the event has welcomed spectators, anglers, sponsors, and advertisers, and it helps support numerous saltwater conservation and marine education projects.

"Rodeo Weekend" officially kicks off on Wednesday night, with a party and a captains' meeting. On Friday and Saturday mornings, the Hillsboro, Boca Raton, and Port Everglades Inlets are filled with shiny, bobbing boats—worth hundreds of millions of dollars—filled with hundreds of anxious anglers checking out their equipment and beseeching Lady Luck to smile upon them. The rodeo competition ends at noon on Saturday, allowing the anglers time to weigh their catches, go home, clean up, and then, hopefully return to claim their prizes (which can range, by the way, up to $10,000) at the Awards Party.

UNIFEST CARIBBEAN CELEBRATION
Vincent Torres Park
4331 NW 36th St., Lauderdale Lakes
(954) 730-8885
www.gcaccoalition.com/index.html

Unifest is the first Caribbean festival in Greater Fort Lauderdale. Every May it draws thousands of people to Lauderdale Lakes, to become Caribbean if only for a day. You'll see and hear well-known musical groups from all over the region, from reggae to ska to Caribbean jazz to calypso. You'll see a battle of the marching bands—and keep in mind that, in the Caribbean, marching bands are often decked out in incredibly colorful costumes with plenty of feathers and plenty of symbols. Many of these costumes, in fact, will be on display in a Parade of Carnival Costumes. The game of dominoes is popular in the region, and there will be a tournament. A "cultural tent" will be filled with opportunities to discover more about this multifaceted region of so many different countries and cultures. Craftspeople from the islands will be proudly showing off their imaginative creations, which are tinged by both Old World and New World influences. And food? Try the spicy jerk chicken and beef from Jamaica, the conch fritters from the Bahamas, and spicy seafood salads from Trinidad.

June

THE BLUE WILD ANNUAL OCEAN ADVENTURE EXPO
Greater Fort Lauderdale/Broward County Convention Center
1950 Eisenhower Blvd., Ft. Lauderdale
(561) 715-0247
www.thebluewild.com

If you love the sea—under the sea, to be precise—this show is for you. Here you can learn about, or buy, everything and

My Fort Lauderdale

I've lived in many places in Florida—Fort Myers, Orlando, Tampa, Jacksonville, and Miami. But—without question—Fort Lauderdale is my favorite spot in this vast state of ours.

I'm a reporter for NBC News, and my job has me traveling the world. I've been to exotic locales like Bhutan, Kosovo, Papua New Guinea, and Kenya, to name just a few. But every time I get off the plane in Fort Lauderdale, I still genuinely relish the moment. It means that I'm home. I'm back in my comfort zone, back in the place I've come to really love.

Here, we have a small town hidden in an urban city. If I long for a meal like the one I had in Chiang Mai, I can find a restaurant here where the chef can not only whip it up to order, but can also tell me about how he grew up in Chiang Mai.

But, just like a small town, I might see that same chef again at the grocery store. And when I do, we'll stop and chat and maybe gossip about the happenings in Fort Lauderdale, the city that we both—after many travels—now call home.

—Kerry Sanders,
Reporter, NBC News,
*NBC Nightly News with
Brian Williams*

videography—and a whole lot more. The weekend's festivities start with a Friday-night Under the Stars Kickoff Party, and, generally, search-and-rescue demonstrations by the U.S. Coast Guard. On Saturday the presentations begin with a diverse and well-known collection of speakers and experts on everything underwater. There are fascinating films by adventurers of all types, from divers to "swamp rats." There's a raffle, in which you could end up driving home with a huge stuffed marlin (or a variety of other awards) in your trunk. Or you just may end up driving home with a compelling piece of art, either oil on canvas or something fusing together various materials from the sea. In addition, there are hands-on workshops and seminars, underwater film shows, and photography exhibits.

FORT LAUDERDALE HOME DESIGN & REMODELING SHOW

Greater Fort Lauderdale/Broward County Convention Center
1950 Eisenhower Blvd., Ft. Lauderdale
(954) 765-5900
Show Information: (305)-667-9299
www.homeshows.net

When it comes to improving or redesigning your home, if you can dream it, you can do it. And this is the place to discover your dreams or to make them come true. There's fine furniture, in a wide variety of styles and periods. There are hundreds of types of accessories you can use in remodeling. There are interior designers and other resources to give you ideas. Kitchen and bath remodeling, of course, can bring incredible value to your home, and you'll find plenty of ways to go about it here. You'll see the newest appliances and the newest advances in home theaters, home improvements, pools

anything having to do with free diving, scuba, spearfishing, marine art, boating, safety, conservation, underwater photography, and

and spas, patios, and landscaping. There are literally thousands of products on display here, all of which can help you improve your home as a place to live and, eventually, as a place to sell. And people are, apparently, taking advantage of it, because show management constantly reports record sales from the Fort Lauderdale show.

July

HOMETOWN FAMILY FOURTH OF JULY: STAR-SPANGLED SPECTACULAR
Hollywood Beach and Broadwalk
Hollywood Boulevard and SR A1A,
Hollywood
(954) 921-3404
www.southflorida.com/events
The city of Hollywood throws an old-fashioned, colorful, patriotic celebration filled with fun and pageantry to highlight America's birthday. And what could be more American than a Fourth on a boardwalk, er, Broadwalk? There are generally two stages—one at Johnson Street at the beach and the other at Tyler Street at the beach. Both stages vibrate with the sounds of great local musicians, ranging from swing or brass bands to popular South Florida groups like the Fabulons (who really make the great sounds of the '60s come alive!) to the Hollywood Philharmonic Orchestra. The entertainment generally goes on until close to midnight. The food is all-American: hot hot dogs and burgers, cold soda, popcorn, ice cream, cotton candy, roasted nuts dripping with honey and cinnamon. And at nine, the skies over the ocean light up with a brilliant fireworks display. Come wish America "Happy Birthday" in style!

September

HOLLYWOOD BEACH LATIN FESTIVAL
Hollywood Boulevard and SR A1A,
Hollywood
(954) 534-3500
www.hollywoodlatinfestival.com
The Latin community has changed South Florida so much over the past 50 years with its culture, its music, its cuisine, its dance, its nightlife, its passion, and its political involvement. And nowhere is this influence more on display than this vibrant celebration of Latin life and culture in America, more specifically, in South Florida. Much of the music, cuisine, dance, and passion will be on display at this annual festival that brings out South Floridians of every culture. Music? There'll be flamenco, salsa, tango, Latin swing, and a dozen other forms. Cuisine? You'll be able to sample Argentine steak, Brazilian *churrasco* and *feijoada*, Cuban arroz con pollo, and, of course, paella, claimed by several Latin cultures. There'll be special areas for the kids. There'll be very special arts and crafts, such as the *casitas* (authentic, handmade and hand-painted little houses) from Colombia. No matter what your ethnic or national background, you've got to come to this festival. It's quintessential Greater Fort Lauderdale. And it's incredible fun!

October

ANNUAL FORT LAUDERDALE INTERNATIONAL BOAT SHOW
(954) 764-7642
www.showmanagement.com/fort_lauderdale_international_boat_show_2010/contact_us
This show started in Fort Lauderdale—"Yachting Capital of the World"—back in 1960. So it's only fitting that the Fort

Lauderdale International Boat Show is now the largest show in the world. The show features more than $3 billion worth of boats and boating equipment With hundreds of boats of all sizes on display—and often for sale—the show is now too big to be contained in just one spot; it now requires five. Between the five venues, it now takes up more than 3 million square feet of space, on land and in the water. Between water taxis, riverboats, and bus shuttles, you won't miss a thing…because transportation between the sites is seamless. The world's finest makers of state-of-the-art luxury watercraft will be represented, along with manufacturers of pretty much every accessory or part you could ever want on (or in) a boat. You'll see it all here. Yachts with so many luxurious touches (including mahogany, gold, brass, marble, and cherrywood) that they seem to be fit for a king—and, indeed, they may actually be owned by one. Sleek, smart, white machines that look like they were born to run. Weekend pleasure or fishing boats. Beautifully restored classic yachts. Motorboats. Sailboats. Schooners. Boats that can hold 40 or 50 people. And boats that can hold two. If you love being out on the water, with the wind in your hair and your cares floating away—or if you've ever dreamed of being out on the water with the wind in your hair and your cares floating away—don't miss this show.

The show is typically held in October or November, and at the following locations: The Greater Fort Lauderdale/Broward County Convention Center (1950 Eisenhower Blvd., Fort Lauderdale; 954-765-5900); the Bahia Mar Yachting Center (Bahia Mar Beach Resort & Yachting Center, 801 Seabreeze Blvd., Fort Lauderdale; 954-627-6309), the Hilton Fort Lauderdale Marina (1881 SE 17th St., Fort Lauderdale,; 954-463-4000), the Hall of Fame Marina (435 Seabreeze Blvd., Fort Lauderdale; 954-764-3975), and the Las Olas Marina (240 E. Las Olas Circle, Fort Lauderdale; 954-828-7200).

FORT LAUDERDALE INTERNATIONAL FILM FESTIVAL
Cinema Paradiso
503 SE 6th St., Ft. Lauderdale
(954) 760-9898
www.fliff.com

When it started in 1986, the Fort Lauderdale International Film Festival was a babe in the woods—another effort by a community that had been called a "cultural wasteland" to expand its cultural horizons. Its origins were modest. But there's nothing modest about this festival any more. And just as Greater Fort Lauderdale has outgrown the "cultural wasteland" designation, its film festival has now reached the cultural big leagues. It now attracts outstanding films—as well as outstanding actors, directors, and producers—from around the world; these people are literally groundbreakers in the cinematic arts. Over a three-week period, from late October to mid-November, the festival shows over 200 new and classic films to packed houses. Many of these groundbreakers will be in attendance at these showings, and many of them will be attending the dozens of parties and special events associated with the festival. If you're here, you'll have the opportunity to meet and speak with them.

During the festival, films are divided into various sectors. Among them are Competition Films, which are judged by panels, in categories such as best film, special jury prize, best director, best actor, best actress, best supporting actor, best supporting actress, best ensemble cast, best screenplay, best cinematography, best score, and best foreign language film. There will be a variety of films from countries all over the world, many of which you would not ordinarily think of as creative cinematic spots. There are compelling, provocative films by American "indies" (remember *Fargo* and *Pulp Fiction*). There are superb documentaries—the original reality shows—putting on celluloid the people, places, and events that have made (or are making) history, and that make us think. There are "shorts." There are home-grown films from Floridians. Children's films, from far and wide. Gay and lesbian films. And there are wonderful retrospectives and tributes to some of the greats in this industry.

VIVA BROWARD! HISPANIC FESTIVAL
**Pompano Citi Centre Mall
Copans Road and N. Federal Highway,
Pompano Beach
(954) 567-0627
www.wedoevents.net**
As discussed in other sections of this book, Hispanic culture has made a profound impact on South Florida and on Greater Fort Lauderdale. And there are many people from different ethnic backgrounds who raptly enjoy Latin song, dance, story, crafts, and foods. Viva Broward! is a great place to see and do and participate in all of the varied aspects of the Hispanic-American experience, particularly during Hispanic Heritage Month. The magnificent Tito Puente headlined the first Viva Broward! in 1995, and renowned entertainers have been making their way here ever since. *NOTE:* the venue may be subject to change as the festival has moved from place to place in recent years.

November

ANNUAL FORT LAUDERDALE BILLFISH TOURNAMENT
**2312 S. Andrews Ave., Ft. Lauderdale
(954) 523-1004
www.miasf.com/billfish**
This fishing tournament was established in 1965 as a competition for genuinely serious fishermen. Now, however, it's one of those events that's become so much so, in fact, that it now takes place in three different inlets—Fort Lauderdale, Miami, and Lake Worth. It's one of the most popular fishing tournaments in a state filled with them. Sailfish are the primary targets of the anglers, but there are also divisions for dolphin, tuna, wahoo, and kingfish. And the winners receive outstanding payouts.

BEAUX ARTS FESTIVAL OF TREES
**Fort Lauderdale Museum of Art
One E. Las Olas Blvd., Ft. Lauderdale
(954) 525-5500**
Christmas-tree decorating, as many of us know, is sort of an art. And it's definitely an art the way it's done by the people whose trees are on display here. In addition, there are other wonderful signs of the season that also could be considered decorative arts, such as wreaths and gingerbread houses. And the kids will love it. There's a Teddy Bear, Trains, and Tea event for them, as well as train rides and a visit from a certain rotund character who will be back down this way again in another month. And this being the Museum of Art, there are some beautiful holiday crafts on display.

BROWARD COUNTY FAIR
10100 Pines Blvd., Pembroke Pines
(954) 922-2224
www.browardcountyfair.com
After more than 30 years at the Pompano Park Racetrack, the fair has been held in downtown Pompano Beach the past couple of years, partially due to the economy, but has a new location in Pembroke Pines. It used to be an enormous enterprise, with a huge midway filled with rides and concessions. The past couple of years, due to downsizing, have focused more on Broward County life and agriculture. Keep looking at the website, or call for more information. Among the features of recent fairs are the Miss Broward County Contest; an agricultural showcase with cows, sheep, rabbits, and other animals; step-team and dance competitions and displays; and art and project exhibits by Broward County students.

CAMELOT DAYS RENAISSANCE FAIR
T. Y. Park
3300 N. Park Rd., Hollywood
(954) 357-8811
Camelot Days brings back the days of yore and puts you right in the middle of them. You'll wander delightedly through a "kingdom" of jesters and jokers, peasants and nobles, kings and queens, knights and knaves, rascals and royalty. The grounds will be filled with musicians playing the instruments of the Middle Ages: flutes, harps, primitive stringed instruments, violins, and harpsichords. Craftspeople will be creating everything from medieval purses to leather books to beaded jewelry to hand-carved flutes. The food will be representative of what the people of those days ate, and, yes, you must experience the Henry the Eighth–type thrill of wandering around the grounds with a giant turkey stick in your hands. After you're done with it—and the accompanying "libation"—watch a game of chess on the living chess board, or participate in one. Shop for fine handcrafted treasures in the Artists' Market. And try your luck at the games and contests played in the time of Sir Lancelot and his fellow Knights of the Round Table, King Arthur, Merlin, Robin Hood (and his Merry Men), and Queen Guinevere. And— just for a day—picture yourself in a mystical land of cliffs darkened by the clouds, dramatic highlands, misty moors, and fog-shrouded lochs.

HOLIDAY FANTASY OF LIGHTS AT TRADEWINDS PARK
3600 W. Sample Rd., Coconut Creek
(954) 968-3880
www.holidaylightsdrivethru.com/index .html
It simply doesn't get any more beautiful than this. And there are very few holiday experiences in South Florida that are as wonderful as this one, which is why people drive from all over South Florida to experience it. From late November through early January, you can drive through the winding roads of Tradewinds Park in the comfort of your own car, past an incredible assortment of structures festooned with strings of brilliant lights of a hundred colors. You'll drive past windmills. Railroad trains. Reindeer (and Santa's sled, of course). Gingerbread houses. Log cabins. Waterfalls. Little Dutch boys and girls with wooden shoes. Castles. Old cars. Elves. Rainbows. And, toward the end of the road, you'll drive through a virtual tunnel of lights.

December

ANNUAL SEMINOLE HARD ROCK WINTERFEST BOAT PARADE

Winterfest, Inc.
Corporate Headquarters
512 NE 3rd Ave., Ft. Lauderdale
(954) 767-0686
www.winterfestparade.com/index.cfm

This, ladies and gentlemen, is it . . . possibly the most-anticipated, biggest, brightest (and certainly, merriest) event in South Florida. More than a million people line the 12-mile route, making the Winterfest Boat Parade into not only the largest one-day, live audience of any event in Florida, but also the seventh-largest one-day spectator event in the country! The International Festival and Events Association has named Winterfest one of the "Top Twenty Parades in the World." The Winterfest Boat Parade is Greater Fort Lauderdale's salute to the holiday season, and it provides colorful holiday cheer to tens of thousands of residents and visitors. On this wonderful night—usually about two weeks before Christmas—a parade several miles long of spectacularly decked-out (and lit-up) boats glides by enthralled crowds gathered on the edge of the Intracoastal Waterway. Each boat is festooned with strings of brilliant lights and decorative seasonal items. Many of them have celebrities on board. Some of them represent local or national companies; others just represent some of the wealthiest people in South Florida. You can hear the oohs and aahs as each one passes by. Many people who are fortunate enough to live along the Intracoastal hold parties on this night, so they can stand outside with their friends and watch. After nearly 40 years, Winterfest is no longer just a boat parade though. The multi-day festival now includes a Golf Tournament; the dazzling Moet & Chandon Champagne Winterfest Black Tie Ball; the Shoreline Decorating Extravaganza, an exciting Grand Marshal Reception, Winterfest White Party, and Family Fun Days, all of which are capped by the boat parade. This parade is a true "Greater Fort Lauderdale" event, right on the water, in the most festive season of all. And it's one you don't want to miss.

HOLLYWOOD BEACH CANDY CANE PARADE

The Broadwalk
Hollywood Beach, Hollywood
(954) 921-3404
www.visithollywoodfl.org/candycane
.aspx

When December rolls around, most of America is bundling up and getting ready for winter. In fact, in most of America, winter has probably already arrived. What better time then to celebrate the season in a place where the winter sun is sweet and warming, and the weather is dreamlike almost every day? Hollywood's been holding the Candy Cane Parade since 1955, so by now it's certainly an important part of the holiday tradition in these parts. More than a hundred colorful entries participate in the parade, from intricate, brilliantly decorated floats to marching bands. And tens of thousands of Greater Fort Lauderdale residents line SR A1A to enjoy it. As you might expect, there's plenty of live music and plenty of good food.

NEW YEAR'S EVE STREET PARTY— DOWNTOWN FORT LAUDERDALE

Esplanade Park, Ft. Lauderdale
(954) 828-4742
www.cbslocal.com

This is one of the largest New Year's Eve celebrations in Florida, and you've gotta be here! More than 120,000 people will gather in downtown Lauderdale to ring in the New Year, with music, games, food, fireworks, costumes, and street parties. The younger set gets a running start on the celebrating, at 5 p.m., with bounce houses, games, contests, balloons, face painting, a DJ, and many other activities. They even get their own New Year's Eve lighted "ball" to count down with. By 8 p.m. the first bands are playing, and by 10 p.m. other bands are playing on a second stage. By 11, you'll be partying with thousands of your closest friends, some of whom will be attired in the craziest costumes you've ever seen. At one minute to midnight, the 8-foot "Downtown Countdown" ball—larger than the one in Times Square—will begin its descent, illuminated by its 7,500 lights. When it hits midnight, you'll hear shouts of joy not only from the street, but also from the surrounding restaurants and clubs as well as neighboring highrises. And you'll be engulfed in a shower of confetti and streamers. It's a great—and very "Fort Lauderdale"—way to ring in the New Year. It's held in Esplanade Park, across from the Museum of Discovery & Science, from SW 2nd Avenue to SW 5th Avenue.

DAY TRIPS & WEEKEND GETAWAYS

One of the best things about Greater Fort Lauderdale is that you're within a few hours of most places in Florida, as well as most places in the Caribbean. True, Florida does have the biggest tourist attractions in the world—within a few hours of Greater Fort Lauderdale—but it's also got so much more than just the major theme parks. In fact, when you're in the area, you'd probably be delighted to learn just how close you are to so many incredible things to do and see. So let's start exploring!

DAY TRIPS

The drive times given below originate from Fort Lauderdale (and they don't take into account rush hour, accidents, etc.).

The Bahamas—Bimini

Yes, this is listed under Day Trips because that's exactly how close you are. You can take a boat from Fort Lauderdale and arrive in Bimini, the closest Bahamian island, in a little more than an hour; and be back in time for dinner. Or you can fly and be there in a half hour. Bimini is a small island full of brightly painted little houses, friendly people, and great seafood (try the conch chowder, fritters, and salad!). Freeport, with its luxury hotels and grand casinos, is also close by. (Visit www.bahamas.com.)

Downtown Stuart

Stuart is a town in Martin County, about an 80-minute drive north of Fort Lauderdale. Stuart restored its downtown area back in the 1990s, and it's now a really pleasant place to walk around. There are cute little shops and restaurants, and a restored old theater that hosts plays and other performing arts productions. And you'll get a kick out of "Confusion Corner," a traffic circle that Charles Kuralt once profiled in his famous *On the Road* series back in the 1970s and '80s. As soon as you drive up to it, you'll know how it got its name! Stuart also boasts the House of Refuge, an old wooden structure on Hutchinson Island that used to serve as a shelter for any shipwrecked sailors who were able to make it to shore. It's now a museum. (Visit www.martincountyfla.com.)

Everglades National Park

The best way to get into the park is to drive down to Miami, then head west on Tamiami Trail, about an hour's drive from Greater Fort Lauderdale. Here you'll find the entrance to a portion of the park known as Shark Valley. There are no sharks here, for sure, and no valley. But there are hundreds and hundreds of square miles of America's only tropical jungle, along with alligators, all kinds of snakes (both poisonous and not), red-shouldered hawks, purple gallinules, and hundreds of other species that you can't see anywhere else in the world. Shark Valley has an 8-mile biking/hiking path if you're the adventurous type. And the entrance to the national park is right at the site of the Miccosukee Indian reservation. The Miccosukee are a branch of the Seminole nation that never actually signed a peace treaty with the United States. Here, you can roam around their village on guided tours, watch craftspeople still creating the traditional crafts (such as the most colorful dresses you ever saw), see the *chickees* (huts of thatched straw), take an airboat ride, watch alligator wrestling, and learn about the history of this matriarchal society. (Visit www.nps.gov/ever/index.htm.)

Jensen Beach

This is a quaint little community about 90 minutes north of Fort Lauderdale, in Martin County. The compact downtown area has colorful, funky wooden shops and restaurants, and it's a fun place to walk around. You can also access the beaches of Hutchinson Island from here, along a beautiful causeway over the Intracoastal that's filled with fishermen cleaning their catches ... and pelicans waiting for the scraps. On Hutchinson Island, besides the great beaches, it's also very interesting to visit the nuclear power plant of Florida Power & Light Company, with its interactive museum. (Visit www.martincountyfla.com.)

Miami

About a half-hour south of Fort Lauderdale, Miami has one of the most impressive skylines in America; it's truly a stunning city. For a good look at this city, take the MetroMover monorail around downtown and through the financial district. Sample some great Cuban food in one of the unassuming but great restaurants in Little Havana, centered around SW 8th Street (Calle Ocho). A must visit is the Bayside Marketplace, a Caribbean-themed collection of open-air shops, cafes, and bistros, along with some of the funkiest kiosks you've ever seen, right on the harbor. If it's basketball season, catch a Miami Heat game across the street in American Airlines Arena. Cross Biscayne Bay to mingle with the international set in the cafes and galleries of Ocean Drive in famous South Beach. Or take a ride to the upscale island of Key Biscayne, right in Biscayne Bay, with an incredible view of this futuristic city on the water as you drive. Family attractions in Miami include Parrot Jungle Island and the Seaquarium. (Visit www.miamiandbeaches.com.)

Palm Beach

About a half-hour north of Fort Lauderdale is the island of Palm Beach, where you will find one of the most beautiful, magical towns in the world, filled with shops, where if you have to ask the price, you can't afford it, and one drop-dead-magnificent waterfront mansion after another. The heart of the island is storied Worth Avenue, lined with Duesenbergs, Bentleys, and Maseratis, and filled with people—both the jet set and mere commoners—from all over the world. On this street, you'll find bistros, boutiques, antiques shops, and galleries, and shaded little alleys and courtyards where artists are working in their studios, along with the most-exclusive international designer names you can find. And even if you do have to ask the prices of the items you see in the shop windows, it's great fun to look. Nearby, and nudging up against the Atlantic, is the legendary Breakers Hotel, built by Palm Beach pioneer/industrialist Henry Flagler in the early 1900s. This small island is filled with superb restaurants, one of the most famous of which is Ta-Boo, a longtime Palm Beach landmark at which you're likely to see local (and sometimes international) celebrities and political figures. And the houses you'll see on SR A1A (the oceanside road) as you drive up from Greater Fort Lauderdale are like mirages from a beautiful dream—you'll see Spanish castles, Moroccan palaces, Greek temples, and Bahamian estates, along with the former estates of families like the Kennedys and the Trumps.

West Palm Paradise

Natural wonders like the Loxahatchee River, Lake Okeechobee, and Everglades National Park provide wonderful day-trip destinations. Plus, Palm Beach International Airport, the Tri-Rail, and Amtrak station are also within a five-minute drive, which can take us anywhere in South Florida—or the world! We also have great city and county leaders, many of whom we know on a first-name basis. Now that retirement is on the horizon, we're looking for a place to buy a second summer home, but it's going to be hard to find any place as great as West Palm Beach. I don't think life gets any better than this!

—Margie Yansura,
Public Relations Consultant,
West Palm Beach

WEEKEND GETAWAYS

If you'd like to get away for more than a day, Greater Fort Lauderdale is close to a variety of interesting—and often exotic—destinations. Within a few hours' drive or boat ride—and less than that in a plane—is a stunning variety of cities, natural wonders, foreign cultures, people, arts and crafts, and entertainment. If you're looking for a place to just kick off your shoes—or just get sand in them—you'll find it close by. And if you're looking for a place to get gussied up for an elegant night on the town at a famous club, restaurant, resort, or casino, you'll find it close to Greater Fort Lauderdale. From the foreign to the domestic, from the familiar to the exotic, it's all just a few hours away.

The Bahamas—Nassau

Nassau, the capital of the Bahamas, is less than an hour away by plane. This is a colorful old colonial town with surprises down every street. Bay Street is lined with international shops. The side streets have rustic-looking (or just plain old!) restaurants and surprisingly good food, with Bahamian specialties such as turtle soup or steak, cracked conch, and peas 'n' rice. At the straw market, you'll see hundreds of women busily creating their one-of-a-kind hats, baskets, and gift items. And Nassau's just across the bridge from Paradise Island, where the resorts are world-class, the dining is gourmet, and the casinos are exciting. Paradise Island is not the original name of this island, however. It's actually Hog Island, but the Bahamian government changed it when they decided to develop the island as a tourism resort. Wonder why! (Visit www.bahamas.com.)

Tampa

Cross the state to Tampa—about five hours—and you'll see a different side of Florida. The west (Gulf) coast of the state is significantly different than the eastern (Atlantic) coast in lifestyles, in outlook, in where most residents came from (the Midwest as well as the East), and, of course, what they see when they look at a sunset or a sunrise. Tampa has a lot to see and do. There's Busch Gardens with great rides, slides, and roller coasters. There's the in-town, colorful section called Ybor City, which was the original home of the Cuban community that first came to Florida in the late 1800s. It's now an authentically restored neighborhood with colorful restaurants and shops and craftspeople—including some who still make real hand-rolled cigars. Near Tampa are the beachside communities of St. Petersburg and Clearwater. (Visit www.visit tampabay.com.)

Cape Canaveral

This is the home of Kennedy Space Center about 3 hours north of Fort Lauderdale. Here, you can see the real space shuttle. You can roam wonderful museum exhibits with hands-on interactive displays. You can see space shows and the launching pads. You can stand in awe at the memorials to those astronauts who did not return from their trips. And, if you're lucky, you can even meet an astronaut or two. (Visit www.kennedy spacecenter.com.)

The Florida Keys & Key West

The first of the string of pearls known as the Florida Keys, strung out into the ocean just south of Miami, is Key Largo, about 90 minutes south of Fort Lauderdale. It's another 3 to 4 hours to Key West. On the way, you'll be driving over the ocean, passing isolated little keys every so often, or a larger key with a town, such as Marathon. On your right will be the Gulf of Mexico, and on your left the Atlantic. All of the keys are great; the inhabited ones often have colorful fishing camps

and old restaurants that serve much better food (especially seafood) than you might think by looking at their exteriors. The resort of Hawk's Cay on Marathon is truly magnificent, restored since the time when Franklin D. Roosevelt used to stay here. And at the end of the line is Key West, the funkiest, coolest, weirdest, wackiest, most colorful town in America, with the shops and restaurants of Duval Street, a thriving literary and arts community, old gingerbread and Victorian homes, and bed-and-breakfasts lining leafy streets. There are the houses of such people as Ernest Hemingway, John Jay Audubon, and Tennessee Williams, as well as President Harry Truman's complex. Be sure to visit the Mallory Docks at sunset; it's a real "event." Not only will you see the most beautiful sunset you've ever seen, but you'll share it with hundreds of people, among them stilt walkers, fire-eaters, jugglers, and snake charmers. (Visit www.fla-keys.com.)

Mount Dora

There's really not a mountain here (or anywhere else in Florida, for that matter). But there is a beautiful old town that dates from the late 1800s, with most of its original buildings still standing and a wood-plank sidewalk in some areas. Many of the graceful old Victorians of the early days have been turned into beautiful bed-and-breakfasts, with period furnishings and down comforters and breakfasts to die for. This town is a few hours north of Greater Fort Lauderdale, not far from Orlando. It's known as one of the best places in America to find interesting old antiques shops, and they have a number of big antiques shows here annually. As you wander around, you'll find atmospheric bookstores and music shops with creaky wooden floors and lace curtains, as well as offbeat restaurants and clothing shops. The town sits on Lake Dora, a huge lake offering a ton of sailing and recreational opportunities. Sitting astride it is the Lakeside Inn, an inn from the 1800s in a Victorian/colonial style, where you can relax in a wooden rocker out on the deck that overlooks the lake, and enjoy gourmet food inside. And the drive around the lake is a pretty one. (Visit www.visitflorida.com/Mount_Dora.)

Naples/Marco Island

Naples is a beautiful small town on the southwest coast of Florida (about 2 hours from Fort Lauderdale), with a magnificent downtown filled with unique shops, restaurants, and galleries. The pace here is slower than on the eastern coast, but there's still a lot to see and do. Walk along Fifth Street and Third Street, elegant boulevards where every doorway holds something interesting. For excellent downtown lodging, stay at the elegant Inn on Fifth. And for a multifaceted beachfront experience, stay at the famed Naples Beach Hotel & Golf Club. You'll enjoy wandering through the one-of-a-kind shops in the woody Tin City marketplace, right on the water. For an unusual gastronomic experience on the water, take one of the charter boats or regular harbor cruises put on by Sip N' Sail; they lay out a buffet of gourmet treats and special wines for you to try, as you cruise at sunset (or other times) past islands inhabited only by eagles. And Marco Island has a variety of good beachside hotels and restaurants. (Visit www.paradisecoast.com.)

Ocala National Forest

About three hours from Greater Fort Lauderdale is another world, pretty much the only place in the United States where you can find both bears and alligators. The Ocala National Forest is an ecological wonderland of dense forest, marshland, beach sand, small hills, and lakes. Here you'll find Wekiwa Springs State Park, where you can paddle along rivers so primeval that you almost feel as if you're the only one who's ever traveled them. There are also hot springs at Wekiwa, said to have restorative powers by some, and hiking paths through the woods. And— nearby Ocala being horse country—you can also see it all from the top of a horse. Wekiwa State Park and the Ocala National Forest are the way Florida was for time immemorial. (Visit www.fs.fed.us/r8/florida/ocala and www.floridastateparks.org/wekiwasprings.)

Orlando

Where do you start when describing a place like Orlando (about 3.5 hours from Fort Lauderdale)? Of course, it's the largest tourist attraction in the world. And the faces you'll see at the various parks of Disney World, Universal, and SeaWorld come here from every country on Earth. If you have kids, the looks of excitement and anticipation that you'll see on their faces will be ones you'll remember the rest of your life. In addition to the world-renowned parks like these, there are also smaller theme and water parks that offer great fun. There are some 4,000 restaurants in the area, with every conceivable type of cuisine. There's downtown Orlando, right on Lake Eola, with interesting museums and old Victorian homes. There's sophisticated dining and shopping at places such as Disney Boardwalk, Downtown Disney, and Universal/Islands of Adventure. And there are some 90,000 hotel rooms for you to choose from. (Visit www.orlandoinfo.com.)

Sanibel Island/Captiva Island

About 3.5 hours from Fort Lauderdale in the Fort Myers area of the west coast of Florida, are two precious little islands. Sanibel Island is a place of cute little shops and restaurants, bicycle paths, and reasonably priced hotels ideally located both for exploring the town and exploring the beaches. It's the kind of place where everyone says Hello . . . and they really mean it. There are also a lot of interesting crafts shops and studios. Captiva Island, on the other hand, has no town and just a few atmospheric motels or lodges. What it does have, however, is peace and quiet, forests, beautiful beaches with little coves where you can watch the spectacular west coast sunsets, and funky beach houses. And it also has the Bubble Room Restaurant, a multicolored, ramshackle old shack filled floor-to-ceiling with Americana, including photos of old Hollywood stars like Frank Sinatra and Lana Turner, cowboy articles, handicrafts from the early 1900s, old songs playing in the background, and an actual choo-choo train that circles around the room overhead as you eat. And the food's incredible, as well, real American comfort food, served by young ladies and men in "Bubble Room" scout uniforms. This is an outrageous place—fun for the whole family. (Visit www.sanibel-captiva.org.)

St. Augustine/Amelia Island

About 4.5 hours drive north of Greater Fort Lauderdale is the historic town of St. Augustine, the first permanent town in America settled by Europeans. Here you can see well-preserved old forts and cannons, in a town over which seven flags have flown. The town is constructed in old-style buildings, some in Tudor style, others in the Spanish-Mediterranean style of the people who first explored this area. The intrepid Ponce de León never did find the Fountain of Youth, but he founded a town that's still with us today. Not far away is Amelia Island, with the restored Victorian town of Fernandina Beach, where a horse-and-buggy with a driver will take you all over town, and tell you the stories of conquerors and the conquered, of Civil War, of winners and losers, traitors and patriots, pirates and privateers, and swashbucklers and scoundrels. (Visit www.staugustine.com and www.ameliaisland.com.)

LIVING HERE

In this section we feature specific information for residents or those planning to relocate here. Topics include real estate, education, health care, and much more.

RELOCATION & REAL ESTATE

South Florida was devastated—there is no other word for it—by the housing meltdown. Fortunes were lost. Savings were decimated. Retirements were ruined. Families were crippled. And lives were destroyed.

In fact, as of May 2010, more than half of the homeowners in Greater Fort Lauderdale—54 percent—owed more on their homes than their homes were worth; in other words, more than half were "under water" on their houses. That same month, some experts came out with an estimate that it would take South Florida some 15 to 20 years for home prices to reach the same levels they were at in 2006.

In the spring of 2010, median prices for existing homes were still falling in Broward County. But for the first time, some experts were seeing a bit of light at the end of the tunnel. Broward County's median price at that time was $186,700, down 13 percent from a year ago, but up slightly from a few months earlier, according to a report by the Florida Realtors Association. And many observers were predicting the end of significant price declines. Just a couple of months earlier, Broward had reported a 6 percent increase in sales over the same period a year earlier.

There was one segment of the Broward County housing market, however, that was actually growing in the spring of 2010. The existing condominium market—especially waterfront condos—was especially hot. Sales were 40 percent higher than the same period a year earlier—although the median price of $71,500 was 17 percent below that of February 2009. Nearly every condo in South Florida lost value in the past four years, with some tumbling 50 percent or more. But waterfront properties have held up better than most. While virtually no buildings have been spared, values in high-end condos hugging the coast have been the most resilient, analysts said, because of the inherent lure of the ocean and Intracoastal Waterway.

OVERVIEW

Waterfront land is, obviously, finite. There's just so much of it to go around. And when it's all built up, there's nowhere else to build. That bodes well if you're a homeowner now in a waterfront area. Because, sure as shootin', when the land for new waterfront condos runs out, the condos already there are going to really appreciate in value. And if you're not yet a homeowner there—but you're thinking abut becoming one—now may be the time to act. Waterfront prices won't remain deflated forever.

Downtown Fort Lauderdale and the periphery of downtown were actually less damaged than the Miami and West Palm Beach core areas during the downturn. Condo units in Miami and West Palm Beach were overbuilt during the crazy speculation of the early 2000s. In Fort Lauderdale, though, city commissioners were more restrained in their approach to downtown development, fearing the effects of overdevelopment. As a result, they didn't rubber stamp every developer's request that came along. Accordingly, Fort Lauderdale's downtown didn't suffer as much as the other two cities' downtowns.

"Held up better than most" is not the same thing as "held up," however. The median price for existing condos in Broward in March 2010 was $73,600—a 66 percent drop from the February 2006 peak of $216,800.

THE OPPORTUNITIES ARE HERE . . . IF YOU LOOK FOR THEM

In the spring of 2010, single-family houses were finally starting to sell, thanks to the low prices and the federal tax-credit program. However, those tax credits were good for only a limited period, so the long-term effects remain cloudy.

Nonetheless, many local experts in the Greater Fort Lauderdale area say that the past two years have presented unprecedented opportunity for buyers and that, if you're thinking at all of buying, there won't be a better time than now. The reason, of course, is simple—a recovering market means higher prices.

For one thing, mortgage rates are still relatively low, in a historical context. For another, Florida's lawmakers have taken steps, over the past couple of years, to finally address the "evil twins"—taxes and insurance. Insurance premiums have, for the most part, come down in this period.

Bob Tenace, owner of Century 21 Tenace Realty in Coral Springs, urges anyone who's considering buying to remember that, for

every seller's horror story, there's a buyer's happy ending.

"Many recent buyers—or people who are now considering a purchase—might have been locked out of the high-flying market of a few years ago," Tenace said. "But now they have opportunities that they didn't have before. Prices are still low. Inventory is still high—affording them a real choice. Mortgage rates are still, for the most part, favorable. And buyers still have so many options as far as neighborhood, town, size, amenities, and style."

Houses that you might not have been able to afford a few years ago are now affordable. Furthermore, they're often affordable in locations that you may not have even bothered considering before, in the belief that you couldn't afford it.

"A few years ago, we were selling houses, quite often, the same week that we listed them," said Tenace, "and sometimes, the same day. Over the past few years, it's often taken up to a year to find a buyer. And properties have often gone for weeks without even as much as a showing, which means that, by this time, there are some mighty desperate sellers out there. If you were to track certain homes in the listings, you'd see that many prices, as the months add up, have gone down significantly."

And even if you're playing a waiting game, Tenace says, in the hope that prices may once again drop, you could still end up paying more—because interest rates may go up.

"All you need, really, is one house in one neighborhood," said Bob Tenace. "And Greater Fort Lauderdale is flooded with 'one' houses, 'one' of which might be right for you."

"Prices are stabilizing now, a bit, as more people are taking advantage of the tax

My Fort Lauderdale

As a native Floridian (actually born in Miami Beach), I am amazed at all the new things I'm constantly discovering in Broward County. Who knew you could watch turtle eggs hatch, and encourage baby turtles to move toward the ocean, at Hollywood Beach? Who knew you could have a butterfly land on your shirt at Butterfly World???

And there are so many interesting people stories here. Rags-to-riches heroes like Wayne Huizenga, who is an unbelievable philanthropist, a great storyteller, and a good friend. Elected officials who work hard every day to make this a better place to live, work, and visit. Community activists who push our elected officials to get it right. And everyday citizens who are willing to offer advice. It's definitely the people that make me most proud of living here. Four of my five siblings are raising families here (one sister fled to Atlanta 40 years ago and returns as often as she can). We really can't imagine life being better anywhere else!

—Nicki Grossman,
President, Greater Fort
Lauderdale Convention & Visitors
Bureau

credits to purchase homes," says Paul Owers, real estate reporter for the *Sun-Sentinel*. "But what will happen when the credits end? No one knows. Some analysts are forecasting that prices may even begin to drop

somewhat again." The general consensus among experts, Owers said, is that prices will bottom out by the end of 2010 or early in 2011.

Some areas in Greater Fort Lauderdale are holding their own. A few, like Parkland—still mostly a refuge of magnificent homes and stables with tree-lined rural streets—are actually doing well. Prices are recovering, and homes are selling. Some areas of Pompano Beach are now also desirable because the town's more modest homes are now more in demand as people downsize. On the other hand, Coral Springs, which was one of the hottest areas in South Florida in the 1980s and '90s, has been badly hurt in the new millennium. So has Miramar, which was a very hot-selling area in the 1990s.

THE CHINESE DRYWALL CRISIS

Another problem—more pronounced in South Florida than in most other areas of the country—is the crisis revolving around Chinese drywall.

"The problem really started at the end of 2008," said Paul Owers. "There was a dearth of domestic drywall, so builders began buying from the Chinese. Because South Florida had been enjoying such a housing boom in previous years, we got a lot of the defective drywall, which was similar to the situation in Louisiana when they started rebuilding after Hurricane Katrina."

The Chinese drywall ruined the electronic systems in homes. It caused a foul sulfur smell. It caused respiratory problems in many people, nosebleeds in others.

"People found themselves in a really tragic situation," Owers says. "They couldn't stay. And they couldn't leave."

The problems were very pronounced in Parkland, Miramar, and Davie, among a number of other communities. And a judge ruled that, in order to fix the homes properly, they needed to be virtually torn down and rebuilt from scratch. One South Florida builder, GL Homes, stood behind the homes they had built, even though the defective drywall was not their fault. They actually rebuilt many of the homes they had put up, as well as providing temporary living quarters for the homeowners that had to move so their homes could be repaired. Most other builders, however, were not as magnanimous. And the values of the homes they had built continued to free-fall.

RECOVERY IS COMING

"Young families are still moving here," says Owers, "because South Florida, in many ways, is still a desirable place in which to live. And some people are moving back into Fort Lauderdale from the western suburbs. Their homes saw big price declines, because they were far from the city, from the entertainment and culture, and from their workplaces. Or in some cases, when they originally bought out west, they were raising a family, wanted good schools, quiet neighborhoods, etc. But now they may have become empty nesters, who want to get back into the excitement and culture of the city, or who want to be closer to the beach."

So, if you're looking for a home in Greater Fort Lauderdale, where does all of this leave *you*?

In a pretty good spot actually. Because the prices are so low, you can find bargains in Broward County that were hardly imaginable only a few years ago. In nice communities. With good schools. And even when prices do start to appreciate, they'll be appreciating so slowly that you'll still be able to find great bargains for several years—at

least. Sellers are eager to deal, so you may even get some nice last-minute incentives thrown in. In fact, since so many would-be sellers have been stuck in their homes for the past couple of years—either unable to get the price they wanted or unable to sell at any price—some of them will be really desperate to get out now.

So, if you've ever thought about owning a home in Greater Fort Lauderdale and enjoying the Florida lifestyle, now may be the best time to do it.

And, if you do decide to buy, where should you buy? Well, that, of course, depends as much on you—and your needs and wants—as it does on the housing market. If you're young and single, or empty nesters, you might want to consider Fort Lauderdale. If you're retired, or if you just *have* to live on the beach, perhaps Lauderdale-by-the-Sea is for you. If you're raising a family, the southwestern suburbs such as Cooper City and Pembroke Pines may be where you want to look. If you need to live near a major highway, such as I-95 or the Florida Turnpike, you might consider Deerfield Beach or Pompano Beach. If you're of a certain age and you like the convenience of high-rise living, you should probably check into Hallandale Beach. (Or, if you're of the same age and like the ease and amenities of a community of retirees, the Century Village developments of Deerfield Beach or Pembroke Pines might be right for you.) If your interest is piqued by a suburb that has many of the cultural, entertainment, and dining opportunities of an urban area, Coral Springs may be your preferred spot. And if money is no object (or not much of an object), take a look at Parkland, which is filled with million-dollar homes (as well as some more reasonably priced ones) and leafy streets, farms where cows and sheep still roam, and an equestrian center, and where you can still pass riders on horseback, right on the street.

"The recovery, which will probably come in early 2011, will be a slow one," Paul Owers says. "And homes will start appreciating at a more traditional rate than they were during the frenzy of a few years ago . . . at about 3 to 4 percent a year."

RETIREMENT

Certainly, you could do a lot worse than retire in South Florida and in Greater Fort Lauderdale. This area offers a lot that retirees love: plenty of great shopping; a wide variety of distinctive (and casual) restaurants; 30 miles of beaches; plenty of golf; an arts scene that's every bit as active and exciting as that where they came from, especially during the Season; the cosmopolitan environment of a growing city as well as the rural green lanes of horse country. And—oh, yes—wonderfully warming sunshine all year long (again, especially during the Season). But even retirees who live here year-round will tell you that summer isn't such an imposition, once you make a few accommodations for it. For example, you can still play golf in the summer; you just have to plan on doing it earlier in the morning. And you won't have to wait for the hordes in front of you to tee off either, because there won't be any hordes in front of you!

There are other advantages as well. Greater Fort Lauderdale has some excellent medical centers and physicians, many of whom specialize in caring for seniors. And, because you're smack in the middle of a metropolitan region of some six million people in South Florida, there also are good facilities just down (or up) the road.

And, if you'd like to be surrounded by other seniors, there are plenty of areas where you can be. There are two huge Century Village communities (senior "villages") in Broward County, in the northeast in Deerfield Beach and in the southwest in Pembroke Pines. There are areas of Coral Springs that cater to seniors, in which there are assisted-living facilities as well as condos with large senior populations. Tamarac, right next to Coral Springs, has a number of senior condo developments (and a lot of parks near them). Lauderhill, also in western Broward, has some areas in which seniors have a large presence. Also, the "condo canyons" along A1A in Hallandale Beach are filled with retirees. And there are plenty of other senior-dense and senior-heavy areas in Greater Fort Lauderdale.

RETIREMENT COMMUNITIES

The two Century Village developments deserve some space of their own—and we'll give it to them! These are virtually towns in themselves. The **Deerfield Beach Century Village** (Century Village East) has some 8,500 condominium units (mostly in low-rises) and, in season, some 16,000 residents living in them. And you could stay busy every day of the week without ever having to leave the premises, if you wanted to. There's a beautiful clubhouse for all sorts of social functions, lectures, presentations, and so on. There's a 1,600-seat theater, which offers a parade of well-known actors, comedians, musicians, and singers. There's a ballroom with seating for 800 (as well as a variety of classes and activities). There's an indoor pool, and 15 outdoor pools (basically, each development has one). There are 17 tennis courts, and an 18-hole executive golf course. There's a fully equipped fitness center. There are also bocce, pétanque, and volleyball courts, saunas, billiards, table tennis, classrooms, card rooms, and a well-stocked library. And there's minibus service to bring you to all of it.

It's the same story at **Century Village in Pembroke Pines,** which has 7,000 apartments. There's a clubhouse in which there's always something—or more than one thing—going on, along with an indoor pool and a 1,000-seat theater with first-rate entertainment. This village boasts a championship golf course and a brand-new fitness center. There are 26 pools, and a lot of different types of clubs enjoyed by residents; no matter what your hobby or passion, you'll probably find a club for it here.

There are retirement communities all over Greater Fort Lauderdale. And Hyatt has become a major player in building them, with **Classic Residences by Hyatt** in Plantation, Pompano Beach, and Hollywood. As you might expect from the Hyatt name, these facilities are comfortable, often-luxurious places, with first-class apartments and amenities.

Here are a few retirement communities in Greater Fort Lauderdale:

ASTON GARDENS AT PARKLAND COMMONS
5999 University Dr., Parkland
(954) 255-0906
www.astongardens.com

CLASSIC RESIDENCE BY HYATT
8500 W. Sunrise Blvd., Plantation
(954) 476-8500
www.plantation.hyattclassic.com

THE HORIZON CLUB
1208 S. Military Trail, Deerfield
(954) 519-2670
www.sunriseseniorliving.com

THE PALACE AT WESTON SENIOR LIVING
4400 Palace Dr., Weston
(954) 217-2000
www.thepalace.org

ASSISTED LIVING FACILITIES

Assisted living communities are also found all over the Greater Fort Lauderdale area—in fact, there are 22 of them in Fort Lauderdale alone, and plenty of others in Hollywood, Margate, Miramar, and many other communities. (According to one dictionary, an assisted living facility is defined as "A living arrangement in which people with special needs, especially seniors with disabilities, reside in a facility that provides help with everyday tasks such as bathing, dressing, and taking medication.")

Here are a few assisted living facilities in Greater Fort Lauderdale:

BAYVIEW RETIREMENT HOME
2625 NE 13th Court, Ft. Lauderdale
(954) 564-3100
www.bayviewretirementhome.com

PRESERVE AT PALM-AIRE
3701 W. McNab Rd., Pompano Beach
(954) 970-2600
www.brookdaleliving.com

VICTORIA VILLA
5151 SW 61st Ave., Davie
(954) 791-8881
www.victoriavilla.com

WILLOW WOOD
2855 W. Commercial Blvd., Ft.
Lauderdale
(954) 739-4200

PERSONAL HOME CARE

If you or your loved one requires personal home care, you can find agencies offering it in Broward County. These agencies can help with the activities of everyday living. They can run errands, such as going to the grocery store or the drug store. They can prepare meals. And they can help with nonmedical types of care, such as trips to the toilet or bathing. These services can cost pretty much anything up to (approximately) $20 an hour, according to the assistance provided. In addition to providing personal care for those needing nonmedical help with daily life, home care assistants can also be of great benefit to family caregivers—if only by relieving them of the burden for a few hours.

Here are a few personal home care agencies in Greater Fort Lauderdale:

A FAMILY MEMBER HOMECARE
2518 N. SR 7, #110, Hollywood
(954) 986-5090
www.afamilymemberhomecare.com

CARE MINDERS
1717 E. Commercial Blvd., Ft. Lauderdale
(954) 771-5450
www.careminders.com

**COMFORT KEEPERS AT FORT
 LAUDERDALE**
1000 W. McNab Rd., Ft. Lauderdale
(954) 825-0155
www.comfortkeepers.com

SENIOR HELPERS
8910 Miramar Pkwy., #316, Miramar
(954) 437-9880
www.seniorhelpers.com

RESOURCES

**AGING & DISABILITY RESOURCE
 CENTER**
5300 Hiatus Rd., Sunrise
(954) 745-9779
www.adrcbroward.org/who.php

BROWARD AGING ALLIANCE
Broward County Health Department
780 SW 24th St., Ft. Lauderdale
(954) 537-2936
www.broward.org/AgingAlliance/Pages/
Default.htm

**BROWARD COUNTY ELDERLY &
 VETERANS SERVICES**
2995 N. Dixie Hwy., Ft. Lauderdale
(954) 537-2936
www.adrcbroward.org/browardco.php

**HEALTHY AGING REGIONAL
 COLLABORATIVE**
Initiative of Health Foundation of South
Florida
2 S. Biscayne Blvd., #1710, Miami
(305) 374-7200
www.healthyagingsf.org/leadership_
council.aspx

HEALTH CARE

You'll find that the county is highly rated for the quality of its healthcare services. In addition to branches of world-renowned medical centers—like the Cleveland Clinic—there are also a number of well-known physicians and researchers working here, to cure many of our most dangerous diseases. There are also several specialty centers, for example, hospitals which might specialize in heart surgery and care.

Many of the hospitals listed below have achieved great distinction. The Cleveland Clinic Hospital in Cooper City, for example, is a branch of the world-famous hospital in Cleveland, to which heart patients come from all over the world for treatment. Holy Cross Hospital, in Oakland Park, also has a good reputation, as do Broward General Hospital and Westside Regional.

The Memorial Health Care System, with 25 branches throughout the county—including a variety of hospitals, surgery centers, and clinics—has won some 70 awards over the years. Broward Health, founded in 1938, is one of the 10 largest public health-care systems in the country, with some two-dozen hospitals, clinics, and specialty-care centers in the county. This company, too, has won numerous awards, including a number from an organization called HealthGrades, which rates hospitals.

Broward County also has a branch (in Plantation) of the Bascom Palmer Eye Institute, probably the most advanced place for treatment of eye diseases in Florida. Bascom Palmer is actually the Department of Ophthalmology for the University of Miami Miller School of Medicine. The Institute is now known internationally as a pioneer in research and has developed one of the most highly sought-after ophthalmology-education programs in the nation.

In addition to hospitals, of course, Greater Fort Lauderdale has a variety of walk-in clinics and emergency centers, all over the county. Some of them are open 24 hours a day.

THERE'S ALWAYS A HOSPITAL NEARBY

There are 44 hospitals in Broward County. And one of them—or in many cases, more than one of them—will be near you.

Cooper City—**Cleveland Clinic Hospital**
Cooper City—**Health South Sunrise Rehabilitation Hospital**
Cooper City—**Humana Hospital Bennett**
Cooper City—**Memorial Hospital West**
Coral Springs—**Coral Springs Medical Center**
Fort Lauderdale—**Broward General Hospital**
Fort Lauderdale—**Coral Ridge Psychiatric Hospital**
Fort Lauderdale—**Doctors General Hospital**

Fort Lauderdale—**Fort Lauderdale Hospital**

Fort Lauderdale—**Imperial Point Medical Center**

Fort Lauderdale—**Kindred Hospital Fort Lauderdale**

Fort Lauderdale—**Las Olas General Hospital**

Fort Lauderdale—**Manor Oaks Nursing & Rehabilitation Center**

Fort Lauderdale—**Provident Hospital**

Fort Lauderdale—**Vencor Hospital of Fort Lauderdale**

Hollywood—**Doctors General Hospital of Hollywood**

Hollywood—**Hollywood Medical Center**

Hollywood—**Hollywood Memorial Walk-In Medical Center**

Hollywood—**Hollywood Pavilion**

Hollywood—**Kindred Hospital Hollywood**

Hollywood—**Memorial Hospital Pembroke**

Lauderdale Lakes—**Florida Medical Center Hospital**

Lauderdale Lakes—**St. Anthony's Rehabilitation Hospital**

Lauderdale Lakes—**St. John's Nursing and Rehabilitation Hospital**

Margate—**Northwest Medical Center**

Oakland Park—**Holy Cross Hospital**

Oakland Park—**North Ridge Medical Center**

Pembroke Pines—**Atlantic Shores Healthcare Center**

Pembroke Pines—**Memorial Hospital West**

Pembroke Pines—**Pembroke Pines General Hospital**

Pembroke Pines—**South Florida State Hospital**

Plantation—**Plantation General Hospital**

Plantation—**Westside Regional Hospital**

Pompano Beach—**Atlantic Shores Hospital**

Pompano Beach—**Humana Hospital Cypress**

Pompano Beach—**North Beach Community Hospital**

Pompano Beach—**North Broward Medical Center**

Sunrise—**HealthSouth Sunrise Rehabilitation Center**

Sunrise—**Sunrise Hospital**

Sunrise—**Sunrise Regional Medical Center**

Tamarac—**University Hospital and Medical Center**

GOVERNMENT & PRIVATE ORGANIZATIONS

BROWARD COUNTY HEALTH DEPARTMENT

780 SW 24th St., Ft. Lauderdale
(954) 467-4700
www.browardchd.org

The Broward County Health Department can be an invaluable resource in helping to familiarize yourself with all the medical and health-care options available here. They are a great clearinghouse for advice. In addition, they run clinics throughout the county.

The department provides medical help to people unable to access private medical care in the county, and it also provides services to children with special medical problems. And it can also provide access to various community resources and social services.

Another possible resource would be the **Broward County Medical Association,** with 1,500 member-doctors in Greater Fort Lauderdale. Among other services, the website (www.bcma.com) offers a physician search directory.

BROWARD COUNTY DEPARTMENT OF HUMAN SERVICES

Governmental Center
115 S. Andrews Ave., #303, Ft.
Lauderdale
(954) 357-6385
www.broward.org/humanservices/
Pages/Default.aspx

The Broward County Department of Human Services can also provide guidance and feedback in community and personal health matters. The department views its mission as enhancing the lives of Broward County's residents through a variety of innovative and integrated health and human-services programs. Human Services has four divisions that are dedicated to the various demographic sectors and populations of the county—Community Partnerships, Elderly and Veterans Services, Family Success Administration, and Addiction Recovery.

EDUCATION & CHILD CARE

Truth be told, Florida is not highly ranked among the states when it comes to education. However, Broward County public—and private—schools—have won notice for the quality of the educational experience offered here.

Broward is the sixth-largest school district in America—and the largest fully accredited school district. Under superintendent of schools James F. Notter and the county school board, the district's motto is "Educating Today's Students for Tomorrow's World." The system has over 255,000 students, 288 schools and centers, three virtual schools, more than 15,000 teachers, and 37,000 full-time employees in all. It's by far the largest employer in Greater Fort Lauderdale, with an annual budget of over $5 billion.

As noted earlier, people around the country have taken notice of the work being done here. Broward County Public Schools (BCPS) was a finalist for the Broad Foundation's Annual Urban Education Award for the second year in a row—receiving its second consecutive award of $250,000 in scholarships. In addition, the district also earned the inaugural Award for Excellence in Financial Management from Washington, D.C.-based Council of the Great City Schools. And—for the 14th consecutive year—the Association of School Business Officials International (ASBO) named the School Board of Broward County as a recipient of its Meritorious Budget Award.

And that's not all. Broward County Public Schools was a finalist for the National School Board Association's Council of Urban Boards of Education (CUBE) Annual Award. Three Broward County schools—Pompano Beach High School, McFatter Technical High School, and City of Pembroke Pines Charter Middle School—were selected as Florida Blue Ribbon Schools of Excellence by the Florida Department of Education. And 10 BCPS high schools and one charter high school were recognized among *Newsweek* magazine's 2009 "Top High Schools in the Nation."

Folks in Greater Fort Lauderdale seem to realize that, to reap real dividends, educating the area's youth must be a cooperative effort among the schools, the parents, and the community. As a result, this school system boasts some 35,000 volunteers. These people gave of themselves to the tune of nearly 600,000 hours, an estimated value of over $11 million in added services to students.

BROWARD COUNTY PUBLIC SCHOOLS

All district classrooms have wireless Internet capability, and more than 3,300 digital classrooms have been incorporated into the district. And there's a special system for forwarding information to teachers and students. It's called the **Broward Enterprise Education Portal (BEEP);** this is a secure, single point of access to digital resources for teaching and learning. Every public-school teacher has access to BEEP. And more than 140,000 students visit the portal every month.

And that's just the tip of the digital connection in Greater Fort Lauderdale. Seventy-four schools, 600 teachers, and more than 15,000 students take advantage of a system called **GLIDES.** These are project-based learning initiatives that afford students the opportunity to exchange ideas and make decisions that affect project outcomes. In addition, the district has 20 elementary and 38 secondary online e-textbooks (which are also available in print) available to teachers and students.

Broward County is always on the leading edge when it comes to testing new ideas and processes. In fact, here a student can even attend a "virtual" school. **Broward Virtual School (BVS)** is an online delivery system offering both part-time and full-time enrollment to students from kindergarten through twelfth grade. BVS has been named the top-performing Florida Virtual School franchise in the state for the school years 2008–2009 and 2009–2010.

In fact, more than 40,000 Broward students are now participating in innovative programs. And the Innovative Programs department now offers 63 programs in 36 subjects, in 50 schools across the district.

In addition, Broward County has pioneered other innovative programs, as well. For example, there's **SEAS (Student Enrichment in the Arts),** an award-winning program that offers every student the opportunity to become involved in theater-based and school-based arts education. Thousands of students take advantage of the program; for example, more than 100,000 students—every year—are transported by the district

to the Broward Center for the Performing Arts in Fort Lauderdale, where they can meet and learn from professional actors, singers, and dancers. And over the years, more than a million Broward students have attended special performances at the Center.

College is the ultimate goal for many Broward families. Nearly half of the graduating seniors in Broward County go on to Florida's **State University System,** or a private, public or Ivy League school—a figure that has improved steadily in recent years. The school district does its part to help get them there. Public high schools offer more than 550 advanced placement (AP) classes, among them 35 college-level courses. AP enrollment has increased for several years in a row now, along with the number of AP examinations taken and the number of AP examinations in which students performed well. Students earning high-proficiency grades also earned college credit for their courses, which are accepted at most major universities.

In addition, there are some 30 charter schools, which are under the direction of the Broward County School Board. Charter schools in Broward County are privately owned, and they contract with the county to provide services for certain types of students. They are responsible for meeting strict guidelines for educational standards. However, the atmosphere at a charter school is a bit more experimental and nontraditional, and teachers are encouraged to explore new techniques. Charter schools serve to increase the reach of the public school system, while at the same time alleviating the crowded conditions in some of the public schools that have resulted from Greater Fort Lauderdale's rapid growth. Educators here say that charter schools also help to provide an

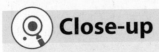

Close-up

School Beginnings

On October 2, 1899, the first two schools in what would later become Broward County threw open their doors. One of them was in Fort Lauderdale, and the other in Pompano Beach. And the teacher who threw open the doors at the Fort Lauderdale school was Ivy Julia Cromartie, who was Broward County's first schoolteacher. (Ivy would later gain fame as the wife of original settler Frank Stranahan, Fort Lauderdale pioneer, trader, entrepreneur, businessman, banker, and ghost.) Ms. Cromartie welcomed nine (presumably eager) students into a little wooden building on what is now South Andrews Avenue. In Pompano, schoolmarm Mary Butler also welcomed nine students. Each of the two women was paid $40 per month. And—since students also had to help out on the farm and in the fields—the school year was only about five months long.

In fact, at that time, going to school wasn't even compulsory here. The needs of family, farm, and fields came first, and this was just a simple fact of life. In 1919, however, just after the end of World War I, compulsory school attendance was mandated. And this helped attract more teachers—and more highly trained teachers—to Broward County.

element of competition amongst schools—thereby raising the levels of education in all schools. The county boasts a number of charter schools that have received "A" ratings from the Florida Department of Education, including the City of Pembroke Pines Charter Elementary, Middle, and High School, Hollywood Academy of Arts Middle School, and City of Coral Springs Charter School.

Strict Anti-Bullying Policy

Broward County Public Schools is a leader in the nationwide trend movement dealing with bullying in our schools, which, as we've seen, can have devastating consequences.

The School Board of Broward County, in fact, was the first district in Florida to approve a specific anti-bullying policy, and the Florida Department of Education will use the policy as a model for the state's other 66 school districts. Broward County

was so far ahead of the game in this matter, in fact, that its policy was developed even before the state legislature enacted a law mandating that all school districts develop such policies.

The district's Anti-Bullying Policy specifically prohibits bullying of or by any district student or employee, and specifies, as well, a range of potential consequences. The policy has firm guidelines for the identification and reporting of bullying. And it requires all staff to utilize prevention and intervention activities, with the tools and resources that the county provides. As is the case with any countywide policy of this importance, community and parental involvement is solicited and encouraged.

Before- & After-School Care

Broward County Public Schools believes its mission is not restricted solely to school hours. Accordingly, there are now nearly 25,000 children being served in 170 Before and After School Child Care Programs. These programs are provided at elementary schools, middle schools, and specific centers, operated either by the school board or by a private provider. Each school's advisory council is charged with recommending the program that best meets its needs, and the principal makes the decision, with the area superintendent's approval.

These programs involve opportunities for the child to do homework, have a snack, and participate in a number of scheduled activities. Among the elements incorporated are academic studies, technology sessions, creative play or dramatic arts, and outdoor activities, as well as opportunities for the child to decide what type of activity to pursue on a given day. You can stop by your child's school to learn more.

Resources

BROWARD COUNTY PUBLIC SCHOOLS
600 SE 3rd Ave., Ft. Lauderdale
(754) 321-0000
www.browardschools.com

PRIVATE SCHOOLS

There are about 160 private elementary schools in Greater Fort Lauderdale, and some 60 private high schools ranging from college preparatory to religious. In the elementary school category, there are a number of private schools with kindergarten-only programs, while some have only kindergarten and pre-K, some go up to specified grade levels, and still others go up to grade eight.

For example, Broward County has three branches of the prestigious **North Broward Preparatory School,** with students from prekindergarten through twelfth grade. These schools focus on providing students with a multifaceted experience that extends far beyond the classroom, involving the arts, athletics, community service, technology, travel-study programs, and environmental studies, with the goal of better preparing them for college. Greater Fort Lauderdale also has a private religious-based school that has achieved fame for its excellent balancing of both academic and religious studies. **St. Thomas Aquinas High School,** in Fort Lauderdale, has been named to the National Catholic High School Honor Roll as one of the top-50 Catholic high schools in the United States. It's the only high school in Florida to achieve this ranking. And, incidentally, its athletic teams are often among the best in the state, and many of its student-athletes go on to win athletic scholarships at major universities.

Another excellent private school is the **American Heritage School** in Plantation, an independent, nonsectarian school for grades pre-K through 12, with approximately 2,400 students. The school was founded in 1965 to serve the fast-growing communities west of Fort Lauderdale, and it sits on a wooded 40-acre campus. It has an award-winning fine arts program. The college preparatory curriculum at American Heritage serves students of bright to gifted intelligence.

Fort Lauderdale's **Pine Crest School** is another school that is considered superb by educators. Pine Crest School is dedicated to academic excellence, as well as developing other aspects of a student's personality and talents. Toward that end, the school provides its students with a wide range of academic, social, community, and athletic opportunities. Its graduates go on to some of the finest institutions of higher learning in the country.

And one of them, Brandon Knight, was the best high school basketball player in Florida during the 2009–2010 season.

The **University School at Nova Southeastern University** is another place that emphasizes preparation for higher learning. And that's an attitude that makes sense as it's located on the campus of Broward's largest institution of higher learning (and one of the largest private universities in the country). Three-quarters of the teachers here have graduate degrees, and the atmosphere is one of innovation and experiment.

HIGHER EDUCATION

Broward County doesn't lack for quality options in higher education. And high-achieving high school students are finding they no longer have to travel far away to receive a good college—and postgraduate—education.

Many branches of Broward County colleges and universities are located in the town of Davie, which has developed over the years into an area called the **South Florida Education Center.** This community is home to main campuses and branch campuses of some of the most-prestigious colleges and universities in Broward County and in the state of Florida. Among them are schools such as **Florida Atlantic University, Florida International University,** and **Broward College** (formerly Broward Community college, now an accredited four-year school), as well as **Nova Southeastern University,** the largest private university in Florida (and sixth-largest in the country).

Davie is not the only city with colleges and universities, however. For example, Broward College, in addition to its Davie facility, also has campuses in downtown Fort Lauderdale (its main campus), Coconut Creek,

My Fort Lauderdale

Broward County is an incredibly diverse community with a variety of activities and opportunities available for residents and businesses. Only in Lauderhill, the city of which I'm mayor, could I play or watch cricket, watch class-A soccer or netball, attend a jazz festival, be a volunteer, listen to great speakers, and have a bagel, among just a few of the activities.

While we can be successful at professional sports—Marlins, Heat, Dolphins, and Panthers—we can also attend the theater, go to the beach, or just enjoy the sunny year-round weather. I personally enjoy the ability to drive a few miles to one of three different seaports and jump on a cruise ship for a quick or long vacation. And when my son was younger, I also enjoyed outdoor activities, such as camping with him.

—Richard J. Kaplan, Mayor, City of Lauderhill

and Pembroke Pines, making a college education within easy geographic reach of anywhere in the county. Florida Atlantic University also has a downtown Fort Lauderdale complex, affording its students at that branch the opportunity to attend school in a vibrant, culturally rich urban environment.

Broward County is also the home of a well-respected art college, which has gained a reputation far beyond the confines of Florida. The **Art Institute of Fort Lauderdale**—less than 2 miles from the beach—not only offers degrees in disciplines such as photography and graphic design, but also in non-fine-art subjects such as culinary arts. And graduates of the Art Institute are working all over the world, on everything from software programs to classic arts to advertising to motion pictures.

In addition to colleges, Broward County also has a variety of vocational and technical centers.

Colleges & Universities

ART INSTITUTE OF FORT LAUDERDALE
1799 SE 17th St., Ft. Lauderdale
(954) 463-300
www.artinstitutes.edu/fortlauderdale

The Art Institute of Fort Lauderdale has become a local landmark since it opened in 1968 . . . and since it began sending so many graduates on to prominent roles in business and the arts. When it opened its doors, it offered only three courses of study—commercial art, interior design, and fashion illustration. Through the years, however, the curriculum has grown dramatically, and now offers a variety of visual, applied arts, business—and even culinary—courses. The Institute is big on hands-on training with leading designers and graphic artists in the community who can help familiarize students with the myriad opportunities in these rapidly growing fields. The school offers both Associate and Bachelor of Science degrees, along with a few other types. And there are now some 35,000 alumni, some of whom you may have heard of.

BROWARD COLLEGE
111 E. Las Olas Blvd., Ft. Lauderdale
(954) 201-7350
www.broward.edu

Broward College was founded as Broward Community College back in 1959 as part of an effort to give as many Floridians as possible an opportunity for post-high-school education. Nearly 50 years later, in 2008, the legislature gave the college the right to offer four-year degrees as well as associate degrees, and Governor Charlie Crist signed an order changing its name to Broward College. Most of the bachelor's degrees offered are in the field of education, in specialties such as middle grades math, middle grades science, secondary math, secondary biology, and exceptional-student education. Broward College has three campuses spread out over the county, as well as several learning centers.

BROWARD COLLEGE–DAVIE BRANCH
Hugh Adams Central Campus
3501 Davie Rd., Davie
(954) 201-6500
www.broward.edu

The A. Hugh Adams Central Campus was Broward College's first permanent campus. When it opened, it had seven buildings; now, however, it has more than 30, including the well-respected Buehler Planetarium and Observatory, a favorite spot of amateur astronomers in Greater Fort Lauderdale. Also here are the Institute of Public Safety, an aquatic complex, the Mayer Gymnasium, a health sciences complex, and the Ralph R. Bailey Concert Hall, another focus of community events. The library is owned jointly by Broward College and Florida Atlantic University. And the Adams Campus also is home to the College Academy at BC, a college preparatory institution run in partnership with Broward County Public Schools.

BROWARD COLLEGE–JUDSON A. SAMUELS SOUTH CAMPUS
7200 Pines Blvd., Pembroke Pines
(954) 201-8997
www.broward.edu

The Judson A. Samuels South Campus is named for a South Broward community leader and one of the college's most influential trustees. It's located on a 100-acre tract just west of the Florida Turnpike, in the southwestern Broward city of Pembroke Pines. This is the home of the college's Aviation Institute, which is located here for a reason—it's next to North Perry Airport, which is used for private planes. Also adjacent is Broward College/Broward County South Regional Library, the first building in Broward County designed to meet the standards of the Leadership in Energy and Environmental Design's (LEED) rating system.

BROWARD COLLEGE–NORTH CAMPUS
1000 Coconut Creek Blvd., Coconut Creek
(954) 201-2240
www.broward.edu

The North Campus of Broward College is in Coconut Creek, on the west side of the Florida Turnpike. Its 14 buildings include the Omni Auditorium (also home to various community events and presentations), the Health Science Center II, the Toski-Battersby Golf Training Center, and the joint Broward Community College/North Regional Broward County Library. This campus is also home to Junior Achievement's largest "Enterprise Village." It's called the Junior Achievement Huizenga Enterprise Village, named after Broward County entrepreneur (and former Miami Dolphins owner) Wayne Huizenga and his wife, Marti, who contributed several million dollars to get the ball rolling some years back.

BROWARD COLLEGE–PINES CENTER
Pembroke Pines Academic Village
16957 Sheridan St., Pembroke Pines
(954) 201-3604
www.broward.edu

The Pines Center serves southwestern Broward; it's on the campus of the Pembroke Pines Academic Village, a 77-acre tract built in the Jeffersonian style. Other entities in the academic village include the Southwest Broward Regional Library, Pembroke Pines Charter High School, an athletic/aquatic complex, and a wetlands preserve.

BROWARD COLLEGE–WESTON CENTER
4205 Bonaventure Blvd., Weston
(954) 201-8501
www.broward.edu

The Weston Center is not a campus. It's located within the Weston Branch Library, and offers a variety of credit and noncredit courses, along with a fast-track associate's degree in Business Administration.

BROWARD COLLEGE MAROONE AUTOMOTIVE TRAINING CENTER
7451 Riviera Blvd., Miramar
(954) 201-8621
www.broward.edu

This facility opened in 2007, just off the Florida Turnpike, in the southern Broward town of Miramar. The center provides classrooms, work bays, and administrative offices for the college's automotive programs.

BROWARD COLLEGE–TIGERTAIL LAKE CENTER
Dania
(954) 201-7350
www.broward.edu

The Tigertail Lake Center is a different kind of college campus. Situated alongside I-95 in Dania Beach, this spot has conference and picnic facilities, as well as aquatic and watersports classes. Here you'll also find the BC Adventure Learning Center, with "challenge" rope-climbing programs and team-building exercises.

FLORIDA ATLANTIC UNIVERSITY–DANIA BEACH BRANCH (SEATECH)
101 N. Beach Rd., Dania Beach
(954) 924-7000
www.fau.edu
This campus is also known as SeaTech, and with good reason. It's the home of a well-regarded research and educational facility for programs in ocean engineering. In addition, the Dania campus is headquarters for two of Florida's Centers of Excellence. The Biomedical and Marine Biotechnology program is dedicated to searching the seas for new medicines to treat disease, and to searching the markets for more expeditious ways of getting them to the people who might need them. And the program in Ocean Energy Technology researches ways of harnessing energy from South Florida's ocean currents.

FLORIDA ATLANTIC UNIVERSITY–DAVIE BRANCH
2912 College Ave., Davie
(954) 236-1000
www.fau.edu
This is FAU's second-largest campus, behind only the main campus in Boca Raton. The Davie campus offers a variety of programs in partnership with Broward College, with which it shares a campus. This campus is the site of the innovative Teaching & Leadership Center, as well as the home of FAU's Everglades research and restoration efforts in partnership with the U.S. Geological Survey.

FLORIDA ATLANTIC UNIVERSITY–FORT LAUDERDALE BRANCH
111 E. Las Olas Blvd., Ft. Lauderdale
(954) 236-1000
www.fau.edu
Located in downtown Fort Lauderdale, this campus gives students the opportunity to enjoy city life (during the daytime), and all the cultural, social, and educational benefits that entails. The campus is home to a range of diverse professional and design-oriented programs, among them architecture, business, computer animation, graphic design, public administration, and urban planning. And, because of the location, students in the urban planning program are able to see first-hand the results of competent (or incompetent) planning.

FLORIDA INTERNATIONAL UNIVERSITY–PEMBROKE PINES BRANCH
17195 Sheridan St., Pembroke Pines
(954) 438-8600
www.fiu.edu
The FIU Broward Pembroke Pines center offers nontraditional students (undergraduate and graduate) a nontraditional college experience.

At this center, four FIU colleges (Arts and Sciences, Business Administration, Education, and Engineering and Computing) offer programs that are in demand in the community—especially in the working community. Many of the programs here are geared toward working adults and built around their work hours. Courses are offered on evenings and weekends, and, to further assist students who are already in the workforce, there are fast-track programs available as well. In addition, community residents can take noncredit courses, just for the intellectual stimulation;

two recent ones, for example, were on the mysteries of the so-called DaVinci Code and on wine tasting (offered by FIU's renowned School of Hospitality Management). The buildings and classrooms here are modern, and the computer labs are state-of-the-art.

NOVA SOUTHEASTERN UNIVERSITY
3301 College Ave., Davie
(800) 541-6682
www.nova.edu

It was a different world back in 1964. The Beatles—now the icons of rock history—were fresh-faced, mop-headed kids then, who made their first visit to America in February that year. The first Mustang rolled off the Ford assembly line in Detroit, setting a new standard for the American sports car. America was still dealing with the death of President John F. Kennedy in November of the previous year. And, in some empty meadows in what was then far-western Broward County, a brand-new college was born.

From the start, Nova was an innovator; in fact, it was a pioneer in the concept of distance-learning programs, starting its first off-campus study course in 1972. And it grew rapidly, gaining students as it widened the scope of its offerings.

In 1981, to the south, Southeastern College of Osteopathic Medicine was inaugurated. This college eventually started programs in other areas of medicine, as well, and eventually became known as Southeastern University of Health Sciences. In 1994, Nova University merged with Southeastern, and the result was Nova Southeastern University.

Today this is the sixth-largest private university in America, with nearly 30,000 students, a major graduate school, and a presence in 23 states and nine countries. It's located on a 300-acre campus. Its reputation for innovation and pioneering programs continues to grow. And there are now more than 100,000 Nova Southeastern alumni.

My Fort Lauderdale

Spending time with someone who has not lived in South Florida very long has made me take a new look at where I live, and I've come to really appreciate its absolute beauty. I've been to a bunch of beach communities here lately, and each one is more gorgeous and unique than the other. We're lucky enough to live, work, and play in a wonderland where the ocean provides a quiet calm and yet an invigorating energy. I'm lucky enough to be able to look at the locale in which I live through the eyes of someone who's new here . . . and he's helped me to see its breathtaking beauty. South Florida, to me, provides so much beauty and uniqueness, from the oceans to gardens, to shopping and dining, to the racetracks, and of course, water parks and boating, to the nightlife, and so much more. I could take a stay-cation for two or three weeks and never run out of things to do.

—Andrea Young,
Teacher, Broward County Schools

WILLIS HOLCOMBE CENTER
111 E. Las Olas Blvd., Ft. Lauderdale
(954) 201-7350
www.broward.edu

The Willis Holcombe Center is on East Las Olas Boulevard, in downtown Fort Lauderdale. It's a joint venture between Florida Atlantic University and Broward College. The Holcombe Center houses Broward College's district administrative offices, along with high-tech classrooms, science and technology labs, and student services. In addition, this campus is the site of the Institute for Economic Development, which offers continuing-education courses, corporate-training services, workforce-development resources, and resources for women transitioning into the workforce.

Vocational, Technical & Community Schools

Atlantic Technical Center—(754) 321-5100, (754) 321-5380; 4700 Coconut Creek Pkwy., Coconut Creek

Bair Community School—(754) 322-2970, (754) 322-2971; 9100 NW 21st Manor, Sunrise

Cooper City Community—(754) 323-0300, (754) 323-0333; 9401 Stirling Rd., Cooper City

Coral Springs Community—(754) 322-3070, (754) 322-3086; 10300 W. Wiles Rd., Coral Springs

Crystal Lake Community Middle School— (954) 786-3566, (954) 786-3776; 3551 NE 3rd Ave., Pompano Beach

Dave Thomas Education Center—(954) 786-7630, (954) 786-7756; 180 SW 2nd St., Pompano Beach

Dillard Community—(954) 797-4800, (954) 797-4857; 2501 NW 11th St., Ft. Lauderdale

Fort Lauderdale High Community School— (954) 765-6939, (954) 765-6180; 1600 NE 4th Ave., Ft. Lauderdale

Hallandale Adult Community Center—(954) 457-2510; (954) 457-2560; 1000 SW 3rd St., Hallandale

Hollywood Hills Community—(754) 323-1150, (754) 323-1185; 5400 Stirling Rd., Hollywood

Lauderhill Middle Community—(954) 497-3813, (954) 497-3974; 1901 NW 49th Ave., Lauderhill

Margate Middle Community—(754) 322-3870, (954) 322-3890; 500 NW 65th Ave., Margate

McFatter Technical Center—(754) 321-5700, (754) 321-5980; 6500 College Ave., Davie

Miramar High Community—(754) 323-1450, (754) 323-1491; 3601 SW 89th Ave., Miramar

Northeast Adult & Community—(754) 322-1650, (754) 322-1680; 700 NE 56th St., Oakland Park

Nova Community School—(754) 323-1741, (754) 323-1709; 3600 College Ave., Davie

Old Dillard Community School—(954) 765-6308, (954) 765-6906; 1001 NW 4th St., Ft. Lauderdale

Piper Community School—(754) 322-1800, (754) 322-1833; 8000 NW 44th St., Sunrise

Plantation Adult & Community School— (754) 322-1850, (754) 6901 NW 16th St., Plantation

Sheridan Technical Center—(754) 321-5400, (754) 321-5680; 5400 W. Sheridan St., Hollywood

South Broward Community—(754) 323-1900, (754) 323-1930; 1901 N. Federal Hwy., Hollywood

Taravella Community School—(754) 322-2400, (754) 322-2433; 10600 Riverside Dr., Coral Springs

Tequesta Trace Community—(754) 323-4470, (754) 323-4471; 1800 Indian Trace, Ft. Lauderdale

Whiddon-Rogers Educational Center—(954) 765-6896, (954) 765-6280; 700 SW 26th St., Ft. Lauderdale

Whispering Pines Off-Campus—(954) 765-6858, (954) 767-8476; 1300 SW 32nd Court, Ft. Lauderdale

Wingate Oaks Center—(954) 797-4260, (954) 797-4264; 1211 NW 33rd Terrace, Ft. Lauderdale

Young Community School—(954) 323-4570, (954) 323-4585; 901 NW 129th Ave., Pembroke Pines

CHILD CARE

As a parent of a young child, you will never make a more important decision—or a more difficult one— than choosing the right child-care center. The first thing you should do is visit several centers so that you can learn what to look for, and what questions to ask. First impressions are very important, so take care to notice several things:

- Does the facility—and the equipment— look safe?
- Do the caregivers/teachers give the impression that they genuinely enjoy their interactions with children?
- When they talk with a child, do they do it at the child's eye level?
- Are there plenty of toys and up-to-date learning materials within the child's reach?
- What does the place sound like? Happy? Solemn? What "vibe" does it give off?
- Do the children sound happy? Involved?
- What about the teacher's voices? Do they seem stressed or agitated? Or calm and in control?
- Does the staff seem cheerful and patient?
- Listen. A place that's too quiet may indicate that not enough meaningful activity

is taking place. A place that's too noisy may mean a lack of control.

- Try to get some idea of the teacher/child ratio. Obviously, the lower the better, particularly with very young children.

There are a number of options available to parents of young children in Greater Fort Lauderdale:

- **Child-Care Center:** This is a facility where care and activities are offered to a group of children in a licensed, nonresidential setting accommodating more than five children. Like most child-care facilities, this type is subject to strict licensing and operating requirements by both Broward County and the State of Florida. There are hundreds of them in Broward County, often called preschools, as well.
- **Family Child-Care Home:** This is a private home owned by the caregiver, where that person oversees a maximum of five children. This center must be licensed.
- **School-Age Child Care:** These are programs for children from ages 5 to 12, taking place both before and after school. Some of them offer child-care on school holidays and vacations. These centers can be situated in a variety of facilities, among them schools, child-care centers, family child-care homes, youth organizations, and religious organizations.
- **Voluntary Pre-Kindergarten (VPK):** A high-quality program focusing on early literacy. There is no charge for children who are Florida residents, and who are four years old on or before September 1.
- **Play Groups:** Play groups are part-week, part-day programs designed to give toddlers and young children an opportunity for socialization with other children their age. These programs may be offered

by licensed child-care centers, church or temple groups, or by local parks and recreation programs. But perhaps the most popular type of play-group is one in which parents are the caregivers.

- **Mommy and Me:** Mommy and Me programs are designed to bring parents and their infants or toddlers together. They generally involve joint activities that help parents learn more about child development in a social, supportive atmosphere.

Many child-care programs are subsidized with federal, state, or local funding. If you need help paying for child care, you should call **Family Central, Inc.'s Child Care Resource and Referral Office** at (954) 724-4609 or (877) 5-FAMILY.

BROWARD COUNTY CHILDREN'S SERVICES SECTION
Governmental Center Annex
115 S. Andrews Ave., #A-360
Ft. Lauderdale
(954) 357-7880
Hearing Impaired/TTY: (954) 537-2882

This department endeavors to improve the quality of life for families and children in Greater Fort Lauderdale, by working with community leaders and other organizations to create and manage programs to care for the county's children. This section is responsible for strategic planning and partnerships with the community, and it administers a budget of $15 million in contracts awarded to public and nonprofit organizations that service children and families.

These services address the needs of children in several program categories, including behavioral health, special health care, children in homeless families, and subsidized child care. Staff also provides support to the Broward County Children's Services Board, which recommends programs in need of funding to the Board of County Commissioners. Open Mon through Fri from 8:30 a.m. to 5 p.m.

MEDIA

For demographic purposes, Fort Lauderdale and Miami are considered one market. And—since they're only about 25 miles apart—they're considered one TV and radio market as well. Whereas West Palm Beach is considered a separate media market, Fort Lauderdale and Miami are one. So TV and radio stations are pretty much always identified as "Miami/Fort Lauderdale."

Newspapers, however, are a different story. Pretty much everyone in Greater Fort Lauderdale/Broward County reads the *South Florida Sun-Sentinel*, while the Miami–Dade County paper is the *Miami Herald*.

REGIONAL NEWSPAPERS

SOUTH FLORIDA SUN-SENTINEL
200 E. Las Olas Blvd., #1000
Ft. Lauderdale
(954) 356-4000
www.sun-sentinel.com

As of April 2010, the *South Florida Sun-Sentinel* was ranked as the 40th-largest newspaper in the United States, with a daily circulation of 180,273. The paper is owned—as are a number of other newspapers across the country—by the Chicago Tribune Company. For many years, Fort Lauderdale had two newspapers; the *Sun-Sentinel,* published in the morning, was the smaller one. The *Fort Lauderdale News* (the afternoon paper) was not only the second-largest newspaper in Florida, but it also used to boast that it had the largest classified section in the state. However, like pretty much every other afternoon paper in America, the *News* began hemorrhaging circulation in the 1980s and eventually shut down. Since then, the *Sun-Sentinel* has reigned supreme in Broward County, except perhaps for a very small number of people on the Broward/Miami-Dade border who get the *Miami Herald.* The *Sun-Sentinel,* originally the *Fort Lauderdale Sun-Sentinel,* changed to the *South Florida Sun-Sentinel* in the 1990s, to reflect more of a regional outlook, since it's also read in southern Palm Beach County. The *Sun-Sentinel* has a good reputation and good writers, and it has the full range of coverage, from local issues and sports to national and international news.

ALTERNATIVE

NEW TIMES
16 NE 4th St., Ft. Lauderdale
(954) 233-1600
www.browardpalmbeach.com

ARTS/ENTERTAINMENT

CITY LINK MAGAZINE
1000 E. Las Olas Blvd., #200
Ft. Lauderdale
(954) 356-4943
www.southflorida.com/citylink

BUSINESS NEWSPAPERS

BROWARD DAILY BUSINESS REVIEW
(305) 347-6612
www.dailybusinessreview.com

SOUTH FLORIDA BUSINESS JOURNAL
6400 N. Andrews Ave., #200
Ft. Lauderdale
(954) 949-7600
southflorida.bizjournals.com/
southflorida
Published every Friday, and sold at area newsstands and bookstores.

LOCAL/COMMUNITY NEWSPAPERS

FORUM PUBLISHING GROUP
1701B Green Rd., Deerfield Beach
(954) 698-6397
www.sun-sentinel.com/news/broward/
cities
The *South Florida Sun-Sentinel* owns a group of weekly community newspapers called the Forum Publishing Group. These papers can be very valuable tools in learning about the community—especially if you're a newcomer. Here is the list of cities which each have their own Forum newspaper:

- Coconut Creek
- Cooper City
- Coral Springs
- Dania Beach
- Davie
- Deerfield Beach
- Fort Lauderdale
- Hallandale Beach
- Hillsboro Beach
- Hollywood
- Lauderdale-by-the-Sea
- Lauderdale Lakes
- Lauderhill
- Lighthouse Point
- Margate
- Miramar
- North Lauderdale
- Oakland Park
- Parkland
- Pembroke Park
- Pembroke Pines
- Plantation
- Pompano Beach
- Southwest Ranches
- Sunrise
- Tamarac
- West Park
- Weston Wilton Manors

OUR TOWN NEWS
11874 Wiles Rd., Coral Springs
(954) 344-5156
www.theourtownnews.com

SPANISH LANGUAGE

EL HERALDO DE BROWARD
1975 E. Sunrise Blvd., #616
Ft. Lauderdale
(954) 792-7402
www.elheraldo.com

EL SENTINEL
(954) 749-4652
www.sun-sentinel.com/elsentinel
Spanish-language paper published by the *South Florida Sun-Sentinel*.

MAGAZINES

COCONUT CREEK LIFE
Life Publications
4611 Johnson Rd., #3
Coconut Creek
(954) 421-9797
www.lifepubs.com

CORAL SPRINGS LIFESTYLE MAGAZINE
Lifestyle Magazines
318 Indian Trace, #246
Ft. Lauderdale
(954) 217-1165
www.lifestylemagazinegroup.com

GOLD COAST MAGAZINE
Gulfstream Media Group
800 E. Broward Blvd., #506
Ft. Lauderdale
(954) 462-4488
gulfstreammediagroup.com

LAS OLAS LIFESTYLE MAGAZINE
Lifestyle Magazines
318 Indian Trace, #246
Ft. Lauderdale
(954) 217-1165
www.lifestylemagazinegroup.com

PARKLAND/CORAL SPRINGS LIFE
Life Publications
4611 Johnson Rd., #3
Coconut Creek
(954) 421-9797
www.lifepubs.com

THE PARKLANDER MAGAZINE
9381 W. Sample Rd., #203
Coral Springs
(954) 755-9800
www.theparklander.com

PARKLAND LIFESTYLE MAGAZINE
Lifestyle Magazines
318 Indian Trace, #246
Ft. Lauderdale
(954) 217-1165
www.lifestylemagazinegroup.com

SOUTH FLORIDA PARENTING
Forum Publishing Group
1701 Green Rd., #B
Deerfield Beach
(954) 747-3050
www.southflorida.com/sfparenting

WESTON LIFESTYLE MAGAZINE
Lifestyle Magazines
318 Indian Trace, #246
Ft. Lauderdale
(954) 217-1165
www.lifestylemagazinegroup.com

TV STATIONS

CHANNEL 2 (PUBLIC TELEVISION)
Community Television Foundation of
South Florida, Inc.
14901 NE 20th Ave., Miami
(305) 424-4002
www.channel2.org

CHANNEL 17 (PUBLIC TELEVISION)
WLRN—Public Radio and Television for
South Florida
172 NE 15th St., Miami
(305) 995-1717
www.wlrn.org

CHANNEL 4 (CBS)
WFOR-CBS4
8900 NW 18th Terrace, Doral
(305) 468-8064
www.cbs4.com

CHANNEL 6 (NBC)
WTVJ
15000 SW 27th St., Miramar
(954) 622-6000
www.nbcmiami.com

CHANNEL 10 (ABC)
WPLG
3900 Biscayne Blvd., Miami
(305) 576-9652
www.justnews.com

SOUTH FLORIDA RADIO STATIONS

Some of the popular radio stations in Greater Fort Lauderdale include:

WAQI RADIO MAMBI—710 AM
Spanish language talk, news

WBGG—105.9 FM
Classic rock

WFLC THE COAST—97.3 FM
Adult contemporary

WFTL—1400 AM
Talk radio

WHOT HOT 105—105.1 FM
Adult rhythm and blues

WHYI—100.7 FM
Top 40

WINZ—940 AM
Fox Sports

WIOD—610 AM
Talk, news

WIRK—107.9 FM
Country and western

WJNA—1040 AM
Nostalgia

WKGR THE GATER–98.7 FM
Classic rock

WKIS—99.9 FM
KISS Country

WLDI WILD—95.5 FM
Top 40

WLRN PUBLIC RADIO—91.3
Jazz, variety

WLYF—101.5 FM
Light adult contemporary.

WMXJ MAGIC—102.7 FM
Oldies

WPBI—1420 AM
Nostalgia

WQAM—560 AM
Sports talk

INDEX